WAR CRIMES IN

BOSNIA-HERCEGOVINA

D1559722

A Helsinki Watch Report

Human Rights Watch

New York • Washington • Los Angeles • London

TABLE OF CONTENTS

ACKNOWLEDGMENTS

This report documents violations investigated by Helsinki Watch representatives during two separate missions to Bosnia-Hercegovina, Croatia, Slovenia and Yugoslavia from March 19 to April 28 and from May 29 to June 19, 1992. It also includes information received from Helsinki Watch representatives who visited several Serbian-run detention camps in Bosnia in August. Refugees, displaced persons and medical and relief personnel were interviewed. Journalists, lawyers, government officials and combatants also were interviewed. This report was written by Ivana Nizich, Research Associate of Helsinki Watch and was edited by Aryeh Neier, Executive Director of Human Rights Watch and Jeri Laber, Executive Director of Helsinki Watch.

Sections of this report which pertain to international law were adapted, in part, from Chapter I of *Needless Deaths in the Gulf War: Civilian Casualties During the Air Campaign and Violations of the Laws of War*, (Middle East Watch, November 1991, pp. 25-68), which was written by Robert Kogod Goldman, professor of law at the Washington College of Law at the American University in Washington, DC. He also is a member of the Middle East Watch Committee, one of the five regional divisions of Human Rights Watch. Jemera Rone, Counsel to Human Rights Watch, also contributed to the international law section. Pamela Cox and others provided invaluable research assistance.

Helsinki Watch expresses its appreciation to the Open Society Fund for its support of our program in the former Yugoslav republics.

FREQUENTLY USED ABBREVIATIONS

EC   European Community

HDZ   Croatian Democratic Union (Hrvatska Demokratska Zajednica)

HOS   Croatian Armed Forces (Hrvatske Oružane Snage)

HV   Croatian Army (Hrvatska Vojska)

HVO   Croatian Defense Council (Hrvatsko Viječe Obrane)

ICRC   International Committee of the Red Cross

JNA   Yugoslav People's Army (Jugoslavenska Narodna Armija)

SDA   Party of Democratic Action (Stranka Demokratske Akcije)

SDS   Serbian Democratic Party (Srpska Demokratska Stranka)

TO   Territorial Defense (Teritorijalna Odbrana)

UN   United Nations

UNHCR   United Nations High Commissioner for Refugees

UNPROFOR   United Nations Protection Force

INTRODUCTION

The full scale war that has been raging in Bosnia-Hercegovina since early April has been marked by extreme violations of international humanitarian law., also known as the laws of war. Indeed, violations of the rules of war are being committed with increasing frequency and brutality throughout the country. The extent of the violence inflicted on the civilian population by all parties is appalling. Mistreatment in detention, the taking of hostages and the pillaging of civilian property is widespread throughout Bosnia-Hercegovina. The most basic safeguards intended to protect civilians and medical establishments have been flagrantly ignored. The indiscrim-inate use of force by Serbian troops has caused excessive collateral damage and loss of civilian life. A policy of "ethnic cleansing" has resulted in the summary execution, disappearance, arbitrary detention, deportation and forcible displacement of hundreds of thousands of people on the basis of their religion or nationality. In sum, the extent of the violence and the fact that it is targeted along ethnic/religious lines raises the question of whether genocide is taking place.

Helsinki Watch calls on the Security Council of the United Nations to exercise its authority under the 1951 Convention on the Prevention and Punishment of the Crime of Genocide to intervene in Bosnia-Hercegovina to prevent and suppress genocide. Helsinki Watch also calls upon the United Nations Security Council to enforce the prohibition of "grave breaches" of the Geneva Conventions by establishing an international tribunal at the highest level to investigate, prosecute, adjudicate and punish those on all sides who have been responsible for war crimes on the territory of the former Yugoslavia.

*   *   *

The findings in this report, and the reports from Bosnia-Hercegovina by independent news media, provide at the very least *prima facie* evidence that genocide is taking place. The "ethnic cleansing" that is being practiced by Serbian forces is directed particularly against Muslims and Croats on the basis of their religion and ethnicity. The victims of such "ethnic cleansing" have been expelled from their homes and villages; rounded up and held in detention camps; deported; killed

1

in indiscriminate attacks; and summarily executed. The murder of 83 Muslim residents of the village of Zaklopača on May 16, on the basis of their ethnicity/religion, is documented in this report and demonstrates in microcosm what has been taking place throughout Bosnia-Hercegovina.

Under Article I of the Genocide Convention, the parties undertake "*to prevent* and to punish" acts of genocide. Article II provides that genocide consists of acts committed "with intent to destroy, in whole or in part, a national, ethnical, racial or religious group, as such." It specifies that the means by which genocide is carried out includes "killing members of the group." Article VIII authorizes the United Nations to take appropriate action "for the prevention and suppression of acts of genocide."

Genocide is the most unspeakable crime in the lexicon. The authorization that the Convention provides to the United Nations to prevent and suppress this crime carries with it an obligation to act. The only guidance the Convention provides as to the manner of action is that it should be "appropriate." We interpret this as meaning it should be effective. Accordingly, Helsinki Watch believes that the United Nations, acting through the Security Council, is under an obligation to act effectively to prevent and suppress genocide in Bosnia-Hercegovina.

It is beyond the competence of Helsinki Watch to determine all the steps that may be required to prevent and suppress the crime of genocide. It may be necessary for the United Nations to employ military force to that end. It is not the province of Helsinki Watch to determine whether such force is required. Helsinki Watch believes that it is the responsibility of the Security Council to address this question.

Whether or not the Security Council determines that military forces is required, Helsinki Watch calls on the United Nations to take steps to ensure that those engaged in genocide will be held accountable for their crimes, and will become aware that they will be held accountable.

Article 146 of the Fourth Geneva Convention of 1949 on the Protection of Civilian Persons in Time of War requires the parties to enact legislation to provide effective penal sanctions for those committing or ordering to commit "grave breaches" of the Convention; and to search for such persons and to bring them to trial. Article 147 states that grave breaches are the following acts committed against protected persons and property:

willful killing, torture or inhuman treatment, including

biological experiments, willfully causing great suffering or serious injury to body or health, unlawful deportation or transfer or unlawful confinement of a protected person, compelling a protected person to serve in the forces of a hostile Power, or willfully depriving a protected person of the rights of fair and regular trial prescribed in the present Convention, taking of hostages and extensive destruction and appropriation of property, not justified by military necessity and carried out unlawfully and wantonly.

Articles 129 and 130 of the Third Geneva Convention Relative to the Treatment of Prisoners of War also require penal sanctions for "grave breaches" and identify many of the same acts as grave breaches.

Article 85 of Protocol I supplements the provisions of the Conventions, stating that "the following acts shall be regarded as grave breaches of this Protocol, when committed willfully, in violation of the relevant provisions of this Protocol, and causing death or serious injury to body or health:

(a) making the civilian population or individual civilians the object of attack;

(b) launching an indiscriminate attack affecting the civilian population or civilian objects in the knowledge that such attack will cause excessive loss of life, injury to civilians or damage to civilian objects as defined by Article 57, paragraph 2(a)(iii);
....

(d) making non-defended localities and demilitarized zones the object of attack;

(e) making a person the object of attack in the knowledge that he is *hors de combat*....[1]

---

[1] Paragraph 3.

Article 85 goes on to define additional acts as "grave breaches" when committed willfully and in violation of the Conventions or the Protocol;

(a) the transfer by the occupying Power of parts of its own civilian population into the territory it occupies, or the deportation or transfer of all or parts of the population of the occupied territory within or outside this territory, in violation of Article 49 of the Fourth Convention;

....

(b) ....inhuman and degrading practices involving outrages upon personal dignity, based on racial discrimination;

....

(d) making the clearly-recognized historic monuments, works of art or places of worship which constitute the cultural or spiritual heritage of peoples and to which special protection has been given by special arrangement, for example, within the framework of a competent international organization, the object of attack, causing as a result extensive destruction thereof, where there is no evidence of the violation by the adverse Party of Article 53, sub-paragraph (b), and when such historic monuments or works of art and places of worship are not located in the immediate proximity of military objectives;....[2]

Paragraph 5 of Article 85 provides that "grave breaches" of the Protocol and Conventions "shall be regarded as war crimes."

Articles 86 and 87 of the Protocol require the parties: to repress grave breaches;[3] provide that superiors are not absolved from penal

---

[2] Paragraph 4.

[3] Article 86, Paragraph 1.

responsibility for grave breaches if they did not take all feasible measures within their power to prevent or repress the breach;[4] and to initiate disciplinary or penal action against violators.[5]

It is now generally accepted that war crimes constitute international crimes under customary international law. There is widespread agreement that war crimes are subject to universal jurisdiction.

The prevailing view of universal jurisdiction in the United States is stated by section 404, Restatement (Third) of the Foreign Relations Law of the United States (1987) (the "Restatement (Third)"):

> A state has jurisdiction to define and prescribe punishment for certain offenses recognized by the community of nations as of universal concern such as piracy, slave trade, attacks on or hijacking of aircraft, genocide, war crimes....

The principle of universal jurisdiction to try war crimes was recognized in the establishment of the Nuremberg Tribunal[6] and in such subsequent cases as the trial of Adolf Eichmann in Israel and Klaus Barbie in France.

In the context of the international war in Bosnia, a tribunal established under the auspices of an appropriate international organization such as the United Nations and affording all those tried before it the protection of internationally recognized standards of due process of law, could exercise jurisdiction over war crimes. Helsinki Watch calls on the United Nations to establish such a tribunal and to prosecute, adjudicate and punish those responsible for war crimes starting with those with the highest level of responsibility for the most egregious crimes.

During two separate missions, Helsinki Watch representatives

---

[4] Article 86, Paragraph 2.

[5] Article 87, Paragraph 3.

[6] Charter of the International Military Tribunal (the "Nuremberg Tribunal"), art. 6(c), as amended by the Berlin Protocol, 59 Stat. 1546, 1547 (1945), E.A.S. No. 472 82 U.N.T.S. 284 (the "Nuremberg Charter").

investigated reports of war crimes alleged to have been committed by Serbian, Croatian and Muslim forces in Bosnia-Hercegovina.[7] Although all sides have committed serious abuses, Helsinki Watch found that the most egregious and overwhelming number of violations of the rules of war have been committed by Serbian forces. Indeed, Helsinki Watch is gravely concerned that the extensive violations documented in this report reflect only a fraction of the abuses being committed in Bosnia-Hercegovina.[8]

Helsinki Watch believes that sufficient evidence is available to warrant the investigation of the following persons to determine whether they have committed the war crimes described in this report:

- Blagoje Adžić, Retired General of the JNA and former Minister of Defense of Yugoslavia and Chief of Staff of the JNA.

- Dragoslav Bokan, a Serbian paramilitary leader.

- Mirko Jović, a Serbian paramilitary leader.

- Radovan Karadžić, President of the Serbian Democratic Party of Bosnia-Hercegovina.

- Slobodan Milošević, President of the Republic of Serbia.

- Ratko Mladić, General of the Yugoslav People's Army

---

[7] This report includes testimony taken by Helsinki Watch representatives from witnesses to, or victims of, serious abuses of the rules of war. Much of the testimony was taken from displaced persons within Bosnia-Hercegovina and from refugees who fled to Yugoslavia, Croatia and Slovenia.

[8] The ferocity of the fighting in parts of Bosnia-Hercegovina prevented Helsinki Watch representatives from travelling to several sites where rules of war violations are suspected to have taken place. In other instances, Helsinki Watch representatives were prevented by Serbian military and paramilitary forces from entering certain areas. For example, Helsinki Watch representatives were denied access to Zvornik and Bijeljina in April 1992.

(JNA), former commander of JNA forces in Knin and Banja Luka, currently Commander of Serbian troops in Bosnia-Hercegovina.

- Života Panić, General and Chief of Staff of the JNA and former Acting Minister of Defense of Yugoslavia.

- Željko Ražnjatović, also known as "Arkan," a Serbian paramilitary leader (also wanted by Interpol for crimes committed in Western Europe).

- Vojislav Šešelj, a Serbian paramilitary leader; President of the Serbian Četnik Movement and the Serbian Radical Party.

Helsinki Watch believes that the murder by Croatian forces of at least 23 Serbs in the city of Gospić in late 1991,[9] should also be investigated by an international tribunal and those responsible should be prosecuted and punished. We do not cite those responsible by name because, up to the present, we have not obtained sufficient evidence to allow us to identify the individual(s) who are responsible.

Insofar as evidence emerges that Muslim or Croatian forces have committed "grave breaches" of the Geneva Conventions and Protocol I, or war crimes, an investigation should be conducted to identify those with the highest level of responsibility for the most egregious crimes so that they may be prosecuted, adjudicated and punished.

BACKGROUND

The former Yugoslav republic of Bosnia-Hercegovina was recognized as an independent state by the international community on April 6 and 7, 1992. Its name derives from the union of two provinces, namely, Hercegovina (a region located in the south/southwest of the republic) and Bosnia (which encompasses all territory not part of Hercegovina.) Bosnia-Hercegovina's total population numbers 4.35

---

[9] The bodies were found in December but the executions are presumed to have occurred in late October, when Croatian soldiers took into custody Serbian residents during the siege of the city by Serbian armed forces.

7

million, of which — prior to the war — 43.7 percent were Slavic Muslims, 31.3 percent Serbs and 17.3 percent Croats. The various ethnic groups were intermingled throughout the country although, in some areas, one ethnic group formed a significant majority. Muslims were a majority in the extreme northwestern corner and eastern parts of Bosnia. The northwestern part of Bosnia and the eastern portion of Hercegovina are dominated by Serbs. Western Hercegovina is primarily inhabited by Croats. All three ethnic groups lived in central Bosnia.

During multi-party elections in Bosnia-Hercegovina in late 1990, three political parties emerged as representatives of the country's various ethnic groups: the predominantly Muslim Party of Democratic Action, the Serbian Democratic Party and the Croatian Democratic Union. Despite Serbian objections, Muslim and Croatian representatives in the Bosnian parliament declared the republic's sovereignty in October 1991. Subsequently, ethnic tensions began to rise. The Serbs supported continued union with Yugoslavia and the Croats and Muslims increasingly supported Bosnia's independence. During the war in Croatia, Yugoslav army soldiers and Serbian paramilitary forces were stationed throughout Bosnia-Hercegovina. In some cases, Serbian and Yugoslav troops harassed non-Serbs and tensions and outbreaks of violence increased in the republic. In late December 1991, Muslims and Croats decided to seek international recognition of Bosnia-Hercegovina as an independent state. Serbs opposed the move and declared their own state within Bosnia-Hercegovina in early January.

On February 29 and March 1, a referendum on independence was held in Bosnia-Hercegovina. Muslims and Croats overwhelmingly voted in favor of independence but most Serbs boycotted the referendum and declared it invalid. Some Serbs in the Bosnian police broke from Sarajevo's command and formed their own police force. Violence broke out during and after the referendum and eventually escalated to full scale war in early April, when the international community recognized Bosnia-Hercegovina's independence.

PARTIES TO THE CONFLICT AND
THE POSITIONS OF THE VARIOUS SIDES

The various ethnic groups and warring parties in Bosnia-Hercegovina are represented by the following political parties and armed forces:

- The predominantly Muslim Party of Democratic Action, led by Bosnian President Alija Izetbegović, supports an independent multi-ethnic state. Bosnian territorial defense units, which are similar to local militia forces, are the main armed forces fighting on behalf of the Bosnian government. Although predominantly Muslim, the territorial defense units also include Croats and Serbs.

- The Serbian Democratic Party, led by Radovan Karadžić, supports the division of Bosnia-Hercegovina into ethnic cantons which would be ruled by the majority group in each area. The Serbian Democratic Party claims seventy percent of Bosnia-Hercegovina's land for Bosnian Serbs, leaving the other thirty percent to be divided between Bosnia's Muslims and Croats. In January, Karadžić proclaimed the establishment of a separate Serbian state within Bosnia-Hercegovina, which would have close ties with and, possibly be incorporated into, Yugoslavia and Serbian controlled areas of Croatia.

When war broke out in Bosnia-Hercegovina, the Yugoslav army initially fought on behalf of Serbian forces in the country. Currently, Serbian armed forces are represented by a newly formed Serbian army of Bosnia-Hercegovina, eighty percent of which is composed of Yugoslav army soldiers and officers who have remained in the republic to fight on the Serbs' behalf after the army was ostensibly withdrawn. A variety of paramilitary groups from the

Republic of Serbia have operated and continue to fight alongside Serbian forces in Bosnia-Hercegovina.

- The Croatian Democratic Union in Bosnia-Hercegovina is divided into two factions. The party's current leader, Mate Boban, is widely regarded to be a puppet of Croatian President Franjo Tudjman. In July, Boban proclaimed an autonomous Croatian state within Bosnia-Hercegovina comprising predominantly, but not exclusively, Croatian areas of the country. Boban represents approximately 35 percent of Bosnia's Croats, most of whom live in the predominantly Croatian area of western Hercegovina.

9

The more moderate sector of the party is represented by Stjepan Klujić, the current Vice-President of Bosnia-Hercegovina. Klujić supports a single, multi-ethnic Bosnian state and is opposed to its division into ethnic cantons. Klujić represents approximately 65 percent of Bosnian Croats, most of whom live in urban areas and outside of western Hercegovina. Klujić's constituency supports the position of the Muslim-led Party of Democratic Action. Croatian armed forces in Bosnia-Hercegovina include the Bosnian-based Croatian Defense Council and members of the armed forces of the Republic of Croatia.

Generally, Muslims and Croats are aligned in the current war. The governments of the republics of Bosnia-Hercegovina and Croatia have signed a military alliance to fight against Serbian forces. Croatian and, to a lesser extent, Muslim forces in Bosnia-Hercegovina receive economic, political and military support from the Republic of Croatia. Similarly, the
Yugoslav government, particularly the government of the republic of Serbia, continues to provide military, economic and political support to Serbian forces in Bosnia-Hercegovina.

VIOLATIONS OF THE LAWS OF WAR

To varying degrees, all parties to the conflict in Bosnia-Hercegovina have violated humanitarian law, or the laws of war. Croatian and Muslim forces have taken hostages, mistreated persons in their custody and harassed Serbs in areas which they control. Serbian forces have committed the same abuses but on a broader scale. Helsinki Watch has found that Serbian forces are summarily executing, detaining and deporting non-Serbs in areas under their control in an effort to "ethnically cleanse" such areas of Muslims and Croats. Such practices were employed in Serbian-occupied areas of Croatia. Similarly, Serbian paramilitary groups are responsible for the forcible displacement of Hungarians, Croats, Ruthenians and others living in Serbia, particularly in the province of Vojvodina.

Summary Executions of Civilians and Persons *Hors de Combat*

10

Helsinki Watch has documented cases in which civilians and disarmed combatants have been summarily executed. On May 16, in the village of Zaklopača, at least eighty-three Muslims were summarily executed by Serbian paramilitaries. The Serbian troops attacked the village and began to kill the village's Muslim residents, primarily the men. Eleven children and sixteen elderly persons were among those executed. Similarly, on May 7, Serbian forces attacked twenty-nine houses in the village of Skelani and killed many of the male residents. Those who survived were expelled from the village.

On May 15, at least fifteen disarmed combatants were tortured and summarily executed near the town of Travnik, most probably by members of the military police of the Yugoslav army. Some of the bodies were mutilated after the victims had been executed. Helsinki Watch also has documented a case in which Serbian paramilitaries opened fire against civilians in the town of Bijeljina on April 1.

"Ethnic Cleansing" and Forcible Displacement

After an area is occupied by Serbian forces, a policy and practice of "ethnic cleansing" often follows. Such a policy aims to remove all non-Serbs from the occupied area, thereby creating an ethnically homogeneous region to be administered by Serbian authorities. The policy of "ethnic cleansing" entails the use of systematic execution, detention, deportation and displacement of non-Serbs from areas under Serbian control in Bosnia-Hercegovina. In some cases, Muslims and Croats are confined to villages which are transformed into ghettos for non-Serbs. Scores of thousands of persons have been victims of "ethnic cleansing" practices in Bosnia-Hercegovina.

Although such atrocities are being committed on a wide scale in Bosnia-Hercegovina, they are by no means restricted to that region. Helsinki Watch has documented similar cases of ethnic cleansing" of non-Serbs in Croatia and in the Serbian province of Vojvodina and, in a different manner, in the province of Kosovo. Such practices are followed in many Serbian-controlled areas, are premeditated and systematically executed. Most of the civilian authorities in the aforementioned areas have not taken steps to stop or prevent such practices. In some instances, they have condoned and encouraged such expulsions. For these reasons, Helsinki Watch is gravely concerned that Serbian civilian and military authorities, as well as paramilitary forces, are implementing a broader policy aimed at the expulsion or extermination of non-Serbian populations in areas under their control.

Disappearances

Thousands of people — mostly men of combat age — remain missing throughout Bosnia-Hercegovina. Although some may have been separated from their families as a result of the war, others appear to have been intentionally taken from their villages or places of detention and subsequently disappeared.

Hostage-Taking

All sides in the Bosnian war hold civilians for subsequent exchanges for combatants captured by an opposing party. In other instances, armed forces have held civilians to extract military concessions from the opposing side. Five thousand women, children and elderly persons were held hostage by Serbian forces in mid-May in a Sarajevo suburb. Approximately three thousand Serbian civilians were held hostage in a tunnel near Sarajevo by Bosnian forces in late May.

Mistreatment in Detention

Helsinki Watch believes that all parties to the conflict are mistreating prisoners — both prisoners of war and civilians — who remain in their custody. Prisoners are routinely beaten and otherwise tortured. Serbian forces also have used prisoners as human shields to ward off attack by Muslim and Croatian forces. Prisoners captured in Bosnia-Hercegovina by Serbian forces also are being detained and mistreated in Serbian-held areas of Croatia.

Indiscriminate Use of Force

Serbian forces have indiscriminately bombed, shelled and otherwise attacked Bosnian towns, cities and villages. Such indiscriminate use of force often serves no military purpose; it appears aimed at terrorizing the civilian population, thereby inducing its surrender or flight from a besieged area. Serbian troops have used force in this

12

manner to displace the non-Serbian population in areas throughout Bosnia-Hercegovina. In other instances, Serbian forces appear to have deliberately attacked medical establishments, cultural monuments and places of worship. Civilians, including children, displaced persons and refugees also have been attacked deliberately. Helsinki Watch has documented cases of indiscriminate use of force in Bijeljina, Mostar, Sarajevo and Tuzla in Bosnia-Hercegovina. A refugee camp on the Croatian and Bosnian border appears to have been targeted for attack by Serbian forces stationed in northern Bosnia.

Attacks Against Medical and Relief Personnel and Vehicles

Domestic and international relief convoys and medical personnel have been attacked, hijacked or obstructed throughout Bosnia-Hercegovina. In most cases, Serbian forces are responsible for such attacks but in other cases, the identity of the attacker cannot clearly be established. Convoys organized by the International Committee of the Red Cross (ICRC) and the United Nations High Commissioner for Refugees (UNHCR) have been attacked on numerous occasions in Bosnia-Hercegovina. Bosnian-based

charitable groups and personnel affiliated with other agencies of the United Nations and with the European Community (EC) also have been attacked.

Helsinki Watch has documented a number of cases in which medical or relief personnel have been attacked, almost exclusively by Serbian forces. Serbian troops also have stolen food and medical supplies destined for civilians in besieged areas. To date, over 600 tons of food, 4.5 tons of medicine and over fourteen truckloads of humanitarian aid have been hijacked or stolen. Helsinki Watch is gravely concerned that Serbian forces are attacking relief convoys carrying humanitarian aid to besieged areas in an effort to discourage or prevent such relief from reaching its destination, thereby exacerbating the severe shortages of food and medicine in parts of Bosnia-Hercegovina and accelerating the starvation or submission of the besieged population.

Attacks Against Journalists

Helsinki Watch has found that, between April 6 and July 23, at least three journalists have been killed while covering the war in Bosnia-

Hercegovina. Four more are missing and at least five have been wounded. At least another five journalists have been physically assaulted or attacked and nine have been otherwise harassed (i.e, threatened, property confiscated). Some of the deaths and injuries may be attributable to cross-fire but some journalists appear to have been targeted because of their professional affiliation. All sides have attacked journalists and Serbian forces have unnecessarily delayed medical attention to a severely wounded journalist, thereby causing his death.

In 13 months, the wars in Croatia and Bosnia-Hercegovina have claimed the lives of at least 24 journalists. At least 33 have been wounded, ten have been captured and subsequently released and six remain missing. At least 68 have been attacked and over 47 have been otherwise harassed (i.e., threatened, property confiscated).

Pillage and Other Destruction of Civilian Property

Helsinki Watch has documented cases of looting, burning and pillage by Serbian forces in Brčko, Bijeljina and Sarajevo. Helsinki Watch is concerned that Croatian and Muslim forces have also pillaged and destroyed Serbian property in areas under their control in Bosnia-Hercegovina.

Other Abuses

Helsinki Watch also has documented cases in which hospitals have been used as depots for armaments, most notably in the military hospital in Sarajevo. Helsinki Watch has also documented a case in which a bridge was deliberately destroyed as civilians were crossing over the Sava River.

STATUS OF REFUGEES AND DISPLACED PERSONS

More than 2.3 million people have been displaced by the wars in Bosnia-Hercegovina and Croatia. The Bosnian war has left one-third of Bosnia's population homeless. Many of the refugees have fled to Croatia while others have fled to other former Yugoslav republics and to Western Europe. Helsinki Watch has interviewed scores of refugees from Bosnia-Hercegovina who were displaced, not as a result the fighting, but

14

rather because they were forcibly deported or expelled by Serbian forces whose aim is to expel Muslims and Croats from areas that they occupied.

Helsinki Watch also interviewed Serbian refugees who had fled as a result of the fighting and who confirmed reports that Serbian forces were indiscriminately shelling civilian targets and forcibly displacing non-Serbs from areas under their control. Many Serbs themselves condemned such attacks. Approximately 850,000 people — including thousands of refugees — remain trapped in the besieged cities of Sarajevo, Goražde, Bihać and Tuzla. Helsinki Watch is gravely concerned that, should those cities fall to Serbian forces, their inhabitants could be victims of "ethnic cleansing" practices.

THE ROLE OF THE INTERNATIONAL COMMUNITY

Efforts by the international community to bring peace to Bosnia-Hercegovina generally have failed. The United Nations, the European Community and the United States have focused attention on negotiating and maintaining cease-fires. Although a series of trade and military sanctions against Serbia have been belatedly applied, the international community has not found a way to stop or prevent egregious violations of the laws of war that continue to occur not only as a result of the conflict but also in occupied areas where there is little or no fighting.

The United Nations

Helsinki Watch is gravely troubled by reports that the United Nations has known about the existence of so-called "concentration" camps in Serbian-controlled areas in north-western Bosnia since at least early July. UN personnel stationed in Serbian-controlled areas of Croatia repeatedly have informed their superiors of the existence, and reports of the existence, of such camps near Bihać, Cazin, Velika Kladuša, Bosanska Dubica, Prijedor and Banja Luka. However, high-ranking UN officials withheld this information from the press and the public and apparently did little, if anything, to stop abuses in these camps. Helsinki Watch believes that UN personnel also withheld information about human rights abuses that occurred during the war in Croatia, particularly the forcible displacement of non-Serbs in Serbian-controlled areas of the country where UN personnel were stationed.

15

UN efforts in Bosnia-Hercegovina have focussed on peacekeeping, delivery of humanitarian aid and imposition of sanctions against Yugoslavia. Unfortunately, UN peacekeeping efforts have been marked by disorganization and political indecision. Disagreements between members of the Security Council and with the Secretary-General have impeded the ability of the UN to speak decisively and with one voice. UN member states have expected much from UN efforts but have not been willing to commit the necessary financial resources to implement plans. Moreover, the parties to the conflict have not always negotiated in good faith, thereby hampering the speedy deployment of UN forces to the region.

UN efforts to deliver humanitarian aid to besieged areas of Bosnia-Hercegovina have been impeded by continued fighting. Serbian forces carry the heaviest responsibility for breaches of cease-fire agreements and for indiscriminate attacks. The UN has been insufficiently outspoken in protesting against such attacks and has been even less vigorous in protesting violations of the laws of war by all parties to the conflict. The consequence has been a failure to promote respect for the laws of war in Bosnia-Hercegovina.

Helsinki Watch supports the imposition of UN sanctions against Yugoslavia. Indeed, we believe that such sanctions are long overdue. UN sanctions should have been imposed against Serbia much earlier for its violations of the laws of war in Croatia, particularly after the city of Vukovar fell and summary executions and the detention of thousands of civilians ensued. Had sanctions been imposed against the Serbian government early on in the Balkan conflict, Serbian and Yugoslav forces may have been discouraged from committing further atrocities in Bosnia-Hercegovina.

The UN should publicly and vociferously condemn all violations of the laws of war committed by all parties, particularizing its denunciations so as to allocate responsibility to the guilty parties. The UN has rightfully stated that all sides are guilty of abuses, but the failure to specify which parties are responsible for particular abuses has diminished the impact of its denunciations. Moreover, the UN has done little, if anything else, to stop, prevent or punish such abuses. The UN has been especially timid in its public condemnation of Serbian forces in Bosnia-Hercegovina. The indiscriminate use of force against civilian targets and continued attacks against UN-escorted relief convoys are particularly unacceptable in the Sarajevo area, where UN forces are most heavily deployed and best equipped to observe and protest such abuses.

16

The European Community

The European Community has been slow and divided in its response to the war in Bosnia-Hercegovina. Germany is the only EC country that has supported an activist policy in Bosnia-Hercegovina. France has supplied much humanitarian aid to Bosnia-Hercegovina but has been restrained in its criticism of Serbian forces in that country. Greece has sought to deflect criticism of Serbia because it views that state as an ally in its effort to deny international recognition to the former Yugoslav republic of Macedonia. Britain has been ambivalent about criticizing human right abuses in Bosnia-Hercegovina and it generally has been passive about the conflict. Most of the EC states have preferred to disengage from the Bosnian war and, with the exception of Germany, have been reluctant to admit fleeing refugees.

The EC monitoring mission to the former Yugoslavia has done much to document abuses and it should be commended for its efforts. However, EC-sponsored peace talks have stalemated in part because of the unwillingness of the parties to negotiate. The EC negotiators generally have refrained from criticizing those parties responsible for gross violations of humanitarian law in Bosnia-Hercegovina, apparently believing that criticism would disrupt peace talks between the warring factions. The EC, like the UN, should not refrain from ascribing responsibility for the atrocities being committed throughout the country. Rather, it should actively and publicly condemn those violations, thereby exerting pressure on those responsible to end abuses.

The United States

United States policy toward the former Yugoslavia has been inert, inconsistent and misguided. For ten months, the US failed to exert its influence on the Serbian authorities to end their intervention in the war in Croatia. Although the US Embassy in Belgrade and the Consulate in Zagreb have done a commendable job of documenting and protesting violations of human rights committed by all sides in the former Yugoslavia, the Bush Administration took no steps to try to quell the violence in Croatia. Only after full-scale war broke out in Bosnia-Hercegovina did the US become involved. However, even then its involvement in Bosnia-Hercegovina has been timid and belated.

17

Despite a lack of leadership and foresight in US policy toward Yugoslavia, the Bush Administration should be commended for mobilizing international support for the imposition of UN sanctions against Yugoslavia. Such a step was long overdue; the US should have undertaken such efforts months earlier. Helsinki Watch supports unilateral US sanctions against Yugoslavia, which were imposed after UN sanctions were approved.

Helsinki Watch endorses the call by Acting Secretary of State Lawrence Eagleburger for a UN investigation of war crimes in Bosnia-Hercegovina. Even so, we believe that this call should have been made earlier and does not go far enough. We believe that it should be coupled with the establishment of an international tribunal to prosecute, adjudicate and punish war crimes and a call for UN action to prevent and suppress genocide. Recent US efforts to garner international armed protection for relief convoys only duplicate failed efforts in the past and will have little or no effect in preventing and suppressing war crimes currently being committed on a mass scale in Bosnia-Hercegovina.

18

BACKGROUND

Bosnia-Hercegovina was established as one of six constituent republics of Yugoslavia after World War II and became an internationally recognized independent state on April 6, 1992. Its name derives from the union of two provinces, namely, Hercegovina (a region located in the south/southwest of the republic) and Bosnia (which encompasses all territory not part of Hercegovina).[1] Located in the west-central part of the former Yugoslavia,[2] Bosnia-Hercegovina is a microcosm of the ethnic, cultural and religious diversity found in the former Yugoslavia. Bosnia-Hercegovina's total population numbered 4.35 million before the war, of which 43.7 percent were Slavic Muslims, 31.3 percent Serbs and 17.3 percent Croats.

Geographically, Serbs constituted a majority in the northwestern areas of the republic, primarily in areas which border Serbian-controlled areas in Croatia (i.e., in the self-proclaimed Krajina region).[3] The Hercegovina region of the country is divided between the Croats and the

---

[1] Generally, Hercegovina includes the municipalities of Stolac, Jablanica, Bugojno, Trebinje, Konjic, Kupres, Čapljina, Čitluk, Ljubuški, Grude, Široki Brijeg, Mostar, Posušje, Neum, Duvno/Tomislavgrad, Livno and Prozor. The republic's remaining municipalities represent Bosnia proper.

[2] The post-war Yugoslav state effectively ceased to exist on June 26, 1991, when Slovenia and Croatia declared their independence. The subsequent secession of Macedonia and Bosnia-Hercegovina led to the further disintegration of the former Yugoslavia. On April 27, 1992, a new Yugoslavia -- composed only of the republics of Montenegro and Serbia, including the provinces of Kosovo and Vojvodina -- was proclaimed. Reference to "Yugoslavia" in this report will signify the present state which is represented by Serbia and Montenegro. The pre-war state of six constituent republics will be referred to simply as the "former Yugoslavia."

[3] Prior to the war in Bosnia-Hercegovina, armed conflict had taken place in Croatia. For developments in the war in Croatia, see the following Helsinki Watch reports as appendices C, D and E: "Yugoslavia: Human Rights Abuses in the Croatian Conflict," September 1991; Letter to Slobodan Milošević, President of the Republic of Serbia, and General Blagoje Adžić, Acting Minister of Defense and Chief of Staff of the Yugoslav People's Army, January 21, 1992; and Letter to Franjo Tudjman, President of the Republic of Croatia, February 13, 1992.

Serbs. The western part of Hercegovina has been primarily Croatian while the eastern part has been primarily Serbian. Croats made up a significant portion of the population in areas of central and northern Bosnia. Muslims generally were a majority in the extreme northwest corner and eastern areas of Bosnia.

Bosnia's Muslims are descendants of Slavic inhabitants who were converted to Islam[4] when the provinces of Bosnia and Hercegovina were taken over by the Ottoman Empire.[5] At the Congress of Berlin in 1878, Bosnia and Hercegovina were placed under the administration of the Austro-Hungarian Empire. In 1908, Austria-Hungary formally annexed Bosnia and Hercegovina. In 1914, the Austrian Archduke Franz Ferdinand and his wife Sofia were assassinated in Sarajevo by Gavrilo Princip, a Serbian nationalist supporting Bosnia's union with Serbia. The event triggered the outbreak of World War I. In 1918, Bosnia and Hercegovina were incorporated into the Kingdom of Serbs, Croats and Slovenes.[6]

---

[4] Most Slavs who converted to the Islamic religion had belonged to the Bogomil heresy, rather than the Roman Catholic or Christian Orthodox religions. (Bogomils were adherents of a medieval religious sect that is believed to have been founded as a reaction against the hierarchy and formalism of the Byzantine church and ruling classes. The Bogomils became heavily concentrated in Bosnia, where Christian elements of the sect became dominant. With the advance of the Turks in the mid- and late-15th century, many Bogomil nobles converted to Islam.)

[5] Prior to Ottoman rule, Bosnia-Hercegovina was ruled by a series of governors (bans) and, later, kings. During the spring of 1463, the Ottoman army seized much of Bosnia and Hercegovina and, by the end of the 15th century, the Bosnian Kingdom ceased to exist.

[6] In 1929, a totalitarian dictatorship was established by the Serbian King Alexandar Karadjordjević and the Kingdom of Serbs, Croats and Slovenes was renamed "Yugoslavia." Inter-war Yugoslavia was divided into regional units. Bosnia-Hercegovina was initially divided into several administrative units. In 1939, Bosnia-Hercegovina was partitioned anew; thirty-eight municipalities were placed under Serbia's control and thirteen municipalities were reserved for Croatia. During World War II, all of Bosnia-Hercegovina was incorporated as part of the Nazi-puppet Croatian state. (Joseph Rothschild, *East Central Europe Between the Two World Wars*, Seattle and London, University of Washington Press,

Bosnia-Hercegovina was incorporated into the Independent State of Croatia, a Nazi puppet state that existed from 1941 to 1945. During World War II, Bosnia-Hercegovina was the scene of much bloodshed between the pro-Axis Croatian Ustaša forces,[7] Serbian royalist Četnik forces[8] and Tito's communist Partisans.[9] The post-war Yugoslav

---

1974, pp. 201-280; and Ivo Banac, *The National Question in Yugoslavia: Origins, History Politics*, Ithaca and London, Cornell University Press, 1984, pp. 359-378.)

[7] With the backing of the Nazi and Italian fascist governments, Croatian fascists (known as Ustašas) established the puppet state of the Independent State of Croatia (Nezavisna Država Hrvatska - NDH). Under the Ustaša regime, thousands of Serbs, Jews, Gypsies and others were killed between 1941 and 1945. Some Muslims were members of the NDH government and Muslim forces fought on the side of the Ustaša regime during World War II. Serbian military and paramilitary forces commonly refer to Croat and Muslims forces in the current war as "Ustašas." Both Croats and Muslims reject the label and vehemently deny that they are Ustaša sympathizers or fascists. Some Serbs also refer to Muslims as "Turks," associating Muslims with the Ottoman rulers who reigned over most of Serbia from 1371 to 1878.

[8] During the Second World War, the Četniks fought against the occupying Axis powers and called for the restoration of the Serbian monarchy and the creation of a Greater Serbia. The Četniks also fought against the pro-Nazi Ustaša forces of Croatia and Tito's communist Partisans and committed atrocities against Muslims and Croats, primarily in Bosnia-Hercegovina. Croats and Muslims both in Croatia and Bosnia-Hercegovina commonly refer to Serbian military and paramilitary forces engaged in the current wars in Croatia and Bosnia-Hercegovina as "Četniks." The Yugoslav army and some Serbian paramilitary groups vehemently reject the label "Četnik," claiming they are merely defenders of their people and their land and that they are not extremists. Others, such as paramilitary units loyal to the ultra-right wing leader of the Serbian Radical Party, Vojislav Šešelj, commonly refer to themselves as Četniks.

[9] Immediately after World War II, Tito's Partisans were responsible for mass executions of thousands of persons, primarily along the Slovenian-Croatian border. Partisans claimed that the killings involved the execution of Nazi collaborators and, therefore, were justified. However, the vast majority of those executed appear to have been civilians, including refugees who had fled from the war and were returning to their homes. Tito's Partisans also were responsible for the execution of Četnik leaders, most notably Draža Mihajlović, the head of the

21

constitution of 1946 reconstructed Yugoslavia as a federation of six constituent republics, including Bosnia-Hercegovina. In addition to the Serbs, Croats and Slovenes, Montenegrins and Macedonians were recognized as constituent nations of post-war Yugoslavia. A Muslim national identity[10] was recognized officially in 1970.[11]

Although the mainly Sunni Muslims of Bosnia and the former Yugoslavia[12] are relatively secular in their religious and social practices, some Serbs claim that an independent Bosnia-Hercegovina will lead to Islamic fundamentalism in Europe and gross abuses of the rights of women and non-Muslims. To date, Helsinki Watch has found no evidence to suggest that Muslim members of the government or leaders of the predominantly Muslim Party of Democratic Action (Stranka

---

Royalist movement during World War II.

[10] Some Croats and Serbs have long denied the legitimacy of the Muslims as an ethnic or national group. Some Serbs claim that the Muslims are Orthodox Christian Serbs who converted to the Islamic religion. Similarly, some Croats claim that in fact the Muslims are Roman Catholic Croats who converted to Islam during Ottoman rule. Muslims categorically reject this argument, claiming not only separate religious affiliation but a distinct Slavic national identity as well.

Helsinki Watch takes the position that a person's identification with a particular national, ethnic or religious group is a matter of personal choice. Any effort to deny an individual the right freely to identify himself or herself as a member of a national, ethnic or religious group is a serious violation of fundamental rights to freedom of conscience, expression and, in this case, religion. The right of the Muslims to identify themselves as a distinct national, ethnic and religious group must be respected.

[11] Patrick Moore, "The Islamic Community's New Sense of Identity," Radio Free Europe, *Report on Eastern Europe*, November 1, 1991, p. 20.

[12] It should be noted that non-Slavic Muslims, such as Albanians and Turks, also live on the territory of the former Yugoslavia. (About 80 percent of Albanians living in the former Yugoslavia practice Islam, while approximately 20 percent are Roman Catholics.) Although Turks, Albanians and Slavic Muslims generally all practice the same religion, they constitute three separate national groups. Most of the Muslims of the former Yugoslavia live in Bosnia-Hercegovina and in the Sandzak region, which is divided between Serbia and Montenegro.

22

Demokratske Akcije -- SDA)[13] have in any way discriminated against, or infringed upon the rights of, non-Muslims in Bosnia-Hercegovina. Moreover, Muslim women enjoy the same rights as women of the Roman Catholic or Serbian Orthodox religions in Bosnia-Hercegovina.

In November and December 1990, multi-party elections were held in Bosnia-Hercegovina.[14] After two rounds of voting on November 18 and December 16, political parties representing the various national groups in Bosnia-Hercegovina were elected to parliamentary and governmental positions.[15]

---

[13] The Party of Democratic Action (Stranka Demokratske Akcije- SDA) is the political party which represents most of Bosnia-Hercegovina's Muslims. A second group, the Muslim Bosniak Organization (Muslimanska Bošnjacka Organizacija - MBO) represents a significantly smaller portion of the Muslim electorate.

[14] All six of the former Yugoslav republics held multi-party elections in 1990. Elections in each of the republics involved two rounds of voting, except in Macedonia, where the electoral process involved three rounds of voting. The first rounds of elections took place in the following republics on the following dates: Slovenia - April 12; Croatia - April 22; Macedonia - November 11; Bosnia-Hercegovina - November 18; Montenegro - December 9; and Serbia - December 9. The elections in Serbia included voting in the provinces of Vojvodina and Kosovo, but ethnic Albanians in Kosovo boycotted the elections in protest of Serbia's repressive rule.

International observers believed the elections were free and fair in all but two of the former Yugoslav republics: Montenegro and Serbia. Unequal access to the media for opposition parties during the election campaigns and voter intimidation (in Serbia) were reported by the U.S. Congressional Commission on the Conference on Security and Cooperation in Europe (see *Report on the U.S. Helsinki Commission Delegation Visit to Hungary, Yugoslavia and Albania*, March 22-28, 1991, pp. 9-26); the U.S. State Department (see "U.S. Policy Toward Yugoslavia," U.S. Department of State, Statement released by Department Spokeswoman Margaret Tutwiler, May 24, 1991); and the National Republican Institute for International Affairs (see *The 1990 Elections in the Republics of Yugoslavia*, February 1991, pp. 7-34).

[15] The Muslim-based Party for Democratic Action (Stranka Demokratske Akcije -- SDA) won a majority 86 seats in parliament, the Serbian Democratic Party (Srpska Demokratska Stranka -- SDS) received 72; the Croatian Democratic Party (Hrvatska Demokratska Zajednica -- HDZ) received 44; and other parties received 33. Candidates from the three aforementioned parties were elected to

In October 1991, Muslims and Croats in the Bosnian legislature joined forces to adopt "a memorandum which, falling short of declaring independence, supported the republic's sovereignty and [its] neutrality" with regard to the war in Croatia.[16] Serbian members of the Bosnian parliament refused to support the measure. Rather, in November 1991, the Serbian Democratic Party (Srpska Demokratska Stranka -- SDS) of Bosnia-Hercegovina "organized its own referendum on remaining in a 'common Yugoslav state,' in which a substantial number of Serbs ... participated and voted favorably."[17]

After the elections and declaration of sovereignty, ethnic tensions in parts of Bosnia-Hercegovina increased for several reasons. Troops belonging to the Yugoslav People's Army (Jugoslavenska Narodna Armija -- JNA) and Serbian irregular forces stationed throughout Bosnia-Hercegovina (particularly those from the Mostar and Banja Luka corps) launched attacks on Croatia from Bosnian territory.[18] Moreover, JNA

---

seats in the republic's collective presidency. (See National Republican Institute for International Affairs, *The 1990 Elections in the Republics of Yugoslavia*, pp. 35-47; "Democratic Action Party Wins Majority" Tanjug Yugoslav News Agency report of December 12, 1990, as reported in Foreign Broadcast Information Service *Daily Report* [hereinafter FBIS], December 13, 1990, p. 47; "Further on Election Results," Tanjug Yugoslav News Agency report of December 12, 1990, as reported in *FBIS* on December 13, 1990, pp. 47-48.)

[16] U.S. Congressional Commission on Security and Cooperation in Europe, *The Referendum on Independence in Bosnia-Hercegovina: February 29 - March 1, 1992*, March 12, 1992, p. 8.

[17] *Ibid.*

[18] For example, the Croatian city of Dubrovnik was attacked from Serbian positions in and around the cities of Trebinje and Mostar in Hercegovina. (Attacks also were launched from the sea and from the republic of Montenegro.) According to a western diplomat interviewed by Helsinki Watch in December 1991 and March 1992, problems in Mostar began after JNA reservists from Montenegro and the Užice corps in Serbia were sent to the city in mid-September 1991. According to the diplomat, the JNA reservists were responsible for "terrorizing Muslim and Croatian villages" in the Mostar municipality. See also "Mostar Garrison Denies Troops Put on Streets," Tanjug Yugoslav News Agency report of December 2, 1991, and "Army Command in Mostar on Peace Problems,"

troops withdrawing from Croatia stationed themselves throughout Bosnia-Hercegovina. Bosnia's Muslim, Croatian and portions of its Serbian communities were alarmed by the escalating military presence of the JNA and Serbian paramilitary groups in Bosnia-Hercegovina. Clashes between Serbian and Montenegrin forces and Bosnian residents occurred throughout 1991 and early 1992. Most notably, JNA reservists in Mostar[19] and in other parts of Hercegovina were accused of harassing non-Serbs and looting and burning property that belonged to Muslims and Croats.[20] In late 1991, the predominantly Croatian village of Ravno[21] was pillaged and burned by JNA reserve soldiers and Serbian irregular troops.[22]

Tanjug Yugoslav News Agency report of December 3, 1991, as reported in FBIS, December 6, 1991.

[19] The population of the municipality of Mostar numbered 126,067. Muslims were 34.8 percent of the population, Croats 33.3 percent and Serbs 19.0 percent. Ten percent of Mostar's population declared itself to be Yugoslav. Prior to the break-up of the former Yugoslavia, some people preferred to call themselves "Yugoslavs" instead of identifying with a particular national or ethnic group. Children of "mixed parentage" frequently refered to themselves as Yugoslavs. Since the break-up of the country, most people now identify as a member of a particular ethnic group, although some still prefer to think of themselves as Yugoslavs. An effort will be made to identify the ethnic make-up of each area throughout this report. The figures cited hereafter reflect the results of the former Yugoslavia's April 1991 census or witnesses' recollections of their villages' demography.

[20] "Tensions Remain High in Bosnia," *Radio Free Europe/Radio Liberty Daily Report*, March 17, 1992, No. 53, p. 6.

[21] Ravno was a predominantly Croatian village in the predominantly Serbian municipality of Trebinje. Recent census results indicate that the municipality of Trebinje (in eastern Hercegovina) was 69.3 percent Serbian, 19.9 percent Muslim and 4.0 percent Croatian.

[22] Helsinki Watch interviewed several foreign diplomats and journalists who had visited the area. They confirmed that Ravno had been destroyed. See also "Destruction of Ravno by JNA Described," *Vjesnik*, November 10, 1991, as reported in FBIS, December 5, 1991, p. 36.

In late 1991, Serbia launched an economic blockade against Bosnia-Hercegovina. The delivery of agricultural products from Serbia and the flow of trade and money between the two republics ceased.[23] Many Bosnians believe the blockade was used as a bargaining chip by the Serbian government to force Bosnia-Hercegovina to remain a constituent part of a Serbian-dominated Yugoslavia.

In late December 1991, Muslims and Croats in the Bosnian government agreed to ask the European Community to recognize Bosnia-Hercegovina along with Slovenia, Croatia and Macedonia on January 15, 1992.[24] Serbs insisted that they wanted to remain part of a federal Yugoslavia and on January 9, 1992, Bosnian Serbs declared that they were forming their own state within the republic, called the Serbian Republic of Bosnia-Hercegovina. The Serbs claimed territory in six regions of Bosnia-Hercegovina where they are the dominant ethnic group and declared that Sarajevo would become their capital.[25]

On February 29 and March 1, 1992, a referendum on independence was held in Bosnia-Hercegovina. While Muslims and Croats participated and overwhelmingly agreed to Bosnia's secession from

---

[23] "Social Democrat on Effects of Economic Blockade," Tanjug Yugoslav News Agency report of December 3, 1991, and "Assembly Plans Reciprocal Measures Against Blockade," Sarajevo Radio broadcast of December 4, 1991, as reported in FBIS, December 5, 1991.

[24] Richard Balmforth, "Serbs in Bosnia Declare Own Republic," Reuters Information Services, January 9, 1992.

[25] Richard Meares, "Bosnian Leader Vows Not to Allow Serbs to Split His Republic," Reuters Information Services, January 10, 1992. On March 27, 1992, the Serbian Parliament of Bosnia-Hercegovina accepted a constitution for the new Serbian Republic, which was to become a "constitutive element of Yugoslavia, together with Serbia, Montenegro and the 'krajinas'" in Croatia." (See Željko Ivanković, "Il Faudra L'Inventer," *East European Reporter*, May-June 1992, pp. 4-5.) On April 16, 1992, the Presidency and the Government of the Serbian Republic of Bosnia-Hercegovina announced that it would seek recognition from the European Community and membership in the Conference on Security and Cooperation in Europe (CSCE). It also declared the establishment of diplomatic and economic relations with the Serbian government in Belgrade. (See "EC Recognition Sought," Tanjug Yugoslav News Agency report of April 16, 1992, as reported in FBIS, April 17, 1992, p. 35.

Yugoslavia, most Serbs boycotted the voting and subsequently claimed that the results of the referendum were invalid.[26]

Both during and after the referendum, armed conflict erupted in parts of Bosnia-Hercegovina.

- On the second day of referendum voting, violence broke out during a Serbian Orthodox wedding in Muslim Baščaršija in downtown Sarajevo.[27] The groom's father, carrying a Serbian flag, was shot and the priest was wounded. This triggered the establishment of barricades, manned by local Serbs, at entrances to the city. Armed Muslims, referred to as "Green Berets," also erected barricades in and around Sarajevo. Barricades were erected near Banja Luka[28] and Serbs there threatened the local television station, demanding that they adopt a pro-Serbian political stance.[29] Armed Serbs at a barricade in Doboj[30] shot a motorist. Twelve people were killed before the fighting died down the evening of March 2.[31]

---

[26] 1,997,644 people (approximately 63.4 percent of the republic's 3.15 million eligible voters) participated in the referendum. 99.7 percent voted in favor of independence and 0.3 voted against. (See *The Referendum on Independence in Bosnia-Hercegovina: February 29 - March 1, 1992*, U.S. Congressional Commission on Security and Cooperation in Europe, March 12, 1992, p. 23.)

[27] Prior to the war, Sarajevo was divided into ten municipalities. In total, Sarajevo's population numbered 525,980 people, of whom 49.3 percent were Muslims, 29.9 percent Serbs, 6.6 percent Croats, and 10.7 percent Yugoslavs.

[28] The municipality of Banja Luka numbered 195,139 people, of whom 54.8 percent were Serbs, 14.9 percent Croats, 14.6 percent Muslims and 12.0 percent Yugoslavs.

[29] "Bosnian Leader Vows Not to Allow Serbs to Split His Republic," Reuters Information Services, January 10, 1992.

[30] The municipality of Doboj included 102,546 people, 40.2 percent were Muslim, 39.0 percent Serbs, 13.0 percent Croats and 5.5 percent Yugoslavs.

[31] Dusko Doder, "Stopping the Bloodshed in the Balkans," *New York Newsday*, March 15, 1992.

- During fighting on the evening of March 3-4, at least 27 people were killed[32] in the towns of Bosanski Brod[33] and Kupres.[34] It is believed that forces from Croatia participated in the March battles in Bosanski Brod.[35]

- On March 17, after a Muslim funeral was attacked by Serbian troops,[36] fighting broke out between Serbian forces who were reportedly members of the White Eagles (*Beli Orlovi*) paramilitary group and Croatian and Muslim troops.

- On March 12, two Muslim police officers were killed near the city of Tuzla.[37] The attackers were unidentified.

---

[32] Chuck Sudetic, "Serbs Attack Muslim Slavs and Croats in Bosnia," *The New York Times,* April 4, 1992, and Chuck Sudetic, "Ethnic Clashes Increase in Bosnia as Europe Recognition Vote Nears," *The New York Times*, April 6, 1992.

[33] The municipality of Bosanski Brod numbered 33,962; 41.0 percent were Croats, 33.8 percent Serbs, 12.2 percent Muslims and 10.6 percent Yugoslavs.

[34] The population of the municipality of Kupres numbered 9,663; 50.7 percent were Serbs, 39.6 percent Croats and 8.4 percent Muslims.

[35] Chuck Sudetic, "Serbs Attack Muslim Slavs and Croats in Bosnia," *The New York Times*, April 4, 1992, and Chuck Sudetic, "Ethnic Clashes Increase in Bosnia as Europe Recognition Vote Nears," *The New York Times*, April 6, 1992.

[36] Željko Ivanković, "Il Faudra L'Inventer," *East European Reporter*, May - June 1992, p. 4.

[37] Slobodan Lekić, "Two Policemen Killed in Bosnia, Barricades Back Up," The Associated Press, March 13, 1992. The muncipality of Tuzla numbered 131,861 of whom 47.6 percent were Muslims, 15.6 percent Croats, 15.5 percent Serbs and 16.6 Yugoslavs.

- In early April, Serbs in the Bosnian police announced that they would no longer recognize the Bosnian government's command and would form an all-Serbian police force.[38]

- On April 4, the presidency of Bosnia-Hercegovina announced a general mobilization of the territorial defense, which is comprised of local militia units.[39]

- On April 5, fighting broke out in Sarajevo. Serbian policemen attacked police stations and then an Interior Ministry training school. The attack killed two officers and a civilian.[40] The Presidency of Bosnia-Hercegovina declared a state of emergency the following day.

- On April 5, thousands of peace marchers in Sarajevo were fired upon by Serbian gunmen inside a captured building. One demonstrator was killed and ten were injured.[41] That evening, local news media reported that an oil truck packed with explosives exploded near a Yugoslav army barracks, killing two people and injuring at least forty.[42]

---

[38] Patrick Moore, "Fighting Continues in Croatia and Bosnia-Hercegovina," *Radio Free Europe/Radio Liberty Daily Report*, No. 65, April 2, 1992, p. 5. (The current police force in Bosnia-Hercegovina is predominantly Croatian and Muslim, although many Serbs have remained and continue to work with their non-Serbian colleagues.)

[39] Željko Ivanković, "Il Faudra L'Inventer," *East European Reporter*, May - June 1992, p. 5.

[40] Chuck Sudetic, "Ethnic Clashes Increase in Bosnia as Europe Recognition Vote Nears," *The New York Times*, April 6, 1992.

[41] Chuck Sudetic, "Shelling by Serbs in Bosnia Intensifies," *The New York Times*, April 7, 1992, and "Factional Battling Intense in Bosnia," Reuters report published in *The Washington Post*, April 6, 1992.

[42] Chuck Sudetic, "Bosnia Calls Up Guard and Reserve," *The New York Times*, April 5, 1992.

Some observers believe that Serbian forces initiated hostilities throughout Bosnia-Hercegovina in an effort to dissuade the international community from granting recognition to Bosnia-Hercegovina. However, on April 6, Bosnia-Hercegovina's independence was recognized by the European Community. The United States followed suit on the next day. Croatia also recognized Bosnia-Hercegovina on April 7 and offered Bosnian Croats dual nationality.[43] Members of the international community, including the Arab world, also extended recognition to the new state in early April.

Full-scale armed conflict in Bosnia-Hercegovina commenced almost simultaneously with Bosnia-Hercegovina's recognition by the international community. On April 7 in Banja Luka, Bosnia's Serbs declared the independence of the Serbian Republic of Bosnia-Hercegovina, claiming two thirds of the new state's territory. Serbian irregular forces from Bosnia-Hercegovina and paramilitary groups from Serbia proper attacked areas of Bosnia-Hercegovina in the hope of preventing all or parts of the republic from seceding. JNA units stationed in Bosnia-Hercegovina, Serbian-controlled territory in Croatia and Serbia proper also launched, or participated in, attacks with Serbian irregular forces throughout Bosnia-Hercegovina. Attacks by Serbian and Yugoslav forces were resisted by Muslim forces of the Bosnian government, Bosnian Croats, and Croatian Army units sent from neighboring Croatia.[44]

On April 27, 1992, the republics of Serbia and Montenegro proclaimed the establishment of a new, truncated Yugoslavia shorn of Macedonia, Croatia, Slovenia and Bosnia-Hercegovina, all of which had proclaimed their independence from the old Yugoslav state. A new Yugoslav constitution was proclaimed on the same day. In a separate declaration, the leaders of the new nation stated that the Federal Republic of Yugoslavia "has no territorial claims" on neighboring republics.[45]

---

[43] Željko Ivanković, "Il Faudra L'Inventer," *East European Reporter*, May-June 1992, p. 5

[44] The following section describes in further detail the parties to the conflict in Bosnia-Hercegovina.

[45] See John F. Burns, "Confirming Split, Last Two Republics Proclaim a Small New Yugoslavia," *The New York Times*, April 28, 1992.

On June 16, Bosnian President Alija Izetbegović announced a formal military alliance with neighboring Croatia[46] against Serbian and Yugoslav forces.[47] On June 20, 1992, the Bosnian government formally declared the country to be in a state of war. A general mobilization of troops, including the draft of all men of fighting age, and compulsory work obligations for public and private enterprises were announced on the same day.[48]

---

[46] Croatia's role in the war in Bosnia-Hercegovina is discussed in subsequent sections pertaining to parties to the conflict and positions of the various sides.

[47] Blaine Harden, "Bosnian Leader Declares Alliance with Croatia," *The Washington Post*, June 17, 1992. The agreement between Croatian President Franjo Tudjman and Bosnian President Alija Izetbegović reads, in part, as follows: "The Republic of Croatia supports the efforts of Bosnia and Hercegovina in the preservation of its independence and its resistance to the aggression and is extending, and will continue to extend, help to the Republic of Bosnia and Hercegovina in this respect. The Republic of Croatia also endorses the efforts of the legal Government and the Presidency of Bosnia and Hercegovina in consolidating the defense of the Republic by joining all forms and components of armed resistance into united armed forces under the command of the Presidency of Bosnia and Hercegovina." (See "Press Release No. 271," Ministry of Information, Republic of Croatia, June 17, 1992.)

[48] "Presidency Declares Bosnia in 'State of War,'" Sarajevo Radio broadcast on June 20, 1992; as reported in FBIS, June 22, 1992.

PARTIES TO THE CONFLICT

Various military and paramilitary forces are parties to the armed conflict in Bosnia-Hercegovina. Generally these forces operate on two opposing sides: the Bosnian -- predominantly Muslim/Croatian -- side and the Yugoslav/Serbian side. However, a variety of troops operate on each side and the political aims and chains of command of each armed force are complex.

Bosnian and Croatian Forces

Bosnian forces are represented by the republic's territorial defense (teritorijalna obrana - TO) structure, which includes local-level militias.[1] Many of the TO's combatants are Muslims, although Croats

---

[1] The armed forces of the Bosnian government are the republic's territorial defense (teritorijalna obrana - TO) units, which comprise local defense forces separate from the federal Yugoslav army. After World War II and during Tito's reign, the official Yugoslav position maintained that Yugoslavia, as a non-aligned state, was surrounded by external enemies, such as the North Atlantic Treaty Organization (NATO) to the west and the Warsaw Pact to the east. In light of these "threats," Yugoslavia had to be prepared to defend its "territorial integrity, unity and independence." In preparation for possible attacks from "outside enemies," weapons for the general population were stored at the local level throughout the country. The weapons were purchased from workers' revenues at local enterprises and kept in various storage areas throughout each locality. Each of Yugoslavia's six constituent republics maintained a territorial defense structure, which included a civilian security force (civilna zaštita) and a local reserve militia. All former soldiers who served in the federal army could be called up to serve as reserve police officers for the republican police force or members of the local territorial defense unit. The TO's weapons could be distributed by the republican government, in consultation with the federal army and the federal government. Most of the weapons stored in territorial defense arsenals in Croatia were confiscated by the Yugoslav Army (JNA) prior to the outbreak of war in that republic. The TO arsenals in Serbian-controlled areas of Bosnia-Hercegovina also have been confiscated by Serbian paramilitaries and the Yugoslav army. With the escalation of armed conflict throughout Bosnia-Hercegovina, the Bosnian Presidency announced a general mobilization of the territorial defense units on April 4, 1992. The current TO units fighting on behalf of the Bosnian government are armed, in part, with weaponry taken from local TO weapons

and some Serbs also fight with Bosnian TO forces. Bosnian troops nominally are commanded by the government of Bosnia-Hercegovina, whose seat is in Sarajevo. However, because the Bosnian capital remains surrounded by Serbian troops and communication has been severed with much of the rest of Bosnia-Hercegovina, the local TOs usually operate under the command of local or regional officers.

Fighting alongside the Bosnian TO's forces are 30,000 Croatian Defense Council (Hrvatska Viječe Obrane -- HVO) troops in Bosnia-Hercegovina. Most HVO troops are armed and trained by the government of Croatia[2] and are Bosnian Croats. Most of the HVO troops are concentrated in areas of Bosnia-Hercegovina where Croats consitute a majority. HVO and TO forces often cooperate both militarily and otherwise.

Despite Croatian government protests to the contrary, forces from the Republic of Croatia have participated in hostilities in Bosnia-Hercegovina. The Croatian Army (Hrvatska Vojska -- HV) is present in western Hercegovina and in the northern Posavina area, particularly in the Bosanski Brod municipality. Most of the HV troops within Croatia are based along the border with Bosnia-Hercegovina but are dispatched to Bosnian areas in which hostilities have commenced. Armed troops of the Croatian Party of Rights, known as the Croatian Armed Forces (Hrvatske Oružane Snage - HOS), also operate in Bosnia-Hercegovina.[3] HOS troops are, in fact, paramilitary forces which the Chief of Staff of the Croatian Army claims to have placed under Croatian government

---

caches.

[2] John F. Burns, "Croats Claim Their Own Slice of Bosnia," *The New York Times*, July 6, 1992.

[3] Leaders of the ultra-right wing Croatian Party of Rights (Hrvatska Stranka Prava - HSP) have frequently criticized the Croatian government for its alleged ill-preparedness for, and laxity toward, Serbian armed forces in Croatia. The Croatian Party of Rights formed an armed wing called the Croatian Armed Forces (Hrvatska Oružane Snage - HOS), which engages in military operations against Serbian forces in Croatia and in Bosnia-Hercegovina. Although these troops operate under the name of the "Croatian Armed Forces," they do not represent the legitimate military forces of the government of the Republic of Croatia. Hereinafter, troops belonging to the Croatian Party of Rights will be referred to by their Croatian acronym, HOS.

control. To date, the visibility and activity of HOS troops in Bosnia-Hercegovina appear to be minimal.

In general, soldiers from the Croatian Army (HV) and the Croatian Armed Forces (HOS) cooperate with soldiers belonging to the Bosnian Territorial Defense (TO) and the Bosnian-based Croatian Defense Council (HVO). It is not uncommon to drive through Croatian- and Muslim-held territory in Bosnia-Hercegovina and encounter members of some or all of the aforementioned Bosnian and Croatian troops at the same roadblock. In many cases, Bosnian and Croatian forces operate together in military operations. The Bosnian police force, which is primarily made up of Muslims and Croats, operates as a single force but conducts certain police duties in conjunction with any of the aforementioned military forces.

The Croatian government denies that Croatian army troops have been dispatched to Bosnia-Hercegovina. Rather, it claims, Croatian army soldiers originally from Bosnia-Hercegovina who wished to return to defend Bosnia-Hercegovina when war broke out in that country have been honorably discharged from the Croatian army at their request. According to the Croatian government, these former Croatian army soldiers have since returned to their homes and joined the Bosnian Territorial Defense (TO) or the Bosnian-based Croatian Defense Council (HVO).

Despite such statements, Helsinki Watch spoke to Croatian soldiers in Bosnia-Hercegovina who claimed that they had been born and permanently resided in Croatia, specifically in the municipalities of Split, Zadar, Slavonski Brod and Županja. All but one of these soldiers wore insignia belonging to the Bosnian-based HVO forces, not the Croatian army. These soldiers included new recruits from Croatia and active members of the Croatian army who claimed that they were fighting on behalf, and in support, of the Bosnian government. However, they were unclear as to whether their military orders were delivered from, and their chain of command resided in, Zagreb, Sarajevo or Grude.[4] The extent to which forces from the republic of Croatia continue to participate in the fighting in Bosnia-Hercegovina remains unclear as of this writing. Nevertheless, because its armed forces are actively engaged in fighting in

---

[4] Grude is a town in western Hercegovina. Most of the current civilian and military leaders of Bosnian Croats are currently based in Grude.

34

Bosnia-Hercegovina, and because it has armed and trained indigenous forces, the Republic of Croatia is a party to the current conflict.

Since the outbreak of armed conflict in Bosnia-Hercegovina, troops and weapons have arrived from Croatia with the knowledge and blessing of the Bosnian government. Since a formal military alliance between Croatia and Bosnia-Hercegovina was forged on June 16, 1992,[5] the short-term goal of all Croatian and Bosnian armed forces in Bosnia-Hercegovina appears aimed at regaining territory lost to Serbian and Yugoslav forces. The ultimate disposition of any regained territory is crucial: if territory regained by Croatian forces is not returned to the control of the Bosnian government but, rather, is annexed to Croatia, the role of the Croatian troops must be seen as that of an occupying armed force rather than of a military ally.[6]

Serbian and Yugoslav Forces

Bosnian and Croatian forces are fighting against local Serbian armed groups from Bosnia-Hercegovina. Paramilitary groups from Serbia and the regular and reserve forces of the JNA have participated in hostilities in Bosnia-Hercegovina.

Prior to May 19, 1992, JNA forces stationed in Bosnia-Hercegovina, Serbian-occupied areas of Croatia, Serbia and Montenegro directly attacked Muslim and Croatian positions throughout Bosnia-Hercegovina. In many cases, the JNA attacks were coordinated and launched in conjunction with Serbian paramilitary groups which either were indigenous or from Serbia proper.

The nominal withdrawal of JNA troops from Bosnia-Hercegovina took place on May 19. However, the Belgrade authorities claimed that 80 percent of the Yugoslav Army troops in Bosnia-Hercegovina were Bosnian Serbs who would be free to remain in Bosnia-Hercegovina and fight on behalf of Serbian forces in the republic after the JNA withdrew

---

[5] The alliance between Croatia and Bosnia-Hercegovina was confirmed on July 21, 1992. John F. Burns, "UN Resumes Relief Flights to Sarajevo," *The New York Times*, July 22, 1992.

[6] Concern that the Croatian and Serbian governments may seek to partition Bosnia-Hercegovina is discussed in the following section.

on May 19. The result was that "a force of at least 30,000 men with tanks, artillery, multiple-rocket launchers and large stocks of ammunition" was left to fight for the Serbian cause.[7] These Bosnian JNA soldiers and their weaponry were absorbed into an army of Bosnian Serbs, the creation of which Serbian Democratic Party (SDS) President Radovan Karadžić and his associates had proclaimed on May 12, 1992.[8] Despite their alleged withdrawal, it is widely believed that both active and reserve JNA soldiers continue to operate in Bosnia-Hercegovina on behalf of Serbian forces in the country. In particular, JNA troops from the Užice corps in Serbia and JNA reservists from Montenegro continue to attack Bosnian and Croatian positions in Bosnia-Hercegovina.[9] Because its armed forces are actively engaged in attacking territory belonging to another state, the Federal Republic of Yugoslavia (i.e., Serbia and Montenegro) is a party to the armed conflict in Bosnia-Hercegovina.

A host of Serbian paramilitary groups also are parties to the conflict in Bosnia-Hercegovina. The self-proclaimed army of Bosnian Serbs -- most of whom are members of the Serbian Democratic Party (SDS) of Bosnia-Hercegovina -- is a predominantly indigenous paramilitary formation. Paramilitary groups from Serbia proper also have participated in hostilities in Bosnia-Hercegovina. These paramilitaries include forces commanded by Željko Ražnjatović (widely referred to by his *nom de guerre*, Arkan), which are most active in the eastern parts of Bosnia. Other paramilitary units are loyal to Vojislav Šešelj, the ultra right-wing leader of the Serbian Radical Party (Srpska Radikalna Stranka) and the Serbian Četnik Movement (Srpski Četnički Pokret). Šešelj's group of paramilitaries operate throughout Bosnia-Hercegovina. The so-called White Eagles *(Beli Orlovi)* paramilitary units, loyal to Mirko Jović, also operate throughout Bosnia-Hercegovina, as do paramilitaries commanded by Dragoslav Bokan. Helsinki Watch interviewed combatants in eastern Bosnia who claimed that they were being trained by yet another Serbian-based paramilitary leader Dragan Vasiljković (a.k.a. "Captain Dragan").

---

[7] John F. Burns, "Cease-Fire Brings Bit of Calm but No Confidence to Sarajevo," *The New York Times*, May 14, 1992.

[8] *Ibid*.

[9] John F. Burns, "A Last Bastion Raided by Serbs in East Bosnia, " *The New York Times*, July 12, 1992.

All the aforementioned paramilitary groups participated in hostilities in Croatia. Helsinki Watch has documented cases in which several paramilitary groups have committed severe violations of the rules of war, including the summary execution of hundreds of civilians.[10]

Several points should be made about the identification and level of activity of Serbian-based paramilitary units in Bosnia. First, the ability to distinguish between the various paramilitary units has become blurred. Although many Serbian combatants wear uniforms belonging to the Yugoslav army, they do not identify themselves as members of the Yugoslav military. Others wear insignia belonging to one paramilitary group but identify themselves as another group. For example, combatants who wear insignia belonging to the White Eagles will identify themselves as members of Vojislav Šešelj's or Dragoslav Bokan's forces. Originally, such forces were commanded by Mirko Jović. Similarly, the term Četnik, originally used to identify Šešelj's forces, now is widely used to refer to paramilitaries belonging to Jović's, Bokan's and, to a lesser extent, Arkan's and Dragan's forces. Many of those who purport to be members of a particular paramilitary group are local Bosnian Serbs/combatants.

There are two reasons why local Serbs identify themselves as members of such paramilitary units. First, these paramilitary units are widely known for their brutality and ruthlessness and local Serbian combatants frequently assume these identities to evoke fear and terror among the non-Serbian population. Secondly, some of the paramilitary commanders have been exalted to "hero" status by the Serbian media and, therefore, identification with such men is viewed as honorable and patriotic. In sum, although combatants may identify themselves as members of a given paramiltary group and/or their victims might do the same, this identification may not always be correct.

The current level of activity of Serbian-based paramilitary groups in Bosnia remains unclear. When fighting broke out in early April, most of the five aforementioned paramilitary groups -- which are otherwise based in Serbia -- were actively fighting on behalf of Serbian forces in Bosnia-Hercegovina. When Helsinki Watch representatives drove through Bosnia-Hercegovina in early April, the presence of Serbian-based paramilitary groups was quite evident and there was little doubt that they

---

[10] See Helsinki Watch letter to Slobodan Milošević, President of the Republic of Serbia, and General Blagoje Adžić, Acting Minister of Defense and Chief of Staff of the Yugoslav People's Army, January 21, 1992.

were commanding and arming local Serbian forces in some areas, including Banja Luka and Zvornik. The extent to which they remain in Bosnia-Hercegovina as of this writing is unclear. During a visit to Serbian-controlled areas of eastern Bosnia in early June, Helsinki Watch representatives interviewed combatants who identified themselves as members of one of the Serbian-based paramilitary groups but, in fact, were local Serbs who had taken up arms. In other cases, Helsinki Watch has interviewed Bosnian Serbs in Zvornik and Bijeljina who claim to have been armed and trained by Dragan and Arkan, respectively.[11] The combatants in Bijeljina claimed that when fighting broke out, Arkan was commanding them but that he had since left the area under the control of Bosnian Serbs whom he allegedly armed and trained.

Although the Serbian government has stated that it will "take measures against illegally armed civilians and groups," paramilitary units continue to operate, recruit and train throughout Serbia.[12] Paramilitary leaders freely roam the streets of Belgrade. For example, Arkan operates a pastry shop near his home in central Belgrade, which is guarded by armed paramilitaries dressed and equipped with full military regalia.

Moreover, it is widely believed that Serbian paramilitary groups conduct military operations in conjunction with, in the presence of, or with the knowledge of JNA forces and commanders. Indeed, almost all displaced persons and refugees from Bosnia-Hercegovina interviewed by Helsinki Watch representatives pointed out that the JNA played a key role in attacking their town or village, either by directly taking part in the hostilities or by the *a priori* arming of Serbian paramilitary units.

---

[11] These interviews were conducted by Helsinki Watch representatives during visits to Zvornik and Bijeljina in early June 1992.

[12] Blaine Harden, "Serbian Leader Retreats from Bosnian Aggression," *The Washington Post*, April 25, 1992. Although Serbian police arrested paramilitary leader Dragoslav Bokan on April 24, he was subsequently released.

POSITIONS OF THE VARIOUS SIDES

Helsinki Watch takes no position on the territorial claims of the various parties to the conflict. This section describing the positions of the various sides is intended to set a context for understanding the actions of the participants.

The Cantonization of Bosnia-Hercegovina

In mid-1991, the European Community began negotiations on the future of Yugoslavia. The EC's efforts were aimed at achieving a peaceful resolution to a variety of crises. The wars in Croatia and Bosnia-Hercegovina, combined with the status of Albanians in Kosovo and Serbs in Croatia, presented a daunting task for the aspiring peacemakers. During an EC-sponsored meeting on Bosnia-Hercegovina held in Brussels from March 7-9, 1992, Croatian and Serbian representatives -- both of whom represented the extremist faction of their constituencies -- favored a division of Bosnia-Hercegovina into various ethnic "cantons." The cantonization of Bosnia-Hercegovina would reorganize the state into three autonomous ethnic regions, one each for Muslims, Serbs and Croats which would maintain a loose confederal association.

Conversely, Muslim representatives argued in favor of a single state for all of Bosnia-Hercegovina's citizens. Muslim representatives were opposed to the division of Bosnia-Hercegovina along ethnic lines. In general, Muslims fear that the division of Bosnia-Hercegovina into three national regions eventually would result in the incorporation of Croatian and Serbian cantons into Croatia and Serbia proper. Most moderate Serbs and Croats support this view.

A March 9, 1992, document, signed by European Community official Jose Cutilheiro, supported Bosnia-Hercegovina's sovereignty but endorsed the concept of national cantonization.[1] The plan did not

---

[1] Željko Ivanković, "Il Faudra L'Inventer," *East European Reporter*, May-June 1992, p. 4, and Judy Dempsey, "Bosnian Carve-Up in the Making," *The Financial Times*, July 8, 1992.

specify how the boundaries of each ethnic canton would be drawn. Moreover, the plan failed to take into account that some areas were so ethnically intertwined that a simple division was not easily possible.[2]

Neither side was satisfied with the EC arrangement. Serbian representatives opposed Bosnia-Hercegovina's sovereignty while Muslim delegates remained wary of cantonization.[3] On March 17, Serbian leaders presented Cutilheiro with a map of the proposed ethnic division of Bosnia-Hercegovina in which Serbs -- who represent 31.3 percent of Bosnia-Hercegovina's population -- claimed 70 percent of the country's land.[4] According to the Serbian plan, the remaining 30 percent of Bosnia-Hercegovina's territory would be divided between Muslims and Croats, who comprise 43.7 and 17.3 percent of the population, respectively.[5]

Since the outbreak of war in Bosnia-Hercegovina in April, Muslim and moderate Croatian representatives have continued to reject efforts to partition Bosnia-Hercegovina into ethnic cantons. Serbian forces continue to support such an arrangement. The position of radical Croatian forces is similar to the Serbian view. The current positions of the various parties to the conflict are described below.

---

[2] Judy Dempsey, "Bosnian Carve-Up in the Making," *The Financial Times*, July 8, 1992.

[3] *Ibid.*

[4] *Ibid.*

[5] In June 1991, Helsinki Watch representatives interviewed Radovan Karadžić, President of Bosnia-Hercegovina's Serbian Democratic Party (SDS) and primary representative of Bosnian Serbs at the EC conference on Yugoslavia. During the interview, Helsinki Watch representatives inquired about the status of the political and civil rights -- especially freedom of the press -- of Serbs in Bosnia-Hercegovina. Karadžić did not answer the question but proceeded to delineate those municipalities in Bosnia-Hercegovina which he sought to claim for Serbs. His calculations in June 1991, were identical to the map presented to EC representatives in March 1992.

The Bosnian Position

In general, Muslims, Croats not from Hercegovina and portions of the Serbian population support an independent, multi-ethnic and democratic Bosnia-Hercegovina. This position is best represented by the current government of President Alija Izetbegović. The Party of Democratic Action (SDA) and the liberal/moderate faction of the Croatian Democratic Union (HDZ), formerly led by Bosnian Vice President Stjepan Klujić, also support this position.

The Croatian Position

The positions of Bosnian Croats, of Croats in Croatia proper and among members of the government of the Republic of Croatia are seriously divided, in particular, about the status of western Hercegovina, a predominantly Croatian region of Bosnia. A total of 752,068 Croats lived in Bosnia-Hercegovina, only 266,815 (or approximately 35 percent) of them in Hercegovina. Approximately 65 percent (485,253 persons) of the republic's Croatian population lived outside Hercegovina.[6]

On the one hand, liberal and moderate Croatian elements support an independent Bosnia-Hercegovina; their views are similar to the Bosnian position, set forth above. Generally, most Croats who live outside of Hercegovina support this position, which is best exemplified by Stjepan Klujić, the former head of the Croatian Democratic Union (HDZ) of Bosnia-Hercegovina and current Vice President of the Bosnian government. Other prominent Bosnian Croats, including Bosnian Defense Minister Jerko Dogo, support Klujić's position. On the other hand, a conservative wing of the HDZ in Bosnia-Hercegovina seeks autonomy for the predominantly Croatian area of western Hercegovina from Bosnia. It is widely believed that this wing of the HDZ seeks the secession of western Hercegovina and its union with neighboring Croatia. This irredentist position is best represented by Mate Boban, the current

---

[6] These figures were calculated by Helsinki Watch representatives on the basis of results from the 1991 census. They reflect the Croatian population in the western (predominantly Croatian) and eastern (predominantly Serbian) halves of Hercegovina. Approximately 7,300 Croats lived in eastern Hercegovina.

leader of the Croatian Democratic Union (HDZ) of Bosnia-Hercegovina.[7]

Klujić was elected by Croats in Bosnia-Hercegovina to represent them in the republic's 1990 elections. At a HDZ party congress in January, conservative elements of the HDZ, most of whom were from western Hercegovina, forced Klujić from office and replaced him with Mate Boban as leader of the party. At the congress, Klujić delivered his resignation saying he was opposed to Bosnia's partition along ethnic lines.[8] It is widely believed that Croatian President Franjo Tudjman engineered Boban's accession as head of the HDZ of Bosnia-Hercegovina and that Boban remains beholden to Tudjman.[9]

The position of the Croatian government with regard to the partition of Bosnia-Hercegovina has been contradictory. On the one hand, Croatia recognized the independence and territorial integrity of Bosnia-Hercegovina on April 7 and in subsequent public statements. Also, Croatia joined a formal military alliance with Bosnia-Hercegovina on June 16, in which Croatia reaffirmed Bosnia-Hercegovina's independence. However, statements made by President Tudjman and actions taken by Mate Boban would indicate that Croatia may have plans to divide Bosnia-Hercegovina with Serbia. In March 1991, Tudjman and Serbian President Slobodan Milošević met secretly in the town of Karadjordje. The topic of their discussion was never disclosed but many have speculated that the two spoke of dividing Bosnia-Hercegovina between Serbia and Croatia.[10] On May 6, 1992, a meeting between Mate Boban and Radovan Karadžić, President of the Serbian Democratic Party (SDS) of Bosnia-Hercegovina, took place in the Austrian city of Graz. Because Boban and Karadžić are widely regarded to be lackeys, respectively, of Tudjman and Milošević, it is widely believed that the meeting was engineered by the Croatian and Serbian presidents to discuss

---

[7] John F. Burns, "Croats Claim Their Own Slice of Bosnia," *The New York Times*, July 6, 1992.

[8] Judy Dempsey, "Bosnian Carve-Up in the Making," *The Financial Times*, July 8, 1992.

[9] *Ibid.*

[10] *Ibid.*

further the partition of Bosnia-Hercegovina.[11] The Croatian government has discounted such "speculations," claiming that the meeting between Boban and Karadžić was one in a series of meetings between the various parties to the conflict in Bosnia-Hercegovina.[12] The Croatian government claims that such meetings were encouraged by the EC and "must be see as part of the bilateral discussions within the framework" of the EC-sponsored Conference on Yugoslavia.[13]

On July 3, 1992, Mate Boban proclaimed a quasi-independent Croatian state within Bosnia-Hercegovina which would include the remaining third of Bosnia's territory which was not occupied by Serbian forces. The new republic is to be called "The Community of Herceg-Bosna" and is to function as an autonomous Croatian territory within the republic of Bosnia-Hercegovina. The territory claimed by Mate Boban for the new Croatian republic is composed primarily of a region about 80 miles long and up to 70 miles wide and includes most of Hercegovina, the Posavina region in northeast Bosnia and a section of Sarajevo called Stup.[14] Although predominantly Croatian, this area incorporates towns and villages where Muslims and Serbs form a majority.[15]

In declaring the "Community of Herceg-Bosna," Boban is widely thought to have acted on behalf of Croatian President Franjo Tudjman, who has made no secret of his territorial ambitions in Bosnia-Hercegovina.[16] President Tudjman denies that Croatia has designs on

---

[11] Blaine Harden, "Serbs, Croats, Agree to Carve-Up Bosnia," *The Washington Post*, May 8, 1992.

[12] "Croatian President Replies to US Senator [Robert Dole] on Croat-Serb Talks on Bosnia-Hercegovina," Ministry of Information, Republic of Croatia, Press Release no. 246, May 9, 1992; and "Don't Lump Croatia with Serbia," Letter to the Editor by Frane V. Golem, Authorized Representative of the Republic of Croatia in the United States, *The Washington Post*, May 16, 1992.

[13] *Ibid*.

[14] John F. Burns, "Croats Claim Their Own Slice of Bosnia," *The New York Times*, July 6, 1992.

[15] *Ibid*.

[16] *Ibid*.

Bosnian land. Rather, he points out that the "Republic of Croatia has recognized the sovereignty and territorial integrity of the Republic of Bosnia-Hercegovina."[17] Tudjman claimed that, in the opinion of the Croatian government, "the crisis in Bosnia-Hercegovina can be solved only by organizing Bosnia-Hercegovina as a community of three constituent nations on a cantonal basis as proposed by the European Community at its conference on Bosnia-Hercegovina."[18]

Indeed, Boban and Tudjman have made repeated statements that would indicate that the Croatian government is laying claim to territory controlled by Croatian forces in Bosnia-Hercegovina. Such statements seriously call into question the role of the Croatian army (HV), Croatian paramilitary groups (HOS) and the Croatian Defense Council (HVO) in Bosnia-Hercegovina, all of which operate there under the pretext that they are aiding Bosnian troops and defending that republic from attacks by Serbian and Yugoslav forces. Recent statements by Boban and Tudjman seem to indicate that the primary role of such troops is to secure territory to be annexed to Croatia.

Prior to the declaration of a Croatian state in Bosnia, Tudjman put pressure on Bosnian President Izetbegović to commit Bosnia-Hercegovina to a confederation with Croatia. Izetbegović's resistance to this idea was met by what amounted to an ultimatum from Boban: Izetbegović would join with Tudjman and proclaim a confederation or Croatian forces stationed near Sarajevo would not come to the aid of the city.[19] Moreover, during most of June and July, Boban increased pressure on the Bosnian government "by blocking delivery of arms that the Sarajevo government, working around a United Nations embargo on all shipments to the former Yugoslavia, has secretly bought."[20] On July 21, President Izetbegović met with President Tudjman and apparently persuaded the latter to resume shipments of arms and ammunition to

---

[17] "Tudjman Sends Letter to Izetbegović," Zagreb Radio broadcast on July 6, 1992, as reported in FBIS, July 7, 1992.

[18] Tudjman News Conference on Current Issues," Zagreb Radio broadcast on July 6, 1992, as reported in FBIS, July 7, 1992.

[19] Ibid.

[20] Ibid.

Bosnian forces, particularly around Sarajevo.[21] Although Bosnia and Croatia have resumed their military cooperation, Croatia's territorial ambitions in Bosnia, and the potential for human rights problems associated with such a partition, remain deeply troubling.

The partition of Bosnia-Hercegovina remains a particularly divisive issue among Croats in Bosnia-Hercegovina and in Croatia. Government officials who are liberal and moderate members of the ruling party (HDZ) and/or other political parties generally oppose the partition of Bosnia-Hercegovina. Franjo Greguric (Croatia's Prime Minister), Milan Ramljak (Vice-President of the Croatian Government) and Zdravko Tomac (former Vice-President of the Croatian Government and current Ambassador to the Republic of Slovenia) have all voiced reservations about the dismemberment of Bosnia-Hercegovina. On the other hand, it is widely believed that Croatian President Franjo Tudjman and Croatian Defense Minister Gojko Šušak (himself from Hercegovina) are the main figures in the Croatian government who support Hercegovina's union with Croatia.

Many opposition parties, the independent press and a substantial portion of the population in Croatia oppose the dismemberment of Bosnia-Hercegovina. It is widely understood throughout Croatia that the Croatian government cannot condemn and call for the return of Serbian-occupied territory in Croatia and, at the same time, seek to annex territory belonging to another state, i.e., Bosnia-Hercegovina. Moreover, prominent Bosnian Croats, such as Stjepan Klujić, have vowed to overturn Boban's proclamation of an independent Croatian state in Bosnia.[22] If sustained, the proclamation, coupled with a similar declaration made by Serbian nationalists in May, would result in the effective partition of Bosnia-Hercegovina between groups whose eventual aim is to annex portions of the republic to Croatia and Serbia.[23]

Helsinki Watch takes no position on the territorial or political construction of the former Yugoslav republics. Our only concern is that

---

[21] John F. Burns, "UN Resumes Relief Flights to Sarajevo," *The New York Times*, July 22, 1992.

[22] John F. Burns, "Croats Claim Their Own Slice of Bosnia," *The New York Times*, July 6, 1992.

[23] *Ibid.*

the human rights of all citizens, regardless of their ethnic, national, religious, political or other affiliation, be respected. Serbian efforts to annex territory in Croatia and Bosnia-Hercegovina have resulted in thousands of human rights abuses and violations of the rules of war in both republics. Helsinki Watch is gravely concerned that steps by Croatia to partition Bosnia-Hercegovina further will lead to additional violence in a conflict already marked by its extreme brutality.

The Serbian Position

For the most part, Serbs living in predominantly Serbian areas of Bosnia-Hercegovina oppose Bosnian independence and are generally in favor of union or close association with Serbia. Many such Serbs are affiliated with the Serbian Democratic Party (SDS) of Bosnia-Hercegovina and claim that their rights would be endangered in an independent Bosnian state. According to SDS leader Radovan Karadžić, "It is impossible for Serbs to live together with other peoples in a unitary state."[24] Karadžić and his followers believe that an independent Bosnian state would be a unitary entity in which a combined Muslim and Croatian majority would persecute a Serbian minority. These Serbs justify their fear of persecution by pointing to history, especially the alliance between Croats and Muslims with the Axis powers during World War II. Some Serbs also claim that they fear the fundamentalist policies of a Muslim government.[25]

The Serbian position also holds that all Serbs have the right to live in one state. Serbs emphasize that nationalities, not republics, have the right to secede from Yugoslavia. They contend that, insofar as other nationalities have sought to secede from Yugoslavia, the Serbs also have the right to secede from Croatia, Bosnia-Hercegovina, or any other Yugoslav republic. Because many Serbs reside on territory belonging to one of the secessionist states, the political and military strategies of Serbian forces in Bosnia-Hercegovina and in Croatia have been to assume control over areas of republics in which Serbs constitute a

---

[24] John F. Burns, "Understanding, and Letting Loose, Dark Distrusts in the Balkans," *The New York Times*, June 28, 1992.

[25] *Ibid.*

46

majority or substantial minority and to fuse those regions with the new Yugoslavia.

Karadžić denies that he and his supporters seek to annex Bosnian territory and become part of a "Greater Serbia."[26] Rather, he contends that they support the division of Bosnia-Hercegovina into communal cantons which would function as autonomous entities under the control of the majority national group in each canton. The cantons would share some responsibilities at the Bosnian level but most government power would be concentrated at the canton level. Under such an arrangement, Karadžić and his followers believe that Serbian-controlled cantons should include 70 percent of Bosnia-Hercegovina's territory despite the fact that Serbs constitute only 31 percent of Bosnia's population. SDS leaders justify such disparity by claiming that Serbs own property on 70 percent of Bosnia-Hercegovina's land and therefore are entitled to those areas.

Serbian President Slobodan Milošević claims that neither he nor his government have in any way intervened, nor are responsible for, the war in Bosnia-Hercegovina. Milošević asserts that the conflict in Bosnia-Hercegovina is a "civil war" between various groups, none of which include forces from Serbia. Moreover, Milošević has claimed that neither the JNA nor the Serbian government have a "single soldier on the soil of Bosnia-Hercegovina and that [they] are not supporting any military action."[27] Rather, he claims, Serbia is supplying indigenous Serbian forces in Bosnia-Hercegovina only with "food and clothes and other things for survival" but not with military support.[28]

Nevertheless, it is well known that the government of Yugoslavia, and in particular, the government of the Republic of Serbia, have provided economic, military and political support to Bosnian Serbs

---

[26] See Karadžić's letter to U.S. President George Bush, dated July 3, 1992, as transcribed by Reuters Information Services, July 3, 1992. See also "Statement by Karadžić to Belgrade Television," April 16, 1992, as reported in FBIS, April 17, 1992, pp. 34-35.

[27] Cable News Network (CNN) Interview with Serbian President Slobodan Milošević, initially broadcast on CNN at 3:00 p.m. EST on June 26, 1992; as transcribed by Reuters Information Services, June 26, 1992.

[28] Ibid.

fighting against the forces of Bosnia-Hercegovina.[29] Many foreign and domestic observers believe that Karadžić, the leader of the SDS in Bosnia-Hercegovina, closely coordinates his actions with Serbian President Slobodan Milošević.[30] The Serbian government has openly supported the political and military aims of the Serbian Democratic Party (SDS) in Bosnia-Hercegovina. The Serbian government also has condoned, and in some cases supported, the formation of at least five paramilitary groups in Serbia which operate in Bosnia-Hercegovina.[31] Lastly, evidence would suggest that the JNA continues to take part in military operations throughout Bosnia-Hercegovina.[32] For example, despite claims by the Yugoslav government that it ceased all military intervention in Bosnia on May 19, air attacks against Sarajevo and other areas continued thereafter. One such air attack on Sarajevo occurred on June 10. According to Lieutenant Colonel Richard Gray, a UN military observer from New Zealand who watched the attack from a window, a Yugoslav army jet "dropped a cluster bomb on a Muslim-controlled hill" near central Sarajevo.[33] Serbian forces in Bosnia-Hercegovina have no aircraft capable of such an attack."[34]

It is important to note that some Bosnian Serbs, primarily those living in multi-ethnic cities such as Sarajevo, do not support the militant position of Milošević, Karadžić or their followers. Many Serbs, including Jovan Divjuk, deputy commander of Bosnian forces, and Nenad Kecmanović and Mirko Pejanović, Serbian members of Bosnia's collective

---

[29] See above section regarding Serbian/Yugoslav parties to the conflict. See also Miloš Vasić "Plan RAM u akciji: Naoružavanje Bosne," *Vreme*, March 1991.

[30] John F. Burns, "Cease-Fire Brings Bit of Calm but No Confidence to Sarajevo," *The New York Times*, May 14, 1992.

[31] See previous section concerning Serbian and Yugoslav parties to the conflict.

[32] *Ibid.*

[33] Blaine Harden, "Sarajevo Greets UN Peace-Keepers," *The Washington Post*, June 12, 1992.

[34] *Ibid.*

Presidency, support the Bosnian position as stated above. Moreover, some Serbs also are members of Bosnia's police force and its territorial defense units and are actively engaged in defending Bosnian territory from militant Serbian and Yugoslav attacks.

Also, portions of the population of Serbia are opposed to the war in Bosnia-Hercegovina. In particular, Serbs in the province of Vojvodina and among independent academic, press and cultural circles in Belgrade have long been opposed to the Serbian government's and JNA's involvement in the wars in Croatia and Bosnia-Hercegovina. Recent demonstrations in Belgrade, which the Serbian Orthodox church has supported,[35] attest to the degree of popular dissatisfaction and opposition many Serbs feel toward Milošević and his policies.[36]

---

[35] Laura Silber, "Serb Regime Rebuked by Church," *The Washington Post*, May 29, 1992, and Michael T. Kaufman, "Thousands Protest Against Serbian President," *The New York Times*, June 15, 1992.

[36] Chuck Sudetic, "Tens of Thousands Call for Removal of Serbia's Leader," *The New York Times*, June 1, 1992; Nikola Antonov, "Big Anti-Milošević Rally in Belgrade," Reuters Information Service, June 28, 1992; Blaine Harden, "100,000 Serbs Demand Ouster of Milošević," *The Washington Post*, June 29, 1992.

VIOLATIONS OF THE RULES OF WAR

Summary Executions of Civilians and Persons *Hors de Combat*

Helsinki Watch has documented cased in which civilians are being summarily executed as part of an "ethnic cleansing" campaign which is being implemented by Serbian forces. Many of the displaced persons who have fled from occupied villages and who could possibly provide further information about such atrocities remain encircled in besieged areas such as Goražde, Tuzla, Bihać and Sarajevo. Helsinki Watch has also received reports that Serbian civilians may have been executed in the municipalities of Sarajevo. However, to date we have not received any evidence that would confirm such reports.

Zaklopača (municipality of Vlasenica)[1]

On May 16, 1992, at least 83 Muslims were summarily executed by Serbian paramilitaries in the village of Zaklopača.[2] At least 11 children (ranging in age from 6 to 16) and 16 elderly persons (over 60) were among those killed,[3] according to eyewitnesses to and survivors of

---

[1] Of the 33,817 inhabitants of the municipality of Vlasenica, 55.5 percent were Muslim and 42.5 percent Serbs.

[2] According to survivors, approximately 200 people lived in the almost exclusively Muslim village of Zaklopača.

[3] On the basis of survivors' accounts, volunteer workers at Zagreb's mosque compiled a list of those killed in Zaklopača. Most of the names on the list were recounted by eyewitnesses during individual interviews with Helsinki Watch representatives on June 5, 1992. According to the list, 30 members of the Hodžić family, nine members of the Hamidović family, eight members of the Salihović family, nine members of the Selimovic family, seven members of the Avdić family and seven members of the Nuskić family were among those killed. The Hreljić family lost three members and the Dugalić, Mušić and Berbić families each lost two family members. Mustafa Mahmutović, Rasim Fetahović and Himzo Vejzović and Bajro Djurić also were killed.

the execution.[4]   The village of Zaklopača is bordered by the predominantly Serbian villages of Gornji Zalkovik, Podbirač, Miloševine, Bakiće, Vukovići, Raići and Milići. At the end of March and the beginning of April, Serbian women, children and elderly persons were evacuated from most of these villages.

According to Najla Hodžić:

> When we asked our Serbian neighbors where and why they were leaving, they refused to tell us. Some made excuses about having to visit relatives but most refused to talk about it at all. After the Bosnian referendum [February 29-March 1, 1992], local Serbs started carrying AK-47s in public. At the same time, businesses began to close, the hospital was temporarily closed and Muslims were being fired from their jobs. For example, 33 Muslim electricians were fired from the Elektrodistribucija plant in Vlasenica and Muslim miners from the Boksita transport plant in Milići also were laid off. Eventually, even the school was closed. During the last week of March, the Serbs erected barricades around their villages. In early May, armed Serbs entered our village searching for weapons but found nothing and left peacefully.

On May 16, at approximately 5:00 a.m., a busload of Serbian soldiers drove through Zaklopača. According to Sena Hodžić:

> The bus was coming from the direction of Milići and was headed toward Gornji Zalkovik. It was full of men in Yugoslav army uniforms who were wearing Četnik symbols on their hats. At first, they only drove through Zaklopača but, once they got to the outskirts of our town, they surrounded it. It was quiet until about noon, when our village was attacked from the Serbian positions which

---

[4] On June 5, 1992, in Zagreb, Croatia, Helsinki Watch representatives interviewed four women who had survived the killings. Helsinki Watch representatives were not able to interview a fifth eyewitness, who was hospitalized due to shock.

had been assumed earlier that morning and from those Serbian villages that encircled ours.

The women claim that no heavy artillery was used; they say they heard only gunfire. The shooting was brief and by mid-afternoon the villagers cautiously began to come out of their homes. Sena Hodžić remembers:

We were scared but we had work to do and I had to till the soil. At approximately 4:30 p.m., I was working my plot and a large automobile passed by me. The car was white but had "massacre" (*pokolj*) written across it in large blue letters. The man who was driving the car was Milomir Milošević from Klještana. Several Četniks with beards also were in the car.

A second witness, Zerina Hodžić, confirmed the above account:

I was taking my cows to pasture when I saw the Četniks. I immediately went into my house from where I saw that three Četniks had gotten out of the car and others were entering the village on foot. About 100 Četniks came from the direction of Zalkovik. Each Četnik had two AK-47s, ammunition strapped across his chest and belt and all were dressed in JNA uniforms but had a Četnik symbol on their hats. Many wore gloves on their hands and stockings over their heads. They broke off into groups that started going from house to house.

According to Najla Hodžić:

They came to my house first because it is the first one at the entrance to the village. Four or five of them came toward my house. It was sometime around 4:30 p.m.. My brother-in-law, Haso Hodžić (age 39) was outside, in front of the house when the Četniks approached. They started calling him an Ustaša. My brother-in-law started to walk toward them and they told him to give up his weapons. He told them that he did not have any weapons

but that they could take his cows. Then one of the
Četniks opened fire and killed him.

The murdered man's wife, Nevresa Hodžić, confirmed her sister-
in-law's account:

> After they killed my husband, we let out
> a scream and they sprayed our house
> with bullets and then machine-gunned
> the entire village. They kept shooting
> for several minutes all over the village
> despite the fact that no one was shooting
> at them.

Similarly Sena Hodžić's husband, Ibrahim, (age 39), was killed as
she and her eight- and ten-year-old sons looked on.

> Three Četniks approached our home. A neighbor from
> the area, Milomir Milošević was with them. My husband,
> my children and I were trying to flee when we saw them
> approaching the house. They surrounded us and we
> hovered in a corner near the house. We were terrified.
> One of the Četniks motioned to my husband with his
> index finger to walk toward him. My husband obeyed
> and started to walk in his direction, only to be sprayed
> with gunfire by the Četnik.

Zerina Hodžić's family faced a similar fate.

> I was hiding in the barn with my husband Rifet [age 35]
> and our two daughters [ages 13 and 7]. Five Četniks
> found us and pointed their index fingers at my husband
> and beckoned him toward them. One of the Četniks shot
> him without ever having uttered a word.

Each of the four women interviewed by Helsinki Watch claimed
to have seen approximately 30 men from the village rounded up into one
group and killed by machine-gun fire. Many others were killed
individually, usually in front of their homes.

During the shooting, those who had survived had hidden in three homes belonging to Haso Hodžić, Alija Hamidović, and Hasko Hamidović. After their husbands had been killed, the four women hid in their family home with 11 other people. In all, approximately 45 people are known to have survived.

After approximately 15 minutes of shooting and killing, several of the paramilitaries headed back toward the village of Milići in their car. The rest of the paramilitaries walked to the other surrounding Serbian villages. When the fighting stopped and the paramilitaries withdrew, the survivors emerged from the houses to find their dead relatives scattered about the village. Several houses had been set on fire. The women interviewed by Helsinki Watch said they had identified the bodies of the following five families:

- Saban Avdić, his two sons, his wife, daughter-in-law and her two children;

- Ibis Hoždić, his wife, their two sons, two daughters-in-law and four grandchildren;

- Enisa Hoždić, her two children, her three sisters, her father, mother and another man they could not identify;

- Fatima Berbić and her husband.

According to Zerina Hoždić:

> We emerged from the house where we had been hiding only to see dead bodies strewn about the village. We remained in the village for a short period of time and I covered my husband, who was lying dead on the ground. Flies were descending over the corpses.

The four women said that the survivors did not bury their dead, fearing another attack by the Serbian paramilitaries. Rather, they headed toward the town of Vlasenica. Because they were afraid of taking the main road, they travelled in the rain through the forest, where they remained for three days without food.

Zerina Hodžić continued:

When the Serbian paramilitaries noticed something moving in the bushes, they shot in our direction. When we got near the village of Damčići, one of the children from our group wandered to the perimeter of the forest only to confront a Četnik. The Četnik asked him where the others were but the child did not answer. The Četnik then shot the boy. His mother ran out of the bushes and another man ran after her. They were both shot dead by the Četnik. I do not know the names of the people but I recognized them as having been from our area.

According to the women, shortly after the child had been killed, some time between 10:00 a.m. and 11:00 a.m., they saw the village of Damčići burning. The women believe that the Četniks set fire to the village. They eventually arrived at Vlasenica and went to the Serbian command center to get permits to travel to Kladanj, a predominantly Muslim town.

According to Zerina Hodžić:

At first they refused to issue the permits and told us to go back to Zaklopača but we refused. They put us on a bus and, when we got to the Serbian village of Luke, we were stopped by about 20 Četniks. They were lined up on both sides of the road, with their guns pointed at us. They told us to get out of the bus and walk along the white line in the center of the road, in a single column. There were approximately 30 of us, including an elderly woman who had been wounded and many children. We walked for two hours in the rain and finally came to the Muslim village of Ravne, from where we were transported to Kladanj. After ten days, we had to leave Kladanj because there was no food left in the town. We went to the village of Živinica, near Tuzla, where we stayed for two days but we were forced to leave because the Serbs started attacking the area. We were driven to Odžak and then to Slavonski Brod in Croatia. Mortars were falling on Slavonski Brod but the locals made every effort to get us some food. When the fighting subsided we were brought here, to Zagreb.

Vlašić Plateau (municipality of Travnik)[5]

Evidence gathered by Helsinki Watch strongly points to the summary execution of at least 15 disarmed combatants probably by members of the military police of the JNA on May 15, 1992. Two of five survivors, Stjepan Dražetić[6] and Nikola Marjanović,[7] were interviewed separately by Helsinki Watch representatives. According to both men, approximately 70 to 100 members of the Bosnian Territorial Defense (TO), the Croatian Defense Council (HVO) and the Bosnian reserve police force were on guard at Vlašić, a plateau on a hill near the city of Travnik. The Bosnian and Croatian troops were armed with AK-47s and other machine guns. Four mortar launchers also were in the vicinity. Fighting between the Croatian/Bosnian and Serbian forces broke out some time between 9:00 p.m. and 9:30 p.m.

According to Nikola Marjanović:

> Some sporadic fighting between our forces and their troops broke out but quickly subsided. Approximately 20 of us [most of whom were HVO soldiers] then took shelter in a nearby barn of sorts. The structure had concrete walls but a wooden make-shift roof. We were preparing something to eat and because it was dark, we couldn't see anyone approaching the barn, but we heard someone coming forward. They told us that they were HVO, but, in fact, they were Četniks. As they approached the door, we saw them aim their guns from the door and then they opened fire. Nikica Žilić, who was wounded, yelled out to them to stop shooting and told them that we would surrender. They stopped shooting and told us to put our hands in the air while we laid down on the

---

[5] Of the 70,402 inhabitants of the municipality of Travnik, 45.3 percent were Muslims, 36.9 percent Croats, 11.0 percent Serbs, and 5.2 percent Yugoslavs.

[6] Interviewed in the hospital in Travnik, on June 12, 1992.

[7] Interviewed in the village of Ovčarevo (municipality of Travnik) on June 12, 1992.

floor. Sḷavko Didak tried to escape but he was shot and killed.

Marjanović said that the JNA soldiers subsequently set fire to the building where the shooting had taken place and that Slavko Didak's body was burned as a result.

Stjepan Dražetić, who had been wounded in the thigh from the shooting said that a second HVO soldier, Mirko Rimac, also was shot but that, unlike Didak, he was not trying to flee. Dražetić recounted what happened after their surrender:

> They told us to form a single column and crawl on our stomachs to a plain on the hill, where we remained on the ground for approximately 15 minutes. We were then told to strip to our undergarments and to crawl for another 15 minutes.

Dražetić claims that a JNA soldier had come to tell their captors that one of their men had been killed during the earlier battle with the Bosnian and Croatian forces. This news supposedly caused the other soldiers to turn violent.

According to Marjanović:

> After we had crawled approximately 30 meters, we were told to lie on our stomachs with our hands behind our heads and to put our faces in the dirt. They kicked and beat us while we were in that position and I heard some shooting; it's possible that someone was killed but I couldn't see who that might have been because my face was in the dirt. I only know that our commander, Zoran Domić, had been killed because I later saw his body nearby.

Marjanović continued:

> At one point, one of the soldiers yelled "Don't kill all of them; we need a few prisoners for exchange purposes." They then told us to get up. Five of us stood up, including Nikica Žilić who had been wounded earlier. Stjepan Dražetić also was wounded, but he managed to

stand up, as did Pero Djepina and Zdravko Brkić.[8] The rest of the men were either dead, crying out or moaning on the ground.

Thirteen corpses were subsequently found on Vlašić plateau. Autopsies were performed on May 23, 1992, in the morgue at the upper cemetery in Travnik. Medical reports[9] indicate that the autopsies were performed eight days after the time of death. The autopsy and medical records of the men -- all HVO soldiers from the municipality of Travnik -- showed many injuries and the causes of death. The reports were as follows:

- Mirko Rimac, from the village of Sipovika, was shot in the legs and subsequently died from blows inflicted to the head by a wooden or metal object.

- The body of Slavko Didak, from the village of Kraljevica, the aforementioned man who was shot when trying to escape, was burned.

- Slavo Babić, from the village of Paklarevo, was beaten to death with a solid object. Most of the blows were inflicted to the face.

- Ivo Sotjak, from the village of Paklarevo, was killed after having been shot in the chest, specifically the heart and lungs.

- Perica Lukić, from the village of Paklarevo, was shot five times in the heart, lung, and stomach. He died from blows inflicted to the head and excessive blood loss.

----

[8] The five men were later taken to various places of detention and mistreated. See section concerning mistreatment in detention below.

[9] Helsinki Watch representatives reviewed medical records and autopsy reports of the 13 men at the hospital in Travnik on June 12, 1992. Also, doctors, including one of the attending forensic pathologists who conducted the autopsies, were interviewed.

- Stipo Jerkić, from the village of Ričica, was shot three times in the chest and subsequently beaten with a solid object on the head.

- Dragan Rimec, from Travnik, was shot twice in the chest, twice in the upper right arm, and twice in the front of the left thigh. He also suffered blows to the head.

- Mato Babić, from Travnik, was killed by bullets fired at his head, specifically the right side of his forehead and his right ear. The upper portion of his head and right eye also were bruised, but doctors concluded that the bruises were caused after Babić fell to the ground once he had been shot.

- Žarko Meljančić, from the village of Ovčarevo, was shot twice in the chest, near the right lung. He also was shot in the forehead. The upper portion of the man's skull was cracked and the bones in his nose were shattered into many fragments.

- Slavko Bendeš, from Travnik, was shot near the right ear and in the right side of his face. His facial bones and crown of the skull were shattered into multiple fragments.

- Tadija Marjanović, from the village of Skulji, was shot below the right eye. An open wound in the back of his neck was a result of his being beaten with a solid object. The upper section of his spine was crushed.

- Luka Babić, from the village of Paklarevo, was shot at the base of the nose. The bones in the upper skull, around the eyes and the nose were broken into many fragments.

- Zoran Domić, from the village of Paklarevo, was shot in the chest three times. The bones in the upper skull, face and lower jaw and his teeth were broken into many fragments.

The autopsy reports conclude that many of these men died from shots fired to the head or chest at relatively close range. They also indicate that most of the beatings were inflicted after the men had been killed or while they were unconscious.

Skelani (municipality of Srebrenica)[10]

According to eyewitnesses interviewed by Helsinki Watch representatives,[11] men in the village of Skelani were summarily executed after the village fell to Serbian forces on May 7. Vahida, Tima and Malida Selimović were married to three brothers -- Azem (age 42), Kemo (age 31) and Rizo (age 27) -- and had a total of seven children. According to each of the three women, Serbs in the area declared Skelani to be a Serbian village on May 1. On the same day, the Serbs demanded that all Muslims relinquish any arms in their possession by 3:00 p.m. that afternoon or risk being attacked. The Muslims complied and relinquished any guns -- mostly hunting rifles -- in their possession.

On May 7, 1992, Vahida Selimović went to work in Bajina Bašta, a village across the Drina River, in neighboring Serbia. She told Helsinki Watch:

> As on every other day, I crossed the bridge to go to work in Bajina Bašta. However, armed Serbs almost didn't let me cross over; they told me that I needed some type of permit. Those in [the village] of Bajina Bašta were all armed with knives, guns and hand grenades. When I returned to Skelani in the afternoon, they wanted to see my passport and I barely got home. There were hordes of armed men on the Bosnian side of the bridge when I crossed over. We were scared of these men so we spent the night in our basement.
>
> In the morning, buses belonging to the Raketa bus company in Serbia came into Skelani and all the Serbs in the village left. The buses had brought Četniks from Serbia and they wore hats with Četnik symbols, helmets and gloves. In our part of Skelani there are 29 houses. The Četniks surrounded those houses and tank and

---

[10] Of the 37,211 inhabitants of Srebrenica, 72.9 percent were Muslims and 25.2 percent Serbs.

[11] Interviewed in Novi Pazar, in the Sandžak region of Serbia, Yugoslavia, on June 20, 1992.

mortar shells were fired at the homes. There were seven men, four women and 11 children hiding in our basement but the Četniks found us and shot and killed all the men in front of us, including our husbands. Then they cursed at us, called us Turks and threatened to kill us.

They then took us to the police station in Skelani, where we were held. One of the Četniks there said, "I am a paid murderer from Montenegro. Your neigbors pay me well to kill you. My only complaint is that I can't shoot women and children." That same man helped us get transferred to Bajina Bašta and then to Novi Pazar.[12]

According to independent Serbian press reports,[13] after the fall of Skelani, 550 Muslims — mostly women, children and elderly persons — were expelled from the village and taken to the Serbian border. Once they crossed 50 meters off the bridge into Serbia, Serbian authorities refused to grant them entry. Rather, when the refugees got to the Serbian side, the authorities turned them back into Bosnia and told them to go home. When the refugees turned back over the bridge, they were met by members of Bosnia's Serbian armed forces. They told the refugees that Skelani was now a Serbian village and that they had no claim to it. Negotiations lasted from 5:00 p.m. to 10:00 p.m. and finally it was decided that some of the refugees would be taken to Macedonia via Serbia. Others were driven from Bajina Bašta to Loznica (in Serbia) in

---

[12] The women have since fled to Turkey. Although some Bosnian Muslims flee to the predominantly Muslim area of Serbia called Sandžak, few remain for long. Many Muslims who have fled to Serbia fear reprisals and are eager to leave. They also regard the situation in Sandžak as volatile and uncertain. During the visit to Novi Pazar, Helsinki Watch representatives saw tanks positioned throughout the city with their turret guns aimed at the city center. Helsinki Watch has received detailed reports concerning the harassment and arrests of Sandžak Muslims by Serbian police and Yugoslav military authorities and is greatly concerned that the human rights situation there will continue to deteriorate. See section concerning "ethnic cleansing" practices in Serbian-occupied areas of Croatia and in the Republic of Serbia.

[13] *Borba*, May 9, 1992.

six buses and two trucks. From Loznica, the refugees were taken back to the Bosnian town of Kalesija.

Bijeljina

According to residents of Bijeljina,[14] Serbian paramilitaries began harassing the town's population on April 1. The witnesses claim that the paramilitaries belonged to Arkan's and Jović's troops. According to a 60-year-old Muslim man:

> Serbian paramilitaries had occupied Bijeljina fifteen days before the town actually fell. They frequently walked around with socks on their heads and took up patrol and sniper positions throughout the city, usually in windows from the top floor of buildings. One day during the first week of April, at approximately 10:00 p.m., I was in the town square, near the bus station. A group of about 15 paramilitaries was roaming the streets. Two of the paramilitary soldiers had stockings over their heads and all were armed, primarily with AK-47s. A Muslim man who appeared to be drunk walked up to the group and said something to them. One of Jović's paramilitaries shot him dead immediately. Thereafter, shots rang out from Serbian positions throughout the city center and I started to run from the gun fire.

The man is unsure if anyone was killed or wounded after the paramilitary forces opened fire. He claims that the paramilitaries' commanders, Mirko Jović and Željko Ražnjatovic (Arkan), were in Bijeljina at the time of the attack.

Bosnian sources claim that civilian populations have also been summarily executed in Foča, Višegrad, Prijedor, Bijeljina, Zvornik, Bratunac, and Brčko. Serbian sources claim that Serbs have been summarily executed in the municipalities of Sarajevo, Srebrenica, Tuzla, Kupres and Livno. Helsinki Watch has not been able to investigate such reports, in part because of continued fighting in some areas and, in part,

---

[14] Six residents from Bijeljina were interviewed individually on June 4, 1992 in Ljubljana, Slovenia. They all confirmed the following account.

because entrance to such areas (particularly Bijeljina and Zvornik) was restricted during our delegation's visit in April.

"Ethnic Cleansing" and Forcible Displacement

After Serbian forces have occupied territory in Bosnia-Hercegovina, brutal measures have been taken to "ethnically cleanse" the area of non-Serbs, removing them from the area and thereby creating an ethnically homogeneous area. The "cleansing" of such areas usually involves the execution, detention, confinement to ghetto areas, and the forcible displacement and/or deportation of non-Serbs, most frequently Muslims, and, to a lesser extent, Croats. Hundreds of thousands of civilians have been the victims of "ethnic cleansing" practices.

Executions

In some cases, Serbian forces have "cleansed" an occupied town or village by summarily executing the non-Serbian inhabitants, particularly men between the ages of 18 and 60. The summary execution of at least 83 Muslims in the village of Zaklopača, described above, appears to be one example in which summary execution was the preferred method used to "cleanse" a region ethnically. Helsinki Watch has received reports that similar mass executions have occurred in the towns of Bijeljina, Foča, Višegrad and Bratunac and in the village of Kozarac (municipality of Prijedor). Helsinki Watch also is concerned that Serbs opposed to such methods of "ethnic cleansing" may also have been executed for treason by Serbian forces.

Detention and "Concentration" Camps

After an area has been occupied by Serbian forces, many of the civilian inhabitants have been imprisoned for various periods. Some have been held in prisons or jails in Serbian-occupied areas of Bosnia. Others have been imprisoned in Serbian-occupied areas of Croatia, most notably in the Stara Gradiška prison and, possibly, in the city of Knin and other areas of "Krajina." Many imprisoned civilians have been exchanged subsequently for Serbian combatants and civilians held by Muslim and Croatian forces.[15]

Muslim, Croatian and Serbian forces contend that areas of detention, which they refer to as "concentration camps," exist throughout Bosnia-Hercegovina. Muslim and Croatian sources say that there are 94 Serbian-operated "concentration camps" and prisons in Bosnia-Hercegovina and that Bosnian non-Serbs are detained at 11 "concentration camps" and prisons in the republics of Serbia and Montenegro.[16] For their part, Serbian sources contend that 17 Muslim- and Croatian-operated "concentration camps" and detention facilities are used to imprison Serbs.[17] Both sides cite schools, military barracks, stadiums and other facilities as sites of such "concentration camps." Muslim and Croatian sources claim that barbed-wire detention facilities, similar to those recently visited by foreign reporters, exist throughout Serbian-controlled areas of Bosnia-Hercegovina. Serbian sources contend that such "concentration" and detention camps include military barracks in Sarajevo and a tunnel near the town of Konjic. (Bosnian troops which had barricaded the Sarajevo barracks have since allowed those JNA soldiers to leave the city. Moreover, because the military barracks are a legitimate military target under international law, they cannot be classified as detention or "concentration camps." The 3,000 Serbs who were held hostage in the tunnel near Konjic[18] have since been released.) When Muslim/Croatian and Serbian forces do not have access to various towns or cities, they often presume that members of their respective ethnic group have been killed, imprisoned or placed in

---

[15] Helsinki Watch has documented the mistreatment of persons who have been detained in prisons and detention centers. See section concerning mistreatment in detention.

[16] This information has been compiled from data collected by various Bosnian government agencies. Helsinki Watch has been forwarded the list of such camps and prisons from Sarajevo.

[17] Helsinki Watch has been forwarded such information from the Ministry of Information of the Republic of Serbia.

[18] See section concerning taking of hostages.

"concentration camps." Some of these assertions cannot be substantiated.[19]

Nevertheless, testimony which Helsinki Watch has taken, reports by the independent foreign media, and UN documents provide at the very least *prima facie* evidence that Serbian-operated camps in northern Bosnia are being used to detain, torture and, possibly, execute non-Serbs.

In early August, Helsinki Watch representatives visited Serbian-run camps in Termokerm, Trnopolje and Omarska. Military officials escorted the representatives to the camps and private individual interviews with the prisoners were not permitted. Access to the camp in the village of Manjača was denied. The ICRC reportedly has visited the camp in Manjača. To date, Helsinki Watch has not been able to investigate thoroughly reports of systematic executions of prisoners. However, beatings and deaths as a result of torture have occurred. Helsinki Watch spoke to an 18 year-old youth who had been captured when he tried to flee from his village of Kozarac. He spent 80 days in the Omarska camp and was subsequently transferred to the Trnoploje camp. According to the youth:

> I was badly beaten when I was caught. I was kneeling with my hands against the wall and they were hitting me from behind for two hours. After that first day, I was

---

[19] Serbian forces, in particular, have consistently made allegations about such abuses against Serbs in Croatia and Bosnia-Hercegovina. Although some of their concerns have proven correct, others have been wildly exaggerated and, in some cases, falsified. For example, in early March, battles around the village of Sijekovac (municipality of Bosanski Brod) took place. Serbian forces were unsuccessful in claiming the territory and alleged that Serbian civilians in Sijekovac had been massacred by Muslim and Croatian forces. Those Serbs who had fled from the area were taken to Vojvodina, where Helsinki Watch representatives interviewed them in mid-March. On the basis of interviews with approximately 20 villagers, it appears that those Serbs who were killed in Sijekovac were armed combatants engaged in hostilities or were civilians who were killed by cross-fire. Under international law, such deaths cannot be classified as "summary executions" or "massacres" of the civilian population. The witnesses claimed that the weapons used by all sides consisted primarily of AK-47s and other automatic rifles and machine guns. At the time of the interviews, Helsinki Watch representatives could not find evidence to substantiate claims of excessive use of force.

beaten at random. People were dying of internal injuries they received from the beatings. I carried out bodies. Then trucks came and took them away.

I was kept on the upper floor and I could see several bodies every day in the field. But I am not sure if this is the place where they disposed of the bodies. It is horrible to say, but we were happy when new priosners arrived because they beat them, not us.

The Omarska camp is an open ore mine and permission to enter the camp is granted from local police officials, not by the military authorities.

According to Serbian military officials in Banja Luka, prisoners are divided into three categories. The first category includes leaders of the predominantly Muslim Party of Democratic Action (SDA) and those who "organized the rebellion against Serbs." The second category includes Muslim combatants. Both categories of prisoners are interrogated at the Omarska camp and are subsequently transferred to the Manjača camp. The third category of prisoners includes "those who could not be found guilty." These prisoners are held in the Trnoplje camp and include women and children. People who had been badly beaten were transferred to the Trnopolje camp. Since foreign journalists have visited the camps, the situation appears to have improved for some of the prisoners, at least temporarily. According to one prisoner in the Omarska camp: "They've turned this into a tourist attraction. Don't believe what you see."

According to international journalists, Serbian forces are detaining prisoners of war and civilians in camps in northern Bosnia. In a series of articles in *Newsday*, written by Roy Gutman after he and freelance photographer Andre Kaiser visited and interviewed prisoners in several camps in the environs of Banja Luka, it was reported that prisoners were held in appalling conditions and are regularly beaten or otherwise mistreated. Others reportedly have been executed or denied food, water or medical care. Thousands of civilians have been deported from Banja Luka, Prijedor and Bosanski Novi in sealed freight or cattle cars.[20]

Gutman interviewed prisoners who had been taken captive after Serbian forces took control of the towns and villages of Mile-kod-Jelice, Skender Vakuf, Ključ, Gornja, Sanski Most, Samica and Kozarac.

Helsinki Watch had previously interviewed refugees from four of the aforementioned villages. The refugees were interviewed in Slovenia and Croatia in June. They had fled either during the siege of their village or immediately thereafter, evading capture by Serbian forces. Many of the refugees interviewed by Helsinki Watch expressed concern that their family and friends had been captured and were being held in camps near Banja Luka.

In an internal memorandum, UN personnel stationed in the UNPAs (i.e., Serbian-controlled areas) of Croatia confirmed the existence of detention centers and expressed their belief that Serbian-operated "concentration camps" exist in Bosnia-Hercegovina. In a July 3 memorandum to senior officials affiliated with the United Nations peacekeeping mission (UNPROFOR) in Belgrade and Zagreb, a UN staffer stationed in the town of Dvor, Croatia, claimed that the football field in the town of Bosanski Novi in Bosnia-Hercegovina was being used as a "holding ground where Muslim groups are detained while their houses are being 'searched,' the men isolated and transported to concentration camps."[21]

---

[20] The information cited here is limited to what Gutman observed directly or was confirmed by Red Cross officials. See the following articles written by Gutman for *Newsday*: "Hidden Horror," July 19, 1992; "Witness Tells of Serbian Death Camp," July 19, 1992; "For Muslims, Misery," July 21, 1992; "Like Auschwitz," July 21, 1992; and "Students Beaten by Serbs," July 29, 1992; and "The Death Camps of Bosnia," August 2, 1992.

[21] Bosanski Novi is clearly visible from Dvor. The two towns are separated by the River Una. Helsinki Watch representatives have made several visits to both towns in the past year where they investigated violations of humanitarian law in relation to the war in Croatia. As early as July 1991, the town of Bosanski Novi clearly was used by Serbian forces and the Yugoslav army as a military base, from where they attacked Croatian military and civilian targets. Helsinki Watch's last visit to the two towns was in late March 1992. The text of the memorandum described here is reproduced as Appendix B. See also Trevor Rowe, "UN Knew of Serb Camps Months Ago, Bosnian Charges," *The Washington Post*, August 6, 1992.

UNHCR representatives and personnel affiliated with the Civilian Affairs section of the UNPROFOR mission stationed in the UNPAs of Croatia had compiled testimony from Muslims fleeing from northern Bosnia who sought refuge under UNPROFOR protection in Dvor and Kostajnica, Croatia. On the basis of this testimony, UN officials informed their superiors that "concentration camps" exist in the villages of Keraterm, Trnopolje, Omarska and Manjača. According to testimony compiled by UN officials, the camps at Keraterm and Trnopolje are located near a railroad station in the town of Prijedor. In Keraterm between 100 to 200 Muslims remain in detention "under extremely bad conditions." Trnopolje appears to be a refugee camp for women, children and old men.

The UN memorandum also mentions camps in the villages of Omarska and Manjaca. According to the memorandum, the camp in the purely Serbian village of Omarska is used to detain Muslim men and local Muslims government officials and authorities in the area, particularly from the town of Prijedor, before the region fell to Serbian forces. The UN memorandum states that, on the basis of refugee testimony, a large camp in Manjaca includes Croatian soldiers who had been taken prisoner during fighting for the town of Kostajnica in Croatia. Kostajnica fell to Serbian forces in early August 1991. The memorandum states that "the treatment of Muslims and other minorities in the camps is reportedly atrocious, with regular beatings, deprivation of food and water, poor shelter, etc.." The memorandum does not mention whether executions are being carried out in the camps.

The memorandum states that the UN personnel stationed in Dvor believe that the existence of a detention camp in Bosanski Novi is "only a tip of the iceberg involving the concerted action of local Serbian authorities in BH [Bosnia-Hercegovina] trying to establish a Serbian Republic of BH [sic], free of Muslims." The UN claims that the mayors, police and local territorial defense units in the Serbian-controlled areas of Croatia (in the towns of Dvor and Kostajnica) are cooperating with their counterparts in Serbian-controlled areas of northern Bosnia (in the towns of Bosanski Novi, Bosanska Dubica, Banja Luka, Prijedor, Sanski Most and Kljuc) to "ethnically cleanse" those areas of non-Serbs, primarily Muslims. The memorandum also states that óther camps exist in Serbian-controlled areas in the municipalities of Bihac, Cazin, Velika Kladusa and Bosanska Dubica.

The UN memorandum states that people have fled to the UNPAs in Croatia, seeking sanctuary with UN personnel. According to the July

3 memorandum, "one Mustafa Ogorinac swam across the river Una at 8 [sic] in the morning [on July 2] from a camp in Bosanska Dubica ... He show[ed] signs of physical abuse and punishment."

Some commentators have implied that if mass executions cannot be substantiated, the situation is not cause for alarm. Helsinki Watch believes that such suggestions depreciate the severity of the abuses which obviously are taking place in the camps. Helsinki Watch will continue to investigate reports of such camps operated by all parties to the conflict in Bosnia-Hercegovina. In the interim, Helsinki Watch strongly believes that the international community must take immediate steps to inspect all such camps. Insofar as prisoners of war are detained in those areas, they must be held under conditions that comply with the (Third) Geneva Convention Relative to the Treatment of Prisoners of War. All civilians held in such camps must immediately be released and guarantees for their safety must be provided.

Confinement to Ghetto Areas

Various villages throughout Serbian-controlled areas of Bosnia-Hercegovina have been reported to serve as places of detention for thousands of non-Serbs. In many respects, these villages have been transformed into ghettos where non-Serbian civilians are held hostage. Serbian paramilitaries or members of the Yugoslav army patrol the perimeters of the villages and maintain a command center within the village, where they conduct interrogations of the interned non-Serbs. The persons confined to such villages appear to be held until they are exchanged for Serbian combatants or civilians held by Croatian and Muslim forces. Others are confined to ghetto villages and have subsequently disappeared. Helsinki Watch interviewed two escapees from one ghetto village.

According to the testimony of two men from the village of Brezovo Polje (municipality of Brčko),[22] their village appears to have

---

[22] Interviewed by Helsinki Watch representatives in Gunja (municipality of Županja), Croatia, on June 3, 1992. Many of the witnesses interviewed by Helsinki Watch asked that their names not be disclosed. Many feared persecution and reprisal attacks should they eventually be able to return to their homes. Still others feared that their testimony would endanger the lives of relatives or friends who remain missing or are believed to be held captive by opposing forces.

been transformed into a detention area for prisoners captured by Serbian forces. Both men were brought to the village on May 3, after they had been captured by Serbian forces during the siege of Brčko. Those detained in this particular ghetto included both civilians and combatants.

According to the two men, the Yugoslav army initially commanded Brezovo Polje but Serbian paramilitaries soon assumed control and the local Yugoslav army soldiers appeared to subordinate themselves to the paramilitaries, most of whom were members of the White Eagles. At the time of the witnesses' detention in the village, approximately 1,500 people were being detained in Brezovo Polje, which is a Muslim village encircled by Serbian villages. According to one of the men:

> We were taken to the home of one of the local villagers in Brezovo Polje and we had to report to the military authorities every two hours. We were allowed to move about the village but could not leave. Paramilitaries and Yugoslav army recruits patrolled the village. We were not mistreated although four to five people were taken from the village every day and never returned. Most of those who were taken away were men under the age of 40. I spent 24 days in Brezovo Polje and every day, at least four men were taken away -- that means that at least 96 men disappeared and were probably killed or taken to a camp.

Both men escaped from Brezovo Polje on June 1, 1992, with the help of a sympathetic JNA recruit. They swam across the Sava river into Croatia, where they were received by members of the Croatian Army.

Serbian and Yugoslav sources claim that Serbs are being held in camps near the towns of Konjić, Novi Grad (near Orasje), and Duvno/Tomislavgrad.[23] To date, Helsinki Watch has not been able to verify such reports from independent sources.

---

[23] "Government Denies Existence of Concentration Camps," Tanjug Yugoslav News Agency report on June 12, 1992, as reported in FBIS, June 16, 1992.

Forcible Deportation

Helsinki Watch has documented cases in which non-Serbs from eastern Bosnia were placed in buses, taken to international border points and expelled from the country by Yugoslav authorities. In one such instance, Helsinki Watch representatives interviewed approximately 30 Muslims from the Zvornik and Bijeljina municipalities in eastern Bosnia who had been forcibly removed from their homes and taken to the city of Subotica, on the Hungarian and Serbian border.[24] The witnesses claimed that they were the fifty-fifth group to have been deported from the Zvornik and Bijeljina areas and that three more groups had stayed behind and would soon also be deported from their homes. They alleged that they were being deported so that Serbian refugees from the village of Janja could occupy their homes.

When they arrived in Subotica, the refugees were told that they had to leave the country. However, in order for an individual to leave the country, he or she had to visit the local police station to apply for a Yugoslav passport. Before the refugees could obtain a passport with which to exit, they had to show proof that they had purchased a train ticket out of Yugoslavia. Because they lacked money, the refugees told Helsinki Watch that they had pawned their wedding rings and other valuables to a local priest for just enough money to buy a train ticket. They also had to pay 8350 dinars (approximately six U.S. dollars) for the passport. After they completed the necessary applications, the refugees were told to come to the train station at 8:00 p.m. that evening, where they picked up their new passports. They then were told that they had between six and eight hours to leave the country. All of the refugees to whom Helsinki Watch spoke did not want to stay in Yugoslavia and followed the instructions of the local police in Subotica. They claimed that they had no intention of disobeying the expulsion order for fear of reprisals. The Hungarian government confirmed the information provided by these refugees. Helsinki Watch has received information from Hungarian government representatives that waves of refugees from eastern Bosnia were deported to Hungary in late June.

---

[24] Helsinki Watch representatives interviewed the refugees on July 2, 1992, in Subotica, in the province of Vojvodina in the republic of Serbia, Yugoslavia.

Forcible Displacement

In addition to the overt tactics used to "cleanse" non-Serbian areas, Serbian paramilitary and Yugoslav army troops often launch mortar attacks against non-Serbian controlled areas for prolonged periods. Such attacks are aimed at forcing the besieged population to surrender or flee from the area. Those non-Serbs who flee from the attacks often take shelter in nearby towns or villages which come under attack only days after the recently displaced persons have arrived.

Helsinki Watch interviewed scores of refugees who had been displaced many times as a result of incessant and advancing mortar attacks. In some instances, after the local population had fled and Serbian forces occupied a non-Serbian village, those forces burned the village before moving on to the next non-Serbian area. One such account taken by Helsinki Watch representatives is illustrative of this phenomenon. Z.S.,[25] a 59-year-old woman from the village of Jeleći (municipality of Foča) was forced to flee 15 times in 40 days before finally finding shelter in a sports hall that has been converted to a refugee shelter in the port city of Split, Croatia. After her village was destroyed and burned after three days of shelling by Serbian troops, Z.S. was forced to flee to Donji Polja where she stayed for five days, after which renewed attacks forced her to flee to Susječino. She remained in Susječino for one night but as a result of a mortar attack, she fled to Danići. She spent three days in Danići but had to flee because of mortar attacks launched by Serbian paramilitaries.

> As I was fleeing Danići, I saw men with Četnik symbols on their hats advancing. Most of them wore shirts belonging to the JNA and civilian slacks. Some wore complete JNA uniforms. As we were fleeing, they began to set fire to the houses and burn the village. I fled to Kozja Luka, where I spent the night and then I left for Kremalusa. I spent three days in Kremalusa but had to leave because of attacks against that village. As we were fleeing, we turned back to see the village in flames. I walked for two hours to Srbotina and spent the night but

---

[25] Interviewed in Split, Croatia, on June 9, 1992. The woman asked not to be identified by her full name.

had to .flee because of yet another attack. Srbotina also was burned. I then fled to Kolum Selo where I remained for three days. On the third day, a Mr. Stanković came to the village and told us that we had to give up our weapons or be killed. He was unarmed and came to deliver a message from the Serbian forces who were positioned in the surrounding hills, waiting to attack us. We then fled to Potkolun for three days but when some villagers went to graze their cows in the pasture, they encountered several Četniks who threatened to attack Golijevići -- which is near our village and Kozje Luke -- so we fled on foot to Smjeće and spent six days there. The Četniks sent word that we had to evacuate the area or be killed so we fled to Basći where we remained for six days. However, a 23-year-old Muslim, Edin Ploco, was killed by a sniper so we got scared and fled yet again. We walked the 40 kilometers to the Bjelašnica area, where we spent six days. Then we went to Konjica for three days, then to Jablanice and finally to Split via bus along dirt roads.

Z.S. claims that no opposing forces were fighting against Serbian and Yugoslav forces during the course of her exodus. She insisted that the attacks were meant to drive non-Serbs from their homes and to destroy Muslim villages in that area, i.e., eastern Bosnia.

In addition to eastern and northern Bosnia, Serbian troops are expelling non-Serbs from western suburbs of Sarajevo under their control.[26] Also, during the afternoon of June 3, non-Serbs were expelled from the Serbian-controlled area of Grbavica in Sarajevo, soon after the arrival of Lord Peter Carrington, the European Community's chief peace broker for the conflict in the Balkans. The expulsion of the non-Serbs from Grbavica also coincided "with the first full working day of a massive international airlift to alleviate shortages of food and

---

[26] Blaine Harden, "Bosnia Bleeds Under Serb 'Purification,'" *The Washington Post*, June 23, 1992.

medicine" in Sarajevo.[27] According to foreign journalists, the non-Serbian residents of Grbavica were confined to their homes for more than two months and non-Serbian men were "forced at gunpoint into labor gangs."[28] Such men included Muslims, Croats and Slovenes who were forced to fill bags with dirt to build bunkers for Serbian troops.[29]

Helsinki Watch is concerned that "ethnic cleansing" by Serbian civilian and military authorities also is taking place in the city of Banja Luka. According to the U.S. State Department, Serbian leaders in Banja Luka mounted an "ethnic cleansing operation aimed at forcibly expelling large numbers of non-Serbs from the area" in early June.[30]

As Serbian and Yugoslav troops advance deeper into Bosnia-Hercegovina, the displacement of non-Serbs continues to accelerate, thereby producing larger swaths of "ethnically pure" areas. Thousands of Serbian civilians also have been displaced by the war in Bosnia-Hercegovina.[31] Some Serbs have been displaced as a result of fighting. Others were told to evacuate the area prior to the commencement of hostilities, usually by local Serbian paramilitary commanders or by Serbian Democratic Party (SDS) leaders. Helsinki Watch representatives interviewed Serbian refugees from Bosnia-Hercegovina who had been told that they had to evacuate an area because Croatian "Ustašas" and Muslim "fundamentalists" were advancing and that their lives would be in danger. In such instances, these Serbian refugees fled their homes before battles began and did not witness the fighting or its aftermath.

---

[27] Blaine Harden, "U.S. Airlift Brings Aid to Sarajevo," *The Washington Post*, July 4, 1992.

[28] *Ibid.*

[29] *Ibid.*

[30] See Margaret Tutwiler, Regular State Department Briefing, June 8, 1992, as transcribed by Reuters Information Service. See also John M. Goshko and Trevor Rowe, "U.N. Votes to Deploy Extra Troops in Bosnia," *The Washington Post*, June 9, 1992.

[31] Interviewed in Belgrade and throughout the province of Vojvodina, Yugoslavia, from June 1 to June 30, 1992.

Nevertheless, Helsinki Watch is concerned that Serbian civilians have been displaced by Muslim and Croatian forces in areas of Bosnia-Hercegovina under the control of these forces. In some cases, these displacements may occur in retaliation for the "ethnic cleansing" policies employed by Serbian forces against non-Serbs. In other cases, Muslim, and particularly Croatian, armed forces may displace Serbs to consolidate their territorial gains.

In areas where members of all three ethnic groups are besieged by attacks by Serbian forces, Croats and Muslims have become suspicious of their Serbian neighbors and have harassed or otherwise persecuted them. As a result of such intimidation, these Serbs then fled to Serbian-controlled areas. Indeed, with the escalation and prolongation of fighting, trust among the various ethnic and national groups has eroded and members of each group have sought to escape to areas controlled by their own group. Such distrust and subsequent flight has facilitated the forcible transfer of the civilian population and the creation of ethnically homogeneous areas throughout Bosnia-Hercegovina.

"Ethnic Cleansing" in Serbian-Occupied Areas of Croatia and in the Republic of Serbia

During the war in Croatia, Serbian forces engaged in practices which closely resemble those used to "cleanse" areas of non-Serbs in Bosnia-Hercegovina. Similarly, such practices are being employed against non-Serbs in the province of Vojvodina, in the Republic of Serbia. Most frequently, non-Serbs are forcibly displaced or deported from Serbian-controlled areas of Croatia and Vojvodina, although in one case, mass executions appear to have taken place. In the province of Kosovo and the region of Sandžak in the republic of Serbia, Muslims and Albanians have been forced to flee for less overt reasons. Helsinki Watch fears that the policy of "ethnic cleansing," which extends beyond Bosnia-Hercegovina, is part of a systematic policy to rid all Serbian-controlled areas of non-Serbs, or at least to diminish their numbers significantly.

Serbian-Controlled Areas of Croatia

In Croatia, Serbian civilian, paramilitary, police and military authorities have systematically expelled non-Serbs from their homes in

Serbian-occupied areas of the country.[32] Serbs from Croatia were subsequently resettled in the homes of expelled non-Serbs in Serbian-occupied areas of "Krajina" and eastern Slavonia in Croatia. Most of the Serbs who were resettled in Croatian, Hungarian and Ruthenian homes had fled from the fighting in Croatia. Others had fled because their property was destroyed, or they faced harassment, by individual Croats or local Croatian authorities in Croatia.[33]

At the very outbreak of war in Croatia, on July 7, 1991, the predominantly Croatian village of Čelija (municipality of Vukovar) fell to Serbian forces, which expelled the inhabitants and burned the village.[34] In the city of Vukovar, many non-Serbs were executed by Serbian paramilitary and Yugoslav military forces when the city and its suburbs fell to Serbian forces in mid-November.

Since November 1991, Helsinki Watch has collected evidence which raises serious concern that mass executions of Croats and other non-Serbian civilians and disarmed combatants occurred between

---

[32] For accounts of human rights abuses and humanitarian law violations by Serbian forces in the war in Croatia, see the following Helsinki Watch reports: "Yugoslavia: Human Rights Abuses in the Croatian Conflict," September 1991, and Letter to Slobodan Milošević, President of the Republic of Serbia, and General Blagoje Adžić, Acting Minister of Defense and Chief of Staff of the Yugoslav People's Army, January 21, 1992.

[33] Abuses committed by Croatian armed forces and individuals are documented in Helsinki Watch's letter to Croatian President Franjo Tudjman, February 13, 1992. Most Serbs displaced from the western Slavonian region had fled after Yugoslav army and Serbian paramilitary groups withdrew from the region in early December. After Croatian forces reassumed control in the area, they destroyed many Serbian houses and predominantly Serbian villages. Moreover, harassment of Serbs and destruction of Serbian property throughout Croatia has hastened the flight of Serbs to the republic of Serbia and to Serbian-controlled areas of Croatia. Although some of the Serbs who have fled from Croatia were combatants or otherwise engaged in hostilities against the Croatian authorities, many Serbian civilians were displaced as a result of harassment they faced from individual Croats or from Croatian authorites, usually at the local level.

[34] For an account of Čelija's destruction, see Helsinki Watch, "Yugoslavia: Human Rights Abuses in the Croatian Conflict," September 1991.

November 19 and 21 in Vukovar. On the basis of evidence Helsinki Watch has collected, approximately 300 Croatian prisoners captured by Serbian and Yugoslav army troops were taken to areas outside of Vukovar (i.e., Ovčara and Petrova Gora) and executed. According to a Serbian journalist who was present during the fighting, fall and surrender of Vukovar, civilians and combatants who emerged from their shelters and surrendered were taken prisoner by Serbian paramilitary and Yugoslav reserve and regular army units. According to the journalist:[35]

> I was with the Yugoslav army reserve soldiers for most of the fighting in Vukovar. When the city fell, I remained with the same troops for several days after Vukovar's fall. Because I am a Serb who spent months with these troops, they thought I was "one of them" and they let me witness most of what they did to their captives after Vukovar's fall. They thought I approved of their behavior but I am appalled at what they have done.

> After Vukovar fell, people were lined up and made to walk to detention areas. As the prisoners walked by, local Serbian paramilitaries pulled people out of the lines at random, claiming that they had to be executed because they were "war criminals." Most of these people were Croats who had spent the duration of the fighting in basements, particularly in the Vukovar hospital. The selection of those who were to be liquidated also was done as these people were leaving the shelters. They were removed from lines under the supervision, and with the apparent permission, of Major Veselin Šljivančanin, the JNA officer in charge of security after Vukovar's fall.

> On the evenings between November 19 and 21, hundreds of prisoners were taken to the Ovčara farm near Vukovar and somewhere near Petrova Gora. I was not permitted to go to the site with the prisoners who were being escorted by drunk Yugoslav reserve army

---

[35] For reasons of safety, Helsinki Watch will not disclose the identity of the journalist. S/he was interviewed in Belgrade in January 1992.

soldiers. As they were leaving for Ovčara, they told me that these people had to be killed because they "worked against Serbs," were members of the Croatian Democratic Union (HDZ) or were somehow believed to have been related to members of the Croatian government.

When they returned in the early morning, they started boasting about what they had done. We were sitting around a fire drinking coffee and brandy and they told me that they executed over 300 Ustašas and that their bodies were dumped in a pit. These soldiers belonged to the first company (*četa*) of the territorial defense unit of Vukovar, which was commanded by Stanko Vujanović. Members of Vojislav Šešelj's paramilitary group and some regular Yugoslav army soldiers also were involved. I believe that Major Šljivančanin organized, or at least was aware of, the executions.

Those who went to the execution site and came back boasting of their crimes were known to me by the following names:

- Dragica, called "Daca," a JNA volunteer from Novi Sad

- Predrag Milojević, called "Kina," a JNA volunteer from Ruma

- Dragoslav Milosavljević, called "Panta," from Negotin

- a young man, a sniper, called "Johnny" (Djani)

- a JNA petty officer called "Hadžija"

- Ivica Andrić, called "Djetić," from Montenegro

- Spasoje Petković, a JNA soldier called "Stuka"

- Milan Lazarević, called "Grozni," a JNA volunteer from Uzdina

78

According to what the soldiers were saying, Stanko Vujanović, the commander of the local Serbian territorial unit, Major Šljivančanin and a JNA Captain Miroslav Radić also were present for the executions. I believe that JNA Captain Saša Bojkoviski also knew about the executions.

Since November, Helsinki Watch representatives have collected scores of testimonies from former prisoners and combatants and Serbian soldiers which support many of the claims set forth in the above testimony. Although no one appears to have survived, and none of those we interviewed actually witnessed the executions, Helsinki Watch has been able to confirm that such prisoners were in fact taken toward the direction of Ovčara and Petrova Gora on the evenings of November 19, 20, and 21 and that they never returned. Their bodies have not been recovered. Approximately 2,000 people remain missing from Vukovar. When Helsinki Watch representatives visited Vukovar in March, they were prevented from going to Ovčara and Petrova Gora. The Yugoslav military authorities cited "security reasons" for denying access to the areas.

Serbian civilian and military authorities also are guilty of forcibly deporting and displacing non-Serbs from their homes in Serbian-controlled areas of Croatia. Helsinki Watch has documented expulsions of Croats, Ruthenians and Hungarians from the following villages between February and April:[36]

| February 17: | 37 persons were expelled from Opatovac |
| February 27: | 11 persons were expelled from Lovas |

---

[36] This information was compiled by Helsinki Watch representatives during a visit to the region of eastern Slavonia in March and April 1992. All the villages enumerated below are part of the municipality of Vukovar except the village of Ernestinovo, which is part of the municipality of Osijek. The information reflected here is taken from interviews with displaced persons who fled from the area, from UN personnel who asked not to be identified and from a Yugoslav army soldier (a Serb) who was present during the expulsion of the non-Serbs from some of the villages. The Yugoslav army soldier condemned, and indeed tried to stop the expulsions, but was unsuccessful. He confirmed and supplemented the information obtained from testimony taken from displaced persons by Helsinki Watch representatives.

March 3:	42 persons were expelled from Ernestinovo and Korodj
March 6:	22 persons were expelled from Bapska
March 16:	138 persons were expelled form Boskić
March 18:	143 persons were expelled from Tompojevci and Šarengrad
March 23:	110 persons were expelled from Petrovci (primarily Ruthenians)
March 25:	101 persons were expelled from Šarengrad
March 27:	63 persons were expelled from Tovarnik
Week of April 3:	105 persons were expelled from the municipalities of Benkovac and Obrovac
Week of April 16:	156 persons were expelled from the city of Vukovar

According to a Yugoslav army soldier to whom Helsinki Watch spoke, non-Serbs also were expelled from the villages of Sotin, Stari Jankovci, Berak and Svinjarevci in March. On the basis of evidence Helsinki Watch has collected, non-Serbs usually were expelled by Serbian paramilitary groups. In most cases, two or three fully armed paramilitary soldiers entered a non-Serbian house, told the inhabitants that they had several minutes to pack some belongings, and then the non-Serbs were placed on buses. The Serbian civilian authorities in the region frequently provided pre-prepared affidavits indicating that the non-Serbian inhabitants of the home were freely relinquishing any claim to their house and belongings contained therein to the Serbian authorities in the municipality. The persons (or the head of household) being expelled were forced to sign such papers at gunpoint.[37] Once on the buses, paramilitaries took their money and jewelry and drove them to the front lines, from where they fled to Croatian-held territory.

In early June, in what was described as a well-documented "criminal act," U.N. officials said that "Serbs who are not private persons" had used threats and intimidation to force twenty-two Croats to flee their

---

[37] Helsinki Watch retains copies, and some originals, of such documents.

80

home village in Serbian-controlled areas of Croatia.[38] Militant Serbian authorities in the Serbian-controlled areas of Croatia not only have displaced Croats but, also, have executed Serbs in Krajina who are willing to negotiate with Croatian government authorities (for example, Dmitar Obradović, the mayor of Vrgin Most.)[39] According to the Serbian Democratic Forum,[40] "a level of totalitarianism in Krajina is getting higher every day, and human rights abuses are everyday events. Violations of human rights first manifested as driving a Croatian minority on the territory of Krajina into exile, and now different-minded persons are being driven into exile as well and even executed." Helsinki Watch representatives have visited Krajina on numerous occasions and persons who live in the region also claim that lawlessness is rife in the area, particularly in the evenings. Members of the Serbian Democratic Forum have been declared "traitors" by Serbian authorities in Krajina and have been banned from the region.

Vojvodina

Serbian paramilitaries, with the apparent blessing of local, provincial and republican governments, are terrorizing and forcibly displacing non-Serbs from Serbia, particularly in the province of Vojvodina.[41] Croats, Hungarians, Slovaks and others have been

---

[38] Blaine Harden, "Hope Seen for End to Sarajevo Siege," *The Washington Post*, June 2, 1992.

[39] Ironically, the Croatian government sentenced Mr. Obradović *in absentia* to eighteen years imprisonment for "endangering the territorial integrity of the Republic of Croatia."

[40] The Serbian Democratic Forum (SDF) is registered as an official organization in Croatia. It is not a political party. The SDF seeks to protect the rights of Serbs in Croatia and its representatives have made numerous trips to the Krajina region with the hope of establishing a dialogue between Serbs in Krajina and the Croatian government.

[41] Vojvodina's population numbers approximately two million; 54.4 percent were Serbian; 18.9 percent Hungarian; 8.2 percent Yugoslav; 5.4 percent Croats; and 3.4 percent Slovaks. Approximately 20 other ethnic groups also lived in Vojvodina. (Figures reflect 1981 census results.)

expelled by Serbian paramilitary forces from the following villages in the province of Vojvodina in the republic of Serbia: Hrtkovci, Šid, Indjija, Beška, Petrovaradin, Slankamen, Novi Sad, Plavna, Golubinci, Kukujevci. Most Serbs who are permanent residents of the aforementioned villages appear not to have supported the expulsion of their non-Serbian neighbors. Rather, Serbian refugees from Croatia and Bosnia-Hercegovina, in conjunction with Serbian paramilitary groups and political extremists have terrorized the non-Serbian population in parts of Vojvodina, forcing them to leave Serbia. Their homes subsequently are occupied by Serbian refugees from Croatia and Bosnia-Hercegovina. The local police and civilian authorities in some of these towns appear to condone and, in some cases, encourage the expulsion of non-Serbs from Vojvodina. Serbian and Yugoslav authorities in Belgrade have done little to prevent or bring to an end such practices.

The displacement of non-Serbs and the resettlement of Serbs in these areas is organized by local extremists and some Serbian refugees from Croatia who seek to change the ethnic structure, names and the local government of multi-ethnic areas in Vojvodina. One example is the village of Hrtkovci where Serbian paramilitary groups and their followers assumed control of the local government in May. The new government has since changed the name of the village and streets to reflect its new Serbian identity. In early May, Hrtkovci's population of 4,000 was approximately 80 percent Croatian; by late July it was approximately 75 percent Serbian.[42] According to anti-war activists in Serbia and to those who have fled the village, the local authorities are resettling Serbs into the homes of Croats and others who have fled or been forced to leave the village.

According to anti-war activists in Belgrade and refugees interviewed by Helsinki Watch representatives,[43] in early April, Vojislav Šešelj visited the village of Hrtkovci and formed a new branch of the Serbian Radical Party, an ultra-right wing political party led by

---

[42] Chuck Sudetic, "Serbs Force an Exodus From Plain," *The New York Times*, July 26, 1992.

[43] Helsinki Watch representatives interviewed refugees from Hrtkovci in Zagreb on June 18, 1992. Helsinki Watch representatives visited the village in late July and have interviewed Ruthenians, Hungarians, Croats, Slovaks and others who have been displaced from Vojvodina since March 1992.

Šešelj. At the meeting, anti-war activists claim that Šešelj stated that "all Croats who had sinned had to leave." The newly appointed secretary of Šešelj's party, a Mr. Zilić, then read the names of those Croats who had to leave the village and announced "cadre" changes in the town's public enterprises. He demanded that several prominent non-Serbs in the community be dismissed from their positions as directors of local firms or from the local government. After the meeting, many residents fled the village out of fear. Those who stayed were verbally and physically harassed and otherwise intimidated. Uniformed and armed men (some with stockings over their heads) have entered the homes of non-Serbs in Hrtkovci, and threatened them at gunpoint or with knives demanding that they pack their belongings, either within days or hours, and leave the village. Some have been forced to sign over their homes and belongings to local authorities. Several people have been beaten, including the local Roman Catholic priest and one man, Milan Stefanac, was found bludgeoned to death in a ditch.[44]

According to M.K., a 27 year-old man interviewed by Helsinki Watch representatives:[45]

> Armed gangs would enter our homes with guns and knives and threaten us, demanding that we leave Serbia. We call the police station and the local police come to see what happens. They can often defuse the situation but claim that they cannot prevent Serbs from taking over houses belonging to non-Serbs who have fled or are about to flee.
>
> When Šešelj came to Hrtkovci in early May, he warned that children of "mixed marriages," i.e., those with Serbian and Croatian parents, were "illegitimate" and that those children have to be "eliminated." He also said that all the Croats had to go to Croatia and all the Serbs had to come to Serbia. Since his visit, that appears to be

---

[44] Chuck Sudetic, "Serbs Force an Exodus From Plain," *The New York Times*, July 26, 1992. See also Florence Hartmann, "Mass Expulsions from Vojvodina," *Le Monde*, June 16, 1992.

[45] Interviewed in Zagreb, Croatia, on June 18, 1992.

the aim of the local extremists who have taken over the village. Most of our Serbian neighbors defended us and now they are being harassed and threatened. They have no choice but to remain quiet now.

Anti-war activists in Serbia have alerted the Serbian Parliament and the Serbian Interior Ministry of the violence against non-Serbs in Hrtkovci. Such complaints were filed in late May by anti-war activists in Belgrade. Some Serbian political parties in Vojvodina continue to pressure the Serbian government to prevent the displacement of non-Serbs from Vojvodina. To date, the Serbian government has done little, if anything, to arrest paramiltaries terrorizing non-Serbs in Vojvodina and has not taken steps to prevent further displacements. Officials at the Interior Ministry told anti-war activists that they should "worry about Krajina" and that they would only accept such a complaint if it was filed by a lawyer who had been appointed by the residents of Hrtkovci.

Serbs affiliated with Serbia's anti-war movement, the independent press and some opposition parties have undertaken steps to protect non-Serbs from persecution and displacement in Vojvodina, often at great risk to themselves. These Serbs have alerted the foreign press to such displacements of non-Serbs, have intervened with the local and republican authorities on behalf of those being persecuted and have maintained contact with non-Serbs they defend to ensure their safety. Moreover, many of the Serbs from Vojvodina support their non-Serbian neighbors and have worked to prevent their displacement. The efforts of such Serbs have been widely ignored in the international community and in the former Yugoslav republics, particularly in Croatia. Serbs who defend non-Serbs in their republic do so at great personal risk of harassment, physical assualt and, possibly, death. Their efforts and courage are to be highly commended and publicly supported.

Serbs have been displaced and forced to flee as a result of harassment and intimidation in Croatia[46] and, to a lesser extent, in Bosnia-Hercegovina. Most often, co-workers and neighbors verbally

---

[46] Violations of human rights and humanitarian law by Croatian civilian and military forces are documented in the following Helsinki Watch reports: "Yugoslavia: Human Rights Abuses in the Croatian Conflict," September 1991, and Letter to Franjo Tudjman, President of the Republic of Croatia, February 13, 1992.

intimidate Serbs and many have fled to Serbia as a result of such harassment. Others have been physically assaulted and some have been murdered. Helsinki Watch has not been able to document, nor has it received reports of, cases in which armed groups have led organized campaigns aimed at forcibly displacing non-Croats from Croatia. Most of the harassment appears to be organized by individual extremists.

The Croatian authorities have investigated, prosecuted and punished perpetrators of attacks against Serbs in Zagreb, Sisak and in other municipalities in Dalmatia and Slavonia. Despite such steps, Helsinki Watch believes that such prosecutions and punishment must be more vigorously pursued in Croatia. In particular, destruction of Serbian property is rampant throughout Croatia and few are prosecuted for such banditry. Moreover, Helsinki Watch believes that Croatian government officials (both at the local and republican levels) and, in particular, Croatian President Franjo Tudjman, should publicly denounce attacks against law-abiding Serbs in Croatia. The Croatian authorities also must make publicly clear that all those found guilty of such attacks will be punished to the full extent of the law.

Kosovo

In the predominantly Albanian province of Kosovo in the republic of Serbia, different methods of "ethnic cleansing" are being employed by Serbian authorities at the local, provincial and republican levels. The Serbian government seeks to resettle Serbs in Kosovo, which is widely regarded by Serbs as the cradle of Serbian civilization. Efforts to increase the Serbian presence in Kosovo are undertaken at the expense of the Albanian poopulation, which comprises ninety percent of the population in Kosovo.[47]

---

[47] Human rights abuses in Kosovo have been documented in the following Helsinki Watch reports: *Increasing Turbulence: Human Rights in Yugoslavia*, October 1989; *Yugoslavia: Crisis in Kosovo*, with the International Helsinki Federation, March 1990; and, Letter to Slobodan Milošević, President of the Republic of Serbia, and General Blagoje Adžić, Acting Minister of Defense and Chief of Staff of the Yugoslav People's Army, January 21, 1992, pp. 23-24. See also Michael W. Galligan, Deborah J. Jacobs, Morris J. Panner and Warren R. Stern, "The Kosovo Crisis and Human Rights in Yugoslavia: A Report of the Committee on International Human Rights," *The Record of the Association of the Bar of the City of*

Albanians are arbitrarily detained, tortured and otherwise mistreated in detention. Hundreds of thousands of Albanians have lost their jobs on the basis of their ethnic affiliation, particularly since 1991. The legal, medical and other professional fields have nearly been purged of Albanians and replaced with Serbs and Montenegrins. The quality of health care has deteriorated so drastically that cases of tetanus, diphtheria and infantile paralysis are appearing among the population. The delivery and receipt of humanitarian aid by local relief groups is impeded. In some cases, stocks of humanitarian aid have been confiscated by Serbian authorities. Over 300 Albanian families have been evicted from their homes without a court hearing, to which they are entitled. Dismissals of Albanians from their jobs and eviction from their homes have led to further economic and social marginalization of Albanians in Kosovo, where reportedly eighty-six percent of the population lives below the poverty line.

Discrimination against Albanians has been codified into many of Kosovo's provincial laws and Serbia's republican laws. For example, laws favor Serbian and Montenegrin ownership of community and private property in Kosovo. A series of laws promulgated in 1990 require those who wish to purchase or rent real estate in Kosovo to obtain special permits from the Serbian government. While such permits are readily available for Serbs and Montenegrins, they are rarely, if ever, issued to Albanians.[48]

New York, Volume 46, Number 3, April 1991.

[48] See "Program za realizaciju mira, slobode, ravnopravnost, prosperitet i demokracije u Socijalističku Autonomnu Pokrajnu Kosovo," ("Program for the Realization of Peace, Freedom, Equality, Prosperity and Democracy in the Socialist Autonomous Province of Kosovo") *Službeni Glasnik Socijalističke Republike Srbije*, Broj 15,30. marta 1990. The following laws either expressly discriminate against, or have been used so as to discriminate against Albanians in Kosovo since the imposition of "special measures" in Kosovo in February 1989: "Zakon o Ograničenju Prometa Nepokretnosti," ("Law Regarding Restrictions of Movement,") *Službeni Glasnik Socijalističke Republike Srbije*, Broj 30, 22. jul 1989; "Zakon o Izmenama i Dopunama Zakona o Ograničenju Prometa Nepokretnosti," ("Law Regarding Revisions and Amendments to the Law Regarding Movement,") *Službeni Glasnik Socijalističke Republike Srbije*, Broj 42, 28. septembar 1989; "Zakon o Postupanju Republičkih Organa u Posebnim Okolnostima," ("Law Regarding the Actions of Republican [Governmental] Bodies in Special Circumstances")

A long-standing record of human rights abuse and discrimination against ethnic Albanians in Kosovo has socially and economically marginalized that population, forcing thousands of Albanians to emigrate. The increasing discrimination against, and abuse of, Albanians in Kosovo appears aimed at decreasing their standard of living, thereby forcing many Albanians into poverty. Serbia's political and economic policies toward Kosovo appear intended to force Albanians to emigrate from Kosovo and to provide Serbs incentives to immigrate to the province.

Sandžak

Helsinki Watch has received numerous reports of beating and other physical abuses of Slavic Muslims in the region of Sandžak in the republic of Serbia.[49] Bosnian refugees who were fleeing to Macedonia, Turkey, Slovenia or Croatia via Sandžak[50] have claimed that Yugoslav army personnel would frequently harass and sometimes beat Muslims in Sandžak, demanding that they leave Serbia.

Službeni Glasnik Socijalističke Republike Srbije, Broj 30, 26. jun 1990; "Zakon o Radnim Odnosima u Posebnim Okolnostima," (Law Regarding Labor Relations in Special Circumstances") *Službeni Glasnik Socijalističke Republike Srbije*, Broj 40, 26. jul 1990; "Zakon o Izmenima i Dopunama Zakona o Radnim Odnosima u Posebnim Okolnostima," ("Law Regarding Revisions and Amendments to the Law Regarding Labor Relations in Special Circumstances") *Službeni Glasnik Socijalističke Republike Srbije*, Broj 54, 27. septembar 1990; and, "Zakon o Izmenama i Dopunama Zakona o Ograničenju prometa Nepokretnosti," ("Law Regarding Revisions and Amendments to the Law Regarding Movement,") *Službeni Glasnik Republike Srbije*, Broj 22, 18. april 1991.

[49] Sandžak is a predominantly Slavic Muslim region in southwestern Serbia and eastern Montenegro.

[50] Muslims displaced from eastern Bosnia who wanted to travel to Croatia would do so first, by travelling to Macedonia and then by travelling through Romania, Bulgaria and Hungary before arriving to Slovenia or Croatia. Many such refugees claimed they feared persecution in Serbia proper and sought to circumvent Serbian-popoulated areas of the republic. Such refugees were interviewed by Helsinki Watch representatives in Ljubljana and Zagreb in June 1992.

Some of the Bosnian refugees to whom Helsinki Watch spoke said that they had been forcibly displaced from eastern Bosnia and had fled to Sandžak, hoping to settle among Muslims in Serbia. However, many fled claiming they felt "unsafe" in Sandžak and that they were frequently subjected to threats and general mistreatment by military personnel stationed in the area. A Helsinki Watch representative visited Novi Pazar, the main city in the Sandžak region, in late June. During the visit, turret guns of Yugoslav army tanks were pointed at the city center. The tanks' presence did not appear to serve a military purpose nor was their heavy presence evident in other civilian areas in Serbia or along the Serbian and Bosnian border. Rather the position and high-level presence of military hardware and personnel in Sandžak appeared aimed at intimidating the local and refugee Muslim population.

Disappearances

Thousands of people -- mostly men of combat age -- remain missing in Bosnia-Hercegovina. While some families may have become separated as a result of the war, many people have been taken to unknown destinations by opposing armed forces. Combatants captured by opposing forces have been held in detention areas for varying periods. Many have subsequently been moved to unknown destinations and their whereabouts remain unknown. In other instances, after a village has been occupied by Serbian forces, the captured civilians have been divided by age and sex. Women, children and the elderly usually have been detained and subsequently deported. The men of fighting age have been separated from the others and are neither seen nor heard from thereafter. In one such case, Serbian paramilitary and JNA soldiers attacked and captured the village of Gravšća (municipality of Doboj)[51] on May 3. They subsequently arrested all the men, whose whereabouts remain unknown.

A 68-year-old woman[52] from Gravšća told Helsinki Watch:

---

[51] Of the 102,546 inhabitants of the municipality of Doboj; 40.2 percent were Muslims, 39 percent Serbs, 13 percent Croats, and 5.5 percent Yugoslavs.

[52] Interviewed in Zagreb, Croatia, on June 2, 1992.

The attack started at 11:00 in the morning. It ended by 8:00 p.m., when Serbian infantry and at least two tanks entered the village and arrested all its inhabitants. The Serbian forces included members of the Yugoslav army and Serbs from the neighboring villages of Sremska Gramska and Prankovci. The local Serbs wore socks over their heads so that no one could recognize them but we recognized their voices.

Anyone who had come outside onto the street was arrested, including myself. Most of the villagers had been rounded up by 9:00 p.m. and we were all taken to Sremska Gramska, where the men were separated from the women and the elderly. The men were taken away but no one knows where they were taken or what has become of them. My son and nephew remain missing.

According to the Bosnian human rights group Save Humanity, at least 100,000 people remain missing throughout Bosnia-Hercegovina. Helsinki Watch has not been able to confirm this estimate independently.

Taking of Hostages

Serbian, Croatian, and Muslim forces are holding civilians for military purposes. Typically, hostages are held and exchanged at a later date for combatants who are held by the opposing side(s). In other instances, civilians are held hostage by one side to extract military concessions from an opposing side. On May 1, 1992, Bosnian TO units blockaded JNA barracks in Sarajevo. The following day, Bosnian President Izetbegović and his daughter, returning from a three day trip to Lisbon, were taken hostage by JNA troops as he disembarked his plane at the Sarajevo airport. In return for his release, the JNA demanded safe passage for JNA soldiers encircled by Bosnian troops.[53]

---

[53] Chuck Sudetic, "Bosnia is Seeking Foreign Military Aid," *The New York Times*, May 5, 1992. Despite guarantees for the safety of the JNA soldiers, made by President Izetbegović and a UN escort, TO forces attacked the JNA troops on May 3 as they evacuated their barracks and killed several soldiers. 180 soldiers were taken prisoner, but were released on May 5.

On May 18, 1992, approximately 5,000 women, children and elderly persons of various ethnic groups were evacuated from Sarajevo by a convoy organized by the "Children's Embassy" charity. The convoy included about 1,000 cars, ten vans and 20 buses and was headed for the Croatian port city, Split. Officials of the relief group claimed to have obtained "written guarantees of safe passage from officials" of the Serbian Republic of Bosnia-Hercegovina.[54] In Ilidza, a suburb of Sarajevo, the convoy was stopped by Serbian paramilitaries and its passengers were taken to a local sports center, where they were held for three days. Their release was contingent upon Bosnian assurances that JNA troops blockaded by Bosnian government forces would have safe passage from JNA barracks in Sarajevo.[55] According to Bosnian officials, young men and parents of the children taken hostage threatened to retaliate against Serbs in Sarajevo if the hostages were not released.[56] The hostages were subsequently freed.

Similarly, evidence suggests that 3,000 Serbian civilians were held in a tunnel near the village of Bradina (near Sarajevo) during the week of May 25, 1992. According to Serbian forces, Muslim and Croatian forces took captive Serbian civilians from the villages of Bradina, Brdjan, Donje Selo, Konjic, Pazarić and Tarcin, near Sarajevo.[57] It remains unclear what the Muslim and Croatian captors intended to do with the detainees.[58] However, since the Serbian civilians were unwillingly in the power of the enemy and appeared answerable with their life or freedom for compliance with the orders of their Muslim and Croatian captors, they must be considered as hostages under international law. The captives reportedly were forced to spend three to five days in the mile-long Ivan-Sedlo railroad tunnel near the village of Bradina, 25 miles

---

[54] Chuck Sudetic, "Serbs Hold 5,000 Hostages Fleeing the War in Sarajevo," *The New York Times*, May 21, 1992.

[55] *Ibid.*

[56] *Ibid.*

[57] John F. Burns, "Serbs Say Muslim Slav and Croatian Gunmen Killed Civilians in Six Villages," *The New York Times*, June 4, 1992.

[58] *Ibid.*

southwest of Sarajevo.[59] After the UN made inquiries, the Bosnian government confirmed that people had been held in the tunnel but that they had been removed. It is unclear what happened to the prisoners after they were removed from the tunnel.[60]

Mistreatment in Detention

Helsinki Watch has documented cases of torture and severe mistreatment of prisoners held in detention facilities.[61] Moreover, Helsinki Watch is gravely concerned that Serbian forces are detaining prisoners of war and civilians in camps where they are held in appalling conditions.

Helsinki Watch has documented the following cases of beatings and general mistreatment of prisoners, including those who had been wounded:

Skender Vakuf and Stara Gradiška -- April 26

On April 26 at 3:30 p.m., Boris Matišić,[62] Travnik's mayor and a combatant in the war, travelled to meet with Lieutenant Colonel Živan Peuličan, commander of Serbian forces on Vlašić plateau, near Travnik. This meeting was to be the eighth or ninth such meeting between Matišić and Peuličan. Matišić said that the meetings were aimed at delaying the outbreak of violence in the Travnik area and that there was never any negotiation meant to prevent hostilities. Peuličan had visited Matišić in Travnik on previous occasions. The April 26 meeting was to have taken place in the Serbian-controlled town of Skender Vakuf.

Along with Zvonko Vuković, a HVO soldier, Matišić travelled to Skender Vakuf, where they were to meet with Serbian military officials

---

[59] Ibid.

[60] Ibid.

[61] This section deals with mistreatment in prisons or make-shift prisons. Detention in camps is described in the section above concerning ethnic cleansing and forcible displacement.

[62] Interviewed in Travnik, Bosnia-Hercegovina, on June 12, 1992.

at the town's post office, which was being used as a headquarters for Serbian troops. Matišić was armed with a 762-caliber handgun and dressed in civilian clothing. His escort, Zvonko Vuković was dressed in a HVO uniform and armed with an AK-47. They travelled to Skender Vakuf in a Renault 21 automobile and surrendered their weapons to the porter at the military headquarters, who gave them a receipt which would enable them to reclaim their weapons after the meeting. They were told to wait while Lieutentant Colonol Peuličan made a telephone call. According to Matišić:

> While we waited, the Serbian soldiers told Vuković to move our car because it was blocking the entrance. He left but did not come back. I continued to wait for Peuličan and then three Yugoslav military police officers approached me and handed me a piece of paper. The paper allowed them to temporarily take possession of our car, which belonged to the municipality of Travnik. I told them that there must be some misunderstanding and asked to speak to their commander. One of the military police officers then punched me in the chest. I then signed the paper hoping to avoid another confrontation. They then threw me against a wall and the other two police officers punched me in the ribs. I was handcuffed and led out of the hallway where I had been waiting for Peuličan.
>
> Vuković had been taken to the basement of the post office. When he returned from the basement, he was badly bruised. He was now dressed in civilian clothing and not his HVO uniform. They handcuffed us together and the same three men beat us in front of the post office for approximately five minutes. We were then taken to an armored personnel carrier, and I thought we were being taken to Banja Luka.[63] However, we ended up in Stara Gradiška. En route, one of the police officers drove the armored personnel carrier while the other two

---

[63] The city of Banja Luka is the second largest city in Bosnia-Hercegovina and the seat of a major Yugoslav military complex.

beat us. The drive lasted for about one and a half to two hours.

When we got to Stara Gradiška, one of the men repeatedly punched Vuković directly in his kidneys. One police officer held him while another beat him. They then started to beat me and concentrated on punching the fifth or sixth vertebra of my spine. This lasted for about 20 minutes, until about 9:30 p.m. We walked through a hallway in the jail, and as we walked by, we were repeatedly hit and punched by soldiers that had lined up along the left side of the corridor. I was punched in the face several times and a tooth was broken. While we were walking through the hallway, we could hear screaming from the cells. We presumed that people were being beaten or otherwise tortured. It took us about 30 minutes to walk through the hallway because we were constantly being hit. They would kick us in the testicles and when we would fall to the floor, they would then kick us again. One of the men, who was dressed in fatigues and wore a red beret, looked at us and said "I am a White Eagle. What you've been through now is nothing compared to what you will soon face."

A soldier of some rank -- possibly an officer or commander -- came into the hallway. The three men who were our escorts, i.e., those who brought us from Skender Vakuf, appeared to show some respect toward this officer. The officer looked at Zvonko and asked him why he looked so disheveled and had he been beaten. Zvonko replied that he had not been mistreated because he feared that he would be beaten again once the officer left us with the three soldiers again. The officer told us to sit in his office. He said that we would be sent home that same evening.

Eventually, we were taken to Banja Luka in the armored personnel carrier. The same three soldiers who drove us to Stara Gradiška now drove us to Banja Luka. They did not beat me during this trip but they did beat Vuković.

93

We went to the Security Center [Centar Službene Sigurnosti] in Banja Luka. It was about 11:00 p.m. when we arrived and we were taken to an office. The mayor of Skender Vakuf, Milan Komljenović, the president of the city council of Skender Vakuf, Vlado Glamočić, and the commander of the military center in Banja Luka, whose name I do not recall, were seated in the office. Komljenović and Glamočić apologized for the ill treatment and misunderstanding and said that this was Peuličan's own doing. We were then released at 5:00 a.m.. Komljenović and Glamočić escorted us to Skender Vakuf and we all went to Travnik and had a cup of coffee together.[64] I then drove them back to their zone of control.

Brčko -- May 3

During the evening of April 30 and May 1, the Yugoslav army had positioned tanks and armored personnel carriers throughout Brčko.[65] The town fell to Serbian forces several days thereafter. The bridge between Brčko and Gunja, Croatia, was destroyed at approximately 5:00 a.m. and, at approximately 10:00 a.m., the JNA disarmed the police in Brčko and many civilians fled that same morning, anticipating fighting. Helsinki Watch interviewed two Muslim men who were in Brčko when the town was attacked.[66] One of the men stated:

---

[64] Many of the combatants on both sides were former acquaintances, colleagues or, in some cases, friends. Matišić, Komljenović and Glamočić were all acquaintances before the war.

[65] The population of the municipality of Brčko was 87,332, 44.4 percent of whom were Muslims, 25.4 percent Croats, 20.8 percent Serbs and 6.4 percent Yugoslavs.

[66] Helsinki Watch interviewed the men two days after their escape from the village of Brezovo Polje, which was used as a detention area for captured non-Serbs. (See the section above on forcible displacement and the section on "ethnic cleansing.") The interviews were conducted on June 3, 1992, in Gunja (municipality of Županja), Croatia.

94

On May 1, the Četniks surrounded the town and an attack was launched on Brčko. Serbian forces attacked the town from the predominantly Serbian villages of Grčice and Ražljevo and from the JNA barracks in Brčko. Cannons, tanks and other heavy artillery were used by the Serbian forces. Muslim forces returned fire from the river with light artillery and concentrated their attacks on the military barracks in Brčko. The battles for Brčko lasted approximately two days and most areas of the town fell to Serbian forces on May 3.

According to another, a 37-year-old man:

After the town fell, some local Serbs and paramilitaries from Serbia -- mostly members of Arkan's and Šešelj's groups -- entered Brčko and captured the remaining inhabitants.

During the attacks on Brčko, I was in the Kolovara section of town, which is populated mostly by Muslims. Our mayor received assurances from a commander in charge of security for the local JNA garrison, a Captain Petrović, that Kolovara would not be attacked because it was predominantly Muslim. Despite such an agreement, the JNA and the Serbian paramilitary forces attacked Kolovara with heavy artillery. We didn't have any heavy weaponry and were forced to take shelter in the basements, which were full of civilians of various ethnic groups.

I hid in a neighbor's basement with approximately 25 other people, mostly elderly persons. My mother, brother and I left the basement and we went to my house -- which was fifty meters away -- to get some food. We were arrested on the street by four or five paramilitaries who did not ask us any questions but they started to beat me until I fell to the ground. Then I was taken to the mosque.

Approximately 100 to 150 men, between the ages of 15 and 80, were already in the mosque. We were forced to sing Četnik songs. At night, we were ordered to squat in a single line and told that if we fell asleep we would never wake up. During the night, local Serbs from Brčko who were dressed in Četnik uniforms would come and beat us with their boots. Usually, three to four Četniks came in every ten minutes; they were not always the same men. They beat people at random, including the old men. Each person was beaten for approximately ten minutes. The president of the local town council and I were beaten together but they beat him more severely. They seemed intent on breaking his bones and knocked out most of his teeth. Seven or eight men were taken out of the mosque but they never returned.

A paramilitary whom they called "Mauzer" from Bijeljina appeared to be in command; he was giving orders to JNA recruits. Later, JNA generals briefly visited the mosque but soon departed, leaving us at the mercy of paramilitaries once again.

While we were being held in the mosque, some hold-out Muslim forces were shooting into Brčko after it had fallen to Serbian troops. At one point, the paramilitaries tied a white ribbon around a prisoner's arm.[67] They then told him to walk about the area to see if a Muslim sniper would shoot him. Because the prisoner wore a white ribbon, our forces could have mistaken him for a Četnik and shot him. The Četniks did this frequently to ensure that no one would shoot at them if they walked out.

The prisoners spent the night in the mosque and were taken to the basement of the local hospital the next morning, where they were interrogated. According to the 37-year-old man:

---

[67] Members of the Serbian Volunteer Guard are identified by the white ribbon which they wear around their arms.

We were questioned every two hours for two consecutive days. Our interrogators were two Serbs from Brčko and two other men whom I did not recognize. Our interrogators would beat us first, then ask us questions. They asked me to identify persons who had weapons in the village and who had shot at Serbian forces. They beat me until I fell unconscious and then threw water on me so that I would wake up. The interrogation resumed and then I was beaten again.

After they got bored with beating me, they took me to the hallway in the hospital and made me stand by a window overlooking Muslim-controlled areas of the town. Muslim forces were trying to take Brčko back and were firing at Serbian positions throughout the town. The Muslims were shooting at the hospital, which the Serbs seemed to be using as a headquarters. I was made to stand in the window for 15 to 20 minutes and could very well have been shot by Muslim soldiers. A Serbian paramilitary stood next to me but his body was protected by a wall but I was made to stand in full-view at the open window. The paramilitary soldier kept a gun pointed at me the entire time to ensure that I would not run away. The shooting from Muslim positions continued but stopped shortly after they saw me standing in the window. I presume that they recognized me and realized that I was being used as a human shield.

The man who was held by the window told Helsinki Watch:

I didn't see any patients in the hospital but Četniks were everywhere. I did not see any medical personnel in the hospital except for two doctors, one was a Muslim and the other was a Croat. I passed by them in the hallway but they appeared to be scared and didn't look at me. Weapons -- mostly machine guns -- were placed throughout the hospital.

I escaped the torture at the hospital only after I gave my watch to a paramilitary in exchange for transport to the village of Brezovo Polje, where I heard that they were keeping all prisoners.[68] I thought my mother might be there. The paramilitary drove me to the village but told me to keep quiet about my transfer. His name was Jelenko Gojaković and he was a local Serb from Brčko.

A similar story was recounted by yet another Muslim man from Brčko:

My home is in the Meraja-Rosulja section of Brčko. About 35 people of various nationalities had taken refuge from the fighting in my basement. We eventually surrendered to Serbian paramilitaries and were taken to the local medical clinic (i.e., *dom zdravlja*). There, we were separated; some of the men were taken to the mosque and the women, children, elders and remaining men were kept in the basement of the clinic. I managed to hide myself and remained with the group in the basement of the health center. Later, the paramilitaries realized that I had stayed behind but they didn't seem to care very much.

We were soon tranferred to the JNA barracks, via bus, where we spent the night. In the morning, we were separated once again. The women and children were sent to the villages of Čelić, Ratković and Štorovići -- all are predominantly Muslim villages in the Brčko municipality. Approximately 50 men remained and we were taken to the gym of the military barracks. At approximately 11:00 p.m., paramilitaries beat some of the men, but they didn't beat me. The Četniks who were beating us belonged to various paramilitary groups; I think the men belonged to Arkan's and Šešelj's groups but they were all working together. The captured men were either beaten in the presence of everyone or were taken outside the

---

[68] The predominantly Muslim village of Brezovo Polje had been turned into a detention center by Serbian forces. (See section above on forcible displacement and the section on "ethnic cleansing.")

98

gym and beaten in the hallway. Approximately ten men who were beaten in the hallway never returned. I presume they were killed.

In the morning we were taken to the predominantly Muslim village of Brezovo Polje, which had been transformed into ghettos for Muslims and Croats by the Serbian paramilitaries.

Skender Vakuf and Stara Gradiška -- May 15

Five men who survived the killing in Travnik on May 15, 1992,[69] were mistreated by their captors who appeared to be JNA officers or soldiers. Two of the men were wounded and required medical attention, which they received three days after their capture.

According to Nikola Marjanović:

From Vlašić [the place of their capture near Travnik], we five were taken one and a half kilometers to a Yugoslav army headquarters office. We were insulted for 45 minutes and then beaten with rifle butts and fists.

We were then taken to the Babanovac hotel, where a larger number of Yugoslav army officers (about eight to twelve) were present. A woman -- either a nurse or a doctor -- came into the room where we were being held. I had a wound on my head but she said it wasn't serious and did not bother with me.

We spent one hour in the hotel, during which time we had to keep our hands up in the air. If we let them down we were beaten. In the evening, we were taken to Skender Vakuf, where those of us who had not been shot

---

[69] Stjepan Dražetić, Nikola Marjanović, Zdravko Brkić, Pero Djepina and Nikica Žilić survived a killing of disarmed combatants on the Vlašić plateau, near Travnik. (See section above on summary executions of civilians and persons *hors de combat*.) Dražetić and Žilić were wounded at the time of their capture.

[i.e., Zdravko Brkić, Pero Djepina and Nikola Marjanović], were held until late afternoon on Sunday [May 17]. During our stay in Skender Vakuf, we received no food, water, blankets or clothing[70] and were beaten by a group of men very frequently. When someone had to go to the bathroom, we were told to wait for five or six minutes and then were beaten en route to the bathroom. We rarely asked to go to the bathroom to avoid the beatings. We were questioned at times, as well.

Stjepan Dražetić also was captured and corroborated Marjanović's story:

The five of us who had been captured were taken to Arambašina voda, which is where cattle usually are brought to drink water. It is approximately 200 meters south, on the lower part of the Vlašić plateau. The Serb[ian troops] put us on a truck and took us to Babanovac, which is a cultural and sports ski center. Once there, a woman dressed my wound. We were kept in a hallway from approximately 4:00 a.m. to 4:30 a.m. and we were still in our undergarments. At approximately 4:30 a.m., we were put on a truck again and taken to Skender Vakuf to the basement of what appeared to be a post office. It was cold and we were beaten there for most of the duration of our stay. We were not given any food, water, clothing or blankets. They beat all five of us, including the two of us who had been wounded [Stjepan Dražetić and Nikica Žilić]. The beatings lasted for about 30 minutes and they would beat all of us simultaneously with their boots, fists and truncheons. Depending on the day, between two to ten men would beat us. We were lined up against a wall, told to face the wall with our hands up in the air and then we were beaten.

---

[70] After the men had been captured, they were stripped of their uniforms. (See section above on summary executions of civilians and persons *hors de combat*.)

The five men were subsequently taken to Stara Gradiška, a town which borders northern Bosnia in the Serbian-occupied area of Croatia and which is the site of a major prison complex.

According to Marjanović:

In the late afternoon, we were taken to Stara Gradiška and were beaten en route in the truck. At Stara Gradiška, they finally gave us some clothing but no boots or shoes. They beat us severely in Stara Gradiška. I fell unconscious two or three times and each time was splashed with water and revived. I was not allowed to change and remained in the damp cell with wet clothes. They told us that we were being treated as "prisoners of war." After that beating, we were not abused for the remainder of our stay in Stara Gradiška.

Dražetić confirmed Marjanović's account:

When we arrived at Stara Gradiška, we were told once again to face the wall and we were then beaten. The men who beat us were dressed in Yugoslav military police uniforms. I fell unconscious from the beatings. We eventually were put in cells, where we received blankets, water and food every morning and evening.

Marjanović and two fellow soldiers who had been captured with him, remained at the Stara Gradiška prison for several days. Dražetić and Nikica Žilić had been wounded at the time of their capture and were separated from the others. Both Dražetić and Žilić later were taken to Banja Luka, where they received medical attention.
According to Dražetić:

Nikica Žilić and I had been wounded at the time of our capture but we had not received any medical attention until we got to Stara Gradiška, where we were kept in a cell with other wounded prisoners. There were eight of us in the cell, which was lined with mattresses. We did not talk to one another because two military police officers stood guard over us and we were afraid that if we spoke to one another we would be killed. We also received first aid from a military officer, who dressed my wounds and gave me 2400 cc's of penicillin in the morning and evening. We were in the cells for three or four days.

During his stay at Stara Gradiška, Dražetić claimed that he saw only Yugoslav military police officers. He claimed not to have seen any regular police officers nor paramilitary units in the prison.

Nikica and I were told we were going to Banja Luka to the military hospital. However, when we got there, the medical personnel refused to accept us; a military officer told us that he could not guarantee our safety in the hospital. So they took us to a civilian hospital but they, too, told us that they could not guarantee our safety. Nevertheless, we were admitted and Nikica and I were placed in a room by ourselves with two armed guards outside our door. We stayed in the hospital where we received surgery. They treated us fairly and we were not discriminated against or treated inhumanely.

On the third day, a military police officer told us to get up and get dressed. A nurse dressed my wound and we were given civilian clothing. Up until that moment, we did not have any clothes besides our undergarments. Three military police officers and one driver came for us and they told us that we were going to be exchanged.

According to Marjanović:

On Friday night, we were told that we would be going home the next morning. They took the three of us to Banja Luka and put us in the jail while they went to get the other two who had been taken to the Banja Luka hospital. We were then taken to Skender Vakuf again.

According to Dražetić:

102

We arrived in Skender Vakuf at approximately 12:00 p.m. and were taken to the same basement [in the post office] where we had been held and beaten before. The treatment there was the same. We were tortured by the same men who had beaten us before. We were beaten for two hours, after which we were told to get on a bus and to put our hands and heads between our knees. We drove on a very badly paved road and, when we got to our destination, the Croats and Muslims were not there for the exchange.

The five prisoners then were taken back to Skender Vakuf. Marjanović said that the men eventually were given some food and water in their cell but that it was taken away from them before they had finished eating. According to Marjanović, the men who beat him at the Skender Vakuf jail and the Stara Gradiška prison were dressed in JNA uniforms.

According to Dražetić:

We spent the night in Skender Vakuf but were not beaten that evening. At 8:00 a.m., the next morning [May 23] we went back to the same exchange point to which we had travelled the day before, an area called Smet. There, we were met by a Lieutenent Colonel Pehulić who gave us some cigarettes and told us that all he wanted was peace. We were exchanged at approximately 10:00 a.m..

A Helsinki Watch representative spoke to the physician who had been in charge of examining the five men after their release.[71] Medical records also were examined to corroborate the witnesses' testimonies. According to the doctor and the patient's medical records, all five men had suffered from severe beatings.

•   Zdravko Brkić (born 1959) suffered from broken facial bones. His tenth and eleventh ribs had been broken. His eyelids had

---

[71] Interviewed at Travnik hospital on June 12, 1992. The doctor asked that his/her name not be disclosed.

been burned. The doctor believed that the injury to Brkić's eyelids had been inflicted by cigarette butts. Brkić also suffered from a damaged right kidney and a mild concussion. The medical report stated that the wounds varied in age, i.e., that they were inflicted at different periods during the nine days of detention, thus confirming that the man had been beaten on several occasions.

- Nikola Marjanović (born 1963) also suffered from a concussion and beatings to the head, especially to the right side of his face.

  His tenth and eleventh ribs were broken. His medical record states that most of his wounds were inflicted by the butt of a gun.

- Pero Djepina (born 1964) suffered from beatings to the face, especially the forehead, the chest and stomach. His medical record states that due to a concussion, Djepina cannot recall all the details of his experience in detention and his equilibrium is uncertain.

- Nikola Žilić (born 1959) had second degree burns on both hands, possibly from cigarettes. The right side of his chest particularly was bruised. He had received prior surgical attention for a gunshot wound on the upper frontal portion of his thigh.

- Stjepan Dražetić (born 1954) also suffered from a bullet wound to the upper thigh and also had received prior medical attention. His upper back and knee caps were particularly injured.

Indiscriminate Use of Force

International law distinguishes between legitimate military targets and civilian objects in armed international conflicts. While not an exhaustive list, the following persons, groups and objects may be regarded as legitimate military objectives subject to direct attack in Bosnia-Hercegovina: active and reserve soldiers of the JNA; members of the armed forces of the Serbian Republic of Bosnia-Hercegovina; members of Serbian paramilitary groups, both full-time and part-time, while the latter are directly participating in hostilities; members of the police of the Serbian Republic of Bosnia-Hercegovina, while they have combat duties; members of the Bosnian territorial defense and the Bosnian police, when the latter assume combat duties; members of the Croatian Defense Council (HVO); members of the Croatian Army (HV); members of Croatian paramilitary groups while they are directly participating in hostilities; weapons, other war materiel, military works, military and naval establishments, supplies, vehicles, camp sites, fortifications, and fuel depots or stores that are utilized by any party to the conflict; and objects that, while not directly connected with combat operations, effectively contribute to military operations, and whose partial or total destruction, in the circumstances ruling at the time, would result in a definite and concrete military advantage to the attacker. Possible objects include strategic portions of transportation and communication systems and facilities, airfields, ports, and otherwise non-military operations, such as manufactured products destined for export.

In the Bosnian conflict, the following should be considered civilian objects and, as such, should be considered immune from direct attack by combatants: structures and locales, such as houses, churches, dwellings, schools, and farm villages that are exclusively dedicated to civilian purposes and, in the circumstances prevailing at the time, do not make an effective contribution to military action; and buildings, monuments and other objects defined as "cultural property" by the 1954 Hague Convention for the Protection of Cultural Property, provided that imperative military necessity does not require waiver of their special protection.[72]

Serbian forces have indiscriminately bombed, shelled or otherwise attacked Bosnian towns and cities with little, if any, regard for civilian life. In many cases, Serbian forces appear to have targeted civilians or civilian objects, including incidents that have been publicized in the Western press and involve people waiting on bread lines, burying their dead in cemeteries or attempting to leave a besieged area for a safer place. On the basis of evidence collected by Helsinki Watch, we believe that such attacks are aimed at terrorizing the civilian population, thereby inducing them either to flee or surrender. According to Jose-Maria Mendiluce, special envoy of the UNHCR, Sarajevo was being

---

[72] Relevant international law is discussed in further detail in a following section of this report.

"systematically destroyed,"[73] and "what we are seeing is something like World War II, with a population center being destroyed and towns and villages attacked, not as military objects, but with the sole purpose of driving the people away."[74]

Helsinki Watch has documented the following cases which indicate that Serbian forces indiscriminately attacked civilian targets:

Bijeljina

A woman who lived in the Zajir area of Bijeljina[75] had taken refuge in her cousin's basement in the Selimović section of Bijeljina during the battles for the town. A lull in the fighting had ensued by morning and she went to the ground floor. The woman told Helsinki Watch:

> On April 4, at about 6:00 a.m., six or seven people were walking toward the mosque to say their prayers for Bairam.[76] All of a sudden, Serbian forces opened sniper fire on the people headed to worship. No one was killed; they just wanted to scare them.

Mostar

Prior to the war in Bosnia-Hercegovina, Yugoslav army reservists, many of whom were from Montenegro, were stationed in the Mostar

---

[73] "Observer Says Violence 'Horrendous,'" Agence-France Presse, May 12, 1992, as reported in FBIS, May 12, 1992.

[74] Laura Silber and Judy Dempsey, "EC Withdraws Its Monitors from Bosnian Capital," *The Financial Times*, May 13, 1992.

[75] Interviewed by Helsinki Watch on June 4, 1992, in Ljubljana, Slovenia.

[76] The lesser Bairam (Id al-Fitr) and the greater Bairam (Id al-Adha) are two major Muslim feasts. Bairam is a three-day feast which concludes the fast of Ramadan.

municipality. According to a woman from Mostar,[77] the reservists stayed close to the Yugoslav army barracks in the city environs prior to the war. However, in early April, tanks were positioned around the barracks and shooting began from the barracks into the city. According to the woman:

> We fled some time around Easter, I believe it was on April 19. At approximately 1:00 p.m., women and children were evacuated via bus. We were going to Split to escape the fighting in Mostar. When we reached the village of Zovnica, we were attacked by gunfire and mortar fire which came from the direction of Hum [a hill] in the Velež area. They opened fire for no reason; there were no military targets in sight and none of us were armed nor were we being escorted by members of the Croatian or Bosnian military. When the shooting started, the bus drove quickly while we all fell to the floor. No one was killed but a child was slightly wounded.

Sarajevo

- According to Munevra Baftić,[78] a woman from Sarajevo, Serbian forces have shot at civilians without provocation. Approximately 20 days ago [April 12], I was standing near a playground in the Dolac Malti area of Sarajevo. Approximately ten children, between the ages of three and ten, were playing in the playground during a lull in the fighting. A green, Yugoslav armored personnel carrier with a Četnik symbol on the door approached and fired into the crowd of people. A woman standing near the pastry shop was wounded but no one was killed. No one attacked them and no one threw stones or otherwise provoked the attack in any way.

- In early May, Serbian forces had captured some western suburbs of Sarajevo. According to international journalists, snipers sat in

---

[77] Interviewed in Split, Croatia, on June 10, 1992.

[78] Interviewed in Zagreb on June 2, 1992.

high-rise apartments and shot at cars passing on a stretch of four-lane highway that separates the Serbian-controlled western areas from the Bosnian-controlled city center.[79] During the week of May 4, 1992, several drivers were found dead "slumped over their steering wheels, each with a single bullet wound in the head."[80]

- On May 27, at least 16 people were killed and more than 100 were wounded after Serbian forces fired three mortar shells at people waiting to buy bread in Sarajevo.[81] The shells were fired from Serbian positions in the hills south of Sarajevo.[82]

- According to foreign press reports, during the "indiscriminate shelling" of Sarajevo on June 21, three Canadian officers belonging to the U.N. peacekeeping mission, were injured after their jeep took a direct hit from a mortar shell in the city's western suburbs. The officers were travelling in a convoy of 18 vehicles that were withdrawing from the Sarajevo airport which was closed at the time.[83]

- After monitoring Serbian radio frequencies, the Bosnian government released a recording of a conversation between a Yugoslav army general and two Serbian colonels which is said to have taken place on May 27. In the recording, the commander

---

[79] Blaine Harden, "In Besieged Sarajevo, Agony and Defiance," *The Washington Post*, May 10, 1992.

[80] *Ibid.*

[81] See Laura Silber, "'The Street Was a River of Blood,'" *The Washington Post*, May 28, 1992; John F. Burns, "Mortar Attack on Civilians Leaves 16 Dead in Bosnia," *The New York Times*, May 28, 1992; and, Blaine Harden, "Serb Gunners Pound Sarajevo in Fierce Attack," *The Washington Post*, May 30, 1992.

[82] John F. Burns, "Mortar Attack on Civilians Leaves 16 Dead in Bosnia," *The New York Times*, May 28, 1992.

[83] Blaine Harden, "Shells Hit U.N. Convoy in Sarajevo," *The Washington Post*, June 21, 1992.

of Serbian forces in Bosnia-Hercegovina, General Ratko Mladić,[84] instructed two Serbian colonels, identified only by Muslim code names "Mustafa" and "Zijo," to attack residential districts of Sarajevo with heavy artillery.[85] Mladić probably was speaking from the Lukavica military barracks in the southwest suburbs of Sarajevo to "Zijo" in Vrača, a hilly suburb to the south of Sarajevo, and to "Mustafa" on Borije Mountain to the northeast of the city.[86] In the recording, Colonel "Zijo" argues that the artillery attacks should be directed at areas with fewer Serbian residents. Mladić disregards the colonel's comment and orders his troops to bomb the Velesiće and Pofalići residential areas of Sarajevo. In regard to Velesiće, Mladić ordered his troops to "burn it all."[87] Moreover, Mladić ordered his troops to attack the civilian targets with the heaviest shells in the Serbian forces' armory, namely 155-millimeter howitzer shells, instead of the lighter 82-millimeter and 120-millimeter shells.[88]

- On June 22, at approximately 11:00 a.m., Serbs launched a mortar attack against Sarajevo. The first mortar shell fell in front of the People's Bank and, in quick succession, five other mortar shells fell in a broad ring around the first target. A mortar exploded in front of a bus on Marshall Tito street, and others exploded in narrow side streets, none more than 300 yards from the others. At least six shells hit in the city center, which was full

---

[84] Initially, Mladić was the Yugoslav army commander in the Serbian-controlled area of Knin in Croatia. He then was transferred to head Yugoslav forces in Bosnia-Hercegovina. Since the nominal withdrawal of the JNA from Bosnia-Hercegovina on May 19, Mladić remains in Bosnia-Hercegovina as commander of Serbian forces in the country.

[85] John F. Burns, "Taped Order Loud and Clear: 'Burn It All,'" *The New York Times*, June 9, 1992.

[86] *Ibid.*

[87] *Ibid.*

[88] *Ibid.*

of civilians who had emerged from their shelters to take advantage of a lull in the fighting. The attack on the city center left three civilians dead and 40 wounded. The continued attack on that day killed a total of 19 civilians and left 87 wounded.[89]

Slavonski Brod

Refugee camps in Croatia have also been targets for Serbian forces stationed in Bosnia-Hercegovina. Muslims and Croats fleeing from Serbian offensives in the Posavina region of northern Bosnia have fled to Slavonski Brod in Croatia. The Bosnian refugees in this region of Croatia include civilians who have been displaced by the fighting and combatants who have retreated from Serbian attacks, particularly since a Serbian offensive in early July. Under the terms of an agreement between the Croatian and Bosnian governments, all Bosnian men of fighting age who have fled to Croatia are to be repatriated. On July 15, a volley of Serbian-launched artillery shells fell on a stadium in Slavonski Brod which was being used as a refugee center. The stadium housed both civilian refugees and men who were to be repatriated to Bosnia. According to foreign press reports, the stadium appears to have been deliberately targeted by Serbian forces in neighboring Bosnia.[90] Approximately 15 shells fell on or just outside the stadium.[91] At least eight people were killed and over thirty-five were wounded.[92] The attack on the stadium was less than a mile from an underground shelter where Croatian Vice-President Mate Granić was meeting with a

---

[89] John F. Burns, "Sarajevo Tries a Normal Life; Bombs Forbid It," *The New York Times*, June 23, 1992.

[90] Peter Maass, "Serb Shelling Hits Crowd of Refugees," *The Washington Post*, July 16, 1992.

[91] *Ibid.*

[92] *Ibid.* The Croatian Government claims that twelve people were killed in the attack and up to sixty were wounded. (See "Press Release No. 288," Ministry of Information, Republic of Croatia, July 16, 1992.)

delegation of two dozen diplomats, relief workers and journalists.[93]

Tuzla

- A 40 year-old woman from Zvornik[94] told Helsinki Watch that an attack on her town came from Mali Zvornik, a town in the Republic of Serbia which is separated from Bosnia by the Drina River. According to the woman, the shooting came from a cannon near the whiting factory and from a tank stationed near the energy plant in Mali Zvornik. The woman said that a tank also was stationed on the bridge between Zvornik and Mali Zvornik. She said that, during the attack on Zvornik, Serbian police officers controlled access between the two republics.[95] The woman fled to Tuzla on April 7 to escape the fighting. She claims that during her stay, Serbian forces deliberately attacked the hospital in Tuzla.

  On May 30, I was standing close to the hospital when an aerial attack was launched. Several airplanes were circling the hospital. The hospital was targeted and hit with a bomb of some sort. Seven people who were standing near me were killed. I do not know how many patients inside the hospital were killed. I left Tuzla the next day because of the increased attacks.

---

[93] *Ibid.*

[94] Interviewed in Zagreb, Croatia, on June 2, 1992.

[95] Two Helsinki Watch representatives were outside of Zvornik on April 7 and can confirm that a Yugoslav army tank was stationed on the bridge between Bosnia and Serbia and that JNA soldiers and members of the Serbian police were controlling access between the two republics. Helsinki Watch representatives were prevented from entering Zvornik on the same day by paramilitaries who identified themselves as members of the Serbian Volunteer Guard (Srpska Dobrovoljačka Garda). The paramilitaries controlled access to and from Zvornik and were in full view of the JNA officers and Serbian police officers stationed on the nearby bridge. Other than denial of access into Zvornik, Helsinki Watch representatives were not abused or harassed by JNA soldiers or the Serbian paramilitaries in Zvornik.

- On June 8, US State Department Spokeswoman Margaret Tutwiler said that "the United States is especially alarmed by the Serbian shelling of Tuzla, a town north of Sarajevo that contains ...one of the largest chemical plants in the Balkans, [including] an extensive inventory of toxic and potentially very hazardous chemicals."[96]

Attacks on Medical and Relief Personnel and Vehicles

Disrespect for the Red Cross emblem and personnel has been pervasive throughout Bosnia-Hercegovina. Armed forces have attacked or otherwise harassed domestic and international medical and relief personnel and a number of people engaged in humanitarian aid have been killed or wounded. Relief convoys have been targeted for attack, primarily by sniper and mortar fire. Hijackings of relief convoys also have occurred. Serbian forces have stolen food, medicine and other humanitarian aid intended for civilians in besieged areas. Vehicles transporting such aid also have been confiscated by Serbian forces. Moreover, Helsinki Watch is concerned that, in some cases, indiscriminate mortar attacks have been launched to dissuade relief organizations from delivering humanitarian aid to besieged Bosnian cities and towns.

- On May 9, a spokesman for the European Community stated that 12 tons of French-donated food which was being stored at Sarajevo's airport for eventual transport to the city center had been stolen by Serbian militiamen.[97]

- On May 9, an ICRC convoy left Belgrade to deliver emergency medical supplies to Sarajevo and Zenica via Tuzla. Two ICRC delegates, Judith Hushagen and Liselotte Bosma, and three local staff members left Belgrade and spent the night in Tuzla, where they

---

[96] John M. Goshko and Trevor Rowe, "UN Votes to Deploy Extra Troops in Bosnia," *The Washington Post*, June 9, 1992.

[97] Blaine Harden, "In Besieged Sarajevo, Agony and Defiance," *The Washington Post*, May 10, 1992.

delivered medical supplies to the local hospital.[98] They proceeded toward Sarajevo the next morning and met their Sarajevo contact, Bernard Oberson, in the village of Olovo, approximately 35 kilometers north of Sarajevo. En route to meet his colleagues, Oberson had informed the guards at the checkpoints he passed that he would be returning with the ICRC convoy. When the group came to Vogošća, about ten kilometers from Sarajevo, the guards at the checkpoint had been replaced and had not been informed about the anticipated arrival of the ICRC convoy. The men at the Vogošća checkpoint wore uniforms, searched the convoy and questioned the delegates for two hours. One of the men who spoke some English apologized for the extensive search, saying that they were not regular soldiers and that he, for example, was an engineer.

The ICRC representatives then were ordered to line up their vehicles on the side of the road and to leave in one of their land cruisers. The ICRC delegates initially objected but eventually obeyed after the guards began to load their rifles. The head of the ICRC Sarajevo delegation tried to have the two vehicles returned but only received the staff's personal belongings, minus their cigarettes and money. Neither the medical supplies nor the trucks in which the aid was being transported were returned to the ICRC.

● In addition to ICRC convoys, Serbian forces are reported to have seized several U.N. trucks carrying food and medicine for

---

[98] The account described here is taken from Judith Hushagen, "On Mission in Bosnia-Herzegovina," *International Committee of the Red Cross Bulletin*, No. 197, June 1992, p. 1, and "Bosnia-Hercegovina: ICRC Striving to Cope as Tragedy Grows," Communication to the Press No. 92/10, May 11, 1992. Press reports identified Serbian forces as those responsible for the confiscation of the medical supplies carried by the ICRC convoy. (See Blaine Harden, "EC Withdraws Ambassadors From Belgrade," *The Washington Post*, May 12, 1992.)

stranded civilians.[99]   UN officials have said that Serbian troops are responsible for delaying, diverting and stealing trucks full of food donated by the US and other Western countries.[100]

- During the week of May 11, 48 truckloads (or 600 tons) of food were unable to reach Sarajevo from Belgrade and Zagreb because Serbian militia commanders repeatedly delayed assurances of safe passage to the UNHCR.[101]

- On May 18, at 2:30 p.m., an ICRC convoy carrying food and medical relief was attacked in the Vranik section of Sarajevo. Bosnian officials and witnesses blamed Serbian forces for the attack, which destroyed 4.5 tons of medicine.[102] Three ICRC staff members, delegates Frederic Maurice and Roland Sidler and their interpreter, Ivan Lalić, were wounded. 39-year-old Frederic Maurice, died the next day in Sarajevo's hospital.[103] According to the ICRC, "security guarantees [had been] obtained from the parties concerned" prior to the convoy's departure for Sarajevo.[104]

---

[99] Blaine Harden, "Hope Seen for End to Sarajevo Siege," *The Washington Post*, June 2, 1992.

[100] Blaine Harden, "Bosnian Siege Endangers Relief Effort," *The Washington Post*, April 28, 1992.

[101] John F. Burns, "As Cannons Roar, UN Leaves Bosnia," *The New York Times*, May 17, 1992.

[102] Tony Smith, "Red Cross Convoy Attacked En Route to Sarajevo," The Associated Press, May 18, 1992.

[103] See "Bosnia-Herzegovina: Three ICRC Staff Injured in Sarajevo," ICRC Press Release No. 1715, May 18, 1992; "Bosnia-Herzegovina: ICRC Delegate Dies in Sarajevo," ICRC Press Release No. 1716, May 19, 1992; "Red Cross Delegate Killed in Sarajevo," Reuters Information Services, May 19, 1992; and, "Bosnian Factions Set New Truce," *The Washington Post*, May 19, 1992.

[104] "ICRC Delegate Killed in Sarajevo," *International Committee of the Red Cross Bulletin*, No. 197, June 1992, p. 3.

- On May 21, Serbian armed units hijacked a dozen UN trucks carrying food and medicine. The next day the UNHCR suspended aid convoys to Bosnia-Hercegovina.[105]

- On June 2, a UN escorted convoy carrying dried milk, baby formula and other foods to the embattled Dobrinja suburb of Sarajevo "was raked with machinegun fire by Serb[ian] militiamen who then made off with the food."[106] The UN forces had been escorting a convoy of humanitarian aid organized by the Children's Embassy charity organization when they were ambushed. The driver and passenger of one of two buses in the convoy were seriously wounded.[107] The bus driver was later reported to have died.[108]

- On June 24, two ambulances came under Serbian machine-gun fire that killed all six occupants.[109] That same day, Morten Hvaal, a 28 year-old Norwegian journalist on assignment for the Associated Press, was leaving the embattled Sarajevo suburb of Dobrinja in a third ambulance. Near a Serbian check-point between Dobrinja and the main road to Bosnian-controlled central Sarajevo, the ambulance was raked by 172 bullets.[110] The driver was hit in the thigh, a severely wounded man on a

---

[105] "Aid Convoys are Suspended," *The New York Times*, May 23, 1992.

[106] Blaine Harden, "Serb Forces Attack Bosnian Food Convoy," *The Washington Post*, June 3, 1992.

[107] *Ibid.*

[108] Blaine Harden, "Starvation Said to Begin in Sarajevo," *The Washington Post*, June 7, 1992.

[109] Blaine Harden, "Land of Peril for Journalists," *The Washington Post*, as reported in *The International Herald Tribune*, July 28, 1992. To date the circumstances of the attack have not been confirmed.

[110] *Ibid.*

stretcher was hit several times and a medic was wounded. Six bullet fragments were found stuck in Hvaal's flak-jacket.[111]

- On June 24, a UN convoy and representatives of the relief group Medecins Sans Frontieres came under repeated sniper fire, on the outskirts of Sarajevo. The UN peace-keeping troops were escorting four doctors, who were driving in a separate jeep. The doctors reportedly were returning from a hospital in Sarajevo's Koševo suburb to the Serbian-held village of Pale. Reportedly, sniper fire came from the Donji Kotorac suburb.[112] One bullet shattered the windows of the jeep and two of the doctors were lightly wounded.[113] The UN troops returned fire and the shooting stopped.[114]

- On June 25, a doctor was killed and two nurses were seriously injured after Serbian troops opened fire with anti-aircraft weapons on a medical vehicle.[115] It was unclear whether the Serbian troops knew they had hit a medical vehicle "because the fusillade came from hillside batteries several miles from the center of the besieged capital."[116] The bus was taking medical employees to a nearby hospital when it was hit.

- On July 2, a UN peacekeeping convoy travelled to the old Jewish Cemetery on a hillside near Sarajevo's city center with local

---

[111] Ibid.

[112] "Two Doctors in UN Convoy Injured by Snipers," Tanjug Yugoslav News Agency report of June 25, 1992, as reported in FBIS, June 26, 1992. See also Charles Lane, "The Siege of Sarajevo," Newsweek, July 6, 1992.

[113] Ibid.

[114] Charles Lane, "The Siege of Sarajevo," Newsweek, July 6, 1992.

[115] "Serbs' Guns Hit Sarajevo Hospital Bus," Reuters Information Services report, as printed in The Washington Post, June 25, 1992.

[116] Ibid.

medical workers to pick up the rotting remains of seven Muslims -- six militiamen and a civilian woman who had been shot there by Serbian troops two weeks before and left for dead. Since then, "the parents of the seven had been able to watch the bodies decompose from the upper floors of nearby buildings."[117] UN officials claim that they first received a request to retrieve the bodies when they appeared still to be alive and in urgent need of medical care. The officials claim that efforts to reach the injured were blocked by the encircling Serbian troops. Later attempts by the parents to obtain "permission from Serbian forces to retrieve the bodies also failed." The July 2 convoy effort went forward without the approval of Serbian forces.[118] Only four of the bodies could be removed before Serbian sniper fire forced the medical workers and the UN troops to leave the cemetery.[119]

In addition to humanitarian organizations, members of the UN peace-keeping force and the EC monitoring mission to Yugoslavia also have been harassed by Serbian forces in Bosnia-Hercegovina.

● In early May, a UN military observer was wounded and an EC onitor was killed in separate attacks six kilometers south of Mostar.[120] The Belgian member of the EC observers' mission was killed by anti-aircraft fire.[121] On the basis of an EC investigation, Belgian Foreign Minister Willy Claes asserted that EC monitor Bertrand Borrey (age 48) had been killed

---

[117] "Terror Not Ended in Sarajevo," *The Washington Post*, July 3, 1992.

[118] *Ibid*.

[119] *Ibid*.

[120] Jonathan Landay, "Fierce Fighting Flares," United Press International, May 19, 1992.

[121] "EC Observers Killed in Bosnia-Hercegovina," Brussels La Une broadcast on May 2, 1992, as reported in FBIS, May 4, 1992.

intentionally by JNA troops.[122]   The JNA had given the monitor express permission to accompany two workers repairing a power plant.[123]

- On May 6, a car carrying United Nations Special Envoy Marrack Goulding and Bosnian President Alija Izetbegović was fired on by snipers in Sarajevo. No one was injured.[124]

- On May 11, two UN jeeps carrying armed members of the UN peacekeeping mission to Yugoslavia were "stopped at a roadblock by Serb[ian] militiamen who stole their weapons and their vehicles."[125]

- The EC monitoring mission withdrew from Sarajevo during the week of May 12 because members of the mission had "been harassed and threatened" by Serbian forces.[126]

- On June 10, a UN convoy was attacked on the outskirts of Sarajevo. The convoy had left Sarajevo and was on its way to meet another UN convoy arriving from Belgrade. One person was injured.[127]

---

[122] "Belgium's Claes Cited," Brussels BRT International broadcast on May 4, 1992, as reported in FBIS, May 4, 1992.

[123] Ibid.

[124] Blaine Harden, "Snipers Hit Car of UN Envoy in Sarajevo," *The Washington Post*, May 7, 1992.

[125] Blaine Harden, "EC Withdraws Ambassadors From Belgrade," *The Washington Post*, May 12, 1992.

[126] Ibid.

[127] "UN Convoy Is Attacked on Edge of Sarajevo as More Units Arrive," Reuters Information Services report, as printed in *The New York Times*, June 11, 1992.

On May 20, the ICRC announced that it was temporarily withdrawing its delegates from Bosnia-Hercegovina. In announcing its decision, the ICRC stated:

> the terrible escalation of violence in this strife-torn republic shows no sign of abating ... [and under] these circumstances, when the most basic rights of the victims and especially vulnerable groups are being constantly
>
> and deliberately violated, the ICRC is no longer in a position to carry out its humanitarian tasks.[128]

After conferring with representatives of Bosnia's warring factions and the governments of Yugoslavia and Croatia, the UNHCR and the ICRC resumed their missions in five cities in Bosnia-Hercegovina (Banja Luka, Bihać, Bijeljina, Grude and Trebinje) in early June.[129] The ICRC subsequently resumed its mission in Sarajevo.

Besieged cities, towns and villages throughout Bosnia-Hercegovina have been faced with severe shortages of food and medical supplies. Prior to the recent delivery of humanitarian aid to Sarajevo, Cedrick Thornberry, chief of civilian operations for the UN peacekeeping operation in Yugoslavia, said that "starvation was beginning" in the suburb of Dobrinja, where an estimated 35,000 residents remain under siege.[130] US State Department Spokeswoman Margaret Tutwiler has stated that "many people are slowly dying of hunger, most reduced to a

---

[128] "ICRC: Humanitarian Situation in Bosnia-Hercegovina Intolerable," ICRC Press Release No. 1719, May 27, 1992.

[129] See "Red Cross Announces Agreement to Allow Operations," Broadcast by Bern Swiss Radio International broadcast on June 7, 1992, as reported in FBIS, June 8, 1992. See also "ICRC Returns to Bosnia-Herzegovina," ICRC Communication to the Press No. 92/16, June 24, 1992.

[130] Blaine Harden, "Starvation Said to Begin in Sarajevo," *The Washington Post*, June 7, 1992.

diet of flour and nettles."[131] Between July 3 and 22, the UN airlift to Sarajevo had provided food to 80 percent of the 450,000 people encircled in the Sarajevo region.[132] Despite world attention focused on the humanitarian needs of Sarajevo's residents, inhabitants in besieged cities, towns and villages throughout Bosnia-Hercegovina remain in dire need of food and medical supplies. Helsinki Watch has interviewed scores of refugees and displaced persons who were forced to leave not only embattled towns but also relatively tranquil areas of Bosnia-Hercegovina because of the lack of food.[133]

Moreover, medical materials are in low supply throughout Bosnia-Hercegovina. Helsinki Watch representatives travelling through Bosnia-Hercegovina were frequently told by local medical personnel that they were in need of antibiotics and, particularly, insulin. David Brauchli, a photographer for the Associated Press, was wounded and needed surgery in Sarajevo. According to Brauchli:

> The hospital couldn't administer general anesthetic because it had no oxygen. All the oxygen was being held by the Serb[ian forces] and, like everything else, was a bargaining chip. The only anesthetic was local and it wasn't strong. Even after numbing my legs with an injection into my spinal cord, I could feel the doctors

---

[131] John M. Goshko and Trevor Rowe, "UN Votes to Deploy Extra Troops in Bosnia," *The Washington Post*, June 9, 1992.

[132] Blaine Harden, "UN Pleads for Help for Bosnian Refugees," *The Washington Post*, July 23, 1992.

[133] For example, refugees who had fled from the environs of Tuzla prior to the Serbian offensive in the area in mid-July told Helsinki Watch that they were forced to leave Tuzla because of the sharp decline in food and medicine. Although the ICRC and UNHCR delivered aid to these areas, it appears that the influx of displaced persons to Tuzla far outpaced the quantity of supplies and the rapidity with which international relief agencies could deliver aid to the displaced.

operating on my hip. The nurse had to tie my arms to the table.[134]

Despite the urgent humanitarian needs of Bosnians, incessant fighting and shelling often prevents humanitarian aid from entering besieged areas. Helsinki Watch is gravely concerned that Serbian forces are deliberately obstructing delivery of humanitarian aid in order to advance their military agenda; i.e., they are trying to force the surrender of Bosnian cities and towns by shelling and, in some cases, starving, the area's civilian population into submission. Ambulances have been unable to cross the line of fire to evacuate those in need of medical care.[135] Prior to the July 3 arrival of UN escorted relief convoys, Serbian forces, which controlled Sarajevo's airport and entrance to and from the city, had refused to allow international agencies to deliver food and medicine that were in desperately short supply in the capital.[136] Even after UN forces assumed control over Sarajevo's Butmir airport and relief supplies were flown in, renewed shelling prevented aid from reaching residents of the embattled city. Although Sarajevo's food shortage has been temporarily alleviated by the recent UN airlift, areas throughout Bosnia which remain under siege by Serbian forces are in chronic need of food and medical supplies.

Attacks on Journalists

In 13 months, the wars in Croatia and Bosnia-Hercegovina have claimed the lives of at least 24 journalists. Between June 26, 1991, and July 31, 1992, at least 33 have been wounded, ten have been captured and subsequently released and six remain missing. At least 68 have been attacked and more than 47 have been otherwise harassed (i.e., threatened,

---

[134] David Brauchli, "Wounded by Shrapnel in Sarajevo, A Photographer's Story," The Associated Press, May 25, 1992.

[135] Blaine Harden, "Street Battle for Sarajevo Intensifies," *The Washington Post*, May 15, 1992.

[136] *Ibid.* See also Laura Silber, "Serbs Cut Off Supplies to Sarajevo," *The Financial Times*, May 11, 1992.

property confiscated.)[137] The escalating violence in Bosnia-Hercegovina severely restricts the ability of journalists to gather, confirm and report the news. The fact that some journalists were killed or wounded by sniper fire would indicate that they were targeted for attack. Indeed, snipers fighting on all sides have "made a practice of firing on vehicles marked to indicate that they were being used by reporters."[138]

A significant number of journalists have been killed, wounded, physically assaulted or otherwise attacked while reporting on the war in Bosnia-Hercegovina. Attacks on journalists have come from all sides in the conflict. Since April 6, 1992, at least three foreign and domestic journalists have been killed while covering the Bosnian war. Four are missing and at least five have been wounded. At least five journalists have been physically assaulted and nine have been otherwise harassed (i.e., threatened, property confiscated, etc.).

After multi-party elections in November 1990, the Bosnian press repeatedly has been criticized by members of the country's three main political parties. The Muslim-oriented Party of Democratic Action (SDA), the Serbian Democratic Party (SDS) and the Croatian Democratic Union (HDZ) have claimed that the Bosnian press did not adequately represent the interests of their respective national constituencies.[139]

Since the November 1991 referendum on Bosnian independence, political pressure, physical attacks and public death threats from political

---

[137] The figures in this section were gathered in Helsinki Watch interviews with witnesses supplemented by information provided by the International and American PEN Centers, the Committee to Protect Journalists and wire and press reports. For information about attacks against journalists in the war in Croatia see the following Helsinki Watch publications: "Letter to Slobodan Milošević, President of the Republic of Serbia, and General Blagoje Adžić, Acting Minister of Defense and Chief of Staff of the Yugoslav People's Army," January 21, 1992; and "Letter to Franjo Tudjman, President of the Republic of Croatia," February 13, 1992.

[138] John F. Burns, "Bosnian Shelling Lifts Civilian Toll," *The New York Times*, July 24, 1992.

[139] In June 1991, Helsinki Watch representatives spoke with leaders of each of the three political parties in Sarajevo, all of whom regarded the Bosnian press as "anti-Muslim," "anti-Serbian" or "anti-Croatian."

leaders against Bosnian journalists have increased dramatically. In mid-May, a memorandum calling for the assassination of Goran Milić, director of YUTEL Television, was broadcast on Bosnian and Serbian television and radio stations. The memorandum, which reportedly was authored by representatives of the Serbian Democratic Party, also listed others alleged to have committed "war crimes."[140] The call sent Milić into hiding in Sarajevo, where he remains, unable to escape the fighting.

Since the outbreak of the war in Bosnia-Hercegovina, journalists working for Sarajevo Television and YUTEL, a Sarajevo-based pan-Yugoslav television program, reportedly have been targeted by paramilitary groups in Sarajevo.[141] Nenad Pejić, editor-in-chief of Sarajevo Television, was forced to flee the country after a public call for his assassination was made by Radovan Karadžić, leader of the Serbian Democratic Party in Bosnia-Hercegovina.[142] On April 8, Bosnian Serbs founded the Serbian News Agency (SRNA) in the Serbian-controlled village of Pale, outside of Sarajevo. SRNA's director, Todor Dutina, alleged that the news agency was formed in reaction to the "banishment" of Serbian viewpoints from the Bosnian media.[143]

With the escalation of violence, attacks against foreign and domestic journalists continue to increase. Although some of the following journalists appear to have been killed or wounded by cross-fire, others may have been deliberately attacked or harassed because of their professional affiliation. At least one journalist died from his wounds because Serbian forces denied him immediate medical attention.

In the cases listed below, mortar shells may have been deliberately fired at journalists, particularly at Ivo Štandeker, the *Mladina* correspondent. Moreover, Yugoslav, Bosnian and Croatian journalists appear to have been arrested solely on the basis of their professional

---

[140] Index on Censorship Briefing Paper, "Bosnian Journalists Face Death Threat in Sarajevo," London, March 22, 1992.

[141] *Ibid.*

[142] *Ibid.*

[143] Tanjug Yugoslav News Agency report on April 14, 1992; as reported in FBIS, April 15, 1992.

affiliation with a particular newspaper or news agency or because of their ethnic or national origin.

Deaths

- Kjafis Smajlović, a Zvornik correspondent for the Sarajevo-based daily *Oslobodjenje*, was shot in his office, reportedly by Serbian paramilitaries, on April 9, 1992.[144] To date, five *Oslobodjenje* reporters have been killed.[145]

- Jordi Pujol Puente, a 25-year-old photographer for Spain's Catalan-language daily *Avui*, was killed by an exploding mortar shell at noon on May 17 in the Sarajevo suburb of Dobrinja. David Brauchli, a photographer for the Associated Press, was wounded by shrapnel in the head, groin and arm.[146]

- Ivo Štandeker, a 30-year-old journalist for the Ljubljana-based weekly *Mladina*, died from injuries incurred during the shelling of an apartment complex in the Sarajevo suburb of Dobrinja on June 16 at approximately 2:00 p.m. Jana Schneider, an American freelance photographer working for the Paris-based SIPA agency, was wounded in the leg. The two journalists were hit by five mortar shells which fell in their immediate vicinity. According to Adnan Abdul Razak, a spokesman for the UN Protection Force (UNPROFOR) mission in Sarajevo, the pair was hit by shrapnel from a Serbian tank shell on June 16 after they

---

[144] Reporters Sans Frontieres, Montpellier, France, to Serbian President Slobodan Milošević, April 28, 1992.

[145] John F. Burns, "Bosnian Shelling Lifts Civilian Toll," *The New York Times*, July 24, 1992.

[146] Tony Smith, "Bosnian Troops Call Off Assault on Army Barracks," The Associated Press, May 17, 1992. See also David Brauchli, "Wounded by Shrapnel in Sarajevo, A Photographer's Story," The Associated Press, May 25, 1992; Manuel Leguineche, "Demasiado cerca" *El Diario*, May 19, 1992; "Un fotografo del Avui muere en los combates de Sarajevo," *La Vanguardia*, May 10, 1992; and "Jordi Pujol Puente, "Una guerra perdida," *El Mundo*, May 19, 1992.

slipped through the Serbian encirclement of Dobrinja. According to Razak, Serbian paramilitaries manning a roadblock "kidnapped" Štandeker and Schneider as they were being rushed from Dobrinja to a downtown hospital. After UN intervention, the Serbian troops agreed to take the pair for medical treatment to Pale, a Serbian-controlled village east of Sarajevo. According to Razak, Štandeker died of massive internal bleeding and Schneider's injuries were "not severe."[147]

Schneider and Štandeker were originally to have gone at 2:00 p.m. to the hospital in Sarajevo's center which is ten kilometers from Dobrinja, the site of the attack. Instead, they were delayed at a roadblock for an unknown period and were then taken to Pale, about 35 kilometers away. Štandeker's death is listed at approximately 10:00 p.m. and he is said to have died before reaching Pale for medical attention.[148] Serbian paramilitaries are responsible for the eight hour delay of medical attention to the wounded Štandeker.

- Twelve employees of the Bosnia-Hercegovina Radio Network have been killed, including reporters, camera operators, drivers and other staff members.[149]

---

[147] "Photojournalist Killed, American Wounded in Sarajevo," United Press International, June 17, 1992. See also, "Wounded Slovenian Photographer Dies," Agence France Presse, June 17, 1992, and Blaine Harden, "Bosnian Leader Declares Alliance with Croatia," *The Washington Post*, June 17, 1992. (*The Washington Post* reports that Schneider was on assignment for the German weekly *Stern*.)

[148] Boris Cibej, Managing Editor, *Mladina*, Ljubljana, to Committee to Protect Journalists, July 22, 1992.

[149] John F. Burns, "Bosnia Shelling Lifts Civilian Toll," *The New York Times*, July 24, 1992.

Disappearances

- Krunoslav Marinović, a correspondent for Croatian Radio, was taken from his apartment in Foča on April 14. Reportedly, he was abducted by Serbian paramilitary or Yugoslav army troops.[150]

- On or about April 16, the Goražde correspondent of the Belgrade daily *Politika*, Ratko Milović, reportedly was arrested in front of his home by armed Muslims. Milovic's whereabouts remain unknown.[151]

- Sead Trhulj, a free-lance reporter for Bosnia-Hercegovina Television, has been missing since May 7. Trhulj and his family left their residence in Sarajevo (at Miške Jovanovića 9) in March, after a bomb had been planted in their home and Trhulj's life had been threatened.[152] On the morning of May 7, his wife and a friend's son told him that his home had been damaged, allegedly by a bomb. At approximatley 10:00 a.m., he went to inspect the damage and has not been heard from since.[153]

- On May 14, Muslim forces reportedly abducted Mirko Carić, *Politika*'s Sarajevo correspondent. According to Serbian sources, Carić and his neighbors had taken shelter from the fighting in Iližda where members of the Bosnian Territorial Defense

---

[150] Croatian Radio and the Ministry of Information of the Republic of Croatia, Zagreb, to the Committee to Protect Journalists, April 28, 1992.

[151] "*Politika* Correspondent Arrested," Tanjug Yugoslav News Agency broadcast on April 16, 1992; as reported in FBIS, April 17, 1992.

[152] Index on Censorship Briefing Paper, "Bosnian Journalists Face Death Threats in Sarajevo," London, March 22, 1992.

[153] Reporters Sans Frontieres, Montpellier, France, open letter of May 11, 1992.

arrested the journalist. Carić's whereabouts remain unknown.[154]

Wounded

- Rob Celliers, chief cameraman for the London-based television service Visnews, was injured in the lower right arm by shrapnel as he filmed battles on the streets of Sarajevo.[155] At the time of the shooting, at 6:00 a.m. on April 21, Celliers was standing opposite the Bosnia Hotel, near a building controlled by Serbian forces. Sniper fire came from a park directly across from the Serbian-controlled building while mortar shells were fired from Serbian positions. The injury could have been caused by sniper bullets, which were breaking up against a wall near Celliers, or mortar shells.

- A car carrying Alfonso Rojo and George Gobet, journalists for the Spanish daily *El Mundo* and Agence France Presse, respectively, came under heavy sniper fire on June 10. Their car swerved and crashed. Rojo broke his arm and Gobet broke a vertebra in his neck. People on the street pulled them out of their car and took them to Sarajevo's University General Hospital. Despite the residents' help, Rojo's flak jacket was stolen.[156]

- On June 30, "Serbian forces opened fire several times on Western reporters seeking to reach" Sarajevo's airport.[157] Jean Hatzfeld, a journalist for the Paris-based *Liberation*, was

---

[154] "Green Berets Kidnap *Politika* Correspondent," Tanjug Yugoslav News Agency report on May 15, 1992; as reported in FBIS, May 18, 1992.

[155] "Two Journalists Wounded in Bosnia and Croatia," Reuters Information Services, April 22, 1992.

[156] Blaine Harden, "Serbs' Shells Make Sarajevo a Man-Made Hell," *The Washington Post*, June 13, 1992.

[157] John F. Burns, "UN Takes Control of Airport at Sarajevo as Serbs Pull Back," *The New York Times*, June 30, 1992.

seriously wounded in the leg. Four other newsmen were lightly wounded.[158]

- On July 23, two CNN journalists were injured in Sarajevo. CNN correspondent Mark Dulmage, 59-years-old, was lightly wounded by bullet fragments and broken glass. Margaret Moth, a 42-year-old CNN camerawoman, was "hit in the jaw by a sniper's bullet" and severely wounded as she rode in a minivan to the Sarajevo airport for a report on the airlift.[159] Moth sustained extensive wounds and was operated on for several hours in Sarajevo's Koševo hospital.[160]

Arrests

- Robert Dulmers, a freelance journalist working for the Dutch ANP news agency, was abducted on May 20 and held for nine days by Serbian militiamen on charges of spying. He was held near the city of Doboj and reportedly beaten and threatened with execution by his captors. He was released after Red Cross intervention.[161]

- On June 17, the Zenica office of Tanjug was broken into and ransacked. Milan Sobić, the Tanjug correspondent in Zenica, was placed under house arrest by the local Muslim and Croatian authorities on June 18. He was taken to a local prison on June 18

---

[158] *Ibid.*

[159] John F. Burns, "Bosnian Shelling Lifts Civilian Toll," *The New York Times*, July 24, 1992, and "Two CNN Journalists Hurt in Sniper Attack, One Seriously," The Associated Press, July 23, 1992. The CNN minivan was clearly marked as a news vehicle.

[160] *Ibid.*

[161] "Serbian Gunmen Free Dutch Journalist," Reuters Information Services, May 30, 1992.

and, reportedly, has not been seen by an investigatory judge nor have any charges been filed against him.[162]

- Slobodan Lekić, a reporter with the Associated Press, Morten Hvaal, a free-lance reporter for the Associated Press, and a cameraman for the British ITN Television Network were shot at by snipers and machine-gunners. The three men escaped injury, either because they wore flak jackets or because they began speeding to dodge sniper fire.[163]

Physical or Other Harassment

- On April 13, the Sarajevo offices of the Belgrade-based Yugoslav news agency, Tanjug, allegedly were demolished and robbed. The Serbian press in Bosnia-Hercegovina and Serbia accuse the "military formations of the former Bosnia-Hercegovina" of the attack.[164] Reportedly, Tanjug correspondent Siniša Ljepojević had his passport and money stolen. The Tanjug office has since reopened.

- On April 28, Željko Magajnić, a reporter for the Split-based daily, *Slobodna Dalmacija*, was beaten by three men in fatigues, presumably members of the Croatian Defense Council (HVO), in Livno in western Hercegovina. Magajnić was dragged from his car, thrown onto the pavement and punched and kicked in full view of several people walking by. A medical report dated April

---

[162] Dušan Župan, Editor-in-Chief, Tanjug World Service, Belgrade, Yugoslavia, to the Committee to Protect Journalists, July 10, 1992.

[163] Blaine Harden, "Land of Peril for Journalists," *The Washington Post* as reported in *The International Herald Tribune*, July 28, 1992.

[164] "SRNA Accuses Authorities of Tanjug Attack," Tanjug Yugoslav News Agency broadcast on April 14, 1992, citing SRNA sources; as reported in FBIS, April 15, 1992.

29 and signed by a Dr. Matić in Split, confirms that Magajnić suffered from contusions and bruises to the head and body.[165]

• Between April 22 and 28, Magajnić and Boris Dežulović, both reporters for the independent Split-based daily *Slobodna Dalmacija*, were verbally harassed, denied travel permits and their movements restricted by the military headquarters in Livno or by individual HVO soldiers in the area. Reporters for the Croatian government-controlled television station did not face such obstacles or harassment and were given ready access to the front lines of battle and a military escort at their request. *Slobodna Dalmacija*'s reporters were denied such cooperation from the Livno military authorities because photographs they had taken and which were subsequently published allegedly "disclosed Croatian military positions." Such pictures included a Croatian soldier photographed against a stone wall, a high-rise building damaged by mortar attacks, a Croatian soldier posing with his AK-47 and a destroyed tank. Some of the pictures taken by the *Slobodna Dalmacija* reporters also were filmed by a Croatian Television crew and shown on the evening news.[166]

• British, Dutch, Irish, Serbian, Canadian and American journalists travelling in three cars had videotapes and other materials confiscated by Serbian troops in Ugljevik on or about May 12, 1992. A flak jacket belonging to Martin Bell, a correspondent for the British Broadcasting Corporation (BBC), was among the items seized.[167]

---

[165] This account is taken from interviews held by Helsinki Watch representatives with Željko Magajnić in June 1992 in Split, Croatia, and from Boris Dežulović, "Ubi Ga Preteška Fotka," *Slobodna Dalmacija*, April 30-May 1, 1992.

[166] *Ibid.*

[167] Blaine Harden, "Teddy Takes a Ride in Bosnia," *The Washington Post*, May 12, 1992.

Obstruction of Freedom of the Press

- Serbian forces have destroyed or seized control of radio and television transmitters throughout Bosnia-Hercegovina. On April 10, a Sarajevo television and radio crew reportedly was told that they were to leave the Plješevica transmitter, which would be placed under the control of Serbian authorities.[168] By April 29, Bosnia-Hercegovina Radio and Television facilities and equipment were seized by Serbian forces in Kozara, Lička Plješevica, Majevica and Velež. The transmitters reportedly are being used to transmit programs of Belgrade-based Serbian Television.[169]

- On the evening of June 20, Serbian forces stationed near Sarajevo's airport fired incendiary shells to set fire to the 12-story building of the Sarajevo-based daily *Oslobodjenje*. When fire crews arrived to extinguish the flames, they were fired upon and one fireman was killed and several were wounded.[170]

- Sarajevo's radio and television broadcasting building has repeatedly been hit by mortar and rocket fire and snipers' bullets. Five hundred of the station's 2,300 employees who manage to go to work are often inside the building at the time of the attacks.[171]

---

[168] "Serbs Control Radio, Television Transmitter," Sarajevo Radio broadcast on April 10, 1992; as reported in FBIS, April 10, 1992.

[169] "'Armed Unit' Said Readying Radio, TV Takeover," Sarajevo Radio broadcast, April 29, 1992; as reported in FBIS, April 30, 1992.

[170] John F. Burns, "Estimates of Bosnia Dead Rising Fast," *The New York Times*, June 22, 1992.

[171] Tony Smith, "Sarajevo Television, Itself a Prime Target, Broadcasts the War," The Associated Press, May 15, 1992.

Pillage and Other Destruction of Civilian Property

Helsinki Watch has received numerous reports of looting, burning and otherwise pillaging predominantly Muslim villages by Serbian paramilitaries. Similarly, Hesinki Watch is concerned that Muslim and Croatian forces are looting and pillaging Serbian property in areas under their control.

Brčko

● According to the A.P., a 47-year-old resident of Brčko,[172] Serbian paramilitaries commanded by Željko Ražnjatović (Arkan), pillaged the town of Brčko during and after its fall to Serbian forces in early May. A.P. reports:

> After Serbian forces attacked Brčko on May 1, I spent three days in the town. During a lull in the fighting, I found that my son-in-law Hajro [age 35] and two friends, Hazem and Mršo, had been killed. I ran to the home of a Serbian neighbor to ask for safe haven but I was turned away. The shooting started again and I fell into a shallow hole and crawled through an open door of another house. Approximately 40 people were hiding in the attic, but I hid in a corridor in the basement because I thought it was safer. Shortly thereafter, I heard shooting and yelling and someone kicked open the front door. Then I heard people running upstairs and shooting throughout the house. The people in the attic were probably killed. Someone asked "Whose house is this," and a second person replied that it belonged to a Muslim. Yet a third person said, "Grujice, don't take anything from the house now; our car is already full. We'll come back later." I managed to look out the window and saw a paramilitary who I believe belonged to Arkan's forces -- one of them was a woman who was

---

[172] Interviewed in Gunja (municipality of Županja), Croatia, on June 3, 1992. The person interviewed asked that his or her name not be used.

laughing as they burned a car nearby. Their car was full of personal belongings and furniture.

Bijeljina

During the Serbian siege of Bijeljina in early April, Yugoslav army and Serbian paramilitaries destroyed property belonging to Muslims. According to a woman from Bijeljina:[173]

> On April 5, some time between 1:00 p.m. and 2:00 p.m., two men dressed in Yugoslav army uniforms and a man in civilian clothing came to our section of town, known as the Selimović section. They stopped before the home of a neighborhood doctor. My cousin recognized the man in civilian clothing as the owner of a neighborhood cafe. I remembered that this man had had an argument with the doctor in the past. They asked a child standing nearby about the whereabouts of the home's owners. The child replied that they were in Brčko. One of the men in the Yugoslav army uniform then sprayed the house with machine gun fire and the second uniformed soldier threw one hand grenade through the window and one through the door. The grenades must have fallen near the gas bottles[174] because the house exploded and burned to the ground.

Sarajevo

Fifteen Roman Catholic priests and seven nuns were kept under armed guard for 30 hours. Fourteen of the priests were professors of theology and all lived and taught at the Franciscan Theology University and Seminary in the Nedjarići section of Sarajevo. According to Father

---

[173] Interviewed by Helsinki Watch representatives in Ljubljana, Slovenia, on June 4, 1992.

[174] In many homes throughout the former Yugoslavia, the gas for stoves is kept in orange steel containers. Many people keep more than one bottle in the home as a reserve gas source for their stoves.

Velimir Valjan,[175] that section of Sarajevo had been occupied by Serbian forces almost as soon as hostilities broke out in Sarajevo in early April.

According to Father Valjan:

We had no problem with the Serbian forces despite the fact that we were under their control. From April to early June, the Serbs launched attacks against Sarajevo's city center from Nedjarići. Up until that time neither Croatian nor Bosnian forces attacked our part of the city.

On June 8, however, mortars fired from Bosnian- and Croatian-held positions fell on Nedjarići and fighting with Serbian forces intensified.

According to Father Valjan:

On June 8, one of the priests noticed that several Serbian soldiers had come into the seminary's garden. One Serbian soldier approached the door and pointed his gun at the building. Then approximately ten to 15 soldiers came to the door and started beating on it. I opened the door and two of the soldiers immediately pointed a gun at me while another two came behind me and pointed their guns at my back. Two soldiers lined up against the wall and pointed their guns to the ceiling, two took up positions on the left side of the hallway while one or two remained outside. Another 15 soldiers began to approach from the garden. They told us that they were members of the Serbian Volunteer Guard and they had white eagles on their hats. One of the soldiers asked me how many people were in the house and I replied that there were 23 in the building. He repeated the number and I confirmed it. He then told me that they were going to search the house and if they did not find exactly 23 people they would shoot all of us. He asked us if there

---

[175] Interviewed in Ovčarevo (municipality of Travnik), Bosnia-Hercegovina, on June 12, 1992.

were any Muslims in the house and I replied that there were not. Again, he told me that if they found one Muslim, they would kill us all. I was escorted through the house by three soldiers, one of whom walked in front of me and two who walked behind me with their guns pointed at my back. I was to summon all of us to come to one area.

We searched the house but it took us some time to find everyone. Some of the priests had retired to their rooms and the paramilitaries were getting impatient. We went to the church where a priest was saying mass for the sisters. I told one of the soldiers that it might not be a good idea for him to enter the Church with weapons but he pushed me aside and yelled at the priest on the altar to finish up and get out.

The 23 residents were told to surrender our identification cards. At 10:55 a.m., we were taken to the seminary basement where we remained under armed guard for 30 hours, but we were not mistreated.

At 7:30 a.m. the next day, a Yugoslav army captain came to the seminary from the military barracks, located across the street. He said that he was aware that a paramilitary unit had come into our home and that he had come to see what should be done with us. He also asked if we had been mistreated, to which we replied that we had not. He said he was going back to the military barracks and we asked to be evacuated out of Serbian-controlled territory.

Before we were evacuated, we were allowed to gather some of our belongings for five to ten minutes from our rooms. We were escorted by an armed guard. My clock, passport, money, batteries and technical equipment had been taken and my computer was on the floor, packaged and ready to be removed as well. The paramilitaries also stole items from the rooms belonging to seminary students. The other priests and sisters had money, radios and personal items stolen from their rooms.

At 2:00 p.m. the priests and nuns were taken to Biljaća mountain, toward Kiseljak, where they crossed over to Bosnian-held territory.

Other Abuses

In addition to the violations of humanitarian law cited above, Helsinki Watch has documented a case in which Serbian forces misused the humanitarian function of a hospital, thereby subjecting patients to unwarranted attack by opposing forces. Helsinki Watch has also collected evidence which suggests that a bridge was destroyed with the intent to kill persons crossing into Bosnia.

Misuse of a Medical Facility

Helsinki Watch interviewed a Muslim doctor from Sarajevo[176] who worked as a psychiatrist in Sarajevo's military hospital.[177] The doctor claimed that the city's military hospital had been used as a storage area for armaments prior to the attack on Sarajevo. According to the doctor:

> I am an officer in the Yugoslav army who lived in the new part of Sarajevo. Most of the families living in my building also were military personnel and, generally, most of the Serbian officers were active members of the Serbian Democratic Party in Sarajevo. I worked at the military hospital in Sarajevo as a psychiatrist and six months before the attack on Sarajevo, the military hospital became an armed camp. Weapons were stored in the hospital and I know of 150 AK-47s and 250 hand grenades that were stored in one area.

---

[176] Interviewed in Ljubljana, Slovenia, on June 4, 1992.

[177] Throughout former Yugoslavia, the JNA maintained hospitals which were devoted primarily to the treatment and care of JNA soldiers, officers and their families. Most of the doctors who were in these hospitals retain military status, usually as colonels or lieutenant colonels.

After the March 2 referendum in Bosnia-Hercegovina, the Serbian doctors separated themselves from their non-Serbian colleagues and weapons were being handed out to the Serbian doctors. Captain Mladen Pušković and Lieutenant Colonels Vugaklija and Otović received sniper rifles.

The doctor's wife confirmed that the Yugoslav Army was responsible for arming radical members of the Serbian Democratic Party in parts of Sarajevo.

Weeks before the attack on Sarajevo, members of the Serbian Democratic Party were armed by military officers. The head of the Sarajevo military police, Captain Momir Tomčić, and another officer, Marinko Djokanović, were the most active in organizing the Serbs in our part of town. About one week to ten days before the April 5th attack on the Bosnian police station, Serbian families started to move out of the area. We sensed that something was wrong so we fled to the Muslim part of town, where we stayed with my sister.

When the attack on Sarajevo commenced, the doctor was at work in the military hospital.

The wing in which I worked was filled with Četnik paramilitaries who were armed and roaming through the hallways. Troops were shooting from the tenth floor. No one seemed to remember that they were in a hospital.

The doctor and his family subsequently fled from Sarajevo and are living as refugees in Slovenia.

Destruction of Bridge Between Gunja and Brčko

On April 30, at approximately 4:50 a.m., a bridge between Gunja and Brčko was destroyed as civilians were crossing. Witnesses estimate that two bus loads of people were killed, although the Bosnian press reports a lower figure.[178]

According to a 23-year-old member of the Croatian Army from Gunja,[179] Bosnian guest workers were returning from Germany to Bosnia. He said that the workers were not armed:[180]

> I was on my usual guard duty on the bridge between Gunja and Brčko the evening of April 29-30. The 800-meter-long bridge was guarded by approximately four to five Croatian police officers and about ten Croatian army soldiers. The bridge had been partially destroyed about two months ago by our forces to prevent the Serbian troops from crossing over into Croatia. However, it was still possible for people to walk over the bridge -- only the center of the bridge had been disabled for vehicle traffic.

---

[178] The Ministry of Internal Affairs of Bosnia-Hercegovina reported that at 4:40 a.m. on April 30, a group of men in camouflage uniforms arrested Bosnian militiamen guarding the bridge near the River Sava near Brčko and took them to an unknown destination. Almost immediately thereafter, two bridges near Brčko were destroyed. According to the report, "several citizens, who were crossing the bridge at Gunja in Croatia into Brčko, were on the bridge at the moment of the explosion. According to information available to [the Ministry of Internal Affairs], four people were killed and several people, including three militiamen, were injured." The Bosnian militiamen who were arrested were released the same day. (See "Internal Ministry Report Bridge Explosion," Bosnia-Hercegovina Radio broadcast on April 30, 1992, as reported in FBIS, May 1, 1992.) Eyewitness testimony taken by Helsinki Watch confirms the Bosnian Interior Ministry's account although the casualty figures cited by the Bosnian government are much lower than the eyewitnesses' recollections, which indicate that nearly two busloads of people were killed as they were crossing the bridge.

[179] Interviewed in Gunja (municipality of Županja), Croatia, on June 3, 1992.

[180] Many Croats and Muslims who live and work in Western Europe are returning to Bosnia-Hercegovina to fight in the war. However, when the guest workers were crossing the bridge, witnesses claim that they were not visibly armed and that at no point did any of them use or display a weapon or ammunition of any sort.

At approximately 4:45 a.m. on April 30, two buses with foreign license plates arrived. The buses were occupied mostly by Bosnian men who worked in Austria and Germany and were returning to Bosnia. According to the soldier:

> We examined their passports and let them walk over the bridge. As the crowd of people began to approach the center of the bridge, a car from the Bosnian side drove onto the part of the bridge that was not damaged -- about 100 to 150 meters onto the bridge. Several minutes later the car exploded. Most of the people on the bridge were killed. The car appears to have been detonated from afar and must have been full of explosives. The next day, Serbian forces overran Brčko.

Two Muslim men from Brčko[181] confirmed that the bridge was in fact destroyed during the early morning of April 30. According to the two witnesses, this took place at approximately 5:00 a.m.; at approximately 10:00 a.m., JNA units disarmed the police in Brčko and many civilians fled that same morning, anticipating fighting.

---

[181] Interviewed by Helsinki Watch representatives on June 3, 1992, in Gunja (municipality of Županja), Croatia.

STATUS OF REFUGEES AND DISPLACED PERSONS[1]

The war in Bosnia-Hercegovina has left one of every three inhabitants homeless. Approximately 10,000 refugees are forced across the border daily.[2] The majority of Bosnia's displaced are Muslims, who have fled to neighboring Croatia.[3] Others have fled to other former Yugoslav republics, Western Europe and Turkey.

As of July 23, 1992, the United Nations High Commissioner for Refugees (UNHCR) estimated that, as a result of the wars in Croatia and Bosnia-Hercegovina, approximately 628,000 internally displaced persons and refugees were in Croatia.[4] 382,500 refugees were registered in Serbia, 70,000 in Slovenia, 48,500 in Montenegro and 31,000 in Macedonia. As of July 29, approximately 2.3 million people had been displaced by the fighting in the Balkans. Over 850,000 persons remained internally displaced within Bosnia-Hercegovina.[5]

---

[1] See also section containing the European Community -- humanitarian aid and refugee assistance.

[2] Blaine Harden, "UN Pleads for Help for Bosnian Refugees," *The Washington Post*, July 23, 1992.

[3] According to the Croatian Government's Office for Displaced Persons and Refugees, as of July 22, 1992, 331,700 Bosnian refugees have been registered in Croatia. (83,708 have been placed in the municipality of Zagreb, 56,002 in the municipality of Split, 44,730 in the municipality of Makarska, 35,553 in the municipality of Slavonski Brod, 19,003 in the municipality of Rijeka. The remaining refugees are placed primarily along the Dalmatian coast, but also in Slavonia and areas north of Zagreb.)

[4] United Nations High Commissioner for Refugees, "UNHCR Daily Estimates of Displaced/Refugees Within Former Yugoslavia," Thursday, July 23, 1992. Of the 629,000 displaced persons and refugees in Croatia, approximately 69,000 remain in Serbian-occupied areas of Croatia, i.e., the United Nations Protected Areas (UNPAs).

[5] Blaine Harden, "UN Pleads for Help for Bosnian Refugees," *The Washington Post*, July 23, 1992.

As of July 24, 1992, Germany had accepted 200,000 refugees, Hungary 60,000, Austria 50,000, Sweden 44,000 and Switzerland 12,200.[6] Italy had accepted 7,000 refugees and the United Kingdom had accepted 1,100 from the former Yugoslavia.[7] The current refugee crisis is the worst in Europe since World War II and UN officials point out that, with the onset of winter, "hundreds of thousands more people" will be forced to leave their destroyed towns and villages in search of food and shelter.[8]

According to UN High Commissioner Sadako Ogata, the flight of refugees "seems not to be just the result but the goal of the fighting.... The vast majority of refugees were brutally forced out of their houses by those damnable practices known as ethnic cleansing."[9]

Helsinki Watch has interviewed scores of refugees from the conflict. Many refugees claimed that they did not flee to escape the fighting but had been forcibly expelled or displaced by Serbian forces. In most cases, the displaced are Muslim women, children and elderly persons who travelled for days, some on foot, to neighboring Croatia.

Some 850,000 people remain trapped in four Bosnian cities besieged by Serbian forces: Sarajevo, Bihać, Tuzla and Goražde.[10] Most of these residents are civilians, including thousands of persons who have already been forcibly displaced by Serbian forces who have occupied nearby towns and villages. If these cities fall to Serbian forces, it is highly likely that the 850,000 people will be victims of "ethnic cleansing" practices.

---

[6] Henry Kamm, "Yugoslav Refugee Crisis Europe's Worst Since World War II," *The New York Times*, July 24, 1992.

[7] *Ibid.* See also Reuters Information Services report, as quoted by Blaine Harden, "UN Pleads for Help for Bosnian Refugees," *The Washington Post*, July 23, 1992.

[8] *Ibid.*

[9] Quoted from an article written by Ms. Ogata in the German newspaper *Die Zeit* and transcribed by Blaine Harden, "UN Pleads for Help for Bosnian Refugees," *The Washington Post*, July 23, 1992.

[10] Henry Kamm, "Aid but Not Homes Offered to Refugees from Balkans," *The New York Times*, July 30, 1992.

While Bosnia-Hercegovina has become a killing field, Croatia has been transformed into a refugee camp. In addition to the 330,000 refugees from Bosnia, Croatia must meet the needs of more than 265,000 people displaced by the war in its own country. Care for the refugees and displaced persons is estimated to cost Croatia $66 million a month[11] or $2 million a day, an outlay second only to Croatia's defense expenditures.[12] In mid-July, Croatia announced that it was closing its borders to more Bosnian refugees because it could not afford to take care of them.[13] Nevertheless, refugees continue to arrive in Croatia almost daily. As a result of the wars in Bosnia and Croatia, approximately 12 percent of Croatia's current population is made up of refugees and displaced persons.[14] In some towns in Croatia and Bosnia-Hercegovina, the refugee and displaced populations equal or surpass the number of indigenous residents. For example, in addition to a peacetime population of approximately 21,000 people, the municipality of Makaraska on the Dalmatian coast is now home to more than 32,500 refugees and displaced persons. In the eastern Bosnian town of Goražde, more than 30,000 of the town's current 60,000 inhabitants, including 10,000 children, have been displaced from neighboring villages which already have fallen to Serbian forces.[15] In other areas, the refugee and displaced population account for a substantial portion of the total

---

[11] Blaine Harden, "We Cannot Go On Like This," *The Washington Post*, July 18, 1992.

[12] Michael T. Kaufman, "Croatia Warns It Will Take Bosnian Refugees to European Borders," *The New York Times*, July 16, 1992.

[13] See Laura Silber, "New Yugolsav Premier Vows Peace Effort," *The Washington Post*, July 15, 1992, and Hugh Pain, "Serbs Boost Attack on Bosnian Town," Reuters report in *The Washington Post*, July 12, 1992.

[14] These figures were calculated by Helsinki Watch representatives by comparing the 1991 census figures and data from the United Nations High Commissioner for Refugees and (as of July 22, 1992) the Croatian Government's Office of Displaced Persons and Refugees.

[15] See Laura Silber, "New Yugoslavia Premier Vows Peace Effort," *The Washington Post*, July 15, 1992, and Hugh Pain, "Serbs Boost Attack on Bosnian Town," Reuters report in *The Washington Post*, July 12, 1992.

population. In Croatia, almost a third of Split's and one-fifth of Osijek's current inhabitants are refugees and displaced persons. Over 25 percent of Dubrovnik's current population consists of persons who have been left homeless by the wars.[16] The municipality Tuzla in Bosnia-Hercegovina, which is also under siege, has a peacetime population of 131,861 and now accommodates thousands of displaced persons.

The conditions under which the Bosnian refugees live vary. Although food is readily available, shelter and hygiene facilites are increasingly difficult to ensure. Some of the refugees who fled from Bosnia at the outset of the war were placed in vacant hotels throughout Croatia, especially in resort areas along the Dalmatian coast. Those who fled later have been housed in gymnasiums, stadiums and sports halls which have been converted into refugee shelters. The conditions in such facilities are cramped and overcrowded and the availability of showers, bathrooms and general hygiene is limited. The most recent refugees into Croatia were transported to the country's border and were forced to sleep and attend to their hygiene needs on the trains. Still other refugees who have fled to Croatia, Slovenia, Macedonia and Yugoslavia have been placed in private homes with families who are willing to house and feed the displaced.

Because of its inability to deal with the increasing number of Bosnians seeking refuge on its territory, Croatia transported newly arriving refugees to the borders of other European nations, many of whom have been reluctant to accept refugees from Bosnia-Hercegovina. Only after Croatia stated that it would leave the refugees at their borders did the Europeans agree to accept a minimal number.[17]

International relief agencies have done a commendable job in aiding refugees and displaced persons from Bosnia-Hercegovina. Medicines, emergency surgical materials, family parcels, hygiene items

---

[16] These figures were calculated by Helsinki Watch representatives by comparing the 1991 census figures and data from the United Nations High Commissioner for Refugees and (as of July 22, 1992) the Croatian Government's Office of Displaced Persons and Refugees. The areas mentioned here refer to municipalities, not individual cities (i.e., the municipality of Split, not the city of Split).

[17] The role of the international community with regard to the Bosnian refugee problem is discussed below.

and food are steadily distributed to hospitals and displaced persons within the former Yugoslavia. The ICRC maintains four delegations[18] and twelve sub-delegations[19] throughout the former Yugoslavia. Representatives of the United Nations High Commissioner for Refugees also have done much to supply humanitarian and medical aid to refugees and displaced persons throughout the former Yugoslavia and have been particularly active in the Sarajevo area. Local Red Cross affiliates, charity groups and church organizations have cooperated with the ICRC and UNHCR to aid victims of the war. Frequently, the conditions under which relief personnel operate are extremely dangerous and some have themselves been victims of the war.[20] The lack of financial contributions from the international community sometimes has impeded the ability of relief organizations to deliver sufficient quantities of aid in a timely manner. The UNHCR has described the relief situation as "critical" and said the shortage of contributions was causing it to delay buying relief supplies and employing people to deliver them. "Money is currently being spent as soon as it is received," it said, "resulting in a virtual hand-to-mouth operation.[21]"

Despite the good offices of international and domestic relief organizations, the flow of refugees and displaced persons from Bosnia-Hercegovina and the need for medical supplies and humanitarian aid continue to increase.

---

[18] In Ljubljana, Slovenia; Zagreb, Croatia; Sarajevo, Bosnia-Hercegovina; and Belgrade, Yugoslavia.

[19] In Rijeka, Knin, Split, Dubrovnik and Osijek in Croatia; in Bihac, Banja Luka, Mostar, Trebinje and Tuzla in Bosnia-Hercegovina; in Herceg Novi, Montenegro; and in Skopje, Macedonia.

[20] See section concerning attacks against medical and relief personnel and vehicles.

[21] John F. Burns, "The Food Gets Through, a Brave but Small Step," *The New York Times*, July 16, 1992.

THE ROLE OF THE INTERNATIONAL COMMUNITY

The United Nations and the European Community have taken steps to bring peace to the former Yugoslavia. The United Nations extended its peace-keeping operation in Croatia to facilitate deliveries of humanitarian aid to areas of Bosnia-Hercegovina. The European Community has tried to broker a political solution to the Yugoslav crisis by bringing the various parties to the negotiating table. While the UN tried to maintain peace on the ground and the European Community explored diplomatic avenues to resolve the crisis, the United States led the effort to impose UN sanctions against Yugoslavia for its use of force in Bosnia-Hercegovina. Although the intentions of the UN, the European Community and the United States are commendable, their actions have had little, if any, effect on the fighting in Bosnia-Hercegovina. The international community has proved unable to bring an end to the conflict or to prevent gross violations of the rules of war throughout Bosnia-Hercegovina. It has done little to date to suggest that those guilty of war crimes will be held accountable for their actions.

The United Nations

The United Nations has sought to achieve three goals in Bosnia-Hercegovina: secure peace, impose sanctions and deliver humanitarian relief. Unfortunately, the well-intentioned efforts of the United Nations in Bosnia-Hercegovina have failed for several reasons. UN peacekeeping and other efforts in Bosnia-Hercegovina, as in Croatia, have been marked by timidity, disorganization, unnecessary delay and political indecision. UN operations in the region have been hampered by political competition between member states and the Secretary-General; unwillingness on the part of member states to commit the necessary financial resources; violation of the arms and trade embargo by several UN member states; and lack of good faith by the parties to the conflict.

Peacekeeping

UN peacekeeping efforts in Bosnia-Hercegovina were at first only symbolic. The presence of UN forces in Bosnia-Hercegovina was part of a larger peacekeeping mission for Croatia, to which the United Nations dispatched a 14,000-member force to monitor and help maintain a fragile cease-fire until a political solution could be found to that country's crisis. The plan was negotiated by Cyrus Vance, Personal Envoy of the Secretary-General. The operation, formally referred to as the United Nations Protection Force (UNPROFOR),[1] was to have been based in Sarajevo and various units were to have been deployed throughout areas of Bosnia-Hercegovina, most heavily in Banja Luka and Mostar.

By establishing its headquarters in the Bosnian capital, the UNPROFOR mission hoped that its presence would discourage armed conflict in that republic. Although valiant, such a hope was somewhat naive. Areas of Bosnia-Hercegovina had been heavily militarized by the

---

[1] The concept for the UNPROFOR plan is set forth in Annex III of the *Report of the Secretary-General Pursuant to Security Council Resolution 721 (1991)*, United Nations Security Council, S/23280, December 11, 1991. (Initially set at 10,000, the number of UN troops was later increased to 14,000. Under the provisions of the plan, the UN troops consist of three groups: infantry units, police monitors and military observers.) The general provisions of the plan call for the establishment of United Nations Protected Areas (UNPAs) in regions of Croatia where Serbs constitute a majority or substantial minority and where armed conflict had occurred. Parts of eastern Slavonia, western Slavonia and the Serbian self-proclaimed "Krajina" region were designated as UNPAs. UN forces were charged with the responsibility for demilitarizing the UNPAs, i.e., ensuring the withdrawal of the Yugoslav army (JNA) and the demobilizing of all armed groups -- both Serbian and Croatian. The UNPROFOR plan calls for the maintenance of the political status quo in the UNPAs, i.e., the continued functioning, on an interim basis, of the existing local authorities and police, which are to be under UN supervision until an overall political solution is reached. Accordingly, the Serbian-controlled local governments in Krajina and eastern Slavonia continue to have jurisdiction over those areas, as do the Croatian-controlled local governments in western Slavonia. Although the existing political authorities in each of the UNPAs remain, the composition of the local police force must reflect the ethnic composition of the community before hostilities commenced. UN forces are to monitor the work of the local police in the UNPAs. Moreover, UN peacekeeping forces are to assist in the repatriation of all persons displaced from their homes in the UNPAs. Lastly, the UN peacekeeping troops are responsible for securing the well-being of the population currently living in the UNPAs and those returning to their homes in those areas.

JNA by late 1991[2] and tensions in Bosnia-Hercegovina were high prior to the arrival of the UN in Sarajevo. If the United Nations hoped to keep the peace in Bosnia-Hercegovina, the deployment of a larger force similar to the one established in Croatia would probably have been necessary for Bosnia-Hercegovina, as well. However, neither the political leadership nor the willingness to commit the financial resources for such a project existed on the part of the UN or its member states. A symbolic presence in Sarajevo did little to prevent the violence in Bosnia-Hercegovina. Rather, it was a half-hearted effort aimed at containing a conflict that was rapidly gaining momentum.

Moreover, UN troops were unable to begin their operations either in Croatia or in Bosnia-Hercegovina because of the operation's lack of resources and subsequent disorganization. UN member states, which called for and approved the plan, spent weeks complaining that the cost of the operation was excessive.[3] Despite the fact that the Croatian and Yugoslav authorities agreed to contribute more toward the costs of the peacekeeping force, the UN's member states have been slow in paying their share of the operation's bill. As permanent members of the Security Council, France, Britain, Russia, China and the United States are responsible for paying more than half of the cost of the peacekeeping operation. Because these countries failed to fulfill their financial obligations, the UNPROFOR mission could not assume its duties in a timely or efficient manner. During Helsinki Watch's missions to the designated UNPA areas in Croatia and to Bosnia-Hercegovina in March, April and June, UN personnel consistently complained that they lacked the most rudimentary materials (including paper, telephones and telefax machines) needed to begin their operation.

In addition to financial and logistical obstacles, Croatian, Serbian and Yugoslav military authorities resisted the deployment of UN forces

---

[2] See background section in which it is pointed out that, in 1991, areas in northern and southern Bosnia-Hercegovina were used by Serbian forces to attack positions in Croatia and that conflict between Bosnian and Yugoslav armed forces had broken out in Mostar.

[3] Initially estimated at $400 million, the projected cost of the UNPROFOR mission was increased to $635 million after the force's troops were augmented in number from 10,000 to 14,000. (See Michael Littlejohns, "UN Worried by Cost of Yugoslav Operation," *The Financial Times*, February 21, 1992.)

in areas under their control. Despite the fact that the Croatian and Serbian governments and the Yugoslav army agreed to the terms of the UN plan, they consistently misrepresented the initial agreement and subsequent negotiations to their domestic constituencies so as to convince them that concessions had not been made to the opposing side. Moreover, after the accord was signed, each side tried to challenge key parts of the plan.[4]

If the United Nations hoped to avert a war in Bosnia-Hercegovina, speed was of utmost importance. Unfortunately, due to the aforementioned obstacles, the deployment of UN forces was slow and disorganized. UN troops began arriving in early March and were to be fully deployed by April 15. However, they did not assume their responsibilities in all designated regions in Croatia until late June. UN forces which were to have been stationed in Bosnia-Hercegovina were withdrawn before they were ever fully deployed. Also, the UN had sent supplies and vehicles to Sarajevo only to have such items destroyed by shelling. While the UN, its member states and the parties to the conflict argued over the cost and terms of the UN plan, thousands of persons were forcibly displaced from the UNPAs, paramilitary and military troops

---

[4] For example, after the the Croatian government had agreed to terms of the UN peacekeeping plan, Croatian President Franjo Tudjman stated that Croatia "could not accept any formula that did not provide for the immediate restoration of the full authority" of its government in the Serbian-held territory of Croatia. Tudjman also insisted that the mandate for the UN peacekeepers should not extend for more than one year, fearing long-term deployment would mean the permanent loss of Krajina to Serbia. These objections conflicted with provisions of the UN peacekeeping plan which provided for the interim maintenance of the political status quo in the UNPAs. Similarly, Milan Babić, then the leader of the Serbian enclave of Krajina, did not accept the withdrawal of the Yugoslav army from Croatia, fearing that Croatian forces would launch an offensive against Serbs in Krajina if the Yugoslav army left the area. Also, Babić demanded that the UN force be deployed on the frontlines, not within Krajina. These objections conflicted with provisions of the UN plan which called for the demilitarization of the UNPAs. (See "Serb Enclave Holds Out Over UN Plan," *The Financial Times*, February 3, 1992; Laura Silber and Judy Dempsey, "Serbian Leaders' Dispute Threatens UN Peace Plan," *The Financial Times*, February 4, 1992; Trevor Rowe, "Croatia Drops Objections to UN Peace Proposal," *The Washington Post*, February 7, 1992; and, Blaine Harden, "Croatian President Renews Objections to UN Peace-Keeping Plan," *The Washington Post*, February 10, 1992.)

were refusing to give up their weapons, the fragile cease-fire was beginning to unravel in Croatia and full-scale war had broken out in Bosnia-Hercegovina. When the UN peacekeeping troops finally arrived in Bosnia-Hercegovina, they no longer had a peace to keep.

Serbian forces took advantage of the UN's delay in deploying and establishing a troop presence by assuming military and political control over parts of Bosnia-Hercegovina. For example, Helsinki Watch representatives travelling to Knin from Belgrade in late March were confronted by Serbian paramilitary units belonging to Arkan on the outskirts of Banja Luka. The paramilitaries had blocked off all roads leading to and from the city. Very few persons, residents of the city or others, were allowed to pass through the barricades. Eventually, the Helsinki Watch representatives were allowed to proceed into the city, where Serbian paramilitaries were roaming the streets with rocket-propelled grenade launchers, AK-47s and Scorpion automatic pistols. Light artillery was placed in several areas throughout the city center and some streets had been sealed off to pedestrian and vehicle traffic. The city's residents claimed that the Serbs had assumed control of the city government that morning. Muslims to whom Helsinki Watch spoke claimed that paramilitaries from Serbia and local extremist members of the Serbian Democratic Party had organized the blockade of the city and the usurpation of the local city government. The Muslims, who were celebrating Bairam, were afraid that military measures would be taken against the city's non-Serbian population. Despite the fact that Banja Luka was virtually sealed off to the outside world and that Serbian forces had effectively executed a coup d'etat on the local level, United Nations troops stationed in the Hotel Bosna did not react. When asked how the UN would respond to the paramilitaries' blockade of the city, how this would affect the city's non-Serbian population and whether this would impede the functioning of the UNPROFOR mission, the local UN commander claimed that he was not aware that the entrances to the city had been sealed off. Moreover, he said that because the UN had not formally and fully assumed its operations in Banja Luka, he could do nothing to prevent the Serbian paramilitary groups from taking up positions within or outside of the city. Lastly, he stated that the UN mandate did not provide him with the right to intervene in such matters.

Although Helsinki Watch appreciates the complexities of the UN operation and understands the limitations of its mandate, we believe that the overall UN mission has been timid in confronting Serbian forces about their military offensives, many of which have resulted in the deaths and forcible displacement of thousands of civilians. Insofar as the UN has issued demands to Serbian forces, such protests have been made in private and veiled by a cloak of secrecy. Helsinki Watch believes actions taken by any party to the conflict which result in gross human rights violations should be vigorously condemned publicly. Although the situation in Banja Luka showed an utter disrespect for the UN's efforts in the region, the UN, by its timidity, encouraged similar actions by Serbian paramilitary and Yugoslav military forces throughout Bosnia-Hercegovina.

After armed conflict had broken out in parts of Bosnia-Hercegovina, UN Secretary- General Boutros Boutros-Ghali ruled out early deployment of an international peace-keeping force in that republic.[5] In a report to the Security Council on May 12, the Secretary-General recommended that UN forces should be evacuated from Sarajevo "because of the ferocity of the fighting and the refusal of the factions to agree to a durable truce."[6]

In response to the Secretary-General's pessimistic report, the Security Council adopted a resolution on May 15 urging the Secretary-General to continue peace efforts in Bosnia-Hercegovina. The resolution also encouraged efforts to reopen Sarajevo's airport for relief flights and measures to protect humanitarian aid workers who had been harassed and robbed by paramilitary groups.[7] The resolution also demanded an immediate halt to the fighting, the withdrawal of Serbian-led Yugoslav federal troops and Croatian army units, and the disbanding of all irregular forces.[8]

---

[5] Laura Silber, "UN Leader Rules Out Peace Force for Bosnia," *The Washington Post*, May 14, 1992.

[6] Paul Lewis, "UN Rules Out a Force to Halt Bosnia Fighting," *The New York Times*, May 14, 1992. See also "Further Report of the Secretary-General Pursuant to Security Council Resolution 749 (1992)," United Nations Security Council, S/23900, May 12, 1992.

[7] Paul Lewis, "Security Council Adopts Measure to Pursue Peace Efforts in Bosnia," *The New York Times*, May 16, 1992.

[8] Reuters report as quoted in "UN Mediates Another Cease-Fire in Bosnia," by Laura Silber, *The Washington Post*, May 16, 1992.

150

The evacuation of the UN troops from Sarajevo -- which was to have taken place on May 14 -- was delayed after fierce fighting trapped the UN personnel in the besieged city.[9] The UN negotiated cease-fires between the warring parties in Bosnia-Hercegovina on May 14 and May 15, but both collapsed within moments. The UN finally evacuated Sarajevo on May 16. Two hundred UN soldiers and staff members left Sarajevo and the UNPROFOR mission's headquarters were moved to Belgrade and Zagreb.[10] One hundred twenty troops remained in Sarajevo to assist relief convoys and to seek a lasting cease-fire in Bosnia-Hercegovina.[11]

Imposition of Sanctions

After the UN troops withdrew from Sarajevo and Serbian forces continued to shell cities and towns throughout Bosnia-Hercegovina, UN member states called for the imposition of sanctions against Yugoslavia, primarily Serbia. For several weeks, the United States and the EC-members of the Security Council (i.e., France, Britain and Belgium) worked on a sanctions resolution but were unable to resolve their differences "about how fast and far the Security Council should go in pressuring the Belgrade government to end its aggression in" Bosnia-Hercegovina.[12] The United States insisted that comprehensive sanctions -- including an oil embargo -- be instituted immediately. Belgium, France and Britain favored a more gradual approach "that would have held the toughest measures, such as an oil embargo, in reserve while the Belgrade government was given a further opportunity

---

[9] John F. Burns, "Intense Fighting in Sarajevo Traps 350 from UN Staff," *The New York Times*, May 15, 1992.

[10] Laura Silber, "UN Peace-Keeping Forces Leave Sarajevo Amid Fighting," *The Washington Post*, May 17, 1992.

[11] John F. Burns, "As Cannons Roar, UN Leaves Bosnia," *The New York Times*, May 19, 1992.

[12] John M. Goshko, "UN Readies Sanctions on Belgrade," *The Washington Post*, May 29, 1992.

to halt violence" in Bosnia-Hercegovina.[13] After a mortar attack on a crowded marketplace in Sarajevo killed at least 20 civilians on May 27, the United States increased pressure on its allies.

Despite efforts by the Serbian government to avert UN action,[14] the Security Council overwhelmingly approved a resolution which imposed economic and trade sanctions on the Belgrade government.[15] The resolution justified the imposition of sanctions against Yugoslavia by citing Chapter 7 of the United Nations Charter, which requires compliance by all UN members with efforts to deal with "threats to international peace and security." The UN sanctions require all member states to cease trading in any commodity, including oil, with Yugoslavia and to freeze all its foreign assets.[16] All air traffic links to and from the country must be suspended and no one may repair, service, operate, insure or provide spare parts for aircraft registered in Serbia or Montenegro.[17] The resolution bans Yugoslavia from participating in any international sporting events and requires all countries to suspend cultural, scientific and technical contacts with Belgrade and to reduce the

---

[13] Ibid.

[14] Serbian President Slobodan Milošević sent a letter to US President George Bush and Russian President Boris Yeltsin appealing to both the US and Russia to place "all the forces involved" in the Bosnian war under their control. He also called on the United Nations to delay voting on sanctions and instead convene an international conference on Yugoslavia. (See John M. Goshko, *The Washington Post*, May 31, 1992.)

[15] Thirteen members of the Security Council (the United States, Britain, France, Russia, India, Cape Verde, Venezuela, Ecuador, Morocco, Belgium, Austria, Japan and Hungary) voted in favor of the resolution to impose sanctions. Two members (China and Zimbabwe) abstained.

[16] Paul Lewis, "UN Votes 13-0 for Embargo on Trade With Yugoslavia; Air Travel and Oil Curbed," *The New York Times*, May 31, 1992. Anticipating some type of punitive measures against its regime, the Belgrade authorities had withdrawn over $1.5 billion of its assets in Western banks between December 1991 and May 1992. See Judy Dempsey and Laura Silber, "Serbs Act to Evade Assets Freeze," *The Financial Times*, May 15, 1992.

[17] Ibid.

size of their foreign diplomatic missions. The May 30 resolution also expressed concern at cease-fire violations and acts of ethnic discrimination in Croatia and called on all the former Yugoslav republics to cooperate with the European Community's peace conference for the region.[18]

The aim of the sanctions is to force compliance by Serbian authorities in Belgrade with UN Resolution 752, which was adopted in early May and called for an immediate cease-fire and an end to ethnic oppression in Bosnia-Hercegovina.[19] Thus, the May 30 resolution required Yugoslavia, particularly the republic of Serbia, "to cease all interference in Bosnia-Hercegovina and to use its influence to promote a general cease-fire, oversee the disbanding and disarming of elements of the JNA and irregular forces and end efforts to create a purely Serbian enclave by driving out other ethnic groups."[20]

One hour after it voted to impose sanctions on Yugoslavia on May 30, the Security Council received a report by the Secretary-General which noted that Serbian militias under the command of Yugoslav army General Ratko Mladić were "independent actors."[21] The report noted that these forces were "subject neither to the authority of Belgrade nor to that of the government of Bosnia-Hercegovina."[22] Western diplomats criticized the report "saying it was imprecise and that its conclusions were based on particular incidents that should not be interpreted on a general basis."[23]

On the basis of evidence collected by Helsinki Watch -- including interviews with Serbian combatants -- Helsinki Watch believes that the Federal Republic of Yugoslavia and, in particular, the Serbian

---

[18] Ibid.

[19] Ibid.

[20] Ibid.

[21] Trevor Rowe, "UN Curbs on Belgrade Questioned," *The Washington Post*, June 4, 1992.

[22] Ibid.

[23] Ibid.

government, exert great military, economic and political influence over Serbian paramilitary and political forces in Bosnia-Hercegovina that are responsible for gross violations of humanitarian law in the current conflict.[24] We therefore consider it appropriate that sanctions have been imposed on the Federal Republic of Yugoslavia, despite the fact that most -- but by no means all -- of the Serbian combatants in Bosnia-Hercegovina are residents of the latter country.

Human Rights Watch (which links Helsinki Watch to the other Watch Committees: Africa Watch, Americas Watch, Asia Watch, Middle East Watch and the Fund for Free Expression) endorses sanctions -- that is, restrictions and prohibitions on military, economic or diplomatic relations -- as an appropriate means for the United States and other governments and intergovernmental bodies to express condemnation of abuses of human rights and as a means to avoid becoming a party to such abuses. In general, Human Rights Watch believes that sanctions should be imposed in circumstances when sanctions are required by US laws or by international agreements that are designed to promote human rights. Human Rights Watch believes that sanctions also should be imposed in circumstances when governments are engaged in, encourage or tolerate a practice of gross abuses of internationally recognized human rights.[25]

---

[24] See section above concerning parties to the conflict.

[25] As used here, the term "gross abuses" refers to genocide; extrajudicial executions or executions for peaceful expression; disappearances; torture; prolonged arbitrary detention; apartheid; and mass forced displacement in such a manner as to cause extensive loss of life. The term "practice" refers to abuses that have taken place with such frequency, or in such a manner, as to signify a policy of conducting, encouraging or tolerating these acts. Our support for sanctions under these circumstances does not preclude our endorsement of sanctions at other times, to be decided on a case-by-case basis.

In situations of internal or international armed conflict, Human Rights Watch favors the application of the same criteria for imposing sanctions. In addition, we favor the application of sanctions against parties to such conflicts that have engaged in a practice of gross violations of humanitarian law (the laws of war) against noncombatants by such means as deliberate or indiscriminate attacks that cause extensive injuries or loss of civilian life, starvation and deprivation of medical care. Here too, "practice" refers to abuses that have taken place with such frequency, or in such a manner, as to signify a policy of conducting, encouraging or tolerating such acts.

We recognize that, in some circumstances, it may be appropriate as a means of expressing public condemnation of gross abuses of human rights, to impose progressively more severe sanctions. In circumstances when the practice of gross abuses becomes extreme -- for example, genocide -- it is important to point this out publicly by extreme sanctions.[26] Egregious abuses committed by Serbian forces in Bosnia-Hercegovina include such gross abuses as extrajudicial executions of civilians and persons *hors de combat*, torture, arbitrary detention, hostage-taking, mass forced displacement and the indiscriminate and disproportionate use of force against civilian targets. The policy of "ethnic cleansing" constitutes a practice of war crimes committed with the intent to destroy or expel non-Serbian national and religious groups from Serbian occupied areas of Bosnia-Hercegovina. This policy and practice raises serious cause for concern that genocide may be taking place. Accordingly, the harshest possible sanctions are warranted.

Helsinki Watch believes that UN sanctions against the Federal Republic of Yugoslavia not only are justified but are long overdue. The abuses committed by Serbian forces in Bosnia-Hercegovina are very similar, if not identical, to those that were committed in the war in Croatia. However, such abuses have been committed on a much wider scale in Bosnia than in Croatia because Serbian forces control greater swaths of territory and are faced with less armed resistance in Bosnia-Hercegovina than in Croatia. Although Croatian armed forces have been

---

In general, we do not favor sanctions that would restrict the provisions of aid or trade that are essential to meet basic human needs for food, shelter, clothing, sanitation or medical care. Also, in general, we do not favor sanctions that would restrict the provision of aid, sales or exchanges for the purpose of disseminating information and ideas; nor do we favor sanctions that would restrict the right of citizens to travel or to speak to or have contact with citizens of any other country. (Human Rights Watch Sanctions Policy, 1990.)

[26] Similarly, in some circumstances, it may be appropriate to lift sanctions progressively as a means of acknowledging a partial alteration of the policies that give rise to abuses. In such circumstances, Human Rights Watch seeks to maintain proportionality between the severity of sanctions and the severity of abuses. (Human Rights Watch Sanctions Policy, 1990)

guilty of serious human rights abuses in the war in Croatia,[27] Serbian violations of the laws of war in both the Croatian and Bosnian conflicts have been extreme, systematic and by far the most numerous. Had sanctions been imposed on the Belgrade authorities in November 1991 - - when Serbian and Yugoslav army troops were committing war crimes on a wide scale in Croatia, particularly in the city of Vukovar -- those same military and political forces might have been dissuaded from, or at least hesitant about, launching a similar campaign in Bosnia-Hercegovina. The fact that the world community did not take decisive action against abuses in Croatia only emboldened Serbian military and paramilitary forces to commit further war crimes in Bosnia-Hercegovina.

Helsinki Watch and Human Rights Watch believe that sanctions, once imposed, should not be lifted unless and until governments have demonstrated that they have altered their policies of gross abuses that gave rise to the sanctions. A reduction in the frequency of abuses, or even the cessation of abuses, are not by themselves sufficient to demonstrate that this alteration of policies has taken place. Rather, we seek evidence of a policy change that will provide reasonable assurances to the potential victims of a practice of gross abuses that the policy underlying the practice has been altered.[28] Therefore, Helsinki Watch believes that sanctions against the Federal Republic of Yugoslavia (including the republic of Serbia) should not be lifted until that government and its armed forces:

- publicly and unequivocally denounce those Serbian forces responsible for war crimes in Bosnia-Hercegovina;

- immediately discontinue all military, economic and political support to Serbian insurgents in Bosnia-Hercegovina;

- facilitate the repatriation, and ensure the safety, of all those displaced or expelled from their homes as a result of the "ethnic cleansing" campaign of Serbian troops in Bosnia-Hercegovina;

---

[27] See "Helsinki Watch Letter to Franjo Tudjman, President of the Republic of Croatia," February 13, 1992.

[28] Human Rights Watch Sanctions Policy, 1990.

- provide compensation to those victims of war crimes which were committed by Serbian military or paramilitary forces;

- allow international observers to monitor compliance with these requirements;

- take immediate steps to arrest those paramiltary and military leaders who are citizens and/or residents of the Federal Republic of Yugoslavia and who are responsible for diverting, training, arming and fighting alongside indigenous Serbian paramilitary units that have committed gross violations of the rules of war in Bosnia-Hercegovina. In cases where evidence that they committed war crimes is available, members of such paramilitary units should be arrested, prosecuted and punished.

- extradite military and paramilitary leaders known to have committed war crimes for the purpose of bringing them to trial before an internationl tribunal, which should be established for the express purpose of adjudicating cases in Bosnia-Hercegovina and Croatia.

Compliance with Sanctions

Interpretation of and adherence to the UN sanctions has varied. The United States has aggressively instituted economic sanctions against Yugoslavia and has imposed further sanctions not specified by the Security Council Resolution.[29] The US froze approximately $450 million in Yugoslav assets, primarily bank deposits, during the first week of June, immediately after UN sanctions were imposed on May 30.[30]

Other states have been lax in their interpretation of the UN sanctions against the Belgrade regime. Greece was the first foreign country to be caught in a large violation of the UN sanctions. During the week of June 1, Macedonia intercepted 66 Greek oil tank trucks bound

---

[29] See relevant section regarding US policy below.

[30] Steve Coll, "Sanctions Unlikely to Affect Transfers," *The Washington Post*, June 7, 1992.

for Serbia.[31]   On June 9, Romania "confirmed that it was allowing oil shipments to reach neighboring Serbia despite UN sanctions."[32] Deputy Transport Minister Valentin Mirescu claims that stopping oil shipments would be a "catastrophe" for Romania.[33]   Constantin Fota, Minister of Commerce and Tourism, said that Romania would lose three billion US dollars as a result of UN sanctions against Yugoslavia.[34] Romania's Ministry of Foreign Affairs reportedly presented a list of such losses and derogaton of certain sanctions to the UN and to European bodies and asked for compensation in mid-June.[35]

Despite the imposition of UN sanctions on May 30, the Cypriot government allowed local banks to continue to permit cash withdrawals and transfers by Serbian individuals and companies, provided such transactions did not directly travel to, or trade with, the rump Yugoslavia. Thus, Serbian companies can withdraw money through their Cypriot subsidiaries and later channel such funds to Yugoslavia through secondary channels.[36]

In addition to the May 30, 1992, sanctions against Yugoslavia, the UN imposed an arms embargo on all the former Yugoslav republics on October 25, 1991.[37]   Although the arms embargo remains in effect, it

---

[31] Blaine Harden, "Greece Blocks Recognition of Macedonia," *The Washington Post*, June 10, 1992.

[32] "Romania Will Break Some UN Sanctions," Radio Free Europe/Radio Liberty *Daily Report*, No. 109. June 10, 1992, p. 4.

[33] *Ibid.*

[34] *Ibid.*

[35] *Ibid.*

[36] Steve Coll, "Serbian Money Trail Leads to Cyprus," *The Washington Post*, June 7, 1992.

[37] Paragraph two, subparagraph six of the report of the Secretary-General, pursuant to paragraph three of Security Council Resolution 713 (1991) states it:

> Decide[d], under Chapter VII of the Charter of the United
> Nations, that all States shall, for the purposes of establishing

has been violated by all sides and, in some respects, has benefited Serbian and Yugoslav forces. Muslims, and Croats to a greater extent, have purchased small arms and some artillery from Eastern European and other countries.[38] Serbian forces have access to a steady clandestine flow of arms.[39] Also, shortly before the UN ban took effect one year ago, the Yugoslav army -- acting through a front company in Nicosia, Cyprus -- purchased 14,000 tons of weapons from Christian militias in Beirut.[40] Moreover, Serbian forces have at their disposal huge caches of weapons that were stockpiled for decades by the Yugoslav army. Before the fighting erupted, Yugoslavia's arms industry produced most of the Yugoslav military's weapons and the country was one of the world's top arms exporters.[41] The UN arms embargo, violated by UN members, has done little but maintain the balance of power in the former

---

> peace and stability in Yugoslavia, immediately implement a general and complete embargo on all deliveries of weapons and military equipment to Yugoslavia until the Security Council decides otherwise...

The EC also implemented a freeze on arms sales and financial aid to Yugoslavia in July 1991. (See "European Community Freezes Arms Sales and Aid," *The New York Times*, July 4, 1991.)

[38] The Croatian government has been seeking to tap the international arms market for American antiaircraft missiles, as well as assault rifles and other arms. Surplus arms of East Germany's military also appear to have been purchased by the Croatian government. Nevertheless, Croatia's efforts to purchase arms -- which are partly financed by donations from Croatian emigres -- have not been very successful. (See Stephen Engelberg with Eric Schmitt, "Serbs Easily Outflank UN Arms Embargo," *The New York Times*, July 5, 1992.)

[39] Stephen Engelberg with Eric Schmitt, "Serbs Easily Outflank UN Arms Embargo," *The New York Times*, July 5, 1992.

[40] A former senior Pentagon official who has handled American covert weapons purchases says that the 14,000 tons involved would be nearly ten times what was provided to the American-supported contra rebels in Nicaragua in 1985 and 1986. (See Stephen Engelberg with Eric Schmitt, "Serbs Easily Outflank UN Arms Embargo," *The New York Times*, July 5, 1992.)

[41] *Ibid.*

Yugoslavia, a balance which overwhelmingly favors Serbian and Yugoslav forces who repeatedly have used their fire power against civilian targets in Croatia and Bosnia-Hercegovina. Although the May 30 UN sanctions have had some effect in rising discontent against the Serbian regime in Belgrade,[42] such measures have had little effect in silencing the guns of Serbian forces in Bosnia-Hercegovina.

Delivery of Humanitarian Aid

After sanctions were imposed against Yugoslavia, the UN undertook efforts to force Serbian forces in Bosnia-Hercegovina to relinquish control of Sarajevo's Butmir airport. UN troops sought control of the airport to allow humanitarian aid to be flown into Sarajevo and delivered to the city, which, after a three-month siege had almost depleted its supplies of food and medicine. On June 8, the Security Council directed Secretary-General Boutros-Ghali to expand the 14,000-

---

[42] Most of the domestic protest in Yugoslavia, particularly in Serbia, is based on the discontent over the worsening of the economic situation after the imposition of UN sanctions. On June 16, the Yugoslav government approved a 79.8 percent increase in the price of electricity and a 105 percent rise in rail transport costs. In mid-June, Serbia's inflation rate was estimated to be 80 percent and is expected to increase. Major enterprises have laid off workers or scaled back on operations. The Zastava Yugo car manufacturer in Kragujevac has sent 18,000 workers on compulsory vacation while 12,000 cars await parts from abroad. The major bus manufacturer, Ikarus of Zemun temporarily laid off 600 of its 1,300 workers and lost a multi-million dollar deal with Turkey for 470 vehicles. In mid-June, the biggest Yugoslav construction company, the Belgrade-based Energoprojekt, announced that it was reducing wages by 60 percent because it only had the capacity for another month's work. Because Yugoslavia's oil output of 79,500 barrels per day can meet only 25 percent of demand, the government rationed petrol to just 30 liters (6.6 gallons) per car per month. Generally, prices of consumer items have risen five- to ten-fold and there has been a rush on stores for food. However, economists claim that food production should not be an immediate problem because of Serbia's rich agricultural land. Moreover, humanitarian aid is exempt from the UN sanctions. (See Jovan Kovačić, "Sanctions Start to Hurt Serbia and Montenegro," Reuters Information Services, June 16, 1992.)

member peacekeeping force in the former Yugoslavia by at least 1,100.[43] The additional UN personnel would include a 1,000-member infantry battalion, 60 military observers, 40 military policemen and whatever civilian technical aides were needed.[44] Once a cease-fire was in effect, the UN team was to reopen the Sarajevo airport and aid in the distribution of relief shipments.

Although Serbian militias agreed to allow relief flights to bring food and medicine to the besieged capital on June 5, those same forces continued to launch mortar attacks against the city until June 30.[45] Because of the continued bombardment, UN troops could not assume control of the airport and relief flights could not land in the city. After Serbian forces continued to defy UN calls to cease the shelling of Sarajevo and allow the opening of the airport, the Security Council issued a 48-hour ultimatum to Serbian forces. The statement, issued in the name of Secretary-General Boutros-Ghali on June 26, demanded that Serbian troops stop fighting in Sarajevo and place their heavy weaponry under UN control. The ultimatum stated that, if Serbian forces failed to comply, the Security Council would meet "to determine what other means would be required to bring relief to the suffering people of Sarajevo."[46] The UN statement generally was perceived as a threat to use force against Serbian troops should they persist in defying efforts to open the airport and obstruct delivery of humanitarian aid to Sarajevo.[47]

---

[43] Frank J. Prial, "UN Council Acts on Bosnia Airport," *The New York Times*, June 9, 1992.

[44] *Ibid.*

[45] See Slobodan Lekic, "50 Observers Arrive in Sarajevo," Associated Press report in *The Washington Post*, June 11, 1992; Blaine Harden, "Sarajevo Greets UN Peace-Keepers," *The Washington Post*, June 12, 1992; Judy Dempsey, "Fresh Fighting in Sarajevo Dashed UN Relief Plan," *The Financial Times*, June 18, 1992; and John F. Burns, "Another Hope Is Dashed in Sarajevo, As Serbs Shatter Airport Truce," *The New York Times*, June 27, 1992.

[46] Paul Lewis, "Serbs Told to End Siege of Sarajevo or Risk UN Force," *The New York Times*, June 27, 1992.

[47] *Ibid.*

Despite continued shelling of Sarajevo for an additional four days,[48] the UN troops finally assumed control of the airport on June 30. On June 29, the Security Council ordered 850 Canadian peacekeeping troops stationed in Croatia to assume control over and reopen Sarajevo's airport.[49] The first relief convoy from the UNHCR carried 15 tons of food, water, milk and medicine that were delivered to Sarajevo's residents on June 30.[50]

Nevertheless, persistent shelling and fighting complicated the airlift and the delivery of humanitarian aid in Sarajevo.[51] Similarly, Serbian forces launched a major offensive throughout Bosnia-Hercegovina in mid-July, taking back the eastern bank of the Neretva River at Mostar from Croatian and Muslim forces. Serbian forces also launched attacks on the towns of Odžak, Doboj and Goražde, the only city in eastern Bosnia not captured by Serbian troops.[52] In response to Bosnian pleas for emergency action to help the besieged areas, the Security Council approved a resolution submitted by the Secretary-

---

[48] See John F. Burns, "Serbs Defy Ultimatum from UN and Persist in Shelling Sarajevo," *The New York Times*, June 28, 1992.

[49] The Canadian troops would thereafter be replaced by three smaller battalions of 400 to 500 troops each from France, Egypt and Ukraine. See Paul Lewis, "UN Votes to Send Troops to Reopen Sarajevo Airport," *The New York Times*, June 30, 1992.

[50] John F. Burns, "First Supplies Reach Sarajevo From Airport as Shelling Continues," *The New York Times*, July 1, 1992.

[51] See "Serbs Still Shelling, Threatening Airlift, UN Says," Associated Press report in *The New York Times*, July 5, 1992; and, Steve Vogel, "Flights to Sarajevo: Airlift Takes Off," *The Washington Post*, July 6, 1992.

[52] See Carol J. Williams, "UN Aid Reaches Sarajevo Neighborhood: Serb Forces Advance On Other Fronts," *Los Angeles Times* report as carried by *The Washington Post*, July 13, 1992; and, Laura Silber, "Serbs Launch New Assaults Across Bosnia," *The Washington Post*, July 14, 1992.

General to add 500 military personnel to UN forces in Sarajevo.[53] Despite the increased UN presence, the Serbian offensive throughout Bosnia-Hercegovina and fighting within Sarajevo continue, and deliveries of humanitarian aid continue to be impeded.

Continued Difficulties

On July 17, a 14-day cease-fire brokered by EC representatives in London called for the three armed factions in Bosnia-Hercegovina to place their tanks, artillery, mortars and other heavy weapons under UN supervision.[54] Bosnian, Croatian and Serbian representatives also pledged to begin indirect talks on a political settlement on July 27 and to permit all refugees and displaced persons to return to places from where they had been expelled.[55] However, Radovan Karadžić, the Serbian representative to the London talks and president of the Serbian Democratic Party in Bosnia-Hercegovina, said that, although Serbian forces would allow UN observers to place heavy weapons under international supervision, they would not relinquish such weapons so that they could be removed from the battle areas and collected at central points.[56] Moreover, the truce never took hold in Sarajevo or elsewhere in Bosnia-Hercegovina, particulary in Goražde in eastern Bosnia, Gradačac in the north, Bihać in the northwest and Mostar and Stolac in the southwest.[57] Due to intense fighting in the vicinity, the UN

---

[53] The new forces would include three small battalions that would replace a larger one and would consist of a helicopter unit, air traffic officers, a medical platoon and a platoon of radar operators to locate artillery. See Seth Faison, "As Fighting Widens, UN Orders Buildup of Troops in Bosnia," *The New York Times*, July 14, 1992.

[54] See Craig R. Whitney, "Factions in Bosnia Accept UN Custody of Weapons," *The New York Times*, July 18, 1992.

[55] *Ibid.*

[56] *Ibid.*

[57] See John F. Burns, "UN Resumes Relief Flights to Sarajevo," *The New York Times*, July 22, 1992; and, "Fighting Forces Closure of Sarajevo Airport," Radio Free Europe/Radio Liberty *Daily Report*, No. 137, July 21, 1992.

suspended the airlift of humanitarian aid to Sarajevo on July 20.[58] Relief flights were resumed the next day, despite continuing ground fire in Sarajevo.[59]

In response to the EC-brokered cease-fire agreement of July 17, the Security Council authorized United Nations forces to take control of all heavy weapons in the region, thereby angering Secretary-General Boutros-Ghali.[60] In a private letter dated July 20, the Secretary-General admonished members of the Security Council for ignoring his objections and expanding the role of the UN force in Bosnia-Hercegovina. In a report issued on July 22, the Secretary-General rejected the Security Council's approval of the EC plan to collect heavy weapons from the three warring sides in Bosnia-Hercegovina. He cited difficulties posed by the incessant fighting but objected most strongly on procedural grounds.[61] Most notably, the Secretary-General was disturbed by the fact that the London agreement had been made, and approved by the Security Council, without his knowledge.[62] As a result of the dispute between the Secretary-General and the Security Council, efforts to disarm the warring factions in Bosnia-Hercegovina apparently have been suspended.

In addition to tensions within the UN, relations between Major General Lewis MacKenzie, the Canadian commander of the UN peacekeeping force in Sarajevo, and Sarajevo's citizens and the Bosnian

---

[58] See "Fighting Forces Closure of Sarajevo Airport," Radio Free Europe/Radio Liberty *Daily Report*, No. 137, July 21, 1992; and, John F. Burns, "Sarajevo Airlift Suspended by UN After Truce Fails," July 21, 1992.

[59] John F. Burns, "UN Resumes Relief Flights to Sarajevo," *The New York Times*, July 22, 1992.

[60] *Ibid*.

[61] Seth Faison, "UN Chief Rejects Plan to Collect Bosnian Arms," *The New York Times*, July 23, 1992.

[62] See Seth Faison, "UN Chief Rejects Plan to Collect Bosnian Arms," *The New York Times*, July 23, 1992; and, Seth Faison, "UN Chief Mired in Dispute With Security Council," *The New York Times*, July 24, 1992.

government were strained for months.[63] General MacKenzie claimed that both Serbian and Muslim forces were breaching the conventions of war "by placing mortars close to hospitals and artillery pieces near schools, ... and by reacting to attacks on military targets by shelling civilians. He did not specify which side was responsible for which offense."[64] General MacKenzie also contends that both Serbian and Bosnian sides in Sarajevo "shell themselves in order to create a particular image."[65] In sum, General MacKenzie holds the Bosnian Government partly responsible for Serbian attacks that have killed and wounded thousands of civilians.[66]

Although some accusations may be true, Helsinki Watch believes that it is a serious mistake to blame both sides for the thousands of civilian deaths in Bosnia-Hercegovina. In fact, blaming all parties for violations has been used by the international community as an excuse to do nothing to stop the gross violations of humanitarian law committed in Bosnia-Hercegovina and, to a lesser extent, in Croatia. With the exception of a few guns captured by Bosnian forces, nearly all of the heavy artillery is in Serbian hands.[67] Insofar as Bosnian forces have attacked Serbian positions, their attacks have not been disproportionate in light of the perceived or actual threat posed by the Serbian forces. Bosnian fire power is no match for the Serbian forces. Conversely, the rule of proportionality and the prohibitions against the indiscriminate use of force have consistently been violated by Serbian troops in Bosnia-Hercegovina. Helsinki Watch has documented numerous cases in which Serbian troops have indiscriminately shelled or bombed civilian areas or

---

[63] General MacKenzie has since been replaced as commander of UN forces in Bosnia-Hercegovina.

[64] John F. Burns, "UN Resumes Relief Flights to Sarajevo," *The New York Times*, July 22, 1992.

[65] *Ibid.*

[66] John F. Burns, "What Is a Team? UN Delays Bosnian Olympians," *The New York Times*, July 23, 1992.

[67] Blaine Harden, "Beset Sarajevo Doubts Will of Blue Helmets," *The Washington Post*, June 19, 1992.

objects. Insofar as Bosnian troops place artillery in civilian areas, under the rules of war, Serbian forces are required to weigh the potential damage to the civilian population before launching an attack. Serbian forces consistently have failed to respect this rule and have tried to justify the total or partial destruction of civilian areas by pointing to the presence of military targets of minor consequence. UN officials, including General MacKenzie, have criticized Serbian troops for their indiscriminate and disproportionate use of force.

During discussions with Radovan Karadžić on June 22, General MacKenzie told the SDS President that the United Nations holds him responsible for attacks on civilians.[68] Also, in his report to the Security Council on May 12, the Secretary-General stated that:

> all international observers agree that what is happening
> is a concerted effort by the Serbs of Bosnia-Hercegovina
> with the acquiescence of, and at least some support from,
> [the Yugoslav army] to partition the republic along
> communal lines. . . . The techniques used are the
> seizure of territory by military force and intimidation of
> the non-Serb population.[69]

Despite such criticisms, Helsinki Watch believes that the UN has not been sufficiently vigorous in condemning abuses committed by all sides in Bosnia-Hercegovina, particularly those violations committed by Serbian forces. Helsinki Watch appreciates the fact that the UN and other international bodies negotiating with the warring factions find it necessary to maintain a level of neutrality in such discussions. However, as a human rights organization, Helsinki Watch believes that all violations should be made known and publicly condemned. The universal tenets set forth in international human rights and humanitarian agreements are not political issues open to compromise, negotiation or arbitration. Those guilty of human rights or humanitarian law violations should be criticized publicly and pressured to conform to their obligations. Helsinki Watch

---

[68] Blaine Harden, "Bosnia Bleeds Under Serb 'Purification,'" *The Washington Post*, June 23, 1992.

[69] Laura Silber, "UN Leader Rules Out Peace Force for Bosnia," *The Washington Post*, May 14, 1992.

commends the UN's criticism of violations committed by Muslim and Croatian forces in Bosnia-Hercegovina and, in the case of the latter, in Croatia. However, Helsinki Watch believes that the UN has not adequately condemned Serbian forces, either in Bosnia-Hercegovina or in Croatia, for their egregious and systematic violations of the most basic rules of war. Indeed, the absence of such vociferous criticism has conveyed the misconception that Bosnian forces share equal blame for the conflict. This has emboldened Serbian forces to continue their offensive, and to commit further war crimes in Bosnia-Hercegovina.

Moreover, the UN has been more concerned with negotiating cease-fires (all of which have been broken) than with seeking a way to end, and to punish those responsible for, the egregious violations of the rules of war in Bosnia-Hercegovina.

Even after the announcement of cease-fire accords in Bosnia-Hercegovina became ludicrous, the UN has inisisted upon negotiating additional agreements. For example, in less than one week in mid-April, the heads of the three national parties in Bosnia-Hercegovina agreed to at least three cease-fires, only to break every one. Croatian and Muslim forces share a portion of the blame for the failure of some of the negotiated cease-fires. However, the overwhelming fault lies with Serbian forces, primarily because they have the largest and most powerful arsenal in Bosnia-Hercegovina. Unfortunately, no mechanism exists to punish those violating such cease-fire agreements. Meanwhile, Serbian forces continue to advance further into Bosnia-Hercegovina, "ethnically cleansing" those areas they occupy; indiscriminately shelling areas occupied by civilians; and summarily executing civilians.

UN Secretary-General Boutros-Ghali is correct in voicing concern that serious disasters in other parts of the world, most notably Somalia, also require the urgent attention of the Security Council. The institution's failures in other parts of the world are no justification for its ineptitude in the former Yugoslavia, however; as Secretary-General, Mr. Boutros-Ghali should not discourage any action anywhere in the world that would lead to a mitigation of abuses.

UN member states, particularly the permanent members of the UN Security Council, have done little but pay lip service to the suffering of the victims of gross violations of human rights and the laws of war in Bosnia-Hercegovina. It is shocking that some member states have even violated the arms embargo and economic and trade sanctions imposed by the United Nations.

Helsinki Watch is gravely concerned that the United Nations has known for some time about the existence of so-called "concentration camps" in Bosnia-Hercegovina.[70] In an internal memorandum dated July 3, 1992,[71] UN personnel stationed in Serbian-controlled areas of Croatia,[72] informed their superiors in Belgrade and Zagreb of the existence of, what the letter refers to as, "detention" and "concentration" camps. The memorandum also indicates that UNHCR representatives and UN Civilian Affairs officers[73] have been collecting testimony from persons fleeing from Serbian-controlled areas of northern Bosnia to United Nations Protected Areas (UNPAs) in Serbian-controlled regions in Croatia.

The author of the aforementioned memorandum implies that communication between UN officials in the field and their superiors in Belgrade and Zagreb had occurred on numerous occasions before July 3. The memorandum states that the officials have "received a stream of reports" from UN personnel in the UNPAs in Croatia of the existence of camps in Bosanski Novi, Bihać, Čazin, Velika Kladuša and Bosanska Dubica. The memorandum describes the frustration of UN field personnel with their superiors' reluctance to take active steps to address the situation in the camps. The memorandum states:

> Our frustration arises from our inability to do anything other than write reports and stand by since UNPROFOR has no operational responsibilities across the border. In recent days, the situation has deteriorated and has now

---

[70] See section concerning detention camps. The text of the letter is reproduced as Appendix B.

[71] See section concerning camps.

[72] The memorandum is written by a UN official stationed in the town of Dvor in the Serbian-controlled Banija region of Croatia. The Banija region is part of an area designated as "Sector North" by the UN peacekeeping mission to Croatia (UNPROFOR).

[73] The UNPROFOR mission to the former Yugoslavia consists of military, civilian, admninistrative and other operational and logistic branches. Cedric Thornberry is head of Civilian Affairs of the UNPROFOR mission.

begun to spill over to the UNPA. We have seen a mounting number of desperate people who have crossed over to seek refuge and protection from UNPROFOR.

Helsinki Watch also is concerned that UN officials withheld information about human rights abuses committed by both Serbian and Croatian forces in Croatia. Complaints about these abuses were presented in separate reports to Croatian and Serbian government officials, but the information was never made public nor were such abuses publicly condemned by the UN.

The violations committed by Croatian forces which the UN has documented include the destruction of Serbian villages and property in western Slavonia, which is now designated as an UNPA in Croatia. The villages were destroyed by Croatian forces after Serbian and Yugoslav troops and the Serbian inhabitants withdrew from the area in late 1991. Helsinki Watch representatives have visited the area several times and have investigated such violations. The abuses have been documented and acknowledged by Croatian government and medical personnel.[74] Although the Croatian government has taken steps to prosecute and punish some Croatian army soldiers responsible for these abuses, Helsinki Watch believes that the Croatian government has not vigorously or thoroughly prosecuted those responsible for the destruction of the villages in western Slavonia. Had the UN made public its findings, the Croatian government would have been under greater pressure to prosecute those responsible for such crimes.

Helsinki Watch is also disturbed that the forcible displacement of non-Serbs from the Serbian-controlled areas of Croatia took place during the UN's presence in these areas.[75] Although Helsinki Watch appreciates efforts by the United Nations since late May to curb such expulsions, we believe that the UN should have taken steps months earlier to prevent expulsions of non-Serbs, when such expulsions were

---

[74] See Ivica Kostović and Miloš Judaš, eds., *Mass Killing and Genocide in Croatia 1991/92*, Zagreb, 1992. The information in this volume includes evidence compiled by the Ministry of Health of the Republic of Croatia.

[75] For a description of these abuses, see section concerning ethnic cleansing and forcible displacement.

carried out on a mass scale throughout Serbian-controlled areas of Croatia and within the designated UNPA areas.

The UNPROFOR mission has divided the so-called "Krajina" region into two administrative zones: sector north (which includes the Banija and Lika regions of Croatia) and sector south (which includes the town of Knin and its environs). UN forces assumed full responsibility in the northern and southern sectors in June. Prior to that, UN personnel were present in the UNPAs. Many were there as observers and as advance teams working on logistic arrangements to facilitate the full deployment of UN forces in the area. Although the UN was to have assumed its duties by April 15, it did not complete its deployment until late June. This was due, in part, to the difficulties posed by the outbreak of war in Bosnia-Hercegovina in early April and the subsequent complications with UN headquarters in Sarajevo. Also, disagreements between UN officials and local authorities in the UNPAs and with the Croatian and Serbian governments prevented the timely deployment of UN troops and personnel in the UNPAs.

Serbian civilian and military authorities in these regions anticipated the full arrival of the UN in April and took advantage of its delayed deployment in May and June by rapidly displacing most of the remaining non-Serbs in areas under their control. Such action apparently was taken by authorities in the Serbian-controlled regions of Croatia to consolidate their position before the UN fully assumed its duties in the region. Most non-Serbs were displaced between mid-February and mid-April. UN officials were aware of and had documented the displacements of non-Serbs but did not publicly condemn these practices.[76] Nor does it appear that UN personnel took any action to prevent further violations.

Helsinki Watch visited the UNPAs in March and April and saw numerous UN soldiers and personnel in Serbian-controlled areas in the eastern Slavonia, Banija and Krajina regions of Croatia. Most of the expulsions of non-Serbs took place at that time. Although UN personnel appear not to have directly witnessed the expulsions, they were aware of the names of the villages from which non-Serbs had been displaced, how

---

[76] In addition to the information compiled above, see John F. Burns, "The Demographics of Exile: Victorious Serbs Repopulate Croatian Villages," *The New York Times*, May 10, 1992. According to Burns, "[T]he recent expulsions have either been witnessed or fully documented by a 1,500 member United Nations contingent that began taking up positions in March."

many had been displaced and when the displacement occurred. This information was never made public by UN officials.[77]

According to Mik Magnusson, Senior Liaison Officer for Civilian Affairs of the UNPROFOR mission,[78] because the UN mission did not fully assume its duties in eastern Slavonia until May 15, UN personnel were not empowered to do anything to stop or prevent expulsions of non-Serbs from that region. Helsinki Watch believes that the delays in deployment of UN forces in Croatia only induced Serbian civilian and military authorities to "cleanse" the areas under their control of non-Serbs. Helsinki Watch appreciates the restrictions of the UN mandate and the need for UN personnel to be adequately prepared to deal with human rights violations. However, Helsinki Watch believes that the failure to address these violations was not in keeping with the spirit of the UN peacekeeping plan. The UNPROFOR mission, as conceived and drafted by Special Envoy Cyrus Vance, provided for UN assistance with the repatriation of all displaced persons from the UNPAs. The forcible displacement of non-Serbs from these areas was against the aim of the peacekeeping mission. If the UN could not fully assume its duties in the UNPAs according to schedule and was aware of the forced displacement of non-Serbs from the UNPAs, steps should have been taken to prevent such expulsions in the interim, for example by forceful public denunciations.

To its credit, since the UN has assumed full responsibilities in the UNPAs, steps have been take to prevent the expulsion of minority groups from those areas. For example, on May 24, UN soldiers intercepted a bus carrying 22 Croats who had been forcibly displaced from the village of

---

[77] Helsinki Watch representatives spoke to UN personnel in Belgrade, Zagreb and in the "field" who were frustrated with the restrictions placed on them by their superiors, denying them authority to speak about or take any action to stop such abuses before the UN assumed its full duties in the areas.

[78] Interviewed by a Helsinki Watch representative in Zagreb on June 17, 1992.

Tovarnik.[79] The displaced persons were placed under UNPROFOR protection after they refused to return to their homes, believing that Serbian forces had already settled in their houses.[80] On June 1, the UNPROFOR mission announced that "it recommended the immediate arrest of five Serbs who had 'terrorized' Croats into abandoning their homes."[81] Helsinki Watch commends such steps, but we believe that UN forces should have taken similar action against expulsions in March and April, when they were most widespread and when the UN had full knowledge of their occurrence.

Non-UN Multilateral Action

In addition to international efforts undertaken under the auspices of the United Nations, several regional organizations and other multilateral institutions have taken steps to punish and isolate Yugoslavia for its support of Serbian forces in Bosnia-Hercegovina. On June 19, the 103-nation General Agreement on Tariffs and Trade (GATT) suspended Yugoslavia's membership. The suspension was largely symbolic and would have little effect since international trade with Serbia and Montenegro had been suspended by UN sanctions on May 30.[82] On July 8, the Conference on Security and Cooperation in Europe (CSCE) suspended Yugoslavia's membership for three months.[83]

On July 16, warships from eight North Atlantic Treaty Organization (NATO) countries and the nine-nation Western European

---

[79] "Attempt to Expel Croats From Tovarnik Intercepted," Zagreb Radio broadcast citing Mik Magnusson, UNPROFOR representative in Zagreb, on May 25, 1992; as reported in FBIS, May 29, 1992.

[80] Ibid.

[81] Blaine Harden, "Hope Seen for End to Sarajevo Seige," The Washington Post, June 2, 1992.

[82] "Trade Group Suspends Belgrade," Associated Press report of July 19, 1992, as reported in The New York Times, June 20, 1992.

[83] Craig R. Whitney, "Belgrade Suspended by European Security Group," The New York Times, July 9, 1992.

Union (WEU) began patrolling the Adriatic and Mediterranean seas to enforce UN sanctions against Yugoslavia.[84] The ships are to watch for possible violations of the UN trade embargo against Serbia and Montenegro but not to stop or board any vessels. Rather, patrol craft crews are to seek to determine any ships' cargo and destination through radio contacts. The two defense alliances created the patrols in an attempt to restrict the Belgrade government's access to weapons and other war materiel it is believed to be funnelling to Serbian forces in Bosnia.[85]

Throughout the war, members of the Islamic Conference (which includes Arab countries, Malaysia, Pakistan and Indonesia) had voiced their concerns about the persecution of Muslims in Bosnia-Hercegovina and of on-going repression against Muslim Albanians in the Serbian province of Kosovo.[86] Two million of Turkey's citizens are Bosnian Muslims and Turkey took the lead in calling the 47-member Islamic Conference Organization to a meeting in Istanbul on June 18. At that meeting, the members of the Islamic Conference agreed "to provide personnel and resources for the UN force to be sent to the region should sanctions against Yugoslavia fail."[87]

---

[84] Six frigates and five destroyers are involved in the operation. The NATO flotilla is positioned in the southern Adriatic sea and ships belonging to the Western European Union patrol the Strait of Otranto at the mouth of the Adriatic. Both forces are under Italian command and include ships belonging to Italy, Britain, Spain, the United States, the Netherlands, Turkey, Greece, Germany and France. (See March Fisher, "Eight Western Navies Cooperating in Watch on Yugoslav Coast," *The Washington Post*, July 16, 1992.)

[85] Marc Fisher, "Eight Western Navies Cooperating in Watch on Yugoslav Coast," *The Washington Post*, July 16, 1992.

[86] Judy Dempsey and Laura Silber, "US Steps Up Effort to Isolate Serbia," *The Financial Times*, May 21, 1992.

[87] Alan Cowell, "Turkey Faces Moral Crisis Over Bosnia," *The New York Times*, July 11, 1992.

The European Community

In general, the European Community has focused efforts on reconciling the warring factions in the former Yugoslavia but has not devoted sufficient attention to preventing gross violations of the rules of war in Bosnia-Hercegovina and in Croatia. Moreover, the EC has not taken adequate measures to punish those responsible for such violations. The Europeans have been divided in their approach to the Balkans and have not spoken with one voice in condemning violations of humanitarian law. According to one Dutch official who characterized EC efforts in the former Yugoslavia: "We are much too divided among ourselves to provide the necessary leadership."[88]

In both the Croatian and Bosnian cases, a lack of consensus, leadership and political will has marred EC efforts to bring an end to the violence. However, in contrast to its activism in Croatia, the EC has played a more restrained role in Bosnia-Hercegovina, preferring to let the US take the lead. Germany is the only EC-country that has supported an active stance toward Bosnia, while France and Britain have preferred to proceed slowly.

The European Community Monitoring Mission

An EC monitoring mission which was launched in Croatia was gradually expanded to include parts of Bosnia-Hercegovina. The EC monitors, most of whom are members of their respective countries' armed forces, were dispatched to Bosnia-Hercegovina to monitor compliance with cease-fire and other EC-negotiated agreements. After a member of the EC monitoring mission was killed near Mostar on May 2,[89] the EC suspended its mission to Bosnia-Hercegovina the following

---

[88] William Drozdiak, "EC Leaders Debate Tougher Policy on Bosnia," *The Washington Post*, June 27, 1992.

[89] See section above concerning attacks against medical and relief vehicles and personnel.

day.[90] On May 12, the last 12 EC monitors withdrew from Sarajevo, declaring it was too dangerous for them to stay in the capital.[91]

European Community-Sponsored Peace Talks

Since the outbreak of armed conflict in mid-1991, the EC has sought to broker a peace in, and resolve outstanding political disputes between and within, the former Yugoslav republics. Former British Foreign Secretary Lord Peter Carrington serves as chairman of the "European Community Conference on Yugoslavia." Initially concerned with quelling the violence in Croatia, the conference also seeks to resolve differences concerning the status of Serbs in Croatia, Albanians in Kosovo and other crisis areas in the former Yugoslav republics. With the outbreak of war in Bosnia-Hercegovina, the EC conference focussed its efforts on trying to negotiate peace between the warring factions.

Lord Carrington chaired several meetings between Serbian, Croatian and Bosnian factions from Bosnia-Hercegovina. Radovan Karadžić and Mate Boban often represent the Serbian and Croatian factions, respectively, at such negotiations while the Bosnian government is represented by President Alija Izetbegović. Frequently, Izetbegović cannot leave Sarajevo for such negotiations because the city remains surrounded by Serbian troops. In such instances, Bosnian Foreign Minister Haris Silajždić has represented the Bosnian government.

Although several EC-sponsored negotiations have taken place since April, the talks were suspended in late May after 20 people were killed in a mortar attack on a Sarajevo breadline.[92] On June 25, talks between the presidents of Serbia, Croatia and Bosnia-Hercegovina took place in Strasbourg. President Izetbegović remained in the besieged capital and was represented by Foreign Minister Silajdžić. According to Lord Carrington, no progress was made at the June 25 meeting primarily because Serbian President Slobodan Milošević refused to take "specific

---

[90] "EC Suspends Action," Paris, Agence France Presse report on May 3, 1992, as reported in FBIS, May 4, 1992.

[91] Laura Silber and Judy Dempsey, *The Financial Times*, May 13, 1992.

[92] "Muslims in Bosnia Lift Blockade of Army Barracks," Associated Press report of June 5, 1992, as reported in *The New York Times*, June 6, 1992.

and substanial steps" toward conciliation with Bosnia-Hercegovina, Croatian President Franjo Tudjman denied reports that Croatian army troops were fighting in Bosnia, and Bosnian Foreign Minister Haris Silajdžić refused to have any future dealings with the leader of Bosnian Serbs, Radovan Karadžić, whom he accused of murdering civilians, specifically children.[93] Talks resumed again on July 27, with little result.

After the tenth round of EC-sponsored peace talks on July 29, an agreement was reached to form a committee to deal with human rights violations. The committee will be led by Commandant Colm Doyle, an Irish Army officer, and will include representatives of Bosnia's three ethnic groups, the United Nations and the International Committee of the Red Cross (ICRC). The committee will work toward establishing a cease-fire, ensuring that humanitarian aid reaches refugees for whom it is intended and freeing all people held in camps or prisons.[94]

EC negotiations have had little success primarily because of the lack of good faith by all parties, but especially on the part of Serbian representatives. As in the case of the UN peacekeeping plan, all parties to the conflict have come to the negotiating table and signed agreements which bound them to uphold obligations which they had no intention of keeping. Croatian and Muslim forces have violated EC-brokered cease-fire agreements which their representatives have signed. Most particularly, Serbian representatives have not negotiated in good faith at EC conferences. Karadžić and Milošević have signed agreements which they have consistently breached. For example, Serbian forces in Bosnia-Hercegovina have extended prior guarantees of safe passage to relief convoys, only to have them attacked by their forces later.[95] Serbian forces continue to shell Sarajevo and its airport. Under UN-negotiated agreements, the airport is to be secured for humanitarian purposes and exempt from attack.

---

[93] See Craig Whitney, "Bosnia, Where Titans Fear To Tread," *The New York Times*, July 16, 1992, and Paul L. Montgomery, "No Progress at Peace Talks," *The New York Times*, June 26, 1992.

[94] "Rights Committee Formed," *The New York Times*, July 30, 1992.

[95] See section concerning attacks on medical and relief personnel and vehicles.

The failure of the EC conference thus far lies, in part, with the EC negotiators. EC negotiators have been more interested in reconciling those parties violating agreements than in taking steps to punish or even denounce such violations. The EC has been mistaken in trying to appease Slobodan Milošević and Radovan Karadžić, both of whom have manipulated the EC's position as a neutral arbiter to advance their own military and political goals. Indeed, many believe that Milošević has "used meetings of an ongoing EC-sponsored peace conference as a smokescreen for his land grabs" and continuing human rights violations both in Croatia and Bosnia-Hercegovina.[96]

The EC has deflected criticisms by saying that all parties to the Yugoslav conflict lack the political will to negotiate.[97] This response, though true, is deficient from a human rights perspective for two reasons. First, it assumes that all parties are equally to blame for the violence and atrocities in Bosnia-Hercegovina. On the basis of our investigations, Helsinki Watch believes that Serbian forces are responsible for the overwhelming majority of violations of the laws of war. By appearing to allocate blame equally among all parties to the conflict, EC negotiators depreciate the severity of such crimes and absolve of guilt those who are responsible for the most egregious violations. Second, by stating that the parties to the conflict lack the will to negotiate, the EC implies that little can be done to stop the slaughter.

Helsinki Watch welcomes efforts by the European Community to bring about a cessation of hostilities in the former Yugoslavia. Moreover, we respect the position of Lord Carrington and his colleagues as neutral arbiters in a very complex conflict. However, we believe that those who are responsible for systematic and egregious violations of humanitarian law should be publicly condemned. Moreover, we believe that the EC must take steps to prevent further abuses and to punish those parties and individuals guilty of gross violations or of failure to abide by their agreements.

---

[96] Roger Thurow and Peter Gumbel, "How Europe's Leaders Let Yugoslav Crisis Gets Out of Control," *The Wall Street Journal*, July 1, 1992.

[97] *Ibid.*

European Community Sanctions Against Yugoslavia

Before the UN imposed sanctions against Yugoslavia, the EC took steps to distance itself from, and to punish, the Serbian government and the Yugoslav military for their use of force first in Croatia and then in Bosnia-Hercegovina. In the fall of 1991, the EC suspended special trade privileges for all the former Yugoslav republics but has since restored such privileges to Slovenia, Croatia, Bosnia-Hercegovina and Macedonia.[98] The EC also has taken steps to distance itself from the state formed by Serbia and Montenegro. Excepting Greece, diplomats of all the EC countries boycotted the ceremonies proclaiming the creation of a new Yugoslav state on April 27, 1992. The United States and Canada also boycotted the ceremonies in an effort to distance themselves from the new state.[99] On the other hand, Russia, China and many non-aligned states attended the ceremony.[100]

At a meeting of EC foreign ministers in Brussels on May 11, the EC member states announced that they were recalling their ambassadors from Belgrade and that they would seek suspension of Yugoslavia from the Conference on Security and Cooperation in Europe (CSCE).[101] In the interim, Yugoslavia would be excluded from certain discussions in the CSCE[102] and the Organization for Economic Cooperation and

---

[98] Alan Riding, "Europe, Weary and Burned, Is Limiting Its Risk in Bosnia," *The New York Times*, May 17, 1992. Slovenia and Croatia were recognized by the EC on January 15, 1992. Bosnia-Hercegovina was recognized on April 6, 1992. The EC continues to withold recognition of Macedonia, due to Greece's objection to the name of the former Yugoslav republic which it regards as part of its historic and cultural heritage.

[99] Laura Silber and David Buchan, "Serbs Raise 'New Yugoslavia,' from the Ashes of the Old," *The Financial Times*, April 28, 1992.

[100] *Ibid.*

[101] Alan Riding, "European Nations to Recall Envoys From Belgrade," *The New York Times*, May 12, 1992.

[102] Yugoslavia was not immediately suspended from the CSCE because of Russia's objections to such a move.

Development (OECD), to which Yugoslavia had enjoyed observer status.[103] Lastly, the EC also declared that it was witholding recognition of the new federation of Serbia and Montenegro as the successor state to Yugoslavia.[104]

On May 22, the European Community's executive commission recommended a trade embargo against Serbia and Montenegro. In its report, the commission said that an embargo on exports from Serbia and Montenegro could have an "important impact" on the two republics since more than 50 percent of their foreign sales are to the EC.[105] The commission recommended freezing Yugoslavia's assets at the International Monetary Fund (IMF), but noted that most other assets had already been withdrawn from western banks.[106] On May 27, the EC imposed a partial trade embargo on Yugoslavia. The EC sanctions covered two-way trade with Serbia and Montenegro, which had sent over half their exports to EC countries and imported 45 percent of their goods from the EC.[107] The EC also announced that it was freezing export credits and suspending scientific and technological cooperation accords.

Moreover, the EC urged the Security Council to freeze financial assets held abroad in the name of the former Yugoslav federation. The EC did not order such a freeze because these assets had already been removed from Europe.[108] The trade embargo did not include a suspension of landing rights to Yugoslav aircraft. However, Germany12 and Italy had already cancelled landing rights for the Yugoslav airline,

---

[103] Paul Lewis, "UN Rules Out A Force to Halt Bosnia Fighting," *The New York Times*, May 14, 1992.

[104] Alan Riding, "Europe, Weary and Burned, Is Limiting Its Risk in Bosnia," *The New York Times*, May 17, 1992.

[105] Barbara Crossette, "After Weeks of Seeming Inaction, US Decides to Punish Belgrade," *The New York Times*, May 23, 1992.

[106] *Ibid.*

[107] Alan Riding, "Europeans Impose a Partial Embargo on Belgrade Trade," *The New York Times*, May 28, 1992.

[108] *Ibid.*

179

JAT, and Germany had banned commercial road and rail traffic with Serbia and Montenegro in December 1991.[109] Efforts to impose the trade embargo had been met with resistance from Greece, which stood to lose sales from Serbia and Montenegro, and from France, which argued in favor of awaiting a decision at the UN Security Council.[110] The trade embargo excluded an oil boycott because EC members felt that, although two of its members supplied Serbia and Montenegro with oil (i.e., Britain and Greece), a global oil boycott would be necessary to cut Yugoslavia off from its main suppliers, namely Russia and China (which each provide 22 percent of Serbia's oil), Romania (which provides 15 percent), and Iran (which provides 13 percent).[111]

Eight days after the EC imposed a partial trade embargo on the Belgrade regime, UN sanctions against Yugoslavia were announced. On July 10, European members of NATO and the Western European Union (WEU) sent frigates and destroyers to patrol Yugoslavia's coast in an effort to ensure enforcement of the UN sanctions. On July 20, the EC accepted the opinion of its legal experts that the state formed by Serbia and Montenegro could not be regarded as the "successor to the former Yugoslavia and thus must be admitted anew" to the UN, the OECD, and more than 40 other international bodies.[112]

Humanitarian Aid and Refugee Assistance

The European Community countries and other European states have contributed millions of dollars in humanitarian relief and medical aid. On April 17, the EC allocated 1.5 million European Currency Units (approximately US $1.8 million) for humanitarian aid to Bosnia-Hercegovina.[113] By mid-July, the 12-nation European Community

---

[109] Ibid.

[110] Ibid.

[111] Ibid.

[112] "Europe's Cold Shoulder," The New York Times, July 21, 1992.

[113] "EC Offers Emergency Aid to Bosnia-Hercegovina," Reuters Information Services, April 17, 1992.

had given US $23 million to the relief effort for Bosnia-Hercegovina. Austria and Switzerland contributed US $172,000 and US $1.5 million, respectively.[114] In late July, EC foreign ministers approved the allocation of an additional US $168 million for Bosnian refugees and each country has individually contributed to the aid effort.[115]

The European Community countries have sent troops to facilitate the distribution of humanitarian aid in Bosnia-Hercegovina. On June 27, at the strong urging of France and Italy, the EC endorsed the use of military force to break the siege of Sarajevo's airport so as to allow delivery of humanitarian aid to the city.[116] Of the EC countries, France has sent the most troops to Sarajevo to help secure the airport. In total, France has dispatched 2,000 troops to Bosnia-Hercegovina and shipped a substantial amount of foodstuffs to the beleaguered country. Moreover, medical teams of the French humanitarian organization, *Medicins Sans Frontieres*, have provided care for refugees.[117] On June 28, President Francois Mitterand made a symbolic trip to Sarajevo to show his solidarity with the citizens of the embattled city.[118]

Despite such notable contributions, European countries have been reluctant to take refugees fleeing the fighting from Bosnia-Hercegovina. Italy, which received a sudden flow of tens of thousands of refugees fleeing Albania last year, has been reluctant to accept Bosnian refugees.[119] In early July, Sweden began turning back Bosnian refugees at its borders and, on July 16, announced that it would end a

---

[114] John F. Burns, "The Food Gets Through, a Brave but Small Step," *The New York Times*, July 16, 1992. By mid-July, Japan had contributed US $437,000.

[115] "Europe's Cold Shoulder," *The New York Times*, July 21, 1992.

[116] William Drozdiak, "EC Endorses Use of Force in Sarajevo," *The Washington Post*, June 28, 1992.

[117] William Drozdiak, "Pressure Rising in Europe For Action on Balkan War," *The Washington Post*, June 25, 1992.

[118] See Blaine Harden, "Mitterand Lifts Spirits In Sarajevo," *The Washington Post*, June 29, 1992.

[119] Alan Cowell, "Italy Cautious on Bosnia Refugees," *The New York Times*, May 24, 1992. In August 1991, Italy forcibly repatriated 20,000 Albanians.

nine-month moratorium on deporting refugees already in the country.[120] On July 2, Austria announced that it would admit only those refugees with visas and Hungary imposed new controls soon afterwards.[121] On July 17, Hungary deported 200 Bosnians who had arrived the night before.[122]

Because European countries have refused to admit refugees fleeing Bosnia-Hercegovina, thousands have been left stranded on international borders. For example, on July 16, a train carrying 2,000 Bosnian refugees was stopped on the border between Croatia and Slovenia because Slovenia refused to admit the train, except for transit. Croatia, already inundated with over 630,000 refugees and displaced persons, claimed that it did not have the resources to accommodate the new refugees. The refugees were taken to international border crossings in the hope that European countries would share the refugee burden. Austria and Italy refused to admit the train, and the refugees were stranded on the Croatian-Slovenian border for 48 hours, during which a child aboard the train died of heat exhaustion.[123] Eventually, Austria agreed to admit the refugees.

Only Germany, and to a lesser extent Switzerland, have shown a willingness to alleviate the refugee crisis posed by the Bosnian war. On July 20, Germany loosened its immigration restrictions to allow more Bosnians to enter the country. In addition to the 200,000 refugees Germany had already accommodated, it agreed to accept an additional 5,000.[124] In the same week, Switzerland agreed to accept 1,000 additional refugees.[125]

---

[120] Blaine Harden, "UN Pleads for Help for Bosnian Refugees," *The Washington Post*, July 23, 1992.

[121] *Ibid.*

[122] *Ibid.*

[123] *Ibid.*

[124] Blaine Harden, "UN Pleads for Help for Bosnian Refugees," *The Washington Post*, July 23, 1992.

[125] *Ibid.*

Germany subscribes to the position that all European and other nations should share the burden of accommodating Bosnian refugees. The United Kingdom has been most opposed to the German position of "international-burden sharing."[126] With the exception of Germany, the EC countries and other European states prefer to send humanitarian aid to Croatia and Bosnia-Hercegovina and make those states responsible for the general care of their refugees and displaced persons.

Sending monetary aid to Croatia to deal with Bosnian refugees only exacerbates the difficulties that Croatia faces in trying to care for refugees. Building tent cities and refugee camps for ever-increasing numbers of Bosnian refugees in Croatia also calls into question the conditions under which some of these refugees will live. Moreover, to claim that those displaced by the war should be housed and cared for within Bosnia-Hercegovina ignores the fact that three fourths of the country is under siege. Sending relief to displaced persons within Bosnia-Hercegovina does little to stave off attacks against the displaced population. Most of the displaced persons within Bosnia-Hercegovina have not been displaced due to the fighting but as a result of Serbian policies aimed at "ethnically cleansing" an occupied region. For example, over 850,000 persons -- many of whom are displaced persons -- remain in the cities of Goražde, Bihać, Tuzla and Sarajevo. Sending humanitarian aid to displaced persons within these cities does not protect them from indiscriminate artillery attacks. Also, sending foodstuffs to displaced Bosnians will do nothing to prevent Serbian forces from further displacing, executing or otherwise abusing those who have already been victims of "ethnic cleansing" practices. Lastly, sending relief supplies to the four aforementioned cities, particularly to Goražde, is becoming increasingly difficult due to the continued fighting. While offers of humanitarian aid are commendable, Helsinki Watch believes that such relief does little, if anything, to prevent violations of the laws of war in Bosnia-Hercegovina. As one newspaper has stated: "What good will it do for [Bosnians] to have food in their stomachs when their throats are slit."[127]

---

[126] Henry Kamm, "Aid but Not Homes Offered to Refugees from Balkans," *The New York Times*, July 30, 1992.

[127] "The Well-Fed Dead in Bosnia," *The New York Times*, July 15, 1992.

The United States

The US position toward the human rights situation in the former Yugoslav republics has been sluggish and inconsistent. The Bush Administration initially misread the situation in the Balkans and then groped to define a policy which swung between complacency and active engagement. The lack of an overall policy toward the former Yugoslav republics undercut the Bush Administration's ability to respond to grave human rights abuses in the former Yugoslavia.

During the first half of 1991, the US devoted too much energy to efforts to preserve Yugoslav unity. As late as June 1991, the US refused to accept the break-up of the country and failed to address the human rights violations in, and potential for violence between, the former Yugoslav republics. During a visit to Slovenia and Croatia in June 1991, Secretary of State James Baker tried to discourage those two republics from seceding. His appeals were rebuffed and both Slovenia and Croatia declared their independence several days after Secretary Baker's visit. The US response to the break-up of the country was disengagement.[128] As a result, during the war in Croatia, the US did little, if anything, to denounce or prevent violations of the rules of war in that conflict. The Bush Administration adopted the position that the war in Croatia was a European problem with which Europe, not the United States, must deal.

When war broke out in Bosnia-Hercegovina, the US was quick to get involved but only in the early stages of the conflict. In attempting to reconcile its complacency toward the war in Croatia with its activist position in Bosnia-Hercegovina, US officials stated that "the Bosnian situation was different because the republic had declared its independence peacefully and in keeping with Western principles and was now being attacked from the outside."[129] Tacitly acknowledging the EC's lack of

---

[128] Some have speculated, and indeed foreign diplomats with whom Helsinki Watch has spoken confirm, that US disengagement from the ensuing conflict in Slovenia and the war in Croatia was due, in large part, to the fact that Secretary Baker was personally offended by Slovenia's and Croatia's refusal to halt their declarations of independence.

[129] Roger Thurow and Peter Gumbel, "How Europe's Leaders Let Yugoslav Crisis Get Out of Control," *The Wall Street Journal*, July 1, 1992.

success in the Yugoslav crisis, the US tried to re-establish its waning credibility in Europe by taking the lead in responding to the Bosnian conflict.

One week after full-scale war broke out in Bosnia-Hercegovina, the United States began efforts to muster international support among its European allies to issue a joint protest to the government of Serbia. On April 14, Secretary Baker sent a letter to Serbian leaders protesting the Serbian offensive and reports of the summary executions of civilians in the town of Višegrad.[130] Also on April 15, State Department spokeswoman Margaret Tutwiler stated that the United States "condemns the use of force, intimidation and provocation to nationalist violence by militant nationalist Serbian, and to a lesser extent, Croatian leaders in Bosnia."[131] The following day, at a CSCE meeting in Helsinki, Secretary Baker warned the government of Serbia that unless it stopped its assault on Bosnia-Hercegovina and withdrew its forces within 14 days, Washington would press for Belgrade's suspension from the CSCE.[132] However, the US chose not to press for such suspension at the CSCE meeting on April 29, mostly in deference to certain European states and to Russia, which was opposed to such moves.[133]

On April 20, Secretary Baker called Western European allies to propose the joint break-off of diplomatic relations with Belgrade but only gained approval from Germany's then Foreign Minister, Hans-Dietrich Genscher.[134] In response to Serbia's accusations that US criticism of its military campaign against Bosnia-Hercegovina was evidence of anti-Serbian bias, the US responded by accusing Serbia of being the

---

[130] David Hoffman, "US Urges Europe To Protect Bosnia," *The New York Times*, April 15, 1992.

[131] Roger Thurow and Peter Gumbel, "How Europe's Leaders Let Yugoslav Crisis Get Out of Control," *The Wall Street Journal*, July 1, 1992.

[132] David Binder, "US Warns Serbia It Faces Reprisals," *The New York Times*, April 16, 1992.

[133] David Binder, "US Frustrated, Backs Off From the Crisis in Yugoslavia," *The New York Times*, May 5, 1992.

[134] Ibid.

"aggressor" in the war in the former Yugoslavia.[135] On May 4, Margaret Tutwiler reiterated that the US "strongly condemns the perpetrators of violence in Bosnia on all sides, including the Serbian side and the Yugoslav army, which clearly bear the heaviest blame and have the greatest responsibility for working to obtain a cease-fire."[136]

The United States sent humanitarian aid to Bosnia-Hercegovina early on in the conflict. By April 19, US airlifts had delivered about 100 tons of aid, including 90,000 ready-to-eat meals, 10,440 blankets and 30,000 pounds of medical supplies worth a total of $1 million.[137] By July 29, the US had contributed $51 million to the aid effort in Bosnia-Hercegovina.[138]

Despite its active engagement when war broke out in Bosnia-Hercegovina, the US retreated into passivity after three weeks, frustrated by its lack of success in dissuading the Serbian forces from launching further attacks in Bosnia-Hercegovina. However, in late May, the US again took an activist position, focussing both on unilateral and multinational vehicles through which to punish Serbian forces for their use of force in Bosnia-Hercegovina. After Serbian authorities rebuffed US appeals to permit safe-passage of humanitarian aid into Bosnia-Hercegovina, on May 20 the US suspended permission for Yugoslavia's national airline, JAT, to land flights in the US.[139] The US Ambassador to Yugoslavia, Warren Zimmermann, was recalled to Washington for consultations on May 16 and, on May 22, Secretary Baker announced

---

[135] John M. Goshko, "US Rejects Bias Charge by Serbia," *The Washington Post*, April 21, 1992.

[136] Laura Silber, "Bosnia Pleads for Help Against 'Aggression,'" *The Washington Post*, May 5, 1992.

[137] Chuck Sudetic, "Serbs Tighten Grip on Eastern Bosnia," *The New York Times*, April 20, 1992.

[138] Henry Kamm, "Aid but Not Homes Offered to Refugees from Balkans," *The New York Times*, July 30, 1992.

[139] John M. Goshko, "Yugoslavia's Airline Loses Its US Landing Rights," *The Washington Post*, May 21, 1992; and Judy Dempsey and Laura Silber, "US Steps Up Effort to Isolate Serbia," *The Financial Times*, May 21, 1992.

that Ambassador Zimmermann would not be returning to Yugoslavia.[140] On May 22, the US announced a series of diplomatic sanctions against Serbia, which included withdrawing military attaches and ordering the expulsion of their Yugoslav counterparts from the US, the closing of Yugoslav consulates in New York and San Francisco, and further reductions in the US Embassy staff in Belgrade.[141] The US also stated that it would withhold recognition of the Serbian-dominated government in Belgrade until Serbian forces were withdrawn from Bosnia-Hercegovina and peace was restored to the former republic.[142]

On May 24 in Lisbon, Scretary Baker called for mandatory UN sanctions against Serbia.[143] In his remarks, Secretary Baker prodded some European countries, particularly France and Greece, which were hestitant about imposing sanctions against Serbia.[144] Also on May 24, Secretary Baker stated that the US would not accept Serbia and Montenegro as the successor state to the former Yugoslavia in multilateral institutions. Secretary Baker claimed that, insofar as the new Yugoslavia wanted to sit in the United Nations, it should be required to

---

[140] "Regular State Department Briefing," Remarks by State Department Spokeswoman Margaret Tutwiler, May 15, 1992, 12:05 p.m., as transcribed by the Reuters Information Service, May 15, 1992; and, Barbara Crossette, "After Weeks of Seeming Inaction, US Decides to Punish Belgrade," *The New York Times*, May 23, 1992.

[141] Don Oberdorfer, "US Places Sanctions on Serbia," *The Washington Post*, May 23, 1992; and, Barbara Crossette, "After Weeks of Seeming Inaction, US Decides to Punish Belgrade," *The New York Times*, May 23, 1992.

[142] Barbara Crossette, "After Weeks of Seeming Inaction, US Decides to Punish Belgrade," *The New York Times*, May 23, 1992.

[143] Don Oberdorfer, "Baker Urges UN to Sanction Serbs," *The Washington Post*, May 25, 1992.

[144] Barbara Crossette, "Baker Puts Pressure on Europeans for UN Penalties Against Serbs," *The New York Times*, May 25, 1992.

reapply for membership "and be held to the same standards as all other applicants."[145]

The United States assumed an active role in initiating, drafting and implementing UN sanctions against the Serbian government. When drafting the UN resolution, however, the US succumbed to European pressure and dropped its explicit challenge to Belgrade's claim that it had inherited Yugoslavia's seat in the UN. Rather, the resolution took a more passive approach of noting that Serbia's claim to the UN seat "had not been generally accepted."[146] Announcing the imposition of UN sanctions against Yugoslavia, Edward Perkins, the US ambassador to the UN, stated that Washington would oppose any effort to award Belgrade a UN seat until Serbia had shown a willingness "to disband, disarm and withdraw" the Yugoslav army and Serbian militias from Bosnia.[147] Moreover, Perkins said:

> By its aggression against Bosnia-Hercegovina and Croatia, and by its repression within Serbia, the Serbian regime can only condemn itself to increasingly severe treatment by a world united in its opposition to Serbian aggression.[148]

The United States moved quickly to implement the UN embargo against Yugoslavia and, on June 1, the Treasury Department announced that it was freezing the assets of the Yugoslav government and the republics of Serbia and Montenegro, including the state-owned airline and banks.[149] On July 10, US warships began to patrol the Yugoslav coast

---

[145] "Regular State Department Briefing," Remarks by State Department Spokesman Richard Boucher, May 24, 1992, 12:12 p.m.

[146] John M. Goshko, "UN Votes Curbs on Yugoslavia," *The Washington Post*, May 31, 1992.

[147] *Ibid*.

[148] *Ibid*.

[149] "US Widens Embargo," Associated Press report of July 6, 1992, as reported in *The New York Times*, July 7, 1992.

as part of a joint NATO/Western European Union flotilla aimed at strengthening enforcement of UN sanctions.[150]

After UN sanctions were imposed, Serbian forces continued to shell Bosnia-Hercegovina, and delivery of humanitarian aid was impossible. Proposals concerning the use of force -- either as an offensive military operation against Serbian forces or as armed protection for humanitarian convoys carrying relief supplies -- were discussed and debated. The US government was divided over the use of force in Bosnia-Hercegovina. On the one hand, the Defense Department was strongly opposed to any direct combat role for US forces and the State Department was willing to use arms only in defense of relief missions.[151] On the other hand, members of the US Congress, particularly in the Senate, pressed the Bush Administration to consider military intervention to halt the Serbian offensive in Sarajevo.[152] Eventually, the Bush Administration adopted the position that it was prepared to send US troops to Bosnia-Hercegovina but only to help supply and safeguard humanitarian aid and only after a durable cease-fire was negotiated.

On June 23, Secretary Baker testified before the Senate Foreign Relations Committee, stating that the killing of civilians in Bosnia-Hercegovina was "an absolute outrage." He announced further US sanctions against Yugoslavia.[153] The sanctions, which are largely symbolic, entailed the closing of the last remaining Yugoslav consulate in the US, in Chicago. Secretary Baker also stated that the US would more actively pursue efforts to suspend Yugoslavia from the UN and other

---

[150] Marc Fisher and Don Oberdorfer, "US, Western Europe Set Patrols in Adriatic," *The Washington Post*, July 11, 1992.

[151] John Goshko, "Bush: We're Not the World's Policemen," *The Washington Post*, June 12, 1992.

[152] "Senate Urges US Action," *The New York Times*, June 11, 1992; "US Senator Urges Force to Curb Serbia," *The Financial Times*, June 11, 1992; and, John Goshko, "Bush: We're Not the World's Policemen," *The Washington Post*, June 12, 1992.

[153] Don Oberdorfer, "New US Sanctions Imposed on Serbia," *The New York Times*, June 24, 1992.

international organizations.[154] The Bush Administration also stated that it would press for the new Yugoslav state to be required to reapply for membership in all international institutions once it had complied with UN Security Council resolutions and met the criteria set for the admission of other new states.[155] The sanctions also withdrew immediate recognition from Belgrade's ambassador to the US.[156] Proposals within the Bush Administration concerning whether to use force to break the siege of Sarajevo were dismissed. Rather, the Administration reiterated its position that it was willing to use Air Force and Navy combat planes to protect international relief missions, but that it would not send ground troops to Bosnia-Hercegovina.[157]

On July 6, the US placed further sanctions on Belgrade. The US Treasury Department went beyond the UN embargo by extending it to all companies in Serbia and Montenegro. According to the Treasury Department, because the violence and rapid changes in the former Yugoslavia had made it difficult to identify ownership of entities subject to the economic embargo, the US "was forced to regard all companies in Serbia and Montenegro and their foreign subsidiaries as either owned or controlled by the Yugoslav government."[158] American citizens and corporations violating the embargo are subject to criminal fines of up to US $250,000 for individuals and US $500,000 for corporations, as well as imprisonment for up to ten years and civil penalties of up to US $10,000 per violation.[159]

---

[154] Ibid.

[155] George Graham, Judy Dempsey and Laura Silber, "US Tightens Sanctions Against Serbia," *The Financial Times*, June 24, 1992.

[156] Ibid.

[157] Eric Schmitt, "Cheney Talks of an Air Role in Bosnia," *The New York Times*, July 1, 1992.

[158] "US Widens Embargo," Associated Press report of July 6, 1992, as reported in *The New York Times*, July 7, 1992.

[159] Ibid.

Once UN and US sanctions against Yugoslavia were in place, the US began to disengage from the Bosnian situation. On July 9, President Bush turned aside a personal appeal from Bosnian President Alija Izetbegović for direct military intervention to stop the siege of his country.[160] Instead, President Bush repeated his call for international efforts to assure the delivery of humanitarian aid to victims of the war.[161] The Bush Administration has, however, refused to pledge further contributions for humanitarian and refugee relief effort for Bosnia-Hercegovina. At a UNHCR conference on July 29, the US claimed that it had already contributed $51 million and refused to pledge additional financial help to alleviate the refugee crisis in the Balkans.[162] US government officials continue to condemn attacks against civilians, the continued shelling of Bosnian towns and cities and the policy of "ethnic cleansing"[163] but such statements have had little effect on those committing such abuses.

Only after reports of death camps appeared in the press did the US resume an active stance. In recent days, the Bush Administration has indicated that it will urge the UN to support the use of force to ensure the delivery of relief to besieged areas of Bosnia-Hercegovina. On August 9, Acting Secretary of State Lawrence Eagleburger emphasized that the US would be willing to use force exclusively for humanitarian, not military, purposes. No US official has proposed ways to bring about an end to the atrocities taking place in Bosnia-Hercegovina.

Moreover, in recent days, the Bush Administration has tried to minimize the severity of abuses taking place in Serbian-operated detention camps in northern Bosnia-Hercegovina. Some officials have

---

[160] Don Oberdorfer and Marc Fisher, "Bush Turns Aside Bosnian Plea for Military Intervention," *The Washington Post*, July 10, 1992.

[161] *Ibid.*

[162] Henry Kamm, "Aid but Not Homes Offered to Refugees from Balkans," *The New York Times*, July 30, 1992.

[163] See "Regular State Department Briefing," State Department Spokeswoman Margaret Tutwiler, July 13, 1992 and July 14, 1992. See also "US Condemns Attacks," *The New York Times*, July 11, 1992, and Eric Schmitt, US Condemns Serbian Attacks; Plans No Force," *The New York Times*, July 15, 1992.

suggested that since the existence of systematic death camps cannot be proven, the camps should not be referred to as "concentration camps" and that, therefore, the conditions in the camps are not as poor as press reports would lead the public to believe. Helsinki Watch believes that this appraisal belittles the suffering of those in the camps and is a rationalization for inaction. On the basis of evidence we have collected, Helsinki Watch believes that even without full evidence about the camps, war crimes are being committed on a massive scale in Bosnia-Hercegovina. Helsinki Watch calls on the US government to act decisively to stop the atrocities in Bosnia-Hercegovina regardless of what may be discovered when the truth about the camps is fully known. Helsinki Watch believes that the information presented here and that gathered by the independent media about "ethnic cleansing," and the manner in which this has been carried out, itself necessitates international action to prevent and suppress genocide and to prosecute and punish war crimes.

The US is correct in exerting pressure on the Serbian government and Serbian forces in Bosnia-Hercegovina and demanding that such camps be opened to international inspection. However, even if the camps are opened to the ICRC, the fate of those imprisoned in them remains precarious. Serbian forces executed those kept in detention in Vukovar and in eastern Bosnia. Helsinki Watch believes that all civilians held in such camps must be released immediately. Prisoners of war who remain in detention must be held in conditions that comply with international law.

Although we support US efforts to ensure the safe delivery of humanitarian aid to besieged areas in Bosnia-Hercegovina, this will not bring to an end the commission of war crimes, and possibly genocide, in Bosnia-Hercegovina. Recent US efforts to garner international armed protection for relief convoys only duplicate failed efforts in the past and will have little or no effect in preventing and suppressing the atrocities currently committed on a mass scale in Bosnia-Hercegovina. On June 26, a statement issued in the name of the UN Secretary- General threatened to use force to ensure that humanitarian aid reaches Sarajevo.[164] Although Serbian forces complied in the short-term, they have since continued to attack relief convoys and forced the closure of the Sarajevo

---

[164] See above section concerning the role of the United Nations -- delivery of humanitarian aid.

airport for a third time in early August. The UN did not follow through on its threats, and delivery of humanitarian aid to besieged areas of Bosnia remains difficult, if not impossible. It is highly unlikely that a renewed threat to use force to ensure delivery of humanitarian aid will stop or prevent the commission of atrocities against the civilian population.

We are pleased that Acting Secretary of State Lawrence Eagleburger issued a public call on August 5 for a war crimes investigation. Though that was a step in the right direction, we believe that more is required. Secretary Eagleburger's call was not coupled, as we believe it should be, by a proposal for the establishment of an international tribunal with authority to prosecute and punish such crimes. The authority that such a tribunal would have is recognized in United States law[165] and by the principles that have been accepted in international law since the establishment of the Nuremberg Tribunal in 1945. Also, Secretary Eagleberger did not refer to the Genocide Convention. As a party to the Convention, the United States has committed that it will "undertake to prevent and punish this crime (Article I)." In addition, the Convention authorizes the United States to call upon the United Nations to take appropriate action under the Charter "for the prevention and suppression of acts of genocide." It should be noted that the Convention specifies that genocide means acts "committed with intent to destroy, in whole or in part, a national, ethnical, racial or religious group" (Article II); and that the acts that are punishable under the Convention include genocide itself; "conspiracy to commit genocide; direct and public incitement to commit genocide; attempt to commit genocide; complicity in genocide" (Article III).

It is beyond the competence of Helsinki Watch to determine all the steps that may be required to prevent and suppress the crime of genocide. Whether or not military force is required is not our province. Helsinki Watch believes that it is the responsibility of the Security Council to resolve that question. Helsinki Watch's position is that, however the question of military force is resolved, those responsible for genocide and other war crimes must be held accountable for their crimes, and must become aware that they will be held accountable. It is to this end that Helsinki Watch calls on the US government to seek action by the United

---

[165] See Section 404, Restatement (Third) of the Foreign Relations Law of the United States (1987).

Nations to prevent and suppress genocide and to establish a tribunal to investigate, prosecute adjudicate and punish war crimes.

Helsinki Watch calls on the United States to take the lead internationally at the United Nations in seeking action that is "appropriate for the prevention and suppression of acts of genocide" as provided in Article VIII of the 1951 Convention on the Prevention and Punishment of the Crime of Genocide. In addition, we call on the United States to take the lead in calling on the United Nations to establish an international tribunal to investigate, prosecute and punish war crimes, or "grave breaches" of the 1949 Geneva Conventions and the 1977 Protocol. The evidence that Helsinki Watch has gathered from victims and witnesses to the conflict, as well as the reports by the independent media, demostrate that international action to prevent and suppress genocide in Bosnia-Hercegovina is required; and that those who have the highest level of responsibility for the most egregious war crimes in the conflict must be prosecuted and punished.

CONCLUSIONS

Helsinki Watch is gravely concerned that the scope and brutality of abuses in Bosnia-Hercegovina far exceeds those that we report here. Witnesses to atrocities in eastern Bosnia remain inaccessible to us in the cities of Sarajevo, Tuzla and Goražde. Helsinki Watch has received reports that Serbian forces have summarily executed civilians on a mass scale in the towns of Zvornik, Foča, Višegrad and Bijeljina. Helsinki Watch is also concerned that Serbian civilians may have been targeted for execution by Muslim and Croatian forces in some areas under the control of the latter groups. Helsinki Watch will continue to investigate reports of humanitarian law violations committed by all sides in Bosnia-Hercegovina.

* * *

Helsinki Watch finds that Serbian forces:

- systematically implement a policy of "ethnic cleansing" throughout Serbian-occupied areas of Bosnia-Hercegovina, i.e., two thirds of the country. Helsinki Watch has also documented cases of "ethnic cleansing" of non-Serbs in Serbian-occupied areas of Croatia and in the republic of Serbia, particularly in the province of Vojvodina. In Bosnia-Hercegovina, "ethnic cleansing" entails the following violations:

    - summary executions of non-Serbian civilians, including children and elderly persons;

    - arbitary detention, torture and general mistreatment of non-Serbs, in prisons, detention camps or ghettos;

    - forcible deportation of non-Serbs from Bosnia-Hercegovina and from Serbia. In some cases, this is coordinated with civilian authorities and police forces of the republic of Serbia and the armed forces of the Yugoslav People's Army (JNA);

195

- forcible displacement of non-Serbs, which is achieved either through terror bombardment and shelling;

- burning of non-Serbian villages and the destruction of Muslim and Croatian homes in ethnically mixed villages.

- summarily execute, torture, beat and otherwise mistreat prisoners of war, civilians and combatants *hors de combat* in their custody;

- "disappear" non-Serbian combatants and civilian males;

- take hostages to exchange for captured combatants or to extract military concessions;

- deny medical care to wounded prisoners of war and civilians, including journalists;

- use prisoners as human shields;

- use hospitals and other medical establishments as military headquarters or as depots for weapons;

- indiscriminately shell and bomb Bosnian cities, towns and villages;

- use disproportionate and indiscriminate force, as well as attacks on civilian targets, to terrorize the civilian population;

- use disproportionate force against Bosnian military targets, thereby inflicting unnecessary and excessive damage on the civilian population;

- target for attack civilians (including journalists), hospitals, heavily populated city centers and cultural and religious objects;

- continue to attack, hijack and obstruct international relief convoys, including U.N. vehicles and personnel, intended for civilians in besieged cities and towns;

- loot, burn and otherwise pillage Muslim and Croatian villages.

Helsinki Watch is also gravely concerned about reports that Serbian forces:

- detain prisoners of war and civilians (possibly including Serbs who oppose Serbian policies) in camps under appalling conditions, where they are tortured, starved or executed;

- deliberately obstruct the delivery of humanitarian aid for civilians to serve military purposes, i.e., to starve, and thereby force, the besieged population to surrender to Serbian troops.

* * *

Helsinki Watch finds that Muslim and Croatian forces:

- take hostages for exchange for captured combatants;

- harass and intimidate Serbs in areas under their control.

Helsinki Watch is also concerned about reports that Muslim and Croatian forces:

- forcibly displace Serbian civilians from areas under their control;

- place artillery and other weapons close to hospitals and other civilian objects;

- loot and destroy property belonging to Serbs;

- shoot at UN vehicles;

- deliberately attack journalists;

- may be executing Serbian civilians and disarmed combatants;

197

Many of these abuses constitute "grave breaches" of international humanitarian law, or war crimes. All of the parties to the conflict have committed such crimes and all should be held accountable and prosecuted for their abuses before impartial tribunals that afford the protections of due process of law. Croatian and Muslim forces are guilty of holding civilians hostage, mistreating prisoners in detention and otherwise harassing Serbs in some areas under their control, but the overwhelming number of crimes are being committed by Serbian forces in Bosnia-Hercegovina which are carrying out a policy of "ethnic cleansing" in systematic fashion, not only in Bosnia-Hercegovina but also in Serbian-occupied areas of Croatia, in the republic of Serbia, the province of Vojvodina and, less visibly, in the province of Kosovo.

APPENDIX A: OTHER RELEVANT PROVISIONS OF INTERNATIONAL LAW[1]

The conduct of armed forces is governed by the rules of war, also called international humanitarian law, which comprise the four 1949 Geneva Conventions, the two 1977 Protocols Additional to those Conventions and the customary laws of war. International humanitarian law distinguishes international and non-international (internal) armed conlicts. The rules governing each type of conflict vary significantly. Under Article 2 Common to the four Geneva Conventions, an international armed conflict must involve a declared war or any other armed conflict which may arise "between two or more of the High Contracting Parties" to the Convention. The official commentary to the 1949 Geneva Conventions broadly defines "armed conflict" as any difference between two states leading to the intervention of armed forces.[2]   For the purposes of this report, the current conflict shall be categorized as an international armed conflict involving two states, namely Yugoslavia and Bosnia-Hercegovina, the latter of which is aided militarily by a third state, namely Croatia.[3]

---

[1] Parts of this chapter are derived from Chapter I of *Needless Deaths in the Gulf War: Civilian Casualties During the Air Campaign and Violations of the Laws of War*, Middle East Watch, November 1991, pp. 25-68.

[2] International Committee of the Red Cross, *Commentary, III Geneva Convention* at 23 (International Committee of the Red Cross: Geneva 1960).

[3] If, in the future, the Republic of Croatia formally annexes territory belonging to Bosnia-Hercegovina and Bosnian and Croatian forces begin to fight against, rather than with, each other, the conflict in Bosnia-Hercegovina would, therefore, be characterized as an armed conflict between three, as opposed to the current two, states. Under the current circumstances, a military alliance between Croatia and Bosnia-Hercegovina is in effect and the current forces of the two states will, for the purposes of this section, be treated as jointly engaged in an armed conflict with another, opposing state, namely Yugoslavia.

Numerous members of the international community recognized Bosnia-Hercegovina's independence on April 6 and 7, 1992.[4] Croatia's independence was recognized by the European Community and non-EC countries on January 15, 1992.[5] The United States recognized both Bosnia-Hercegovina and Croatia as independent states on April 7, 1992. Moreover, both Bosnia-Hercegovina and Croatia meet the standards of statehood as prescribed by international law.[6] Thus, we treat Croatia's and Bosnia-Hercegovina's independence from Yugoslavia as complete as of January 15 and April 6, 1992, respectively.

On April 27, 1992, the republics of Montenegro and Serbia joined to form a new Yugoslav state, which also meets the standards of statehood as prescribed by international law. Although some states have not recognized the current Yugoslav state as the legitimate successor to the former Yugoslavia,[7] for the purposes of this section, the current

---

[4] As of July 22, 1992, the EC, the UN, the United States, Albania and Saudi Arabia and others have recognized Bosnia-Hercegovina's independence. Bosnia-Hercegovina was admitted as a Member State to the United Nations on May 22, 1992. Slovenia, Croatia and Macedonia have recognized Bosnia-Hercegovina's independence. Yugoslavia -- the new state formed by the union of Montenegro and Serbia on April 27, 1992 -- has refused to extend formal recognition to any of the former Yugoslav republics.

[5] As of May 29, 1992, 78 countries have recognized Croatia's independence. Croatia was admitted as a Member State to the United Nations on May 22, 1992.

[6] "Under international law, a state is an entity that has a defined territory and a permanent population, under the control of its own government, and that engages in or has the capacity to engage in, formal relations with other such entities." (See Section 201, *Restatement of the Foreign Relations Law of the United States*, Volume I, Sections 1-488, as adopted and promulgated by the American Law Institute at Washington, D.C., May 14, 1986.) Although both Bosnia-Hercegovina and Croatia do not have control over portions of their territory, their territorial integrity has been recognized by the international community, and, for the purposes of this report, they shall be treated as sovereign states with legitimate jurisdiction over their territories.

[7] As of July 12, 1992, Russia, China, and most non-aligned states have recognized the new Yugoslav state. Greece, is the only member of the European Community to extend recognition to the new Yugoslavia. The other EC member states and the US have refused to extend recognition.

Yugoslavia will be treated as an independent state, under whose control the JNA operates.

Of the three parties to the conflict, only two states (Croatia and Yugoslavia) are High Contracting Parties to the Geneva Conventions and their Protocols. The four Geneva Conventions and the 1977 Protocols Additional to those Conventions were ratified by the former Yugoslavia in 1950 and 1978, respectively. The current Yugoslav state (now made up of Montenegro and Serbia) has expressed its wish to be recognized as the successor state to the former Yugoslavia and thereby retain membership in international organizations. Such a declaration also implies that the current Yugoslav state is willing to succeed to international agreements to which the former Yugoslavia was a party. Therefore, for the purposes of this report, all international obligations assumed by the former Yugoslavia will be transferred to the current Yugoslav state, including its obligations under international humanitarian law.[8]

Croatia became a High Contracting Party to the Geneva Conventions and their Protocols on May 11, 1992, ten months after armed conflict broke out on its territory and approximately five weeks after hostilities commenced in Bosnia-Hercegovina. Plenipotentiary representatives of the parties to the conflict in Croatia (i.e., the governments of the Republics of Croatia and Serbia and the Yugoslav People's Army) met in Geneva on November 26-27 and December 19-20, 1991, and agreed to comply with the all provisions of international

---

[8] According to Section 208 of *The Restatement of the Foreign Relations Law of the United States*, "When a state succeeds another state with respect to particular territory, the capacities, rights and duties of the predecessor state with respect to that territory terminates and are assumed by the successor state, as provided in sections 209-10." The relevant aspect of section 210(3) states, "When part of a state becomes a new state, the new state does not succeed to the international agreements to which the predecessor state was party, unless, expressly or *by implication*, it accepts such agreements and the other party or parties thereto agree or acquiesce." (See *The Restatement of the Foreign Relations Law of the United States*, Volume I, Sections 1-488,as adopted and promulgated by the American Law Institute at Washington, DC, May 14, 1986, at pp. 100-114.) Because the new Yugoslav state has expressed a wish to be recognized as the successor state to the former Yugoslavia, it has implied that it is willing to succeed to the international agreements to which the former Yugoslavia was a party, including the four 1949 Geneva Conventions and the two 1977 Protocols Additional to those conventions.

humanitarian law. Given that declaration and ratification of the Geneva Conventions and their Protocols, both Croatia and Yugoslavia can reasonably be held responsible to adhere to the tenets of international humanitarian law in Bosnia, as in Croatia. Moreover, the customary laws of war bind all parties to respect the fundamental principles of humanitarian law.

As of July 22, Bosnia-Hercegovina has not formally ratified the Geneva Conventions or their Protocols. However, when the government of the Republic of Bosnia-Hercegovina declared a state of war, it also agreed to respect and abide by international humanitarian law. The June 20th declaration states, in part:

> The Republic of Bosnia and Hercegovina will observe the requirements of international law and of the international conventions which regulate the behavior of States in a State of War, and in accordance with Article 51 of the United Nations Charter, will respect the decisions and initiatives of the Security Council concerned with the establishment and maintenance of peace and security.[9]

On the basis of this declaration, and the universally binding principles set forth in the customary laws of war, we hold the Bosnian government responsible for violations of humanitarian law committed by its troops.

On the basis of the reasoning set forth above, the requisite conditions for the existence of an international armed conflict are satisfied and, therefore, the four Geneva Conventions of 1949, the 1977 Protocols to those Conventions and customary international law apply to the conflict in Bosnia-Hercegovina.

---

[9] "Declaration of a State of War," signed by Alija Izetbegović, President of the Republic of Bosnia and Hercegovina, June 20, 1992.

Customary Law and Protocol I: Civilian Immunity and the Principle of Distinction

United Nations General Assembly Resolution 2444

United Nations General Assembly Resolution 2444,[10] adopted by unanimous vote on December 19, 1969, expressly recognized the customary law principle of civilian immunity and its complementary principle requiring the warring parties to distinguish civilians from combatants at all times. The preamble to this resolution clearly states that these fundamental humanitarian law principles apply "in all armed conflicts," meaning both international and internal armed conflicts. United Nations Resolution 2444 affirms:

> ...the following principles for observance by all government and other authorities responsible for action in armed conflicts:
>
> (a) that the right of the parties to a conflict to adopt means of injuring the enemy is not unlimited;
>
> (b) that it is prohibited to launch attacks against the civilian population as such;
>
> (c) that distiction must be made at all times between persons taking part in the hostilities and members of the civilian population to the effect that the latter be spared as much as possible.

Protocol Additional to the Geneva Conventions of 12 August 1949 and Relating to the Protection of Victims of International Armed Conflicts (Protocol I)

Protocol I contains detailed rules, mostly reaffirmations or clarifications of existing customary law, which implement the customary principles that a distinction should be made between combatants and

---

[10] *Respect for Human Rights in Armed Conflicts*, General Assembly Resolution 2444, 23 U.N. GAOR Supp. (No. 18) p. 164, UN Doc. A/7433 (1968).

civilians and that civilians and civilian objects may not be the object of attacks. Four different sections of the Protocol are devoted to this task. First are provisions designed to revitalize and strengthen the legal requirement to distinguish military objectives from civilians and civilian objects and to limit attacks to military objectives. Second are provisions clarifying practical steps to be taken in the selection of targets to prevent attacks on civilians and civilian objects, including the rule of proportionality and a prohibition on indiscriminate attacks. Third are provisions regulating the means and methods of *both* attack and defense to avoid or minimize civilian casualties and damage to civilian objects. Fourth are specific provisions limiting or prohibiting attacks on particular objects and specified areas.

Basic Rule: The Immunity of Civilians and Civilian Objects

The rules of war dictate that civilians may not be subjected to deliberate individualized attack since they pose no immediate threat to the adversary.[11] Article 48 of Protocol I is a paraphrase of the basic rules stated in paragraphs 2 and 3 of United Nations General Assembly Resolution 2444. It states:

> In order to ensure the respect for and protection of the civilian population and civilian objects, the Parties to the conflict shall at all times distinguish between the civilian population and combatants and between civilian objects and military objectives and accordingly shall direct their operations only against military objectives.

Article 51(2) reaffirms this mandatory distinction by providing: "The civilian population as such, as well as individual civilians, shall not be the object of attack. Acts or threats of violence the primary purpose of which is to spread terror among the civilian population are prohibited." This general immunity does *not* prohibit attacks which may cause civilian casualties. For example, civilians who are located within or near legitimate military targets, while still immune from individualized attack,

---

[11] M. Bothe, K. Partsch, and W. Solf, *New Rules for Victims of Armed Conflicts: Commentary on the Two 1977 Protocols Additional to the Geneva Conventions of 1949*, Geneva 1982, p. 303. (Hereinafter referred to as *New Rules.*)

may be at risk of death or injury as a result of lawful attacks against such targets, although, as noted later, such civilians would retain the benefits of the rule of proportionality as it applies to collateral civilian casualties.

Terror and Morale Attacks

Article 51(2) also prohibits attacks, and threats of such acts, which are launched or threatened with intent to terrorize the civilian population. Specifically, the second sentence of that section provides: "Acts or threats of violence the primary purpose of which is to spread terror among the civilian population are prohibited." This provision is intended to make clear that terror bombing or shelling targets for the sole purpose of terrorizing civilians violates the laws of war. However, the fact that attacks upon legitimate military objectives may cause terror among the civilian population does not make such attacks unlawful.

This article also prohibits bombing or shelling to attack civilian morale. Although technically there may be a distinction between morale and terror bombing, they are, in practice, treated the same. It often has been observed that what is morale bombing to the attacking force is terror bombing to the civilians who are targeted. Some attacks may be carried out by strategic bombardment or shelling of the enemy's economic infrastructure. This infrastructure may include a mix of military and civilian targets. To the extent that these attacks are launched or threatened solely or primarily for political ends, they violate the principles of civilian immunity, proportionality, and humanity. Attacks intended primarily to induce the civilian population to rebellion or to overthrow its leadership would be examples of unlawful attacks.[12]

Civilians and Civilian Population

Article 50 of Protocol I defines the term "civilian population" as comprising "all persons who are civilians" and defines a civilian as anyone who is not a member of the armed forces or of an organized armed

---

[12] See generally Remarks of Hamilton De Saussure delivered at the American Red Cross - Washington College of Law Conference on International Humanitarian Law in 31 *The American University Law Review*, Summer 1982, pp. 883-889; J. Spaight, *Air Power and War Rights* (3d ed. 1947) p. 275; and J. Spaight, *Air Power in the Cities* (1930) p. 110.

group of a party to the conflict.[13] Thus, civilians and the civilian population comprise all persons who are not entitled to, or do not directly, participate in hostilities. This article also stipulates that the "presence within the civilian population of individuals who do not come within the definition of civilians does not deprive the population of its civilian character."[14] Therefore, "[t]he presence of a small number of off-duty combatants, or even of some engaged in the transaction of business for the armed forces within a community of civilians would not subject that community to attack."[15]

Insofar as they are solely engaged in their professional duties, journalists are considered civilians.[16] The term "civilian" also includes

---

[13] Protocol I, Article 50(l) defines a civilian as "any person who does not belong to one of the categories referred to in Article 4A (1),(2),(3) and (6) of the Third Convention and in Article 43 of this Protocol." In pertinent part the persons listed in Article 4(A) of the Third Geneva Convention are: members of the armed forces of a Party to the conflict as well as members of militias or volunteer corps forming part of such armed forces; members of other militias and volunteer corps, provided that they fulfill certain conditions; and members of regular armed forces who profess allegiance to a government or an authority not recognized by the detaining power.

Article 43(1) of Protocol I defines the armed forces of a party as consisting of "all organized armed forces, groups and units which are under a command responsible to that Party for the conduct of its subordinates, even if that Party is represented by a government or an authority not recognized by an adverse Party. Such armed forces shall be subject to an internal disciplinary system...."

[14] Protocol I, Article 50(3).

[15] New Rules, p. 296.

[16] Protocol I, Article 79 states:

> 1. Journalists engaged in dangerous professional missions in areas of armed conflict shall be considered as civilians within the meaning of Article 50, paragraph 1.
>
> 2. They shall be protected as such under the Conventions and this Protocol, provided they take no action adversely affecting their status as civilians, and without prejudice to the right of

some employees of the military establishment who are not members of the armed forces or militia but assist them. While as civilians they may not be targeted, these civilian employees of military establishments or those who indirectly assist combatants assume the risk of death or injury incidental to attacks against legitimate military targets while they are at or in the immediate vicinity of military targets.

Insofar as any side utilizes, as part-time combatants, civilians who are otherwise engaged in civilian occupations, these civilians lose their immunity from attack for as long as they directly participate in hostilities.[17] "[D]irect participation [in hostilities] means acts of war which by their nature and purpose are likely to cause actual harm to the personnel and epuipment of enemy armed forces," and includes acts of defense.[18]

"Hostilities" not only covers the time when the civilian actually makes use of a weapon but also the time that he or she is carrying it, as well as situations in which he or she undertakes hostile acts without using a weapon.[19] Examples are provided in the United States Army Field Manual which lists some hostile acts

> as including sabotage, destruction of communication facilities, intentional misleading of troops by guides, and liberation of prisoners of war.... This is also the case of a person acting as a member of a weapons crew, or one providing target information for weapon systems intended for immediate use against the enemy such as

---

war correspondents accredited to the armed forces to the status provided for in Article 4 A (4) of the Third Convention.

[17] *New Rules*, p. 303.

[18] International Committee of the Red Cross, *Commentary on the Additional Protocols of 8 June 1977 to the Geneva Conventions of 12 August 1949* (Geneva: Martinus Nijhoff Publishers, 1987) p. 636. (Hereinafter referred to as ICRC *Commentary*.)

[19] ICRC *Commentary*, p. 618-19. This is a broader definition than "attacks" and includes at a minimum preparation for combat and return from combat. (*New Rules*, p. 303.)

artillery spotters or members of ground observer teams. [It] would include direct logistic support for units engaged directly in battle such as the delivery of ammunition to a firing position. On the other hand, civilians providing only indirect support to the armed forces, such as workers in defense plants or those engaged in distribution or storage of military supplies in rear areas, do not pose an immediate threat to the adversary and therefore would not be subject to deliberate individual attack.[20]

Once their participation in hostilities ceases, that is, while engaged in their civilian vocations, these civilians cannot be attacked.

Designation of Military Objectives

To constitute a legitimate military objective, the object or target, selected by its nature, location, purpose or use must contribute effectively to the enemy's military capability or activity *and* its total or partial destruction or neutralization must offer a definite military advantage in the circumstances.[21]

The official ICRC *Commentary* on Article 52, Protocol I, notes that the concept "definite military advantage in circumstances ruling at the time" means that "it is not legitimate to launch an attack which only offers *potential or indeterminate advantages*. Those ordering or executing the attack must have sufficient information available to take this requirement into account; in case of doubt, the safety of the civilian population, which is the aim of the Protocol, must be taken into consideration."[22] The other authoritative commentary, the *New Rules*, similarly indicates that the adjective "definite" which modifies "military advantage" "is a word of limitation denoting in this context a concrete and perceptible military advantage rather than a hypothetical and

---

[20] *New Rules*, p. 303 (footnote omitted).

[21] Protocol I, Article 52(2).

[22] *Ibid.* (Emphasis added)

speculative one."[23]   The requirement that the definite military advantage must be present "in circumstances ruling at time" imposes an additional significant limitation on the attacker's target selection. The *New Rules* states in this regard:

> This element emphasizes that in the dynamic circumstances of armed conflict, objects which may have been military objectives yesterday, may no longer be such today and vice versa. Thus, timely and reliable information of the military situation is an important element in the selection of targets for attack.[24]

Whether the required definite military advantage under prevailing circumstances would accrue from a particular attack "must be judged in the context of the military advantage anticipated from the specific military operation of which the attack is a part considered as a whole, and not only from isolated or particular parts of that operation."[25]

Types of Military Objectives

Though Protocol I does not delineate specific categories of persons or property as military objectives, it is clear that enemy combatants and civilians who assume a combatant's role are legitimate targets.

The ICRC *Commentary* contains the following proposed list of military objectives:

(1) Armed forces...and persons who...take part in the fighting.

(2) Positions, installations or constructions occupied by the forces...as well as combat objectives (that is to say, those objectives which are directly contested in battle between land or sea forces including airborne forces).

---

[23] *New Rules* p. 326.

[24] *Ibid.*

[25] *New Rules*, pp. 324-25.

(3) Installations, constructions and other works of a military nature, such as barracks, fortifications, War Ministries (e.g. Ministries of Army, Navy, Air Force, National Defense, Supply) and other organs for the direction and administration of military operations.

(4) Stores of arms or military supplies, such as munitions dumps, stores of equipment or fuel, vehicles parks.

(5) Airfields, rocket launching ramps and naval base installations.

(6) Those of the lines and means of communication (railway lines, roads, bridges, tunnels and canals) which are of fundamental military importance;

(7) The installations of broadcasting and television stations; telephone and telegraph exchanges of fundamental military importance;

(8) Industries of fundamental importance for the conduct of the war:

> (a) industries for the manufacture of armaments . . . ;
>
> (b) industries for the manufacture of supplies and material of a military character, such as transport and communications material, equipment for the armed forces;
>
> (c) factories or plants constituting other production and manufacturing centers of fundamental importance for the conduct of war, such as the metallurgical, engineering and chemical industries, whose nature or purpose is essentially military;
>
> (d) storage and transport installations whose basic function it is to serve the industries referred to in (a)-(c); and
>
> (e) installations providing energy mainly for national defense, e.g. coal, other fuels, or atomic energy, and

plants producing gas or electricity mainly for military consumption.

(9) Installations constituting experimental, research centers for experiments on and the development of weapons and war material.[26]

Members of the Yugoslav, Croatian and Bosnian armed forces and paramilitary groups are legitimate military targets and subject to attack, individually or collectively, until such time as they become *hors de combat*, that is surrender or are wounded or captured.[27] Some armed groups operating inside Bosnia-Hercegovina have identified themselves as "civilians." This nomenclature is not accurate under the rules of war. Whatever their original occupation, members of such groups interviewed by Helsinki Watch were combatants, armed and operating under responsible command and engaging in full-time military duties, defensive as well as offensive. Accordingly, those Serbian, Croatian and Muslim "civilians" that participate in hostilities are combatants and subject to attack.

Policemen without combat duties are not legitimate military targets. The drafters of the Protocols Additional to the Geneva Conventions intended to exclude policemen as well as certain other government personnel authorized to bear arms (e.g., customs agents) from the definition of "armed forces." Policemen with combat duties, however, would be proper military targets and subject to direct individualized attack.

Unofficial paramilitary groups, like other civilians, lose their immunity from attack whenever they assume a combatant's role. Thus, when they prepare for, actively participate in and return from combat (while carrying a weapon or committing hostile acts without using a weapon), they are proper military targets. To the extent that paramilitaries have not been incorporated into the operations of the Bosnian, Croatian or Yugoslav governments' armies but retain a separate

---

[26] ICRC *Commentary*, pp. 632-33.

[27] This explains why killing a wounded or captured combatant is not proper: it does not offer a "definite military advantage in the circumstanecs" because the soldier is already rendered useless or *hors de combat*.

command structure, they are legitimate military targets while actually participating in hostilities.

Civilian and "Dual-Use" Objects

The ICRC's model compilation includes objects that have "dual-uses or functions" in that while they serve the needs of the civilian population, they also are used by the enemy. These objects typically include bridges, power plants, chemical and other factories, fuel-storage depots, railroad and other transportation facilities and systems, vehicles and communications facilities.

It is important to understand that, under customary law, civilian objects enjoy general protection against direct attack. Article 52(l) defines civilian objects negatively as all objects that are not military objectives as defined in paragraph 2 of that same article which sets forth the two-fold test for military objectives. Therefore, Article 52 implicitly characterizes all objects as civilian, unless they make an effective contribution to the enemy's military action and unless destroying, capturing or neutralizing them offers a definite military advantage in the prevailing circumstances.

In doubtful situations, Article 52 creates a presumption that objects normally dedicated to civilian use, such as churches, houses or schools, are not employed to contribute effectively to military action. This presumption attaches only to objects that ordinarily have no significant military use or purpose, not to dual-use objects.[28]

Cultural Property

Protocol I, Article 53 explicitly prohibits committing any "acts of hostility directed against historic monuments, works of art or places of worship which constitute the cultural or spiritual heritage of peoples." It also prohibits using these objects in support of the military effort or as objects of reprisals.

Cultural property, as defined in Article 1 of the Hague Convention of 1954, includes monuments of architecture, art or history, whether religious or secular; groups of buildings which, as a whole, are of historical or archaeological interest; works of art; manuscripts, books and other objects of artistic, historical or archaeological interest and

---

[28] *New Rules*, p. 326.

buildings whose main and effective purpose is to preserve or exhibit the movable cultural property such as museums and large libraries. Article 4(2) of the Hague Convention of 1954 states that this obligation may be waived only in cases "where military necessity imperatively requires such a waiver."

The ICRC *Commentary* notes that if such objects were used in support of the military effort, the right to attack them

> should not be accepted without duly taking into account the fact that the objects concerned are of exceptional interest and universal value. All possible measures should be taken to endeavor putting a stop to any use in support of the military effort (by giving due warnings, for example) in order to prevent the objects from being destroyed or damaged. In any case, this is the spirit of the provision: it is an invitation to safeguard the heritage of mankind.[29]

Prohibition of Disproportionate and Other Indiscriminate Attacks

The Rule of Proportionality

Even attacks on legitimate targets, however, are limited by the principle of proportionality. This principle places a duty on combatants to chose means of attack that avoid or minimize damage to civilians. In particular, the attacker should refrain from launching an attack if the expected civilian casualites would outweigh the importance of the military target to the attacker.[30] For example, an attack on an entire town or village in order to destroy a number of clearly separate military targets that could be attacked separately would be indiscriminate. Attacks carefully directed at each military target within that location would not be indiscriminate.

---

[29] ICRC *Commentary*, p. 1470.

[30] Article 51(5)(b) formulates this rule as follows: "an attack which may be expected to cause incidental loss of civilian life, injury to civilians, damage to civilian objects, or a combination thereof, which would be excessive in relation to the concrete and direct military advantage anticipated."

Concrete and Direct Military Advantage

The *New Rules* notes that the rule of proportionality imposes "an additional limitation on the discretion of combatants in deciding whether an object is a military objective under paragraph 2 of Article 52."[31] If an attack is expected to cause incidental casualties or damage, the requirement of an anticipated "definite" military advantage under Article 52 (one of the minimum requirements for an object to be a proper military target) is heightened to the more restrictive standard of a "concrete and direct" military advantage set forth in Article 51(5)(b). According to the *New Rules*:

> "Concrete" means specific, not general; perceptible to the senses. Its meaning is therefore roughly equivalent to the adjective "definite" used in the two pronged test prescribed by Article 52(2). "Direct," on the other hand, means "without intervening condition of agency." Taken together the two words of limitation raise the standard set by Article 52 in those situations where civilians may be affected by the attack. A remote advantage to be gained at some unknown time in the future would not be a proper consideration to weigh against civilian losses.[32]

The ICRC *Commentary* provides a similar interpretation, stating:

> The expression "concrete and direct" was intended to show that the advantage concerned should be substantial and relatively close, and that advantages which are hardly perceptible and those which would only appear in the long term should be disregarded.[33]

---

[31] *New Rules*, p. 360.

[32] *Ibid.*, p. 365.

[33] ICRC *Commentary*, p. 684.

214

While allowing a fairly broad margin of judgment, the *Commentary* notes,

> even in a general attack the advantage anticipated must be a military advantage and it must be concrete and direct; there can be no question of creating conditions conducive to surrender by means of attacks which incidentally harm the civilian population. A military advantage can only consist in ground gained and in annihilating or weakening the enemy armed forces. In addition, it should be noted that the words "concrete and direct" impose stricter conditions on the attacker than those implied by the criteria defining military objectives in Article 52 . . . . [34]

The term "concrete and direct military advantage" refers to the advantage expected "from the specific military operation of which the attack is a part taken as a whole and not from isolated or particular parts of that operation."[35]

Excessive Collateral Damage

The other side of the proportionality equation is the requirement that the foreseeable injury to civilians and damage to civilian objects not be disproportionate, i.e., "excessive" to the expected "concrete and definite military advantage."

Excessive damage is a relational concept, not quantifiable in terms of a fixed number of civilians dead or injured, or houses destroyed. Such damage need not be so great that it "shock the conscience" of the world. Rather, its avoidance requires a good-faith balancing of disparate probabilities -- the foreseeability of collateral damage and the relative importance of a particular military target.

The ICRC *Commentary* provides examples of "excessive" damage: (a) the presence of a soldier on leave cannot serve as a justification to destroy the entire village, and (b) "if the destruction of a bridge is of

---

[34] *Ibid.*, p. 685.

[35] *New Rules*, p. 311 (footnote omitted).

paramount importance for the occupation or non-occupation of a strategic zone, it is understood that some houses may be hit, but not that a whole urban area be levelled."[36] Of course, the disproportion between losses and damages caused and the military advantages anticipated "raises a delicate problem; in some situations there will be no room for doubt, while in other situations there may be reason for hesitation. In such situations the interests of the civilian population should prevail...."[37] However, the ICRC *Commentary* makes it clear that there is never a justification for excessive civilian casualties:

> The idea has also been put forward that even if they are very high, civilian losses and damages may be justified if the military advantage at stake is of great importance. This idea is contrary to the fundamental rules of the Protocol; in particular it conflicts with Article 48 (*Basic rule*) and with paragraphs 1 and 2 of the present Article 51. The Protocol does not provide any justification for attacks which cause extensive civilian losses and damages. Incidental losses and damages should never be extensive.[38]

Ultimately, compliance with the rule of proportionality depends on the subjective judgment of military commanders in specific situations. Recognizing that decisions are taken in battle "under circumstances when clinical certainty is impossible and when the adversary is striving to conceal the true facts, to deceive and to confuse,"[39] the *New Rules* states:

> The standard for judging the actions of commanders and others responsible for planning, deciding upon or executing attacks, must be based on a reasonable and

---

[36] ICRC *Commentary*, p. 684.

[37] ICRC *Commentary*, p. 626.

[38] *Ibid.*, p. 626.

[39] *New Rules*, p. 279.

honest reaction to the facts and circumstances known to them from information reasonably available to them at the time· they take their actions and not on the basis of hindsight.[40]

In view of the subjective nature of such decisions, the *New Rules* suggests that parties to the conflict "should curtail the limits within which commanders of operating units exercise their discretion by issuing rules of engagement tailored to the situation prevailing in the area of conflict involved."[41]

---

[40] *Ibid.*, p. 279-80.

[41] *Ibid.*, p. 310.

Other Indiscriminate Attacks

In addition to disproportionate attacks, Article 51(4) and (5)[42] defines and prohibits other kinds of "indiscriminate" attacks. Examples of such attacks are those that are not directed at specific military objectives or that employ a method or means of combat that a party cannot direct at a specific military objective. Thus, the article prohibits parties from attacking military objectives and civilians or civilian objects without distinction.

---

[42] The relevant sections of Article 51 state:

> 4. Indiscriminate attacks are prohibited. Indiscriminate attacks are:
>
> > a) those which are not directed at a specific military objective;
> >
> > b) those which employ a method or means of combat which cannot be directed at a specific military objective; or
> >
> > c) those which employ a method or means of combat the effects of which cannot be limited as required by this Protocol; and consequently, in each such case, are of a nature to strike military objectives and civilians or civilian objects without distinction.
>
> 5. Among others, the following types of attacks are to be considered as indiscriminate:
>
> a. an attack by bombardment by any methods or means which treats as a single military objective a number of clearly separated and distinct military objectives located in a city, town, village or other area containing a similar concentration of civilians or civilian objects; and
>
> b. an attack which may be expected to cause incidental loss of civilian life, injury to civilians, damage to civilian objects, or a combination thereof, which would be excessive in relation to the concrete and direct military advantage anticipated.

218

Article 5l(5)(a) characterizes an attack as indiscriminate when it treats a number of clearly separate and distinct military objectives located in a city, town, village, or other area containing a concentration of civilians or civilian objects as a single military objective. A ground assault on a single military objective within that locale, on the other hand, would not constitute an unlawful indiscriminate attack. An attack on an entire populated area to destroy several military objectives that a party could have attacked separately, however, would be indiscriminate under this test. This provision, therefore, would prohibit the target-area aerial bombardment of densely populated civilian centers that occurred during World War II.[43]

Verification of Military Objectives

The attacker must do everything "feasible" to verify that the target(s) to be attacked is not civilian in nature.[44] "Feasible" means "that which is practical and practically possible taking into account all the circumstances at the time, including those relevant to the success of the military operation."[45] The means used to attack legitimate military targets must be carefully chosen and feasible precautions must be taken in choosing targets, with a view to avoiding, and in any event to minimizing, incidental loss of civilian life, injury to civilians and damage to civilian objects. Effective advance warning must be given of attacks that might affect the civilian population, unless circumstances do not permit this.[46]

---

[43] The *New Rules* indicates that for this rule to apply the "concentration" of civilians must actually be endangered by the attack. "[T]he rule would not be violated if the civilian population has evacuated the town or city before the attack or if the entire locality is used for military purposes." *Ibid.*, p. 309. However, civilians remaining in the town or city would retain the benefits of the rule of proportionality.

[44] Protocol I, Article 57(2)(a)(ii).

[45] *New Rules*, p. 362.

[46] Protocol I, Article 57(2)(c).

Other Prohibited Acts

In addition to the aforementioned prohibitions concerning attacks on civilian targets and the indiscriminate and disproportionate use of force, international law also prohibits the following kinds of practices, orders or actions:

- Orders that there shall be no survivors and such threats to combatants or directions to conduct hostilities on this basis.

- Murder or attacks against combatants who are captured, surrender or are placed *hors de combat*.

- Torture, any form of corporal punishment or other cruel treatment of persons under any circumstances.

- Mutilation.

- Outrages upon personal dignity, in particular humiliating and/or degrading treatment of civilians or combatants who are captured, have surrendered or are *hors de combat*.

- Collective punishments.

- Shielding.

- Hostage-taking.

- Attacks upon the wounded and sick.

- Attacks upon medical units and transports.

- Forced displacement of the civilian population for reasons connected with the conflict.

- Starvation of the civilian population.

- Threats to commit any of the foregoing acts.

Shielding

Principles of international humanitarian law forbid the parties from "shielding," that is, using the presence of the civilian population to immunize areas from military operations, or to favor or impede military operations. In addition, the parties may not direct the movement of civilians in order to attempt to shield legitimate objectives from attack or to favor military operations.[47]

Hostage-Taking

International law explicitly forbids hostage-taking. "Hostages" are defined by the ICRC *Commentary* as follows:

> Hostages are persons who find themselves, willingly or unwillingly, in the power of the enemy and who answer with their life or their freedom for compliance with the orders of the latter and for upholding the security of its armed forces.[48]

Civilians captured and held for exchange purposes are hostages, since they answer with their freedom for compliance with the orders of their captors.

Protection and Care of the Wounded and Protection of Medical Units and Transports

The wounded and sick shall be respected and protected, whether or not they have taken part in the conflict. In all circumstances, they shall be treated humanely and shall receive, to the fullest extent practicable and with the least possible delay, the required medical care. It is forbidden to distinguish between them on any grounds other than medical ones.[49]

---

[47] Protocol I, Article 51(7).

[48] ICRC *Commentary*, p. 874.

[49] Protocol I, Article 10.

It is forbidden to attack medical units and transports. Their protection may cease only if they are used to commit hostile acts outside their humanitarian function and after a warning has been given with reasonable time limits, and remains unheeded.[50] The distinctive emblem of the Red Cross shall be respected in all circumstances.

Interference with the transport of sick and wounded to the hospital, by stopping an ambulance and removing patients, does not comply with this duty to respect and protect the sick and wounded. Where the patients are gravely wounded, such intervention can so delay their care as to cause a serious deterioration in their condition, if not their death. The duty is to treat such patients with the least possible delay, which in the majority of cases will mean permitting the ambulance to continue on its way, with patients.

---

[50] Protocol I, Article 13(1) on the protection of medical units states:

1. Medical units shall be respected and protected at all times and shall not be the object of attack.

2. Paragraph 1 shall apply to civilian medical units, provided that they:

    (a) belong to one of the Parties to the conflict;
    (b) are recognized and authorized by the competent authority of one of the Parties to the conflict; or
    (c) are authorized in conformity with Article 9, paragraph 2, of this Protocol or Article 27 of the First Convention.

3. The Parties to the conflict are invited to notify each other of the location of their fixed medical units. The absence of such notification shall not exempt any of the Parties from the obligation to comply with the provisions of paragraph 1.

4. Under no circumstances shall medical units be used in an attempt to shield military objectives from attack. Whenever possible, the Parties to the conflict shall ensure that medical units are so sited that attacks against military objectives do not imperil their safety.

222

While it is proper to halt a medical vehicle briefly for purposes of establishing its non-combatant role, it is a violation of Protocol I to attack a medical vehicle without warning.[51]

Protection of Civilians from Displacement for Reasons Related to the Conflict

There are only two exceptions to the prohibition on displacement, for war-related reasons, of civilians: for their security or for imperative military reasons. "Imperative military reasons" require "the most meticulous assessment of the circumstances"[52] because such reasons are so capable of abuse. One authority has stated:

> Clearly, imperative military reasons cannot be justified by political motives. For example, it would be prohibited to move a population in order to exercise more effective control over a dissident ethnic group.[53]

Mass relocation or capture of civilians for the purpose of changing the ethnic composition of territory, in order to later justify annexation, is a political, not a military move, and does not qualify as an "imperative military reason." Destruction of civilian homes as a means to force those civilians to move is as illegal as a direct order to move.

---

[51] Protocol I, Article 13(1) states:

> The Protection to which civilian medical units are entitled shall not cease unless they are used to commit, outside their humanitarian function, acts harmful to the enemy. Protection may, however, cease only after a warning has been given setting, whenever appropriate, a reasonable time-limit, and after such warning has remained unheeded.

[52] ICRC *Commentary*, p. 1472.

[53] ICRC *Commentary*, p. 1472.

Prohibition Against Starvation of the Civilian Population

Article 54 of Protocol I expressly forbids starvation of civilians as a method of warfare, "i.e., a weapon to annihilate or weaken the population."[54] The ICRC *Commentary* states:

> To use it as a method of warfare would be to provoke it deliberately, causing the population to suffer hunger, particularly by depriving it of its sources of food or of supplies. It is clear that activities conducted for this purpose would be incompatible with the general principle of protecting the population, which the Diplomatic Conference was concerned to confirm and reinforce.[55]

Moreover:

> it is prohibited to attack, destroy, remove or render useless objects indispensable to the survival of the civilian population, such as foodstuffs, agricultural areas for the production of foodstuffs, crops, livestock, drinking water installations and supplies and irrigation works, for the specific purpose of denying them for their sustenance value to the civilian population or to the adverse Party, whatever the motive, whether in order to starve out civilians, to cause them to move away, or for any other motive.[56]

This prohibition applies only when such action is taken for the specific purpose of denying these items for their sustenance value to the civilian population of either party, or to a combination of the enemy's forces and the civilian population, but not when damage is the collateral

---

[54] ICRC *Commentary*, p. 653.

[55] *Ibid.*

[56] Protocol I, Article 54(2).

224

effect of an attack on a military target. The *New Rules* states in this regard:

> This paragraph does not prohibit the incidental distress of civilians resulting from otherwise lawful military operations. It would not, for example, be unlawful to attack or destroy a railroad line simply because the railroad was used to transport food needed to supply the population of a city, if the railroad was otherwise a military objective under Article 52 [of Protocol I]. Such incidental effects are regulated to some degree by Article 57 and Articles 68-71 dealing with relief actions.[57]

Article 54(3) specifies the two situations in which the objects covered lose their special protection from direct attack, destruction or removal.[58] Subparagraph 3(a) permits supplies of foodstuffs intended for the *sole* use of the enemy's armed forces to be attacked or destroyed. The *New Rules* indicates that this exception generally applies "to supplies already in the hands of the adverse party's armed forces because it is only at that point that one could know that they are intended for use only for the members of the enemy's armed forces."[59] However, it would not

---

[57] *New Rules*, p. 339.

[58] Protocol I, Article 54(3) states:

> The prohibitions in paragraph 2 shall not apply to such of the objects covered by it as are used by an adverse Party:
>
> a) as sustenance solely for the members of its armed forces; or
>
> b) if not as sustenance, then in direct support of military action, provided, however, that in no event shall actions against these objects be taken which may be expected to leave the civilian population with such inadequate food or water as to cause its starvation or force its movement.

[59] *New Rules*, p. 340.

be permissible to destroy objects "in the military supply system intended for the sustenance of prisoners of war, the civilian population of occupied territory or persons classified as civilians serving with, or accompanying, the armed forces."[60]

The ICRC *Commentary* indicates that this permission to target enemy armed forces' foodstuffs "is undoubtedly concerned with foodstuffs and the agricultural areas producing them, crops, livestock, and supplies of drinking water, but not with installations for drinking water or irrigation works."[61] The *Commentary* notes, however, that while "some supplies of foodstuffs or drinking water can serve to sustain the armed forces, this possibility does not seem sufficient reason for depriving such objects of the protection it was agreed to afford them."[62]

Secondly, Article 54(3)(b) of Protocol I permits attacks against objects when used for a purpose other than the subsistence of the enemy's forces and such use is "in direct support of military action." The ICRC *Commentary* provides examples of military objects used in "direct support of military action": "bombarding a food-producing area to prevent the army from advancing through it, or attacking a food-storage barn which is being used by the enemy for cover or as an arms depot, etc."[63] The *New Rules* suggests that this exception "is an extremely narrow one" not likely to be invoked frequently.[64]

Even if action is taken against covered objects under this exception, other provisions of Article 54, paragraph 3(b) limit such action by prohibiting those "which may be expected to leave the civilian population with such inadequate food or water as to cause its starvation or

---

[60] *Ibid.*, p. 340-41.

[61] ICRC *Commentary*, p. 656.

[62] *Ibid.*, p. 657.

[63] ICRC *Commentary*, p. 657. The *New Rules* gives the following examples of direct support: "an irrigation canal used as part of a defensive position, a water tower used as an observation post, or a cornfield used as cover for the infiltration of an attacking force." (p. 341.)

[64] *New Rules*, p. 341.

force its movement."[65] The *New Rules* indicates, however, that "Article 57 provides the limitations on the effects of the attack, if the purpose of the attack is to deny the adverse Party the direct support to military action afforded by the object (other than its sustenance value) and if the two-pronged test of Article 52 [military objectives] is met."[66]

Both the ICRC *Commentary* and the *New Rules* agree that the term "civilian population" referred to in paragraph 2(b) does not refer to the civilian population of the country as a whole, but rather to the population of "an immediate area," although the size of the area was not defined by the Diplomatic Conference.[67]

---

[65] *Ibid.*

[66] *Ibid.*

[67] *New Rules* p. 341; ICRC *Commentary* p. 656.

APPENDIX B: UN MEMORANDUM[68]

SECTOR NORTH
03 July 1992

MEMORANDUM

Subject: Humanitarian Aid

I refer you to your subject memo of 1 July 1992.

The football field in Bosanski Novi (BH) is clearly visible from the town of Dvor in the UNPA. Further to our many previous reports on this, let me clarify that our sense of frustration is not, as stated in Mr. Magnusson's subject memo to the FC, our "inability to investigate this matter." I believe you have received a stream of reports not only of Bosanski Novi, but also for other flash points along the border with BH (Bihac, Cazin, Velika Kladusa and Bosanski Dubica). In those reports, we highlighted the following points.

We believe the football field detainees are only a tip of the iceberg involving the concerted action of local Serbian authorities in BH trying to establish a Serbian Republic of BH, free of Muslims. In that process, the Mayors, the Milicija and TDF of Bosanski Novi, acting in unison with their counterparts, not only in the UNPA (Dvor and Kostajnica), but also with Bosanski Dubica, Banja Luka, Prijedor, Sanski Most and Kljuc. The Serbs appear to be engaged in a determined process of forcefully disarming Muslims where they are clearly a small encircled minority, such as in Bosanski Novi, or besieging their city totally, such as in Bihac. Apparently the football field is the holding ground where Muslim groups are detained while their houses are being "searched," the men isolated and transported to concentration camps.

The UNHCR representative and Civil Affairs have pieced together reports from Muslims who recently have taken refuge under UNPROFOR protection in Dvor and Kostajnica. There are reported concentration camps at the following locations:

> KERATERM: Located at a railroad station in Prijedor en route to Banja Luka. 100-200 Muslims believed to be here under extremely bad conditions.

---

[68] Reproduced by Helsinki Watch. Original available from Helsinki Watch upon request.

- TRNOPOLJE: Also located at a railroad station in Prijedor, direction Banja Luka. A refugee camp for women, children and old men.

- OMARSKA: Located in a purely Serbian village. Reportedly a camp for Muslim men and local Muslim authorities prior to Serbian take-over of control, particularly in Prijedor.

- MANJACA: Outside Banja Luka. A large camp reportedly including Croatian soldiers taken prisoner during the fighting in Kostajnica.

The treatment of Muslims and other minorities in the camps is reportedly atrocious, with regular beatings, deprivation of food and water, poor shelter, etc.

Our frustration arises from our inability to do anything other than write reports and stand by since UNPROFOR has no operational responsibilities across the border. In recent days, the situation has deteriorated and has now begun to spill over to the UNPA. We have seen a mounting number of desperate people who have crossed over to seek refuge and protection from UNPROFOR. Yesterday, one Mustafa Ogorinac swam across river Una at 8 in the morning from a camp in Bosanski Dubica. He is now under UNPROFOR protection along with two other persons. He shows signs of physical abuse and punishment.

In a separate communication (CIV\AFF\06\96, dated 30 June 1992) I appealed to the Special Envoy of the UNHCR for one temporary measure to help cope with the situation while waiting for the ICRC and UNHCR to resume their operations in BH. We have requested a minibus with driver to help in transporting the escapees to safety since UN vehicles are not to be used for humanitarian purposes. Any assistance you can lend on the acquisition of the 16-20 seater minibus and driver is most appreciated.

Regards,

TO: Ms. Y. Auger, DDCA (BELGRADE)

CC: Mr. M. Magnusson, ZAGREB

Appendix C: Helsinki Watch Report on Human Rights Abuses in the Croatian Conflict

September 1991

Helsinki Watch is gravely concerned about the deteriorating human rights situation in Croatia. Since July, human rights abuses have been committed by the Serbs, the Croats and the Yugoslav People's Army. These abuses include using civilians as human shields, taking hostages, deliberately destroying civilian property, displacing civilians, beating prisoners, shooting at medical vehicles and personnel, firing employees because of their nationality, and failing to vigorously prosecute a killing.

Helsinki Watch calls on all parties to the conflict--Serbs, Croats, and the Yugoslav army--to call a halt to these abuses and to respect their obligations under international humanitarian law.

Introduction

Croatia, one of Yugoslavia's six republics, held its first democratic election in April and May 1990. The Croatian Democratic Union (Hrvatska Demokratska Zajednica--HDZ) won a majority in Parliament and thereafter elected HDZ president Franjo Tudjman president of Croatia. With Tudjman's election Croatian nationalism soared. The new Croatian government resurrected Croatian national symbols (including the traditional Croatian flag and national anthem) which had been banned by Yugoslavia's Communists for 45 years. With the election of Tudjman's HDZ party, many former communist bureaucrats--many of whom were Serbs--were replaced with Tudjman's appointees. A Croatian Interior Ministry strengthened the republican police force, hiring thousands of new recruits, the vast majority of whom were ethnic Croats. In May 1991, a National Guard was formed to serve as the republic's army.

However, with the rise of Croatian nationalism, the Serbs in Croatia became increasingly intolerant of, and frightened by, the new Croatian government, equating it with the puppet fascist government that existed during World War II. In June 1990, Croatia's Serbs demanded cultural autonomy. Tudjman acceded and drafted a plan for cultural autonomy for ethnic Serbs, the largest of Croatia's ethnic minorities. Thereafter, the Serbs demanded political autonomy, including control over local police stations in areas where Serbs constitute a majority; this, however, was unacceptable to the Croatian government. Since then, some Serbs have refused to recognize the new Croatian government or to participate in the Croatian Parliament as an opposition group.

Serbs constitute 11.5 percent (550,000) of the 4.5 million people in Croatia. Of Yugoslavia's 23.5 million people, Serbs (the largest ethnic group) account for 36 percent of the population while Croats (the second largest) account for 20 percent. Throughout 1990, Serbs developed their own institutions of government in some areas where they constitute a majority. In August 1990, in the predominantly Serbian town of Knin (population 15,000), Serbs held a referendum to proclaim an autonomous region, "Krajina." In subsequent months, other Serbian-populated areas of Croatia held similar referendums. These towns also declared themselves to be part of Krajina, now formally called the Independent and Autonomous Region of Krajina (Samostalna Autonomna Oblast Krajina--SAOK). Rejecting Croatian rule, the Serbs created their own institutions of government, including a police force and an army.

231

Throughout Croatia, Serbs erected barricades and checkpoints on roads leading into their villages in an effort to assume control of the region and to prevent the Croatian authorities from exercising their jurisdiction.

Since August 1990, the Serbian protest against the Croatian government has become an armed insurrection. In March 1991, Serbian insurgents occupied the police station in Pakrac and tried to take over the Plitvice National Park in Croatia. In April through July, fighting between Serbian insurgents and Croatian police escalated in frequency and intensity.

Since coming to power, the Croatian government has moved toward greater independence from the Yugoslav federal government. Initially, Croatia advocated the transformation of Yugoslavia from a single federal entity to a union of sovereign states. In 1991, the impetus for complete independence intensified. In February 1991, the governments of Croatia and neighboring Slovenia declared that their respective republican laws took precedence over federal Yugoslav laws. On June 25, 1991, Slovenia and Croatia declared their independence. Since then, battles between Serbs and Croats have become commonplace in Croatia.

Since June 1991, militant Serbs have gone on the offensive to establish military control in areas which have substantial Croatian minorities. Croatian authorities have played a defensive role in most cases and resisted Serbian military advances. Differences between the Serbs and Croats have led to an escalation in violence against civilians: displacement of thousands of people, abuse of humanitarian personnel, taking of hostages, use of human shields, brutal beatings, discrimination and other abuses.

In many cases, there is evidence pointing to army complicity on the side of the Serbian insurgents. The Yugoslav People's Army (Jugoslavenska Narodna Armija--JNA) was authorized to act as a buffer between the two sides in order to prevent further bloodshed. However, the JNA, whose officer corps is predominantly Serbian and whose interests lie in the preservation of a Yugoslav state, has continued to intervene in the conflict apparently without authorization from its civilian commander-in-chief, the Yugoslav Presidency. These interventions have had the effect of preserving territorial gains made by the Serbs in Croatia.

232

This newsletter briefly highlights the main abuses currently being committed by both sides in the conflict in Croatia.[1]

Positions of the Serbs and the Croats

Although contemporary socio-economic and political problems divide the Serbs and Croats, a tumultuous and bloody history has left deep scars on the consciousness of both peoples. During World War II, while Yugoslavia was occupied by the Nazis and Italian fascists, a fierce civil war was waged among Croats, Serbs and communists. The Independent State of Croatia (Nezavisna Drzava Hrvatska--NDH) was a fascist state run by the Nazis and Italian fascists. Under the NDH, Croatian fascists (Ustasa) massacred thousands of Serbs, Jews, Gypsies and others. Similarly, Serbian Cetniks, a group loyal to the Serbian king in exile, massacred thousands of Croats, Muslims and others. The Cetniks advocated the creation of a "Greater Serbia," in which Serbia would annex most of Croatia and all of Macedonia, Montenegro and Bosnia-Hercegovina. Both the Cetniks and the Ustasa were defeated by Marshal Tito's communist partisans. After the war, Tito massacred thousands of civilians as part of a campaign to purge all "enemy elements" in the new-found communist Yugoslavia.

The atrocities committed during World War II have left bitter memories in both Serbs and Croats. Indeed, the war continues to be a subject of constant debate; memories of the war are among the many obstacles blocking reconciliation. Both sides stress that the current conflict is not an ethnic conflict but the result of rabid nationalist activities by the opposite side. Each is willing to believe gruesome tales of atrocities committed by the other, but such stories can rarely be substantiated. The Serbian and Croatian press exaggerate and often misrepresent the news, exacerbating the fears of both Serbs and Croats.

---

[1] This newsletter documents violations investigated by Jemera Rone, Counsel to Human Rights Watch, and Ivana Nizich, Consultant to Helsinki Watch, during a mission to Yugoslavia from July 23 to August 14. Elliot Schrage, a New York attorney, participated in the mission from July 24 to August 1.

The Serbian Position

Serbs living in Croatia feel threatened by the resurrection of Croatian nationalism--both within the Croatian government and among the general populace. The Serbs claim that such fervent nationalism is a prelude to the resurrection of the World War II Nazi puppet state under which thousands of Serbs were killed. They believe that an independent Croatia would be a fascist state. They particularly object to the strengthening of the police force and the formation of the National Guard, which in their view are Croatian instruments of terror to be used against the Serbian population in Croatia. They do not want to live in areas where the traditional Croatian flag flies, claiming that thousands of Serbs were massacred under that flag during World War II. They view traditional Croatian songs as fascist, anti-Serbian and anti-Yugoslav.

The Serbs, 11.5 percent of Croatia's population, do not want to be labeled as an ethnic minority in Croatia. They fear that, as an ethnic minority, they would be treated as second class citizens. In particular, the Serbs vehemently oppose the new Croatian constitution of December 1990 and its preamble which states that "...the Republic of Croatia is comprised as the national state of the Croatian people and all minorities who are citizens of Croatia, including Serbs, Muslims, Slovenes, Czechs, Slovaks, Italians, Hungarians, Jews and others, for whom equality with those citizens of Croatian nationality is guaranteed, as is the realization of national rights in accordance with the democratic norms of the United Nations and all countries in the democratic world." The Serbs reject their relegation to minority status and have demanded that the preamble read as follows: "...the Republic of Croatia is comprised as the national state of the Croatian and Serbian peoples and all other nationalities and minorities who are citizens of Croatia, including Muslims, Slovenes, Czechs, Slovaks, Italians, Hungarians, Jews and others." According to the Serbs, such language would guarantee them equal status as a nationality.

Some Serbs claim that the Serbian people have contributed much to the freedom of the Croats because the Serbs "liberated" the Croats from the horrors of fascism during World War II. As "liberators," the Serbs believe that the Croats are indebted to them and that the relegation of Serbs to a minority status denigrates their contribution to Croatian society.

The Serbs claim to have been persecuted since the new Croatian government came to power. They claim that they do not have the right to use their Cyrillic alphabet and language throughout Croatia; they reject Croatian as the official language of Croatia and ask that both the Latin and Cyrillic alphabets be used throughout the republic, not just at the local level. While conceding that they held a disproportionate number of high-level positions while Croatia was under communist rule, they assert that they are now being dismissed from their jobs because of their national origin. Many Serbs have quit the Croatian police force and others claim that they were pressured to leave. Under the communist regime, Serbs made up the vast majority of the Croatian police force. Now they comprise less than 25 percent. Indeed, many Serbian police officers have joined the Krajina police force and insurgent army. Serbs also complain of ethnic harassment on the job and of being required to sign loyalty oaths to the Croatian government in the work place. Others claim that the Croatian government wants to create an "ethnically pure" state and, therefore, is trying to drive the Serbs from Croatia.

Politically, Serbs in Croatia and elsewhere call for the preservation of Yugoslavia as a strong federal state. The Serbs in Croatia have declared that they will secede from Croatia if Croatia secedes from Yugoslavia, and that they will take large areas of Croatia's land with them. The position of many Serbian insurgents is: "If the Croats want to secede from Yugoslavia, good riddance to them. But if they secede, they will not take one Serb, or any land on which a Serb lives, with them." Other Serbs have called for a "Greater Serbia," in which Serbia would rule all of present-day Yugoslavia, except for Zagreb (the Croatian capital) and its environs, and Slovenia.

The Croatian Position

The Croats seem bewildered by Serbian fears of the resurrection of Nazism in Croatia. "If we've lived together for forty-five years, why can't we do so now? What do we have to gain from killing thousands of Serbs who were our neighbors until yesterday?" is a frequent refrain among Croats. The Croats point to their December 1990 constitution which guarantees equal civil and political rights to all ethnic minorities. They note Article XXI of the Constitution, which expressly grants the right of the Serbian population to use both the Latin and Cyrillic alphabets in areas where Serbs constitute a majority.

Many Croats believe that the current Serbian insurrection is the creation of the federal government in Belgrade, whose aim is to bring about the fall of the Croatian government and to re-instate Serbian and communist control over its territory. They believe that Slobodan

235

Milosevic, the president of the Republic of Serbia, is manipulating the cause of human rights to achieve an "imperialist" goal. A frequently cited example is Kosovo, where the Serbian government justified its repression of the majority ethnic Albanian population and suspension of Albania's political rights on the basis of purported human rights abuses by Albanians against local Serbs and Montenegrins.

Many Croats explain the resurrection of Croatian nationalism in the past year as a reaction to forty-five years of communist repression and Serbian hegemony. The Croats are particularly bitter about Tito's crackdown against nationalist Croats who called for greater autonomy from the central government in the early 1970s. They also feel that although they constituted a majority in their own republic, they had little control over their own fate and that Croatia was in fact a vassal of Belgrade. They say that Serbs held a disproportionate number of high-level government and commercial positions in Croatia during the previous communist regime, partially because the Serbs joined the League of Communists[2] in far greater numbers than did the Croats.

Many Croatian government officials have insisted that the current Serbian insurgency involves only a fraction of the Serbian population in Croatia. They claim that only 24 percent of the Serbs in Croatia live in areas controlled by the insurgents while the remaining 76 percent live side-by-side with Croats and are active participants in Croatia's political, cultural and professional communities. According to the Ministry of the Interior, of the 550,000 Serbs living in Croatia, only 10,000 to 15,000 have joined the insurgency.

The Croats do not regard the current fighting as an inter-ethnic conflict; they view it as a conflict between democratic forces that were legitimately elected and old-guard communist forces fearful of losing their privileges under a new regime. Croats assert that their democratically-elected government represents the forces of democracy, free market economics and restored Croatian pride. The vast majority of Croats support the present government and Croatian independence.

Conversely, many Croats consider the Serbian government of Slobodan Milosevic to be the real cause of the Serbian insurrection. Croats fear that Milosevic wants to preserve communist rule in Yugoslavia and to create a "Greater Serbia." For these reasons, Croats believe that Milosevic waved the banner of Serbian nationalism and

---

[2] The official name for Yugoslavia's former ruling communist party.

planted the seed of fear of persecution among Croatia's Serbs through his propaganda, amplified by the Serbian media, claiming that an independent Croatia would be a reincarnation of the Nazi puppet state. Moreover, the Croats accuse the Serbian government and the Yugoslav People's Army of materially aiding the Serbian insurgents in Croatia with weapons, ammunition, fuel, and monetary support.

Croats are particularly angry at the JNA, which they view as a Serbian, rather than a Yugoslav, army. Croats claim that by acting as a "buffer" between the insurgents and the Croatian police, the JNA has in fact prevented the legitimate Croatian government from regaining control over territory it lost to the Serbian insurgents. They claim that the JNA supplies the Serbian insurgents with advanced weaponry and intelligence and provides them sanctuary and reinforcements when it appears that Serbian insurgents are losing a battle to the Croatian police and National Guard. The Croats claim that the JNA is now a party to the conflict. They accuse the army not only of actively fighting on the side of the Serbian insurgents but also of unilaterally assaulting Croatian security forces and innocent civilians.

International Law

Protocol II of 1977 to the 1949 Geneva Conventions governs the conduct of internal armed conflicts. Yugoslavia has ratified Protocol II. Its provisions apply not only to the conduct of the federal army but also to the republican armies and police forces that participate in hostilities, such as the Croatian National Guard and the Croatian police.

The provisions of Protocol II apply equally to the conduct of the Serbian insurgents, regardless of their legal capacity to ratify the Protocol, because they qualify under Protocol II, Article 1 as "dissident armed forces or other organized armed groups which, under responsible command, exercise such control over a part of ... territory as to enable them to carry out sustained and concerted military operations and to implement this Protocol."

The Serbian resistance to the Croatian government is well-organized and well-armed. It extends to three different regions of Croatia, 1) the so-called "Krajina" region of eastern Dalmatia and Lika, 2) Banija and 3) Slavonija and Baranja. The Krajina region has been under Serbian control since mid-August 1990. Within a period of two months (June-August 1991), Serbian insurgents took over government buildings and gained substantial territory by force in Slavonija, Baranja, and Banija.

A Serbian-run government parallel to the Croatian government has existed since August 1990 in Krajina. The Serbian command thus is sufficiently well-organized and controls sufficient territory in Croatia to be held responsible for the conduct of Serbian combatants. This is true regardless of whether, as Croatian officials uniformly allege, they are funded and controlled by the government of the Republic of Serbia and receive arms from the Yugoslav Army.

Both Croatian and Serbian villagers set up armed patrols to protect their communities from attack from the opposite side. Both sides consistently refer to combatants who are villagers as "civilians," although when asked they concede that the "civilians" are armed, but only with "pistols and hunting rifles," and that they are only "defending the village."

Under the rules of war, those actively participating in hostilities lose their civilian status and become combatants during the period of their combat participation, which includes defensive, as well as offensive action.

Human Rights and Humanitarian Law Abuses

Human Shields

International humanitarian law forbids the use of human shields in warfare. "The presence of civilians...shall not be used to render certain points or areas immune from military operations, in particular in attempts to shield military objectives from attacks or to shield, favor or impede military operations." (See Protocol I, Article 51 (7), to the 1949 Geneva Conventions.)

On July 26, Serbs organized an offensive from the town of Dvor (85.6 percent Serbian)[3] to dislodge the Croatian police in the village of

---

[3] An effort will be made to identify the ethnic make-up of each area throughout this report. The figures cited reflect the results of Yugoslavia's April 1991 census or witnesses' recollections of their villages' demography. (Official census results were excerpted from "Popis Stanovnistva, Domacinstva, Stanova, i Poljoprivrednih Gospodarstvo u 1991. Godini; Pucanstvo Republike Hrvatske po Nacionalnom Sastavu, Vjerskoj Pripadnosti i Materinskom Jeziku," Zagreb: Republickog Zavoda za Statistiku Republike Hrvatske, Broj 21.4, 19.07.1991.)

Kozibrod (predominantly Croatian). En route to Kozibrod, the Serbs captured 30 to 50 villagers, including women and handicapped and elderly persons, from the Croatian villages of Struga and Zamlaca. The insurgents forced their captives to walk in a long column, shoulder-to-shoulder, with their hands held high, in front of the advancing Serbian insurgents. The villagers were used as human shields for approximately six hours until a village defender threw a hand grenade and the captured civilians scattered. One of the hostages, a 75-year-old woman, was killed. According to hostages interviewed a week after the assault, their houses were ransacked and robbed by the Serbian insurgents and several hostages were beaten, including a 20-year-old woman who lost three teeth. In addition, in front of the hostages, Serbian rebels abused and humiliated three Croatian police officers who surrendered, and then forced them to run, shooting and killing all three.

One month before the attack, the Serbs in Dvor had erected barricades to control entrance and exit from their town. In response, the villagers in Struga had done the same, fearing a Serbian attack. On July 26, at approximately 9:30 a.m., the Serbs started to mortar Struga for 90 minutes and then proceeded to enter the village of Zamlaca, which is situated between Dvor and Struga. According to witnesses, two Serbs were manning light artillery on a truck. The Serbian insurgents entered each house, ransacked the premises and dragged the occupants out to the street. Helsinki Watch interviewed a woman and her daughter, both of whom had been used as human shields, as was their 75-year-old grandmother, who later was killed in the fighting. The mother described the assault on Zamlaca:

> The Serbs started pulling people out of the houses and lining them up as a buffer zone. People were taken at random; some managed to escape. Others hiding in the houses were not found when the Serbs searched them. . . . The Serbs opened fire on our house and we ran out, scared.

The daughter added:

> We captured civilians were made to walk with our hands lifted in the air. We were not allowed to look back: we could only look straight ahead. We were made to stand in a long line, a phalanx, shoulder to shoulder, like

cattle. Some 50 civilians, men and women, were rounded up in Zamlaca and made to walk toward Struga; we were used as human shields. The civilians included young and old women, including my 75-year-old grandmother and a mentally retarded woman who they refused to let go. We in the phalanx walked ahead with two Serbs pointing automatic weapons at us from behind. Behind those two, the truck with the artillery was being driven. Behind the truck were armed Serbs, I do not know how many. It looked like quite a lot.

It took us six hours to get through Zamlaca and halfway into Struga because they stopped in front of each Croatian house in Zamlaca and shot it up, forcing people to come out, then harassing them and making them join the line-up. This took a long time. We kept our hands above our heads the whole time and were not given food or water. We were not allowed to sit down.

During the assault, the Serbian insurgents beat their captives, including two women, cousins aged 19 and 20. The witnesses recounted the beatings:

Visnja Blazevic was wearing a crucifix which they made her take off and throw to the floor. Then they demanded that she stomp on it. They beat her on the arms with rifle butts and now she has difficulty moving her fingers. I think her nerves have been damaged.

After they beat Visnja, they turned to the other girl, Milita Blazevic. Her brother was one of the men defending Struga and he had oil for a gun in their house. When the Serbs found the oil, they took her out of the column. They beat her because they found the gun oil in her house. We did not see the beating because we were not allowed to turn around, but we heard her screaming. Then they sent her back to the column. She was black and blue, her mouth was swollen and she could barely walk. They beat others as well during this ordeal.

Two young Croatian men (aged 23 and 27), on patrol in Struga at the time of the assault, confirmed the mother's and the daughter's stories:

> During the time they were taking hostages in Zamlaca, Struga was being attacked from the forest and we could not see what was happening in Zamlaca. However, when they entered Struga, we saw that they had captured people to use as human shields. They put the people in front of the truck, making them march ahead. There were about 30-40 people; I think 37 in all. They filled up the entire width of the street. They had their hands up in the air, although many had been beaten and could not keep their hands up.
>
> We [in Struga] did not know what to do. Some of our relatives were captured and used as shields. My mother and his sister [referring to his friend] were being used as shields. We could not shoot at our
>
> families. We retreated to the center of the village so we could consolidate our forces.

Both the mother and the daughter interviewed by Helsinki Watch claimed that they knew many of their assailants. They recounted the names of ten Serbs they recognized guarding, beating and harassing them that day. According to the hostages, after the Serbs finished beating the two women, one of the Serbs found three Croatian police officers in a house in Struga. According to the daughter, the Serbs

> made the Croatian police officers get down on their hands and knees while they rode on their backs. Then they made the three captives strip down to their underwear and told them to run. While they were running, they shot them and hit them. Then they laughed and said, "You see, we had to shoot. They were trying to escape!" After they were wounded, the Serbs shot at them again. They made us move on and we did not see the rest.

The two men defending Struga saw part of this ordeal as well:

> The Serbs encircled the house where three Croatian
> police officers were on the roof. These three saw that
> they did not stand a chance since they were vastly
> outnumbered. They went downstairs and surrendered.
> I saw the three police officers running through the fields.
> They [the Serbs] shot and killed them. We know the
> names of the dead police officers. They were all between
> 21 and 26 years old.

According to the witnesses and captives, the Serbian insurgents
were shooting at houses and over the heads of the civilian shields. They
received no return fire during this entire period. When the insurgents
entered Struga, they continued their pillaging; a civilian, Manda Ulakovic,
was shot in the shoulder.

The 23-year-old Struga defender continued to recount the
advance into Struga:

> The Cetniks[4] continued their advance through the
> village, dragging women and children out of their homes,
> stopping to smash up houses and cars. Behind them, I
> saw cars and trucks that were carrying out televisions and
> other items from the houses.

As the Serbs advanced through Struga, they passed a wall behind
which were hidden a Croatian police officer and a civilian from Struga.
The 23-year-old continued:

---

[4] During World War II, the Cetniks were a band of Serbian extremists
engaged in the civil war against both the Ustasa and the communist partisans.
The Croats commonly refer to the current Serbian insurgents as Cetniks because
they equate their current actions with those committed against Croats and
Muslims during World War II. Some of the Serbian insurgents Helsinki Watch
interviewed vehemently reject the label of "Cetnik," claiming they are merely
defenders of their land and not extremists. Others speak with praise of Vojislav
Seselj, leader of the right-wing Serbian Cetnik Movement, which is gaining
adherents, particularly among the young, in Serbia.

242

After the hostages passed the wall, the police officer and
the villager jumped out from behind the wall and threw
a grenade at the truck with the artillery. The hostages
ran into the ravines and the Serbs shot at them but
missed. The Croatian police opened fire after the
hostages began running away and anarchy resulted.

The villager who threw the grenade had three more grenades
strapped around his waist and they exploded on his body. Both he and
the police officer were killed. The mother and the daughter who had
been used as human shields told Helsinki Watch that the villager had
saved their lives. "The villager sacrificed himself for us. He was 37 years
old with a wife and two children. The police officer who sacrificed
himself was Zeljko Filipovic, a Serb. Both were very brave."

As the gunfight between the Croats and Serbs ensued, the 75-
year-old grandmother was badly wounded in the leg. However, given the
ferocity of the battle, no one could come to her aid and she died about
one hour later, having bled to death. After about ninety minutes of
fighting, the army intervened. The 23-year-old defender described the
army's actions:

The army had a post close to the village. Our side did
not call the army in. It is quite ironic that the army did
not intervene when the Serbs were pillaging the villages
and using people as human shields but did get involved
when it appeared that the Serbs were losing the fight to
the Croats in Struga. Where was the army when they
[the Serbian insurgents] were taking the civilians?

The Zamlaca villagers spent the night in Struga and returned to
their village the next day to look at their homes.

We found that everything had been wrecked; the door
was broken, the windows were shattered, the mattresses
and pillows on the couch were ripped, there were holes
in the wall, the telephone and television were smashed
and even the bird cage was destroyed and the birds were
killed.

243

My neighbor came to tell me that my husband had been killed. People who managed to escape capture in the village spent the night in hiding in Zamlaca. At one point, they heard my husband say "You're not going to fire at me?" and then they heard shots. We think he knew his attacker.

The villagers believe that when the Serbs retreated from Struga to Dvor, passing Zamlaca en route, they killed one man and took five men and one child hostage. The whereabouts of the six were unknown at the time of our interview. The villagers returned to Struga but fled to Red Cross shelters shortly thereafter. The mother told Helsinki Watch what happened after they returned to Struga:

The army took all our weapons and went off into the hills to negotiate with the bandits. They did not show us any compassion or offer any help, so we were afraid. Why were they constantly negotiating with the bandits if they were supposed to be protecting us? The army told us "If we hear one gunshot from within Struga, we will destroy the village." We left out of fear.

The mother added emphatically, "The Serbs are not refugees. They are fleeing to safety before they pick a fight. We are the refugees."

Taking of Hostages

Protocol II, Article 4 (2)(c) strictly forbids the taking of hostages. Hostages are defined by the International Committee of the Red Cross in its commentary on this article as "persons who are in the power of a party to the conflict or its agent, willingly or unwillingly, and who answer with their freedom, their physical integrity or their life for the execution of orders given by those in whose hands they have fallen, or for any hostile acts committed against them."[5]

---

[5] Commentary on the Additional Protocols of 8 June 1977 to the Geneva Conventions of 12 August 1949. International Committee of the Red Cross. Geneva: Cz Nijhoff Publishers 1987.

Three categories of hostages are being held by the Serbs. The first is those captured after combat, such as the 16 Croatian police officers who surrendered when their police station in Glina was overrun by Serbian rebels on June 26. They were told they were being held for exchange. They were all taken to the Knin jail, where beatings administered to them and other prisoners, including electric shock, ceased a week before our visit, after complaints to the International Committee of the Red Cross.[6]

The second category of hostages is those captured at home or at insurgent checkpoints, including unarmed civilians and off-duty police officers.

The third category of hostages is those Croats who are not held in any jail but who are not permitted to leave old Tenja in Slavonija. At the time of Helsinki Watch's visit, these included elderly people and one Catholic priest. There may be 30 to 50 people who want to leave but have been refused permission by the Serbian insurgents. Some Croats living in old Tenja apparently remain voluntarily.

Prisoners Held for Exchange

As of August 12, 51 Croats were held in the Knin jail for exchange (some of whom were released the next day), and as of July 27, 13 were held in Borovo Selo, in Slavonija. During the July 26-29 fighting in the Banija region of Croatia, some 15 prisoners were held in a mountain base, all of whom were released (some in exchanges) by July 31. Others may be held in other locations. Although almost all Croatian hostages were exchanged for imprisoned Serbian insurgents between August 10 and 15, the insurgents resumed taking hostages almost immediately afterwards.

Judge Dozet, the criminal court judge of Knin, told Helsinki Watch on August 12 that none of the 51 prisoners held in the Knin jail had been charged with a crime, nor did they have defense attorneys. The judge said that because of the confused political situation in Krajina the Knin government is in the process of expanding its court and deciding what law to apply, whether Croatian, Serbian or federal Yugoslav statutes. Helsinki Watch regards this as a pretext.

---

[6] Helsinki Watch interviewed some of the Knin prisoners privately in jail on August 12 and a prisoner released from Borovo Selo on July 30.

The Croatian prisoners held by the Serbs in Knin are, in most cases, treated as prisoners of war by their captors, with regular access to them by the International Committee of the Red Cross and Helsinki Watch. The Geneva Convention makes detailed provisions for prisoners of war in international armed conflict. But humanitarian law does not recognize such a status in an internal armed conflict, and the government is free to arrest and try rebels for common crimes who would be immune from prosecution if they were involved in an international armed conflict. Thus, the killing of combatants by rebels in the course of conflict is still murder under domestic law.

On the other side, Croatian authorities have not waived their right to try Serbian detainees as common criminals. They protest that there is a big difference between people held hostage by insurgents and persons held in regularly constituted jails in Croatia charged with violations of the criminal code and protected by all due process guarantees (none of which have been suspended). Their willingness to participate in these exchanges makes it likely, however, that the Serbs will continue to capture Croats for purposes of exchange.

Hostages Confined in Old Tenja

Between 30 and 50 Croatian residents living in old Tenja, in Slavonija, want to leave the Serbian-controlled town but are not permitted to do so by the Serbs. They have been told that they are being held as hostages. At the time of our visit, the insurgents were holding hostage a Catholic priest, Tomislav Cvenic.[7] During Helsinki Watch's interview, the chief of police of Knin, capital of the SAO Krajina, and insurgents in old Tenja in Slavonija openly admitted that they have taken persons captive in order to exchange them for Serbs held in jail in Croatia. They also informed the prisoners that they are being held for exchange.

Tenja, a village of 8,500, six kilometers from the district capital of Osijek, is divided into two sections, the old and new sectors. New Tenja's 35 percent Croatian population evacuated the village in haste on June 29-30 after violence escalated. Some Croats living in predominantly Serbian old Tenja were prevented from leaving because the Serbs had set up barricades to defend against an anticipated attack. The attack came

---

[7] Cvenic was released on August 15.

246

on July 7 from a combined force of Croatian police and National Guard and lasted five hours until the army intervened.[8] In the current stalemate, new Tenja remains uninhabited, separated by a one-and-a-half kilometer stretch of no-man's land from old Tenja, a garrison town with only defenders and support personnel. All of the children have been evacuated. Sporadic fighting continues from behind barricades on both sides, with casualties.

Old Tenja is isolated by mutual barricades only from Croatian-controlled territory. Serbs come and go by car through Serbian-controlled villages to the Republic of Serbia across the Danube, where we interviewed displaced persons who had taken this route before and after fighting broke out in their communities.

According to several different sources, Croats asked the Osijek chapter of the Red Cross to help their trapped relatives leave old Tenja. The Red Cross was allowed to contact many of these people on July 17, but the action was terminated by the Serbian insurgents and the Red Cross had to leave without without taking with them any Croats who wanted to be evacuated.

Helsinki Watch visited old Tenja on July 29, escorted everywhere by insurgent officials. Among other things, we asked and were permitted to interview, in private, the Catholic priest remaining in town, a Croat. The priest, Father Tomislav Cvenic, said:

> Those who wanted to leave have not been able to leave. I am sure you know this. They will not let me leave. My mother was living here and she is diabetic. The first time the Red Cross came [on July 10], they evacuated my mother. I thought that I could leave at the same time and that is when they told me that I was being held hostage.

> After the Red Cross arrived, I went out on the street. They had a gun. Then they told me, "Pastor, go back in the house." I could not leave. It was clear to me that I was a hostage. "We're not really savages," they told me. "Fine, then let me go. There's

---

[8] The army did not side with the elected republican government of Croatia to defeat an armed challenge to its authority but positioned itself between the two forces.

no point in me staying, all my parishioners have left," I said. "That might be true, but we have to use you as a hostage." Those were their exact words. They did not tell me why they were holding me hostage. I think that they are waiting for a situation to come up so that they can use me if they need me.

According to the priest, on the second visit of the Red Cross the local Serbian command accompanied the Red Cross on its interviews of those Croats who wanted to leave. "About 20 to 30 people got in the Red Cross bus to go. There was some misunderstanding and the Red Cross effort was cut off. No one left."

The priest has not been physically mistreated and neighbors bring him food.

Their relations with me have been quite good. There has been no harassment. But they will not let me go anywhere. They do not say I am under house arrest but none of us can go outside because we are afraid of being shot because we are of the wrong ethnic group. All the Croatian phones except for mine have been taken away by the local Serbian command. All I can do is call Osijek. The command told me that my telephone would be take away soon.

He does not say mass at the church because all his parishioners are too afraid to attend.[9] "We cannot walk on the streets. We are afraid because all of them are armed. Since July 1, I have not been out of this house at all."

The Serbian spokesperson, a military advisor nicknamed "Djilas," said that they did not release the priest and other Croats in old Tenja because

You have to remember, this is a war. We have to take precautions and we may take the priest's phone away. This is far

---

[9] Our escort asked the priest to unlock the church to show us that Croatian publicity about the desecration of the Catholic church was a lie. It did not appear that any damage had been done to the interior portions of the church we saw, including the altar.

different from beating and killing him, however. You have to remember that the Croatian Democratic Union (HDZ) started in this town in the Roman Catholic Church. This priest helped organize the HDZ with his sermons and homilies.

This suggests the priest is being held on account of his prior exercise of free speech.

According to "Djilas," Serbs were holding the Croats because 1) their release would result in bad publicity since they would denounce "Serb abuses" and 2) the release would jeopardize Serbian military security.

Destruction of Civilian Property

In Croatia, the destruction of civilian property has been used as a means of fear and intimidation. In many cases, the damage to civilian property is used as a method to drive people out of their village. On July 7, the village of Celije in Slavonija was burned and destroyed by Serbian insurgents. Celije, a Croatian village of 158 individuals, is surrounded by Serbian villages.

In May 1991, Serbs in the neighboring villages isolated Celije by putting up roadblocks and, in some cases, prevented the Croats from travelling to Vukovar or Osijek. The nearest commander in the neighboring Serbian village of Bobota (population 3,000) demanded that the Celije residents surrender their arms or face the consequences. Fifty members of the Croatian National Guard were sent to Celije to defend the village and they patrolled Celije with the local residents from June 25 to July 7, repelling sporadic attacks by Serbian insurgents in neighboring villages.

On July 7[10], a strong attack was launched against Celije. After fighting between the Croats in Celije and the Serbian insurgents, the Croats fled the village under army escort. Two days later, those from Bobota burned 70 percent of the homes in Celije. Helsinki Watch

---

[10] This was the day of a concerted attack by the Croatian National Guard and police forces on the nearby Serbian-controlled village of old Tenja for the purpose of dislodging the Serbian barricades from the village and making it possible for those Croats who had fled to return to their homes. Tenja is approximately 6 kilometers from Osijek.

reviewed photographs taken by a Spanish photographer in Celije. Houses were in fact burned and it appeared that explosives had blown off the roofs. Some walls were left standing and burn marks from the fire were visible. There was damage to cars, tractors, and the local church, whose altar had tumbled over. Graffiti was written on the school wall, which read "Ustasa[11], we will return and massacre you."

Serbian insurgents in Bobota admitted to outsiders that they burned the houses in Celije because the Croats refused to hand over their arms and because they claimed that the Croats were occupying Serbian land. In addition, they said that one of the Celije villagers arrived in Celije on foot through the fields after the evacuation. An outside observer was told by the Bobota insurgents that the victim "had a gun and shot at those from Bobota, who returned fire, thus killing him. They threw his dead body in his house and burned it all down."

In other regions, Croats have destroyed the homes of Serbs as a means of intimidating and driving them out. In the town of Trpolje, near Sibenik, Helsinki Watch representatives examined the remains of three apartment buildings which were severely damaged by explosives. Graffiti and derogatory remarks demanding that all Serbs, Muslims, Albanians and Gypsies leave the area were scrawled on the walls.

Explosions have become commonplace in Croatia and, in most cases, property is destroyed for revenge. For example, if a Serb destroys a Croatian house one evening, a Croat will destroy a Serbian house the next evening. In Knin, Croatian and Albanian homes and places of business have been systematically destroyed since August 1990. In Tenja, Helsinki Watch representatives saw an Albanian-owned kiosk which was burnt by a riot of Serbs celebrating the victory of the Serbian Red Star soccer team at the European championship games. In May 1991, after Franko Lisica, a Croatian police officer from the village of Bibinje, was killed, the Croatian villagers came to the nearby city of Zadar and, in a riot, destroyed places of business owned by Serbs and Serbian and Yugoslav firms, such as the Yugoslav Airlines (JAT) offices.

In most cases, the Croatian authorities have sent inspectors to the scene of the damage, but few perpetrators have been apprehended. The Croatian insurance company has agreed to cover the losses suffered by

---

[11] The Ustasa were Croatian fascists who killed thousands of Serbs during World War II. The term is considered to be derogatory and today's Croatia's nationalists vehemently deny that they are Ustasa sympathizers.

the Serbian places of business destroyed in Zadar. Despite these steps, Helsinki Watch is concerned that not enough is being done to prevent individual destruction of civilian property and calls upon respective authorities in Croatian- and Serbian-controlled regions to take measures to punish those found guilty of such crimes and to prevent such violence in the future.

Displacement of Persons

Protocol II, Article 17, forbids the forced displacement of civilians for reasons connected with the conflict, with two exceptions: their personal safety or imperative military reasons. It specifically states that "civilians shall not be compelled to leave their own territory for reasons connected with the conflict."

Using military means to force members of an ethnic group from their homes and villages as was done to the Croats in Banija and Slavonija is forbidden since it is done on a discriminatory basis and not on the basis of individual security. Furthermore, there is no imperative military reason that overrides prohibitions on such ethnic discrimination.

In Slavonija, the residents of Celije and new Tenja have been forcibly displaced. In Celije, the Croats were attacked repeatedly by people from surrounding Serbian villages between June 25 and July 7. After the assault on July 7, the residents of Celije fled and were prevented from returning to their homes because 70 percent of their homes had been burned on July 9 and a member of their village had been killed after he returned to the village. Of the 158 people who lived in Celije, 154 were placed by the Red Cross. Fifty-three families lived in Celije before the attack and now the village is deserted. Zlatko Kramaric, the mayor of Osijek, believes that the Serbian insurgents are trying to purge Croats from areas which are ethnically mixed. Kramaric told Helsinki Watch that "Celije was the first case of burning of a Croatian village. It appears that they [the Serbs] may try to do this in Banija as well, to ethnically purify the districts, so as to convince the United States and the European Community that they are fighting to keep what appears to be ethnically pure Serbian territory."

Also, in new Tenja, a series of shooting incidents and explosions forced the villagers to flee either to Osijek or Serbian-controlled old Tenja. In peacetime, Tenja's population totals 8,000. Of the 4,500 who live in the old part of Tenja, 90 percent are Serbian. Of the 3,500 people who lived in new Tenja, 60 percent were Serbian and 40 percent were

Croatian. Of the 3,500 people who lived in new Tenja, 60 percent were Serbian and 40 percent were Croatian. Currently, 4,000 people live in Serbian-controlled old Tenja and only a Croatian police station operates in new Tenja. In late June, shootings throughout Tenja began to frighten the local population. The majority of the population of new Tenja fled on June 29. A Croatian reserve police officer interviewed by Helsinki Watch claimed that his house was hit by a rocket-propelled grenade (RPG) in late June:

> On June 26, for no reason, the Serbs opened fire at the houses on my street, which is predominantly Croatian. Although old Tenja is majority Serbian, there are two streets that are populated by Croatian families. From June 26 to 30, there was shooting at night, with only a few shots during the day. After June 30, there was shooting during the night and day. We could not sleep. Most of the Croats fled to Osijek out of fear.

In Banija, the residents of Struga and Zamlaca were forcibly displaced by a Serbian assault aimed at the village of Kozibrod.[12] Moreover, it appears that the army required that all the villagers of Struga and Zamlaca evacuate. Those who had been used as human shields returned to Zamlaca the next day, only to be told by the army that they could not remain in their village. According to the mother who had been used as a shield:

> We took some clothes and returned to Struga. We left everything behind. But we stayed in Struga for only two days because we were frightened. The army demanded that those in Struga surrender their weapons, which they did. The army then went to talk to the bandits in the hills and showed little interest in protecting us.

According to a Croatian defender of Struga during the Serbian assault:

---

[12] See above section concerning human shields.

252

The army stayed in the village until the entire village evacuated, which happened three days later. We had no electricity and no water. In fact, there was a lot of pressure from the army to leave and so we left.

According to the Serbian Red Cross, as of August 19, 1991, 57,047 Serbs from Croatia have fled to Serbia. According to the Red Cross of Bosnia-Hercegovina, as of August 16, 1991, 14,922 people from Croatia (both Serbs and Croats) have fled to Bosnia-Hercegovina. According to the Croatian Red Cross and the Croatian Ministry of Labor and Social Security, as of August 19, 1991, 35,938 people have been internally displaced in Croatia; of this number, 96.5 percent are Croats, 2.3 percent are Serbs, and 1.5 percent are Hungarians, Italians, or others.

Beating of Prisoners

Protocol II, Article 4 (2) (a), strictly prohibits "violence to the life, health and physical or mental well-being of persons, in particular...cruel treatment such as torture, mutilation or any form of corporal punishment." It also forbids "outrages upon personal dignity, in particular humiliating and degrading treatment." (Protocol II, Article 4 (2) (e))

Helsinki Watch has documented the following cases of prisoner beatings in recent weeks:

A. Elderly Croats and Albanian youths were beaten by Serbian insurgents in Borovo Selo jail, July 1991:

Ante Gudelj, a 72-year-old Croatian man,[13] was captured by Serbian rebels in Tenja on July 1. When interviewed, this elderly man still had many black and blue bruises covering large areas of his back, chest and arms. "The worst are the bruises on my back and kidneys. I was hit with police batons. They also hit me in the groin with their legs."

---

[13] Gudelj was interviewed in the intensive care unit of the hospital in Osijek, Croatia, on July 30, 1991, three days after his release. The beatings required hospitalization, but he was in intensive care because of a serious prostate condition caused by age.

According to the doctor, the patient's left lung was punctured and filling with water.

Gudelj was captured outside his house before noon on July 1 by masked men.[14] He and six other elderly Croatian captives (ranging in age from 58 to 72 years, all grandparents) were blindfolded and held in a dark basement in nearby Bobota for three days before being moved to Borovo Selo.

> There they started to beat us with everything they had. The room where we were held was dark. They would open the door, flash a light in our faces, and say, "Why don't you come over here." The light blinded us. In that direction three men were waiting for us, holding clubs. They hit me and the others. We were beaten for 10 days consecutively, mostly in the evening and at intervals throughout the day. The men beating us would say, "Ustasa murderers, you came to this land to kill. We will get Tudjman."

They were beaten by a group of three men who took turns, and questioned by another group. Each beating lasted approximately thirty minutes.

> Later five Albanians came, and they beat them terribly, almost killing them. I do not know what happened to them. The terror was much worse against them. They were younger men, about 18 and 20. They were not police but the Serbs did not believe that. They kept beating them to get them to admit that they were police officers.[15]

---

[14] Gudelj's son was manning a barricade where, shortly after learning of his father's capture, he opened fire on a negotiating team, killing three. (See section concerning failure to prosecute a killing.)

[15] The Serbian insurgent military advisor interviewed in old Tenja on July 29 said that they were holding "five Albanians who came from Kosovo to join the Croatian National Guard" and that they wanted an exchange, but the offer was refused.

The jail is in the center of Borovo Selo, three doors to the left of a restaurant, which is across the street from the city council. According to Gudelj, they were held in "what looked like a storage room. On the door there was a window with bars. The door was of green steel. There were no other windows." The 15 were kept together in one room with no light, where they slept on the floor.

He and a 58-year-old female prisoner (who was not beaten but was confined to the same one-room jail as the men) were evacuated by an army officer on July 27 in a civilian car with a white flag the Serbs provided. Seven Croats and five Albanians remained in jail.

B. Serbian prisoner beaten by Croatian National Guard, near Djakovo, July 7, 1991:

Djordje Rkman[16] was in charge of weapons inventory at the local territorial defense unit[17] for 15 years. He lived in the village of Sodolovni with his parents, wife and two children. While on vacation on July 7, at approximately 10:00 A.M., he was tending to chores in the fields when he heard fighting at the entrance to the village. He ran to the closest house, 300 meters away, for shelter. There were eight people inside the house, two grandmothers, one young woman, a boy, and four men. When they saw that the National Guard was shooting at the house, they ran upstairs for shelter.

There had been some men in the attic of this house with a machine gun who fled through the roof when the National Guard opened fire, he said, but he did not see them. The machine gun was abandoned in the room next to the civilians' hiding place.

Fifteen to twenty National Guards came into the attic, followed by a second group which beat the men.

---

[16] Rkman was interviewed in private in the Osijek jail on July 30, 1991. We requested to speak with him by name and the prison authorities complied.

[17] During Yugoslavia's communist era, territorial defense units consisted of a local reserve militia and armaments stored at the local level. See section concerning discrimination below for a description of territorial defense units and their significance in the current conflict.

All were in uniforms, all were National Guards. I could not see who they were. I was on the floor while they were beating me. I heard the verbal harassment and threats. "Kill them now," one was saying.

The beating was really hideous. They put a gun to my forehead and were yelling "Cetnik" at me. We were beaten for half an hour. We were then brought downstairs and they made us go out in the yard, where they made us lie down on our stomachs, hands on our heads. Then they randomly hit and kicked whoever they wanted. The women were not hit.

About 20 to 30 National Guards hit us, kicking us too. I have not been to the doctor. It is hard for me to breathe. My lip and my head were cut and I cannot open my mouth very much.

His upper right lip had a white scar on it.

While they were beating us, they were insulting us, saying we were Cetniks, although my father was a major officer in the partisans fighting against the Cetniks -- as if that made any difference to them.

We were then made to walk one to two kilometers with our hands behind our heads to their cars, where they beat us again.

They were handcuffed and taken to Djakovo, where the women were released. In Djakovo, they were individually interrogated.

When they saw I was beaten up, they took me to the hospital. While they were taking me down the hall in the police station, some of the police were yelling "Cetnik" at me, kicking me in the sides as I went down the steps. It still hurts. I was also kicked in the courtyard of the hospital. But it was in the house where they broke my lip and my head. My left temple still hurts, as well as my ribs and back.

At the first aid station [in the hospital] they gave me two injections and stitched my face. I got two stitches on my mouth, two on my head, and two on my left cheek.

At the Osijek jail, although he complained through his attorney that his ribs still hurt, he did not receive further medical attention. The four men arrested with him also remained in jail at the time of Helsinki Watch's visit.

C. Croatian prisoners beaten at the Serbian military base, Samarica Mountain, Banija, July 26-29:

- Predrag Vucicevic, a 29-year-old attorney who was chief of police of Dubica, Croatia,[18] was ambushed returning to Dubica from Croatian Kostajnica[19] on July 26 and captured by Serbian insurgents, who beat him at their camp. At the time of the interview, he had extensive bruises on his body, left shoulder, face, neck, and torso, and his left eye was swollen and red. His neck also bore rope marks.

  There were six armed men in the two ambushed cars, of whom four were injured in the ambush. Two were taken for medical care and a third, who received no medical attention, died en route to the base.[20] The fourth wounded man, the only one uniformed, was not captured or seen again.

---

[18] Vucicevic was interviewed at the Sisak hospital on August 3, 1991.

[19] The following incident took place in Croatian, not Bosnian, Kostajnica. Croatian Kostajnica and Bosnian Kostajnica are two separate villages which lie within their respective republican borders and are separated by the Una river.

[20] Vucicevic reported, "One of the wounded died from excessive bleeding because he was not able to get medical attention. He was Srecko Kitonic, 27, single, an engineer of forestry. An artery in his leg was hit and he did not get any first aid. He lay dying next to me in the truck. I could not do anything. I do not know what they did with his body. It was left in the truck when we got out."

257

The two not wounded were blindfolded and tied up: the police commander's hands were tied behind his back to a rope fastened around his neck. Vucicevic said, "I was badly beaten at their base, which is on Cavic Brdo in the Spomen Dom, in Samarica," a recreational area. They were held in a bowling alley, where the Serbian command post was also situated.

I was kicked with their military boots. While I sat on a chair, they would kick me. I would fall to the floor, and then others would kick me. I could barely eat because I could not open my mouth. They had kicked out one tooth. My head was all beaten, too. I have bumps and scars on my head. It was not so much the physical pain because I am strong, but the psychological pressure that came from their constant threats to massacre us. They yelled that I was an Ustasa, that they would kill us all. When the armed civilians came back from the field, they would come in and kick us. Just for revenge.

The Serbian insurgent police did not hit the prisoners but let others beat them. However, when their commanding officer came in one day, he saw how we looked and he started screaming that this was not supposed to happen, but things did not change. We were all beaten. I was beaten the worst, because I was the only police officer.

They used electric shocks on me, on my feet and hands. They did this for torture. They gave me these shocks after questioning, when I did not know anything. Five or six of them were standing around laughing when I screamed. Each shock lasted three or four seconds. This all happened every day, two or three times a day, whenever they got bored.

One of a team of three medical workers, held at the same time, confirmed Vucicevic's account.[21] There were 13 to 15 prisoners in all who for two days and nights were kept sitting up in chairs, hands tied, blindfolded. They were questioned, beaten, and slept in the same room. The civilians were given electric shock once.

> The Croatian police commander [i.e. Vucicevic] got the worst of it. They were questioning and beating us. This questioning was conducted by a horde yelling at us, provoking us. One would interrupt the other, saying, "It's my turn to question him." They were getting a kick out of our screaming. It was just "Ustasa, go to Hell."

> The problem was that the armed men would come in from the field and be angered by a bad turn in the fighting. Then they would take out their anger on whoever was there, beating us all.

All the prisoners were released by Wednesday, July 31.

D. Beating and humiliation of three surrendered Croatian police officers by Serbian insurgents in Struga on July 26, and beating of two young women in Struga on July 26.[22]

Shooting at Medical Vehicles and Personnel, Denial of Treatment to the Wounded, and Holding Medical Personnel Hostage

Protocol II, Article 12, provides that the distinctive emblem of the Red Cross shall be displayed by medical personnel and on medical transports. It shall be respected in all circumstances. "Medical units and transports shall be respected and protected at all times and shall not be the object of attack" (Article 11 (1)). Moreover, "medical and religious

---

[21] This witness was separately interviewed on August 3 in Sisak. (See section concerning shootings at medical vehicles and personnel, denial of treatment to the wounded, and holding medical personnel hostage.)

[22] See section on human shields for detailed account of this incident.

personnel shall be respected and protected and shall be granted all available help for the performance of their duties " (Article 9 (1)).

These provisions of Protocol II to the Geneva Conventions were violated when Serbian insurgents ambushed and hit a clearly marked ambulance belonging to the medical center of Sisak in a village near Croatian Kostajnica in the Banija region, on July 26, 1991. The ambulance was carrying three wounded Croatian police officers and three hospital personnel -- a doctor, a medical technician, and an ambulance driver -- all long-time employees of the Sisak hospital.

The three medical personnel, who were wearing their white hospital uniforms, were held captive for five days in a mountain base where for two days Serbian insurgents returning from the field of battle took turns beating them. They were told that they were being held for exchange, that is, as hostages,[23] and were later released.

Protocol II also stipulates that the wounded shall be respected and protected, and that in all circumstances they shall be treated humanely and shall receive, to the fullest extent practicable and with the least possible delay, the medical care and attention required by their condition, and that no distinction shall be founded on any grounds other than medical ones (Article 7). Despite this provision, the three wounded persons being evacuated in the ambulance, one of whom was seriously wounded, were denied the medical care to which they were entitled under Protocol II. They were separated from the doctor providing them care and their emergency trip to the nearest hospital, in Croatian Kostajnica, was cut short by the ambush. They were removed in the ambulance to an unknown location. Whether they ever received further medical care is unknown.

The ambulance and all of its medical supplies were never returned to the hospital; this was the second ambulance the Serbian insurgents captured in the field from the Sisak hospital, which had 12 ambulances. This too violates the mandate of Protocol II that states that medical transports shall be respected and protected at all times.

Helsinki Watch interviewed one of the medical personnel who was ambushed and taken prisoner. He said that the three left Sisak hospital with a fully equipped ambulance on Wednesday, July 24. The white van had a red cross on the door next to the driver and was

---

[23] The holding of hostages, a separate violation of Protocol II, Article 4 (2) (c), was explained in the relevant section above.

prominently marked "Medical Center of Sisak." The van flew a flag with the Red Cross emblem on it as well.

The hospital had established an arrangement by which hospital personnel would spend three-day shifts in one of the small villages between Dvor (held by Serbian insurgents) and Kostajnica (then held by the Croats) to supply medical aid to all the villages between the two towns, all of which had been isolated. The three medical personnel arrived on July 24 and relieved their colleagues, who had completed their three-day shift and were now returning to Sisak. On July 26, at approximately 10:15 A.M., mortars were fired for nearly 90 minutes.

During a 10 to 20 minute pause in the fighting,

> two wounded civilians came in cars to the medical outpost and received first aid. They had both been injured in their lower legs, by shrapnel from a mortar, not serious injuries. They were cousins and had not been defending the village. One was hiding in the basement when the mortar fell on the asphalt outside the house; the other was making a call to Sisak during the lull in the fighting; the phone was opposite the police station. He was injured by the same mortar.

The medical personnel also set the broken arm of a 20-year-old Croatian police officer. Another police officer was brought in, already dead.

At about 3:00 P.M., when the shooting had stopped, a column of tanks, heading in the direction of Dvor, passed through the village. The ambulance driver ran out, waiving the Red Cross flag as a sign for the tanks to stop. He wanted to ask them what the medics should do. The column passed by quickly, without stopping.

The villagers came to tell the medical unit that there were two badly wounded police officers in the village in the direction of Dvor. The ambulance arrived and found the two men inside a house to which the villagers had moved them.

> The one on the bed had severe wounds to the head and chest. He was not coherent but he could see us. The other was injured but capable of walking. We put them in the ambulance. We were very careful that they did not put any guns in the ambulance and that the wounded

261

did not have on their uniforms.

Two medical personnel sat in the back with the patients, giving transfusions and cleaning the wounds. They passed by their post and picked up the 20-year-old Croatian police officer with the broken arm, without his uniform or gun.

> We all had on white Red Cross uniforms, including the
> driver. The Red Cross flag was flying on a stick as we
> drove out to Kostajnica. The driver turned on the lights
> and the siren, trying to draw attention to the fact that we
> were a medical emergency vehicle. We got about 500
> meters to one kilometer from the police station when the
> other side opened fire on us.

> The shooting smashed all the windows of the ambulance,
> and the two medical personnel in the back hit the floor
> with the two patients to avoid being shot. Bullet holes
> were all over the ambulance. The windows were hit, as
> was the driver's seat.

The ambulance driver, a veteran of the emergency ward, continued to drive quickly past the open cornfield from which they were ambushed and came to a stop next to some houses. The driver, medical technician, and the Croatian police officer with the broken arm ran out and took cover near the houses. The doctor and two patients stayed in the back of the ambulance.

After about 15 minutes, they were called on to surrender and were captured by about ten men in yellow camouflage uniforms, with no patch or insignia. The three medical personnel, in their white uniforms, were "ordered to lie down on the ground, face down and hands stretched out."

> They took away the ambulance with the two wounded
> inside. I think they put the police officer with the broken
> arm in there too. That was the last time we saw the
> three wounded men. We could not say anything. Our
> captor kept telling us to keep quiet. That was the last
> time we saw the ambulance, too, on July 26. They kept
> it.

All of the medical supplies in the ambulance were confiscated as well.

> We got very scared when we saw that we were prisoners despite the fact that we were medical personnel. They did not believe that we were medical workers. They thought that we were Croatian police officers.

The three were blindfolded and their hands were tied behind their backs. "There was the normal amount of kicking in that situation," the victim added.

> When we asked later why they opened fire, they said, "Croatian police officers had used the Red Cross before, and we thought that you were one." We asked, "Why didn't you put up a barricade if you wanted us to stop? You shouldn't have opened fire, even if we were suspicious."

After changing vehicles once, they were driven several hours to their destination, an insurgent base in a mountainous area, where they were put in a large room with several other prisoners, perhaps 15 in all. They were beaten by groups of armed men. "The problem was that the armed men would come in from the field and be angry at the way the fighting was going. Then they would take it out on whoever was there."[24]

They were released on July 31 at 3:00 P.M. Although no one would confirm this, it appears that they were indeed exchanged for Serbian prisoners held by the Croatian authorities.

Discrimination

Yugoslavia, including Croatia, is in economic crisis. In recent months, many workers of different nationalities have lost their jobs for economic reasons, while thousands continue to work without pay or receive their pay one to four months late. Given the insolvency of many

---

[24] See above section concerning the beating of prisoners.

firms, closures and layoffs are becoming commonplace throughout Yugoslavia. However, many claim that they have lost their jobs for ethnic, as opposed to economic, reasons.

Helsinki Watch has received reports of discrimination in the work place in Croatia. Much of the discrimination is not government-sponsored, but privately organized. For example, individual Croats, particularly in the coastal cities of Split and Sibenik, have authored and organized the signing of "loyalty oaths" to the Croatian government. The loyalty oaths are typically written by Croatian workers and presented either to all employees or only to Serbian workers for signatures. Those who refuse to sign -- mostly Serbs -- are threatened with dismissal or are, in fact, fired from their jobs.

The "loyalty oath" campaign originated with Croats who claimed that Serbian colleagues who worked with them were the same individuals who fought on the side of the Serbian insurgents, particularly in Knin. They accused their Serbian colleagues of manning barricades and shooting at Croats in the evening and then coming to work the next day with the same Croats at whom they shot the night before. One man told Helsinki Watch:

> How can someone who is breaking the law, shooting at mc and at my children in the evening, expect to be treated as a common worker? Our government has done little to arrest these people and I refuse to work with them. Yes, we organized the signing of loyalty oaths to separate the bandits from the honest workers. If they want to work for the bandits, let [Krajina president Milan] Babic give them a paycheck.

The Croatian Ministry of Labor and Social Security has documented cases of loyalty oath signature campaigns in ten enterprises throughout Croatia, including the TEF (Tvornica elektroda i ferolegura) and TLM (Tvornica lakih metala) plants in Sibenik, the ship-building factory in Split, the Slavija enterprise in Zagreb. Helsinki Watch has also received reports of such campaigns in the Zadranka firm in Zadar and at the Jadrantours enterprise in Split.

The Croatian government and the Parliamentary Committee for the Protection of Human Rights has condemned the signing of loyalty oaths and has required the reinstatement of those who have lost their jobs because they refused to sign the loyalty oaths. Helsinki Watch welcomes the condemnation of loyalty oaths by the Croatian government. We also urge the authorities to take disciplinary actions against those who have required the signing of loyalty oaths and to take steps -- at the republican and local levels-- to prevent similar campaigns in the future. Dismissing a worker because of his or her failure to sign a loyalty oath to a government violates the right to freedom of expression. Moreover, using loyalty oaths to weed out "dishonest Serbs" is discriminatory. If individuals are engaged in illegal activity, the authorities should conduct an investigation, rather than firing an individual because he or she is suspected of supporting Serbian insurgents. In addition, Serbs and Croats have lost jobs because of their ethnic origins. Croats have been dismissed from their jobs in Knin, the Krajina "capital." Knin is predominantly Serbian, and Croats comprise only 8.6 percent of Knin's population. According to the Croatian Ministry of Labor and Social Security, Croats have been dismissed from the hospital, steel plant and TVIK (Tvornica vijaka Knin) factory in Knin. In other areas of the Krajina region, Croats have reportedly lost their jobs, specifically in the Gracac hospital and in Glina, where 175 Croats were dismissed from administrative positions at the local city council and elementary school. Helsinki Watch condemns the use of nationality as a criterion for job dismissal and urges Serbian leaders to refrain from, and to punish, such actions.

Similarly, Helsinki Watch is concerned that ethnic criteria are applied by the Croatian Ministry of the Interior to hire and dismiss Serbian police officers. During the communist era, the vast majority of the police officers in Croatia were Serbian. According to the Croatian Ministry of the Interior, Serbs accounted for approximately 75 percent of the Croatian police force despite the fact that they comprised only 11.5 percent of the republic's population. Since the new Croatian government has taken power, the police forces have been greatly enlarged and the ratio between police officers of Serbian and Croatian origin has been reversed. Whereas Serbs comprised approximately 75 percent of the Croatian police force during the communist regime, they now constitute approximately 23 percent.

The Croatian Ministry of the Interior contends that the numbers have not been reversed because Serbs were fired from their jobs but because more Croats were recruited. Slavko Degoricija and Milan Brezak, both Deputy Interior Ministers, told Helsinki Watch that no one has been fired from police jobs simply because of their nationality. They contend that three factors have influenced the reversal in the composition of the police. First, after the new Croatian government decided to change the insignia on the police uniform from a communist red star to the traditional Croatian coat of arms, many Serbs quit claiming that they would not wear the new insignia because they equated the coat of arms with the fascist period during World War II. Second, according to Brezak and Degoricija, some Serbs quit the Croatian police force to fight on the side of the Serbian insurgents in Croatia. Third, when the Croatian police force was being augmented, an effort was made to rectify the disproportionate representation in the police forces by establishing "national parity and equal representation" in the police force.

Indeed, in the past year, the Croatian police force has been greatly enlarged. The Croatian government justifies the increase in their security forces by pointing to the Serbian insurgency, the Serbian bias of the Yugoslav People's Army and the Army's dismantling of Croatia's territorial defense units. In 1990, the Yugoslav Army confiscated most of the weapons which were part of Croatia's territorial defense (teritorijalna obrana - TO), a local defense force separate from the federal army. After World War II and during Tito's reign, the official Yugoslav communist position was that Yugoslavia was surrounded by external enemies, such as NATO to the west and the Warsaw Pact to the east. In light of these "threats," Yugoslavia had to be prepared to fight for its "territorial integrity, unity and independence."

In preparation for possible attacks from "outside enemies," weapons for the general population were stored at the local level. The weapons were bought by individual firms and kept in various storage areas throughout a respective locality. Each republic maintained a territorial defense structure, including a civilian security force (civilna zastita), a local reserve militia. All former soldiers who served in the army could be called up to serve as reserve police officers for the republican police force of civilian security forces for the local territorial defense unit. The TO's weapons could be distributed by the republican government, in consultation with the federal army and government.

When the federal and republican governments were communist, it was clear that the territorial defense units were controlled by the Communist Party. However, a few weeks before Slovenia and Croatia voted out their communist regimes in 1990, the Yugoslav Army made efforts to confiscate weapons which were part of Slovenia's and Croatia's territorial defense units. In April 1990, just prior to the Croatian elections, the army confiscated most of the republic's weapons. It was less successful in Slovenia, where the local population blocked such action. After the army depleted Croatia's territorial defense arsenal, the Croatian

266

government tried to buy new weapons for the government-owned armaments plant but was refused permission by the federal army, who had to approve all weapons purchases. During the summer of 1990, the Croatian government bought weapons on the international market. In justifying such purchases, the Croatian government claimed that while all republics had maintained their territorial defense units, Croatia had been depleted of its weapons at a time when the Serbian insurgency was beginning. Also, with the election of a non-communist government, the Croats feared reprisals by the army or other republics whose interests lie in the preservation of a communist Yugoslavia.

Similarly, the new Croatian government undertook efforts to strengthen both the active and reserve police units. Within the active police units, a special division was created. At the time, these distinct police units were commonly referred to as "specials" (specijalci), and were meant to serve anti-terrorist, S.W.A.T.-type functions. Most of the "special" police forces have now been incorporated into the Croatian National Guard. According to Milan Brezak, Croatia's security forces currently number approximately 25,000 active police officers, 30,000 armed reserve police officers and 15,000 National Guard members.[25]

Although Helsinki Watch does not dispute the Croatian government's right to increase and strengthen its police force, it is concerned that Serbs are being excluded and dismissed because of their nationality. Helsinki Watch interviewed several insurgents who admitted that they had quit their jobs with the Croatian police to join the Serbian insurgency. However, it is difficult to believe the Ministry of the Interior's assertion that of the 11,000 Serbs who worked for the Croatian police during the communist regime, 6,000 left of their own accord. Helsinki Watch believes that potential recruits should not be excluded on the basis of national origin or political affiliation. Moreover, Helsinki Watch is concerned that Serbian police officers have been dismissed from their jobs because they were suspected of being supporters of the Serbian insurgency.

---

[25] The National Guard is not part of the Croatian police force and, therefore, is not under the control of the Ministry of the Interior. Rather, the National Guard, formed approximately three months ago, serves as the Croatian army and is responsible to the Croatian Defense Ministry. However, during the course of battles with Serbian insurgents, the National Guard and the Croatian police operate jointly.

Failure to Prosecute a Killing

On July 1, the Chief of Police of Osijek, Josip Reichl Kir (a Croat), and two elected officials (one Serb and one Croat) were killed. One other Serbian official was wounded by a Croatian reserve police officer.[26] This officer, Antun Gudelj, was known to be a Croatian extremist. He shot at the officials' car from behind a police barricade in Tenja. Although many reserve and regular police officers were at the scene, no one detained the killer, who is still at large. The victims, seen as moderates, were trying to negotiate a peaceful settlement to the violent Tenja disputes.

Background to the Killing

After the HDZ won a majority in the republic-wide elections in 1990, local HDZ representatives in Tenja reportedly became aggressive. According to a young Serbian displaced woman, "About three times each week, Croatian nationalists would come around waving flags and provoking Serbs with threats, dragging their fingers across their throats." A military advisor to the Serbian insurgents[27] said:

> Those who joined the HDZ were exclusively Croats. The HDZ had more rights than others. They had special identification papers that allowed them to become part of the police force. They were armed civilians. They made changes in the major enterprises and factories. The Croats took over the best positions and the Serbs were not allowed into management positions. When it came

---

[26] Those killed with the Chief of Police were Goran Zopundzija (a Croat), vice-president of the executive branch of Osijek's government, and Milan Knezevic (a Serb), president of Tenja's town council and member of Osijek's district council. Wounded at the same time was Mirko Tubic (a Serb), a member of Tenja's town council.

[27] Serbian military advisor, nicknamed "Djilas," interviewed in old Tenja on July 29, 1991.

to making promotions of directors, the Serbs were excluded.[28]

Old Tenja is currently controlled by Serbian insurgents, whose press attache, Milan Trbojevic,[29] claimed that a few months before this "war" started, harassment of Serbs increased.

> The Serbian people were being arrested for small things. The entrances and exits to Tenja were tightly controlled and Serbian cars and people were constantly searched.

After Gudelj's election as HDZ president in old Tenja, inter-ethnic tensions rose dramatically; these tensions continued to worsen even after Gudelj was removed from his position. The mayor and police chief of Osijek came to Tenja to hold monthly town meetings to air disputes and resolve conflicts. The Croatian mayor of Osijek, Zlatko Kramaric[30] said:

> Tenja? Everything has happened there. Tenja is 70 percent Serbian and 30 percent Croatian. But it is part of the larger picture, in which Serbia has not relinquished its role as a mini-imperialist power. Croatia has a 12 percent Serbian population and the 14 districts of eastern Slavonija are 30 percent Serbian. In the three districts around Osijek, their population is only 35,000 and they occupy a lot of territory with few people. Although none of their villages are 100 percent Serbian, the Serbs are pressuring the Croats to leave in order to create a pure Serbian zone for use as a bargaining chip to justify the amputation of Croatia.

---

[28] This claim is part of a republic-wide dispute over the Croatian government's policy of restoring ethnic parity. (See section concerning discrimination.)

[29] Interviewed in old Tenja on July 29, 1991.

[30] Kramaric was interviewed in his office on July 29, 1991. He is a university professor and member of the Croatian Liberal Party, not the majority HDZ.

The Osijek mayor continued:

I thought everything would work out but the Serbs were arming quickly and provoking the Croats in Tenja. The Croats there were emotional and took the bait and got into tiny conflicts here and there.

One night, a Serbian house was blown up. The next, five Croatian houses were burned in retaliation. Because of this type of problem, the 3,000 Croats in new Tenja evacuated.

A Croatian mother from new Tenja said:

I do not remember when, some time near Easter, the Serbs put up their barricades and their flag and announced that they were part of Serbia. We were astounded because that was such a stupid thing to do, on a piece of land in a tiny village.

They posted signs on the walls. They held meetings for three days proclaiming their union with Serbia. There was a barricade in the center of old Tenja made up of tractors around the city council and other buildings.

The Croatian police called up the reservists in Tenja on June 27 and the next day they received weapons and were posted near Osijek, according to the wife of one reservist.

That Saturday, June 29, it was very tense in new Tenja because the people were saying that they would not accept the declaration that old Tenja had joined with Serbia. A man from the Croatian police force rushed into town and told his mother she had to get ready to leave, since something evil was about to happen.

It was really pitiful to watch Croats run away from the village like rabbits. Between 3:00 and 6:00 P.M. on Saturday [June 29], the entire village of new Tenja left.

270

The Serbs say the armed conflict started with an assault by seven armed Croatian HDZ men on one Serbian house at 7:45 P.M. on June 29, occupied by two couples. The armed men, allegedly looking for "Cetniks" and weapons, "opened fire through the windows and doors at the Serbs in the house," who shot back while other Serbs joined in. After this event, new Tenja was evacuated; the Serbian residents fled to Serbian-controlled old Tenja and the Croats retreated to Osijek. According to Osijek mayor Kramaric,

> The Serbs asked for a meeting with Kir, but Kir did not use his political acumen when he agreed to talk to the Serbs in Tenja [on July 1]. The Croats there, who are pretty radical, would view that as aiding the Serbs.

> The man who shot Kir, Antun Gudelj, had just had his house burned and his father captured on that day[31] and he was psychologically unstable. One can understand but not exonerate his anger.

During Kir's visit, three barricades had been erected in Tenja: one was manned by the active Croatian police, another by the Croatian reserve police, most of whom were HDZ members, and a third was controlled by the Serbian insurgents. Kir and his colleagues passed through these barricades without difficulty on their way to Tenja. While Kir was at the Serbs' headquarters, he was reportedly warned of an impending attack by the Croatian police. Kir, claiming he had no knowledge of this, agreed to return to talk to his men. He was reportedly told that no attack was planned.

On his way back to deliver this reassuring message to the Serbs, as he passed again through the HDZ-controlled barricade, Kir and two others were shot dead.

The Mayor of Osijek said:

> Gudelj knew who he was shooting at. He has not been arrested. You have to talk to the police about this. These are times when the police do not have control over such things.

---

[31] See section concerning the beating of prisoners.

A Croatian reserve police officer[32] said:

> I was there on July 1 when Kir was shot and I saw the
> bodies. I was about 100 meters away on patrol. I did not
> have a good view of the scene but I heard the shooting
> and ran over.
>
> Kir was killed at the entrance to new Tenja. A reserve
> police officer killed them because the Cetnik driver
> refused to stop the car. Many others were there and saw
> it, including the Croatian police.

The investigating magistrates of the district court in Osijek have
reported that a warrant is out for Gudelj's arrest but that the police have
not forwarded any investigation in this case nor had an arrest been made
as of July 30.

The Croatian government has a duty to investigate crimes such
as the killings of Police Chief Kir and the other two officials. It has a
duty to apprehend and charge those responsible. Because they called up
and armed reserve police officers, they have a heightened duty to
prosecute acts allegedly committed by these officers.

Helsinki Watch calls on Croatian officials to vigorously prosecute
the killer of Chief Kir, Goran Zopundzija and Milan Knezevic.

Conclusion

The current conflict in Croatia between Croats, Serbs and the
Yugoslav army has resulted in many civilian deaths and human rights
abuses. The majority of abuses committed by the Croats involve
discrimination against Serbs: the Croats' beating of prisoners in police
custody and their failure to rigorously prosecute a killing are also serious
violations. The abuses committed by the Serbs involve physical
maltreatment -- including the beating and use of electric shocks against
prisoners-- and egregious abuses against civilians and medical personnel,
including the use of human shields and the taking of hostages. The
Yugoslav army is also committing serious human rights violations by
attacking civilian targets in coordination with the Serbian insurgents.

---

[32] Interviewed on July 30, 1991, in Osijek.

Recent examples ·of such attacks occurred during the week of August 19th, when the Yugoslav army indiscriminately attacked civilian targets in Osijek and Vukovar.

The current conflict is spreading from the countryside to the major cities in Croatia, heightening concern that more civilians will be killed and more abuses will be committed. Helsinki Watch condemns such abuses and urges all sides to refrain from committing further violations of international humanitarian law. Helsinki Watch calls upon all parties to the conflict -- Croats, Serbs, and the Yugoslav army -- to respect their obligations under the Geneva Conventions of 1949 and the Second Protocol of 1977.

Appendix D: Helsinki Watch Letter to Slobodan Milošević, President of the Republic of Serbia and General Blagoje Adžić, Acting Minister of Defense and Chief of Staff of the Yugoslav People's Army

January 21, 1992

His Excellency Slobodan Milošević
President of the Republic of Serbia
Marsala Tita 14
11000 Belgrade
Serbia

General Blagoje Adžić
Acting Minister of Defense and
Chief of Staff of the Yugoslav People's Army
Kneza Miloša 35
11000 Belgrade
Serbia

Dear President Milošević and General Adžić:

The U.S. Helsinki Watch Committee is deeply troubled by reports of serious human rights abuses by the Serbian government and the Yugoslav Army. Our own investigations of these reports, conducted during a series of fact-finding missions to Yugoslavia over several years, indicate that many of these reports are well founded. We call upon you to investigate the abuses enumerated in this letter and to punish those responsible for them. We call upon you to take immediate measures to ensure that such violations of human rights do not occur again.

The abuses described in this letter include violations of the laws of war in the Croatian conflict, including the summary execution of civilians; the indiscriminate and disproportionate use of force against civilian targets; the torture and mistreatment of detainees; disappearances and the taking of hostages; the forced displacement and resettlement of civilian populations; and the killing of journalists covering the war. In addition to violations connected with the armed conflict in Croatia, Helsinki Watch has also documented restrictions on the press and on free

274

expression in Serbia and the harassment and repression of opposition political figures and people who have spoken out against the war. Finally, we object to the continuing persecution of the Albanian population of Kosovo.

Rules of War Violations in the Croatian Conflict

We hold the government of the Republic of Serbia responsible for violations of the rules of war by two groups of rebels -- local Serbian irregulars organized in Croatia, and those organized in Serbia and sent to Croatia.

The government of Serbia has provided military, economic and political support to locally-based insurgents in Croatia. Moreover, President Milošević has asserted that if Croatia were to secede from Yugoslavia, the Serbs in Croatia and the territory on which they live could not be part of an independent Croatian state. The Serbian government's statements that Serbs in Croatia need protection from Croatian government persecution has stirred up fear and hysteria among the Serbian population and contributed to the tension that has led to violence.

The Serbian government has also condoned and, in some cases, supported the formation of at least three paramilitary groups in Serbia which operate in Croatia. What appears to be the most brutal of these groups is led by Vojislav Šešelj, leader of the Serbian Radical Party (Srpska Radikalna Stranka) and the Serbian Četnik Movement (Srpski Četnički Pokret). Šešelj's group of paramilitaries call themselves "Četniks" and operate throughout Croatia. A second paramilitary force is commanded by Željko Ražnjatović (a.k.a. Arkan) and a third group is led by Mirko Jović. Both Arkan's and Jović's forces are most heavily concentrated in the eastern Slavonian region of Croatia. In addition, various Serbian paramilitary groups are organized and trained by the so-called Captain Dragan, described by the *Washington Post* as "a half-Serb mercenary with Australian citizenship who refuses to give his real name."[1]

We hold the Yugoslav People's Army (JNA) and the federal Yugoslav government responsible for the conduct of these groups as well,

---

[1]Mary Battiata, "Serbian Guerrilla Camps Operate Inside Croatia," *The Washington Post*, July 22, 1991, p. A1.

since the JNA has conducted military operations in which it commands the irregulars or operates in conjunction and/or in coordination with them. Both local insurgents and Serbian-based paramilitary groups have been armed, either directly or indirectly, by the JNA and provided with army uniforms and possibly military intelligence.

We therefore request a response from both the Serbian President and the Chief of Staff of the Yugoslav People's Army to the following very serious and credible reports of violations of humanitarian law during the conflict in Croatia.

Summary Executions

Serbian rebel forces appear to be responsible for the extrajudicial executions of at least 200 civilians and disarmed soldiers in at least 14 separate instances in five months, committed in areas where these forces had exclusive military control or shared that control with the JNA. In several cases, the victims were tortured before their execution. Some were captured because they were not to able to flee before advancing Serbian insurgent forces due to advanced age or physical incapacity.

July 22, 1991 - Benkovac

Three Croats were arrested in Benkovac by Serbian paramilitary police. Ivica Knez, 39, was beaten to death and the whereabouts of the other two men, Tomislav Čeranja and Tomislav Kolerić, remain unknown.

July 26, 1991 — Struga (municipality of Dvor)

During a Serbian assault against the predominantly Croatian village of Struga (population 254), three Croatian police officers surrendered after Serbian insurgents encircled a house in which they had taken up positions. According to eyewitnesses,[2] the police officers were

---

[2] Interviewed by Helsinki Watch in late July 1991. Serbian insurgents launched an offensive from the town of Dvor against Croatian police in the village of Kozibrod. En route, the insurgents captured approximately 40 civilians, including some of these witnesses, and used them as human shields during their advance through the villages of Struga and Zamlača. Their testimony is contained

stripped of their clothing, humiliated and ordered to run through a field, where they were shot and killed by the insurgents.

August 1 — Dalj (municipality of Osijek)

On August 1, Serbian insurgents attempted to take over the local police station in Dalj.[3] Police trapped inside the station refused to surrender to JNA troops and a battle for the town ensued. After the JNA occupied Dalj, Serbian paramilitary groups reportedly searched the village for Croatian soldiers, police officers and civilians, and killed many of those who were found wounded. Some victims had been killed by a bullet to the head at close range, apparently after being wounded or beaten, according to autopsy reports.[4] Pjetar Djevelekaj, a baker of Albanian origin was first beaten and then executed by two close-range gunshots to the head.

Between August 5 and 14 — Lovinac (municipality of Gračac)

Serbian paramilitary groups attacked the village of Lovinac (population 499) on August 5 and reportedly kidnapped five Croats (Ivan Ivezić, 38, Stejepan Katalinić, 55, Marko Pavičić, 75, Jure Sekulić, 57, and Martin Sarić, 40). Their bodies were found 10 days later.

---

in "Yugoslavia: Human Rights Abuses in the Croatian Conflict," Helsinki Watch, September 1991, pp. 6-10.

[3] Dalj has a population of 5,492, in which Serbs constitute a slight majority over Croats and Hungarians.

[4] The information was obtained from reports of autopsies performed by doctors from the Department of Pathology and Forensic Medicine at Osijek Hospital and the Department of Anatomy at Zagreb University's School of Medicine. The autopsy reports cited herein were performed by Croatian and non-Croatian doctors, including Serbian pathologists and forensic experts. Helsinki Watch interviewed some of the doctors who performed the autopsies in Osijek and Zagreb.

August 16 — Pecki (municipality of Petrinja)

After the village of Pecki (population 374) was occupied by Serbian forces, four Croatian men were killed when they returned to the village to feed their livestock. Three of the men appear to have been tortured prior to their execution. According to autopsy reports,[5] Ivica Bugarin, 23, was shot and stabbed repeatedly, most probably with bayonets. His left arm was amputated, probably with an ax.

Hand axes were probably used to kill Djuro Horvat, 28, and Mate Horvat, 32, whose skull was fractured after his head was held firmly to the ground while heavy blows were inflicted with a blunt object. Stjepan Horvat, 70, died as a result of multiple gunshot wounds.

September 3-4 — Četekovac, Čojlug and Balinci (municipality of Podravska Slatina)

On September 3-4, the villages of Četekovac (population 310) Čojlug (population 86) and Balinci (population 295) were attacked by Serbian forces. After the villages fell to Serbian forces, two policemen and 21 civilians (16 men and five women) were killed. The dead ranged in age from 18 to 91 years. According to autopsy reports,[6] 15 civilians were killed by gunshots to the chest or neck. J.B., 65, died from two wounds inflicted by a sharp object, presumably a knife. The body of M.S., 36, was set on fire.

A man from Četekovac recounted how his 58-year-old sister was shot in the knees and then killed with a knife by local Serbian insurgents, many of whom were known to him. A 67-year-old man said that he was dragged from his home and then witnessed his house and barn set on fire by Serbian paramilitaries.[7] Four separate witnesses interviewed by

---

[5] The following information is contained in reports of autopsies performed by doctors from the Department of Pathology and Cytology at Sisak Hospital and the Department of Anatomy at the Zagreb University School of Medicine.

[6] The autopsy reports were prepared by doctors from the Department of Pathology and forensic Medicine at Osijek Hospital and the Departments of Forensic Medicine and Anatomy at the Zagreb School of Medicine.

[7] Interviewed in the village of Četekovac and Balinac on January 7, 1992.

Helsinki Watch all identified Boro Lukić, a Serb from a nearby village, as the main perpetrator and organizer of the massacres in Četekovac and Balinac.

October 13 — Široka Kula (municipality of Gospić)

Reportedly 13 people (mostly elderly persons and at least one child) were shot or burned to death after a mob, led by a Serbian police officer, looted Croatian homes and set them on fire. Eight remaining survivors identified their attackers and those who looted their homes.

Of the 536 people who lived in the village of Široka Kula, approximately half were Serbs and half Croats. According to eyewitness statements, most of the Croats had fled by late September after being threatened and intimidated by local Serbian authorities, who had occupied the village. On October 13, the Serbian leader of the local police, Iso Poskonjak, promised to evacuate the remaining Croats from the village and instructed Dane Orešković (a Croat) to gather the Croatian villagers in two houses. As the Croats assembled in the buildings, Serbian paramilitary groups began looting the homes and shot at the assembling villagers. Most of those killed were members of the Orešković family. They were killed with shotguns and their bodies were thrown into their homes which had been set on fire.

Mande Baša and Ana Niksić, both over 70, were reportedly found with their throats slashed in Mande Baša's home.

October 31 -- Grubišno Polje and other villages in western Slavonia

Reports by the news agency Tanjug accused Croats of having committed war crimes against Serbs in the areas near the town of Grubišno Polje[8] in Croatia. The allegations were investigated by members of the European Community (EC) monitoring mission who found that Serbian forces, not Croatian forces, were guilty of summary executions and destruction of civilian property in the area. The monitoring mission's report concludes:

---

[8] The population of the municipality of Grubišno Polje is 14,186, of which 42.3 percent are Croatian, 32.1 percent are Serbian, 13.7 percent are Czech, 3.5 percent are Hungarian, and 4.5 percent are Yugoslav.

We established evidence of crimes which were committed by the [Serbian forces] during the two- and three-month period that they controlled that particular zone [western Slavonia]. Our team did not find evidence of killings later, nor of the systematic destruction of Serbian property by the Croatian National Guard or Croats from the area.[9]

The EC report also found that Czechs and Croats were killed in 16 villages visited by the mission, homes were destroyed and residents were terrorized.

November 10-11 -- Bogdanovci (municipality of Vukovar)

A 46-year-old Albanian woman, Z.B.,[10] had lived in Bogdanovci (population 1,208) for 18 years with her family. In early July, members of the Croatian National Guard had taken up positions in the village and many slept in the cellars of people's homes, reportedly with the proprietors' permission. After hostilities in the surrounding areas commenced in early July, many villagers fled. When the JNA and Serbian paramilitary groups launched a mortar attack against Bogdanovci on July 24, only about 100 people remained in the village. Z.B. hid in the cellar of a house with nine other people ranging in age from 46 to 83. At the time of the attack, approximately 50 members of the Croatian National Guard were stationed in the village. Z.B. recounted the attack:

> We were shelled from the Serbian-controlled villages of Petrovci, Bršadin and Pačetin. We hid in a basement for nearly two months, including my blind 83-year-old mother-in-law. The Croatian Guardsmen would bring us food during that time. On November 10, the village fell

---

[9] Excerpts of the European Community monitoring mission's report were published by the Paris-based newspaper *Liberation* on November 20, 1991, and Stephen Engelberg, "Villagers in Croatia Recount Massacre by Serbian Forces," *The New York Times*, December 19, 1991, p. A1.

[10] The woman was interviewed on December 12, 1991, in the village of Drsnik (municipality of Klina) in Kosovo.

to Serbian insurgents and the JNA and they told us to leave the cellar.

After three hours of detention in a local store,[11] the Serbian forces told us to go home. When we got outside into the yard of the store, they told us to form a line. Two elderly Croats -about 80 years old - who they had evidently found in the village, were also put in the line with us. One of the soldiers started shooting at each person in the line with a machine gun. When he got to me, he said "I am going to spare this one" and I was the only one who wasn't killed. During this shooting, a crowd of [JNA] soldiers stood by but did nothing to stop him from killing us.

They left me alone and I hid behind a wall. I saw them loading videos and televisions into a truck; they were confiscating property from abandoned homes. A soldier later saw me and they put me into a house. I was taken to a room where I was interrogated and raped repeatedly for twelve hours by several men. One of the men raped me twice and took away my wedding ring.

At 9:00 the next morning, two soldiers took me out of the house and I saw that the dead bodies had been covered with blankets during the night. I was then interrogated by a Serbian lieutenant colonel in his mid-fifties who greeted me in Albanian. He told me that he was a friend of my late husband's and that he was from the village of Lukavac in Kosovo. He saw the bodies of the people who had been killed the night before and asked me who these people were and I identified the bodies. He told me that maybe the Croatian Guardsmen had killed them but I replied that I saw a man in Yugoslav army uniform shoot them. The lieutenant colonel frowned and appeared angry. He said that he

---

[11] Four men who had hid with the witnesses and others were severely beaten by Serbian forces. The beatings are described below.

would spare my life because he knew my husband. The two soldiers and the lieutenant colonel drove me to the predominantly Ruthenian village of Petrovci, where I stayed with a Ruthenian couple for ten days. I was then put in a truck full of soldiers and driven to Valjevo [in Serbia]. Two soldiers gave me money for a bus ticket to Belgrade, from there I took a train to Kosovo.

November 18 — Vukovar

The city of Vukovar[12] was under constant siege by Serbian forces for three months. When the city fell on November 18, 15,000 people who had not fled the fighting emerged from the basements in which they lived for 12 weeks. After Vukovar's fall, civilians and soldiers *hors de combat* were beaten or arrested by Serbian paramilitary groups and the JNA. On the basis of interviews with displaced persons from Vukovar and foreign journalists and humanitarian workers who visited Vukovar immediately after its fall,[13] Helsinki Watch has reason to believe that many Croatian men, both civilians and combatants who had laid down their arms, were summarily executed by Serbian forces after Vukovar's fall.

November 18 — Škarbrnje (municipality of Zadar) and Nadin (municipality of Benkovac)

On November 18, at approximately 7:15 a.m., the JNA and the Serbian paramilitaries launched a mortar and artillery attack against the Croatian village of Škabrnje (population 1,964). At 11:00 a.m., a JNA tank reached St. Mary's Church in the center of town and fired a mortar

---

[12]Prior to its occupation, Croats comprised a majority of the population of the city of Vukovar (population 44,342) while the villages surrounding the city are predominantly Serbian. Croats comprised 43.7 percent and Serbs 37.4 percent of the population of the entire Vukovar municipality (population 84,024). Hungarians, Ruthenians, Slovaks, Ukrainians and Yugoslavs accounted for the remaining 18 percent of Vukovar's population.

[13]These interviews were conducted in Belgrade and Zagreb on December 14-19, 1991 and January 2-6, 1992, respectively.

at the main door. Serbian paramilitaries then sprayed the church with machine gun fire and one paramilitary took up position in the bell tower and shot at the village from the tower. On November 19, at approximately 1:30 p.m., the same forces attacked the neighboring Croatian village of Nadin (population 678). By 4:30 p.m., both Škabrnje and Nadin had fallen to Serbian forces.

Reportedly after Croats[14] destroyed a Yugoslav army tank at the western end of Škabrnje, the Serbian forces turned against the civilians. Serbian paramilitaries began plundering and shooting throughout the villages, killing 48 civilians (41 from Škabrnje and seven from Nadin). Most of those killed were elderly persons and, according to autopsy reports, the vast majority were killed by a bullet to the head shot at close range.[15] A tank crushed the head and chest of K.R., a 59-year-old woman. B.S., F.R., and S.S., were severely beaten and were subsequently killed by blows to the head with a blunt instrument.

A 19-year-old woman recounted her experience during the attack on Škabrnje:[16]

> About 500 insurgents and 20 tanks entered Škabrnje and occupied the village. They told us that we were all Ustašas and that they were going to kill us. Approximately 35 of the villagers were taken to the basement of the local church, where the insurgents beat many of the men, most of whom were elderly, with fists, rifle butts and sticks. My 80-year-old grandfather was beaten to death. We were later removed from the basement and taken to a detention center in Benkovac. When we emerged from that cellar, I saw approximately 10 bodies in a pile. The victims were both men and

---

[14] Eyewitnesses claim that neither members of the Croatian police force nor the Croatian army were stationed in Škabrnje or Nadin at the time of the attack. The resistance with which the Serbian forces were met was apparently organized by local Croats.

[15] The autopsies were performed by the Pathology Departments at Zadar Hospital and Sibenik Hospital (three bodies).

[16] Interviewed by Helsinki Watch on January 7, 1992, in Zagreb.

women and I recognized one of the dead women. I also saw that my house had been ransacked and sprayed with machine gun fire.

The local Zadar Red Cross and members of the European Community monitoring mission were denied access to the area after Škabrnje's and Nadin's occupation. Despite the fact that Nadin had been under control for over 24 hours, the JNA claimed that access to the villages was restricted because fighting continued. After a week of negotiations, the JNA agreed to deliver several corpses from Škabrnje to the Croatian authorities. Thirty-five bodies were delivered on November 23, and 13 more bodies were delivered on November 26.

Mid-December - Joševica (municipality of Glina)

Serbian paramilitary groups reportedly killed 20 Croats (ages five to 65) in the village of Joševica (population 120), which is part of the Serbian-controlled municipality of Glina.

Reportedly, members of the JNA and Serbian paramilitary units attacked Joševica and conducted a house-to-house search. Twenty people were taken from their homes and brought to the center of the village, where they were subsequently executed. According to the Serbian press, the killing of civilians in Joševica was meant to avenge the recent deaths of 21 Serbian paramilitaries killed during a Croatian offensive in the village of Gračanica, near Pokupsko. The Serbian authorities in Glina are said to be conducting an investigation of the killings.[17]

December 19 - Hum and Voćin (municipality of Podravska Slatina)

In August, Serbian insurgents seized control of several villages in the western Slavonian region of Croatia, including the predominantly Serbian villages of Hum (population 245) and Voćin (population 1,558). The area was reportedly held without any support from the JNA.[18]

---

[17] "Ubijeno 20 Hrvata," *Borba*, December 18, 1991, p. 7.

[18] Stephen Engleberg, "Villagers in Croatia Recount Massacre by Serbian Forces," *The New York Times*, December 19, 1991, p. A1.

After Croatian forces launched an offensive to regain lost territory in western Slavonia in early December, over 20,000 Serbian civilians and an undetermined number of paramilitaries fled the area. As the Serbian forces withdrew from the villages, they killed 43 Croats and burned many Croatian homes in both Hum and Voćin. The Catholic Church in Voćin, which served as a storage area for the Serbs' munitions, was completely destroyed after the paramilitaries exploded the ammunition to prevent it from falling into Croatian hands.

Eyewitnesses[19] claim that members of the "White Eagles" (Beli Orlovi) paramilitary group, were responsible for the massacre and destruction. According to one witness:

> Serbian irregulars from Valjevo and other parts of Serbia came to our village by bus on December 1. Using these same buses, they evacuated the Serbs from our village; they were reportedly taken to Bosnia and then to Belgrade. Četniks [members of a paramilitary group led by Vojislav Šešelj] were coming in small trucks packed with trunks of body bags. They spread rumors throughout the village that hundreds of Serbs had been massacred by Croats in Podravska Slatina and that they [the Serbs] would retaliate.

Another witness from Hum recounted her father's murder:

> Some time around December 1, 1991, my children and I were at my parents' and brother's home. Five or six police officers from the Krajina region came to our door dressed in army camouflage uniforms. They had driven in a car with "Z-101 - SAO Krajina" registration plates. They demanded that we turn over a radio transmitter which we did not have. They did not believe us and searched the entire house but found nothing. They took me, my parents, my children and my brother to Voćin. They put my brother in handcuffs and called him an

---

[19]Interviewed by Helsinki Watch on January 5, 1992, in Voćin, Hum and Podravska Slatina.

Ustaša, because our other brother was in the Croatian Guard in [Podravska] Slatina. When we got to the Vočin police station, they told us that "this is where you will be seeing throats slashed." We were put in a room and periodically people would come in and say, "Ustaša, we are going to cut your throats and kill you." We were kept in detention from 2:00 pm to 8:00 pm and were periodically interrogated by an inspector who was in his early 30s and claimed to be from Daruvar. At 8:00 pm, we were released and we went to our friend's home in Vočin. We were told to report back to the police station at 8:00 am the next morning.

The next morning we went to see the police inspector. A second man in a white overcoat was also present and he told us that he had to kill us because we were all Ustašas. At 3:30 pm they took us back to Hum and we saw that my father's home had been burned. More Četniks then arrived in the village. My mother, children and I were forced into the house and my father was left in the yard. When we got into the house, they threw something that sounded like a bomb outside. Three Četniks were yelling "The old man stays." I recognized one of the voices as that of Jovan C., with whom I went to school for many years. I heard my father say, "Don't shoot," but shortly thereafter, we heard shooting and when we came out into the yard we saw my father's body; only half of his head remained. We then hid at the home of B.D., a Orthodox [Serbian] man who helped us remove my father's body from the yard.

286

According to autopsy reports,[20] many of the victims had multiple gunshot wounds to the face and neck, usually from the back. Some also were shot in the legs and arms. Ten bodies were badly burned. I.S. had his hands bound, was strangled and then stabbed in the thorax. M.S. and V.A. were hit on the crown of the head with a sharp object, probably an axe. F.M. and M.M. were both shot in the eyes with a 9mm handgun. T.M. and M.M. appear to have been chained to a table and then set afire while still alive, according to the autopsy report.

The body of a 77-year-old Serb, S.N., was severely beaten and bruised; his arms appeared to have been branded with a hot iron. S.N.'s body was found a few meters from the bodies of an elderly Croatian couple who were chained and burned in their backyard. The village priest believes that the Serb may have been beaten and then killed for coming to the defense of the Croatian couple.

Among the civilian victims was a 72-year-old American citizen, Marija Majdanžić, nee Skender, who was born in Erie, Pennsylvania, but moved to Croatia at an early age. She appears to have died of smoke inhalation after being trapped in her burning home.

December 16-17 -- Jasenice and Zaton Obrovački (municipality of Obrovac)

In the evening of December 16, five civilians were executed in the village of Jasenice (population 1,280). The predominantly Croatian village was situated between the Maslinički bridge and the town of Obrovac, which had been under the control of Serbian forces for several months. Two men (Stipe Žubak, 71, and Ive Maruna, 71) and three women (Zorka Žubak, 67, Božica Jurjević, 66, and Manda Maruna, 67) were killed in Jasenice. On the same day, Luka Modrić, 66, was killed in the town of Zaton Obrovaćki (population 464). Reportedly, the bodies remained unburied 15 days after the murder.

---

[20] This information is taken from autopsy reports from Osijek Hospital and photographs of the dead bodies. When a Helsinki Watch representative visited Hum and Voćin on January 7, a local parish priest who had identified the bodies at the site of their murders also described the condition of the bodies and houses one day after the massacre. The bodies of burned animals and remains of the victims' clothing were still visible when Helsinki Watch visited the villages in January. Chains with which some victims were reportedly shackled also were found at the site where the bodies of the dead were burned.

December 21 - Bruška (municipality of Benkovac)

Ten Croats and one Serb were reportedly killed in the village of Bruška (population 366), in the Serbian-controlled municipality of Benkovac. All 10 Croats were surnamed Marinović and were between 20 and 70 years of age. A deaf woman was among the dead.

Reportedly four Serbs entered the Marinović home, where the Serb was having dinner with the Marinović family. They stabbed four victims and shot the other seven with rifles, according to autopsy reports.

General Vladimir Vujović, the commander for the Knin-based corp of the JNA, reportedly confirmed that the killings had taken place and that he had formed a commission to investigate the matter and send a written report to the Croatian authorities in Zadar.[21]

Court Martial and Execution

It was reported that Nemanja Samardžić, an advocate against Serbian extremist groups, was hanged after a court-martial for urging the expulsion of Četniks from Mirkovci in late August.[22] Such grounds for condemnation to death violate free speech and due process.

Torture and Mistreatment in Detention

Serbian forces maintain approximately 36 detention camps throughout Vojvodina, Serbia, Bosnia-Hercegovina and Krajina (where approximately 18 such camps exist).[23] Helsinki Watch has received reports that the conditions in these detention areas are often appalling

---

[21] *Vjesnik*, December 27, 1991.

[22]"Report on Civilian and Non-Combatants Killed as of 31.08.91," United Nations, Center for Human Rights, Geneva, p. 21.

[23] According to an international humanitarian organization, some of the camps are located in the following places: Niš (about 500 prisoners), Sremska Mitrovica (about 1,000 prisoners), Stajičevo, Bjeliči, Stara Gradiška, Marinj, Kotor, Knin, Glina, Begejči, and Manjača (near Banja Luka). See also Mary Battiata, "Serbian Guerrilla Camps Operate Inside Croatia," *The Washington Post*, July 22, 1991, p. A1.

and in many cases, detainees are tortured and beaten by their captors and guards.

Begejči Camp, Vojvodina

Dr. Malden Lončar, who worked at the Novi Sad hospital in the Serbian province of Vojvodina, was arrested by Serbian police reportedly after a package of medicine he was carrying to his parents in Ilok, Croatia, was found on his person. Lončar was beaten for 30 hours and then released. He was subsequently arrested several times thereafter and finally ended up in Begejči camp near Zrenjanin, Vojvodina. According to Lončar's written statement received by Helsinki Watch:

> The camp was an old barn filled with hay. There were over 550 people packed in this camp and we had to sleep on our sides for lack of space. People were tortured and beaten regularly. They would even put a barbed wire around your neck and beat you: if you moved, your throat would be cut from the wire. One old man died before my very eyes after he had been severely beaten.

> Over 90 percent of the people held were Croats and many were old. Some people were sick, some were paralyzed while others just needed immediate medical help. This maltreatment was not the work of individuals acting on their own accord. The orders came from above, from the commanders.

Lončar was released on December 10.

Sremska Mitrovica camp, Serbia

Helsinki Watch interviewed people who had been released from Serbian detention centers, many of whom were tortured, beaten and otherwise maltreated. Dr. Jure Njavro, a surgeon at the Vukovar Hospital, was taken to a detention camp in Sremska Mitrovica by Serbian forces after the fall of Vukovar on November 18. During his 22-day detention, Dr. Njavro was also physically maltreated and was forced to attend to people who had been severely beaten in the prison on a daily basis.

289

Every day I was called to attend to someone who had been badly beaten by his or her captors. I was usually awakened at night, which is when many people were beaten. I saw a prison guard beat and kick a medical technician. When I examined the technician, I saw that he had four broken ribs and that he was badly bruised.[24]

Bogdanovci

On November 10, as Serbian forces were advancing on the village of Bogdanovci, three grenades were thrown into the cellar in which Z.B. and nine other people had hidden for over three months during the conflict. Z.B. told Helsinki Watch:

> None of us were killed [by the grenades] because we hid in a narrow concrete corridor in the basement. A tank also fired at the house. At 9:00 the next morning, two bearded men dressed in Yugoslav army uniforms told us to leave the basement and go to our homes. We put my mother-in-law in a cart and started to move toward our house only to be stopped by a crowd of about 50 soldiers who kept asking us why we came to Bogdanovci and did we come because of our Catholic faith. They shouted vulgarities at us and took us to a store where the army had set up a headquarters. They searched all of us and I saw a soldier drop a bullet into the pocket of Nikola Palushi who had hidden with us in the basement the entire time. When they searched Palushi and found the bullet in his pocket, the four men who had been hiding with us in the basement for over three months were beaten. They separated me from the rest of the crowd and put me in a room where I could see them beating Krist Lleshi in the corridor with machine gun butts and fists: he was also kicked repeatedly. I never saw Krist

---

[24] Interview by Helsinki Watch on January 4, 1992, in Zagreb.

again and I presume that he died from the beatings.[25]

Benkovac

On July 22, 1991, three Croats were arrested in Benkovac by Serbian paramilitary police. Ivica Knez, 39, was beaten to death and the whereabouts of the other two men, Tomislav Čeranja and Tomislav Kolerić, remain unknown.[26]

Vukovar

One week after Vukovar's fall, only 128 of a total of about 440 patients from the Vukovar Hospital were handed over to the Croatian authorities. In some cases, it is feared that medical treatment was denied to the sick after their capture. More than 200 members of the hospital staff were captured and removed to Serbian detention centers.[27]

Disappearances

Vukovar

According to independent humanitarian organizations, at least 3,000 prisoners, including many noncombatants, were captured after the fall of the city of Vukovar on November 18. During half the day on November 20, the JNA denied journalists and the ICRC access to Vukovar Hospital. Helsinki Watch interviewed medical personnel who were in the hospital when it was sealed off to outside observers by the

---

[25]Interviewed by Helsinki Watch on December 12, 1991 in Kosovo.

[26] "Report on Civilian and Noncombatants Killed as of 31.08.91," United Nations Center for Human Rights, Geneva, p. 14.

[27]An American journalist who visited Vukovar two days after its fall saw two Serbian irregulars beat a man's head against a concrete wall while she looked on. Thereafter, a JNA officer ordered the two to stop beating the man.

JNA.[28] According to these eyewitnesses, the JNA interrogated the director of the hospital, Dr. Vesna Bosanac, and other doctors. In the interim, Serbian paramilitaries evacuated male medical personnel and wounded individuals who were identified as Croats by some Serbian members of the hospital staff.

Helsinki Watch is concerned about the arrests and disappearances of wounded Croatian forces and civilians, most of whom are males between the ages of 16 and 60. While most of the disappeared come from Vukovar, many Croatian males were captured by Serbian paramilitary groups after the fall of other villages, towns or cities.

Families have not been notified of their whereabouts and many missing are feared to have been the victims of extrajudicial executions. Ljubo Voloder was captured by Serbian forces after having spent three months in a basement in Vukovar. According to Ms. Marija Voloder, five army soldiers abducted her 58-year-old husband on November 19. She was forced to join a group of women, children and elderly persons who were being led away from the city. Ms. Voloder claims that her husband was not a member of the Croatian security forces or a combatant during the siege of Vukovar. Because she has not seen or heard of her husband since, she fears that he has been either imprisoned or executed.

As of January 10, 1992, about 3,000 people from Vukovar remain missing, according to the Association of Evacuated Vukovar Residents in Zagreb, which is keeping a list of names.

Hum and Vočin

Approximately 100 villagers from Hum and Vocin have been missing for over four months, according to the local parish priest in Vočin.[29] Local Serbs from the village raided Croatian homes and took some Croats prisoner in early September. According one witness:

> Franjo Banovac and Drago Jukić were taken to Gudnog,
> near the village of Sekulinac. Those who weren't
> captured fled and hid in the forests and cornfields. In

---

[28] The interviews were conducted between January 2-6, 1992, in Zagreb.

[29] Interviews by Helsinki Watch were conducted in Hum and Vočin on January 5, 1992.

292

later raids, Serbs came in trucks and entered only Croatian homes. The local Serbs stayed in their homes and did not help the others hunt down the Croats.

Zadar

The whereabouts of over 110 people from Serbian-controlled villages in the Zadar municipality remain unknown.

Benkovac

Some 1,500 persons residing in the villages of Bruška, Popovići, Lisičić, Rodajlice, Šopot and Podlug in the Serbian-controlled municipality of Benkovac are missing. On July 22, 1991, three Croats were arrested in Benkovac by Serbian paramilitary police. Ivica Knez, 39, was beaten to death and the whereabouts of the other two men, Tomislav Ceranja and Tomislav Kolerić, remain unknown.[30]

Obrovac

Some time around December 20, many of the 354 Croats who remained in the Obrovac municipality (from the villages of Kruševo, Jasenice, Zaton Obrovački and Medvidja, including the town of Obrovac itself) were reportedly taken to Knin jail. Most were elderly persons who had remained in their homes after Serbian insurgents assumed control in the Obrovac municipality.

Dalj

The fate of over 100 police officers and 200 civilians after the August battle for Dalj remains unknown.

---

[30] "Report on Civilian and Noncombatants Killed as of 31.08.91," United Nations Center for Human Rights, Geneva, p. 14.

Hostages

Hostages are defined as "persons who find themselves, willingly or unwillingly, in the power of the enemy and who answer with their freedom or their life for compliance with the orders of the latter and for upholding the security of its armed forces."[31]

Helsinki Watch has received many reports of persons who have been captured for the purpose of exchange, as set forth in our publication "Yugoslavia: Human Rights Abuses in the Croatian Conflict."

Indiscriminate and Disproportionate Attacks
Against Civilians and Civilian Targets

Serbian forces indiscriminately shelled the cities of Dubrovnik, Vukovar and Osijek for prolonged periods. The Yugoslav military justified its attack against these and other Croatian cities by claiming that it aimed to protect the Serbian population in Croatia and to liberate JNA barracks encircled by Croatian forces. However, such an argument cannot explain the shelling of Dubrovnik, a municipality in which the local Serbian population numbers only 6.7 percent and in which no JNA barracks exist. Dubrovnik was shelled from the beginning of October and the shelling of Osijek and Vukovar began in late August. The shelling of Vukovar lasted until November 18, when Croatian forces capitulated to Serbian troops, who occupied a city that had been reduced to rubble. Although the attacks against Dubrovnik and Osijek have subsided since the recent cease fire took effect, the shelling of the two cities was indiscriminate and caused much damage to civilian, historical and cultural objects. In all three cases, the use of force by Serbian troops was disproportionate to the threat posed by Croatian troops, and the indiscriminate shelling resulted in hundreds of civilian deaths and casualties.

Approximately half of those killed and one-third of those wounded in the conflict in Croatia are estimated to have been civilians. Most independent observers believe that at least 10,000 people have been killed since hostilities began in late June 1991 although Croatian officials say that less than 3,000 people died.

---

[31] International Committee of the Red Cross, *Commentary on the Additional Protocols of 1977* (Geneva 1987) at 874.

In addition, considerable civilian property, including hospitals, churches, and cultural monuments have been damaged or destroyed by the JNA's and Serbian rebels' shelling of towns.

Hospitals

Yugoslav armed forces have shelled hospitals in Croatia. Hospitals in Osijek, Pakrac, Vinkovci, Vukovar and Zadar have all been damaged or destroyed by aerial, mortar and artillery attacks. During the course of three days, from September 14-17, Osijek hospital was hit 56 times by mortar shells, 21 times by tank shells, and 17 times by rockets from multiple rocket launchers. The hospital was also hit by bullets from light weaponry. During one attack a 38-year-old nurse was killed and two doctors were wounded. Most of the hospital wards, including the intensive care unit, were damaged during the attack.

Dalj

Reportedly, at least 80 Croatian police officers and 195 civilians were wounded during or after the battle for Dalj on August 1. The JNA restricted access to journalists and the local Red Cross for several days after the attack. Initially, only 25 cadavers (only two of whom were civilians) were taken to Osijek hospital. By August 5, 70 dead and 195 wounded civilians were received by the Osijek morgue and hospital. More people were reportedly killed as they fled Dalj into the nearby town of Erdut during the siege.

Vukovar

During the four month siege against Vukovar, the hospital was repeatedly attacked and badly damaged, forcing the medical personnel to grant medical assistance, and even perform surgery, in the basement of the hospital.

International and local medical personnel have been hampered from evacuating the dead and wounded and delivering humanitarian aid because of continued fighting and disrespect for the red cross emblem.

Churches

Z.B. from the village of Bogdanovci said:

> Although there were no Guardsmen in the Catholic Church at the time of the attack, the shells seemed to be aimed at it. All the other shells fell indiscriminately throughout the village. Planes bombed the village and at one point 12 people were killed from aerial bombardment.

In addition, members of the Croatian Catholic Bishops' Conference have compiled a list through November 1991 of 348 churches destroyed or damaged during the conflict.

Osijek

In mid-1991, a woman travelling in a trolley car was killed after a mortar fell in Osijek's city center during rush hour.

Split

On November 15, 1991, three crew members on board a ferry in the port of Split were killed when federal gunboats opened fire.[32]

Indiscriminate Use of Land Mines

A 12-vehicle convoy, organized by Doctors Without Borders, evacuated 108 seriously injured people from the besieged town of Vukovar on October 19. Leaving the town on a road designated for their travel by the JNA, one of the trucks hit a mine and two nurses (from Luxembourg and Switzerland) were injured.

---

[32]"Yugoslavia Says Withdrawal Offer Made; Split in Command Seen," The Associated Press, November 15, 1991.

Targeted Attacks on European Community Helicopter

On January 7, 1992, a helicopter carrying five members (four Italians and one Frenchman) of the EC monitoring mission was shot down by a Yugoslav Air Force MIG fighter. The clearly marked helicopter had left Belgrade for Zagreb via Hungary and was shot down over Novi Marof, Croatia (30 miles east of Zagreb). All five persons aboard the plane were killed.

Shortly after the attack the Yugoslav military command announced that that air force chief, Zvonko Jurjević, ASC, had been suspended pending an investigation.[33]

Robbery

Dalj

Four days after Dalj's fall to Serbian forces on August 1, the army command put local Serbs in charge of all civilian functions. As of October 7, 533 non-Serbs (about 165 families) remained in Dalj and were forbidden from leaving the town. Families from Dalj were forcibly made to sign over their belongings and property to the local Serbian authorities before they were finally allowed to leave the town.

According to a written statement by Stjepan Papp, a member of the town council before Dalj's occupation, armed men in Yugoslav army uniforms entered his home on October 8. The Papp family was ordered to lock up their home and go to the local defense center, where Milorad Stričević, appointed by the Yugoslav Army as Minister for Ethnic Affairs for Dalj, Erdut and Aljmaš, took the Papp's car and apartment keys. Their belongings were subsequently confiscated by Serbian paramilitaries. While at the defense center, Ms. Ruža Papp was robbed of gold coins, money and a bank book which she had in her purse. The Papps were forced at gunpoint to sign over all their belongings to the defense center of Dalj. The statement claimed that the Papps were giving all their belongings to the local Serbian authorities as "gifts." After they signed the statement, they received passes allowing them to leave Dalj.

---

[33] Slobodan Lekic, "Five EC Observers Die in Yugoslav Attack," Associated Press, *The Washington Post*, January 8, 1992, p. A16.

Forced Displacement and Resettlement

The JNA and Serbian paramilitary groups are responsible for the displacement of thousands of people.

Helsinki Watch is concerned that Croats, Hungarians, Czechs and others are being forced by Serbian rebels from their homes in Serbian-occupied territory in order to create purely Serbian regions in areas that are otherwise of mixed population. We are concerned that this non-Serbian population is being discriminated against and being forcibly displaced on the illegal grounds of ethnic origin. We are also concerned that displaced Serbs are being resettled in Serb-occupied territory in Croatia to consolidate Serbian control over regions captured from Croats and prevent the original non-Serbian inhabitants from returning.

According to *The Washington Post*, displaced Serbs who fled from western Slavonia in November "have since been advised by Serbian officials in Belgrade to resettle" in Serbian-occupied territory in the region of Baranja,[34] where the most active resettlement campaign is currently taking place. Serbia plans to resettle 20,000 Serbs into 17 occupied villages in Baranja, some 4,000 homes and 100 stores are to be taken over by prospective Serbian settlers in Baranja and Serbian officials say "they have no intention of allowing tens of thousands of displaced Croats and ethnic Hungarians to return to their Baranja homes and force out Serbian settlers . . . . People are to be moved to conform to the Serbian notion of where a new border" between Croatia and Serbia should be drawn.[35]

We are also concerned that Serbian insurgents have evacuated Serbian women and children, presumably for reasons of safety, just prior to the launching of an offensive against Croatian positions or prior to an attempt to take over Croatian government institutions and the police station in various localities, particularly in eastern Slavonia. In almost all such cases, no non-Serbs were told to evacuate an area prior to a Serbian

---

[34]Blaine Harden, "Serbia Plans Resettlement of Croatian Region," *The Washington Post*, November 25, 1991, p. A14. Baranja is located north of the city of Osijek, between the Danube and Drava rivers. This fertile region is populated by Croats, Serbs and Hungarians and has been occupied by Serbian forces since late August.

[35]Ibid.

offensive. In instances where a Croatian offensive was anticipated (such as in western Slavonia in late November, for example), Serbian forces evacuated occupied territory and demanded that the local Serbian population flee with them. In almost all cases, Serbian insurgents frightened the villagers into fleeing, claiming that Croatian "Ustašas" were planning an attack and slaughter of the Serbian population and the burning and looting of Serbian homes, a fear reinforced by the Belgrade press. In television interviews, Serbian refugees from western Slavonia "have themselves disputed that it was the Croats who forced them to leave their homes. . . . [Rather,] Serb refugees said the federal army gave them 48 hours to flee."[36]

Killing, Assault and Harassment of Journalists

Helsinki Watch is concerned about the large number of journalists who have been killed, wounded, physically assaulted or otherwise attacked while reporting on the war in Croatia. According to the International Federation of Journalists (IFJ), Yugoslavia was "the most perilous site for journalists" in 1991.[37] According to the IFJ, some of the journalists killed in Yugoslavia were deliberately targeted because of their professional affiliation.[38]

Since July 26, 1991, at least 16 foreign and domestic journalists have been killed while covering the war in Croatia. Nine journalists have been captured and subsequently released by Serbian forces and four remain missing. At least 28 journalists have been wounded while covering

---

[36]Ibid.

[37]"Record Number of Journalists Reported Killed in 1991," Associated Press, January 6, 1992. According to the IFJ, of the 83 journalists killed worldwide in 1991, 21 were killed in Yugoslavia alone. More journalists have been killed since the IFJ released its report in late December.

[38]Ibid.

the war in Croatia. At least 63 have been attacked and over 38 have been otherwise harassed (i.e., threatened, property confiscated).[39]

Deaths

The following journalists were killed while covering the war in Croatia under circumstances in which Serbian forces or JNA were or may have been responsible:

- On July 26, Egon Scotland, a 42-year-old German reporter for the Munich-based *Sueddeutsche Zeitung* and his colleague, Peter Wuest, were fired upon reportedly by armed Serbs. The two men were driving in a clearly marked press car when they were attacked as they left the village of Glina. Scotland was wounded by gunfire and bled to death on the way to the hospital.

- Stjepan Penić, a Vukovar radio producer and correspondent for *Glas Slavonije*, was killed on August 4 near the town of Dalj. His body was discovered on August 19.

- Gordan Lederer, a cameraman for Croatian Television, was critically injured in Kostajnica on August 9. Despite a request by his colleagues, the Yugoslav army refused to transport the wounded Lederer to the hospital and he died.

- Žarko Kajić, a cameraman for Croatian Television, was killed in Osijek on August 28, reportedly after he was fired at by an armored Yugoslav army vehicle.

- On August 29, Djuro Podboj, a technician for Croatian Television, was killed in the town of Beli Manastir reportedly during an attack by Serbian forces.

---

[39] The figures in this section were gathered in Helsinki Watch interviews with witnesses and information from the International and American PEN Centers, the Committee to Protect Journalists, the Foreign Press Bureau in Zagreb, Croatia, and non-Yugoslav press and wire reports.

- Nikola Stojanac, a technician for Croatian Television, was killed on September 15 in the Gospić area reportedly while he was trying to film Yugoslav army jets.

- On September 19, Pierre Blanchet, a correspondent for the French weekly, *Nouvel Observateur*, and Damien Ruedin, a correspondent for Radio Suisse Romande, were killed when their vehicle hit a mine outside army barracks near Petrinja.

- Zoran Amidžić, Bora Petrović, Dejan Miličević and Sreten Ilić of Belgrade Television were killed on October 9 on the road between Petrinja and Glina in circumstances still unclear.

- Živko Krstičević, a cameraman for WTN, was killed in the town of Turanj, near Karlovac, on December 30, by a mortar reportedly launched by Serbian forces.

Arrests

On September 4, two French journalists, Jean-Pierre Musson and Eric Micheletti, were captured by Serbian paramilitaries and taken to Yugoslav army authorities in Banja Luka. Although their equipment was confiscated, both men were released three days thereafter.

On September 6, Maciej Maciejewski and Marcin Kowalczki, journalists for the Polish *Dziennik Lodzki*, were captured by armed Serbs near Vrgin Most and were accused of spying. Their release was negotiated by diplomats. On September 26, WTN reporters, Diviek Quemener and Jacques Languein, their guide, Alan Bubalo, and two French journalists reportedly were captured by Serbian paramilitaries near Pakrac. After three days, they were handed over to the Yugoslav army and were subsequently released.

Disappearances

The whereabouts of four journalists remains unknown. On September 1, Viktor Nogin and Genadi Kurinoj, a reporter and cameraman for Soviet Television, left Belgrade for Zagreb, via Osijek, and have not been heard from since. They were driving a dark blue Opel Omega with diplomatic license plates. They are presumed to have been killed.

Radio Vukovar correspondent Siniša Glavašević and cameraman Branimir Polovina have been missing since the city of Vukovar fell to Serbian forces on November 19. It is believed that they were removed from a column of civilians evacuating Vukovar Hospital and that they are being held by Serbian forces within Vukovar or in a detention camp in Serbia.

Restrictions on Free Expression

Forced Mobilization

Helsinki Watch is alarmed by what appears to be an effort by the Serbian government to silence anti-war activists and opposition figures by sending them to the battlefields in Croatia. This practice is most widespread in Vojvodina and Belgrade. The most notable example of such forced mobilization is the case of Nenad Čanak, President of the League of Social Democrats of Vojvodina/Yugoslavia (Liga Socijaldemokrata Vojvodine/Jugoslavije - LSV/J) and a vocal anti-war activist and opposition figure. On November 7, Čanak[40] was arrested by local police and taken to the police station: he was subsequently transferred to military police custody and taken to a military detention center. Čanak was then sent to Ilok, Croatia, as a member of the volunteer corps of the army. Čanak's arrest and forcible mobilization was vehemently protested by many domestic and foreign organizations and he was subsequently released on December 12.

Although Čanak's case received much publicity, Helsinki Watch has received reports of similar cases of arrests and subsequent mobilization of anti-war activists by Serbian authorities and the Yugoslav army, particularly in the province of Vojvodina and among independent-minded journalists in Belgrade. Repression against ethnic Hungarian anti-war activists is also taking place. Reportedly, after peaceful anti-war demonstrations were held in the Hungarian communities of Zenta and Temerin, special police forces intimidated ethnic Hungarians in Zenta and Ada, the seat of the Hungarian community in Vojvodina. The organizers of the demonstration, Janos Szabo, Jozsef Bodo, and Jozsef

---

[40] Čanak was interviewed by a Helsinki Watch representative on December 17, in Novi Sad.

Papp were arrested and their whereabouts were not disclosed to their families.

Criminal Charges

The Serbian government has also tried to silence and intimidate opposition politicians and political groups by bringing criminal charges against them. In early January, charges were brought against Vuk Drašković, leader of the Opposition Serbian Renewal Movement (Srpski Pokret Obnove -- SPO) that has criticized President Milošević's policies in Croatia and Serbia. On March 9-10, 1991, demonstrations were held in Belgrade to protest Serbian government control of the media. Excessive police force and an ensuing riot resulted in the deaths of a 17-year-old youth and one police officer. At least 203 were wounded. Demonstration participants and organizers -- including Drašković -- were arbitrarily arrested and harassed.[41] Almost one year later, charges have been brought against Drašković purportedly because of his role in organizing the March demonstrations. Drašković is charged with bearing the responsibility for the deaths of two men, the injuries of 29 individuals and 15.5 million dinars worth of material damage. If convicted, Drašković could face fifteen years in prison.

Helsinki Watch believes that the charges brought against Vuk Drašković are unjustified and are being used as a means of political intimidation. Although Drašković was one of the main organizers of the March demonstrations, it was the excessive use of force by the Serbian police against demonstrators that resulted in the ensuing riot. Criminal charges were filed against Drašković after he and other Serbian opposition figures voiced their discontent regarding President Milošević's policies toward Croatia, continued government control of the media and stifling of the Serbian opposition. Helsinki Watch believes that Drašković's arrest is being used as a means to intimidate opposition groups in Serbia and cow them into submission.

---

[41]For an account of human rights violations and the excessive use of force by the Serbian police, see "Yugoslavia: The March 1991 Demonstrations in Belgrade," Helsinki Watch, May 1, 1991.

Persecution of Anti-War Activists

The Serbian government now portrays anti-war activists as fascists and traitors to the Serbian nation. Many prominent intellectuals such as Mirko Kovač, Bogdan Bogdanović and Filip David have been threatened with bodily harm and are otherwise harassed for their opposition or anti-war activities.[42] In some cases, groups and persons who refer to themselves as "Yugoslav," rather than "Serbian," are targets of attacks and harassment. The Serbian government's propaganda campaign has resulted in the political marginalization of Serbia's once-active opposition movement.

Moreover, members of Serbian paramilitary groups and individual vandals have harassed members of the Serbian opposition, the anti-war movement and the independent or non-Serbian press. In some cases, Serbian authorities appear to have condoned, if not encouraged, such harassment and assaults. In November, the headquarters of the Center for Anti-War Activities was vandalized. On November 11, five men vandalized the headquarters of the Reformist Party of Serbia, an opposition group that advocates the maintenance of a single, democratic Yugoslavia.[43] The Belgrade headquarters of Yutel, a pan-Yugoslav television program based in Sarajevo, was also ransacked and members of its staff were physically assaulted. Helsinki Watch is not aware of any arrests by the Serbian authorities of individuals responsible for such violence.

Press Restrictions

Helsinki Watch is concerned about reports that the Yugoslav army is forcing local newspapers in Kragujevac and other areas in inner Serbia to print lists of persons whom the JNA claims are army deserters who fled from the battlefields in Croatia. Military authorities reportedly intended to post such lists in public areas. At anti-war rallies in Serbia, petitions were signed protesting such action by the Yugoslav military.

---

[42]See Slobodan Kostić, "Grafit na jasenovačkom cvetu," *Borba*, December 12, 1991, p. 22.

[43]See Dušan Stojanović, "Yugoslav Military Bombards Dubrovnik, Appears Near to Capturing Vukovar," Associated Press, November 11, 1991.

According to the Center for Anti-War Activities, 680 people signed such a petition at an anti-war meeting in Belgrade on December 29. Thereafter, the military authorities revoked their demands that such names be publicly disclosed. Helsinki Watch does not question the JNA's role in maintaining discipline in the army. However, Helsinki Watch is concerned that the public disclosure of the names of purported deserters could lead to reprisals against them or their families by paramilitary groups or individual extremists. Moreover, by demanding that local newspapers publish such lists, Yugoslav military authorities are interfering with freedom of the press.

The Albanian-language press in Kosovo has either been banned by the Serbian authorities (as in the case of the Albanian-language daily *Rilindja*) or completely subordinated to the Belgrade media (as in the case of Radio/Television Priština). The governments in Vojvodina and Montenegro have effectively wrested all control of the press from journalists. Journalists, regardless of their national or ethnic affiliation, have been harassed throughout Vojvodina for their support of the political opposition. The managing directors and editors of the Radio/Television Novi Sad were replaced by the provincial government. In addition to Vojvodina's Serbian-language media, Hungarian-, Ruthenian-, Romanian-, and Slovak-language presses also were purged. Directors, editors and journalists unsympathetic to the provincial government or Belgrade's politics were replaced at the following newspapers: *Dnevnik, Poljoprirednik, Hlas Ljudu, Libertatee, Ruske Slovo, Het Nap* and *Magyar Szo.*

Continuing Human Rights Abuses in Kosovo

The Serbian misdemeanor law, which allows for up to 60 days imprisonment, has been grossly abused by Serbian authorities in Kosovo. Instead of prolonged detention, ethnic Albanians are being imprisoned several times for short periods. Many Albanians are arrested for committing so-called "verbal crimes," such as "insulting the socialist, patriotic, national and moral feelings of the citizenry," "insulting a public official, institution or organization," and "conveying disturbing news." In many cases, Albanians are charged with such "crimes" for their support of Albanian nationalism, of independence from Serbia and of republic status for Kosovo or union with Albania. Those convicted are usually given 30- to 60- day prison sentences and by the time an appeal is filed and a hearing is granted, an individual has already served his or her prison term. Many Albanians have served multiple misdemeanor sentences, and the practice is being abused so as to silence, intimidate and harass opponents and critics of the Serbian regime in Kosovo. Moreover, some Albanians are summoned by the police for interrogations or, what is commonly referred to as an "informative discussion" (informativni razgovor). In some cases, ethnic Albanians have been beaten during such interrogations.

Rilindja, the only daily Albanian-language newspaper in Kosovo, remains banned; it has been eighteen months since its forcible closure in July 1990. From October 25 to December 1, 1991, four Albanian journalists were arrested and imprisoned for publishing a book, a map and two articles which were deemed to be subversive by the Serbian authorities. Journalists who have been imprisoned for similar "offenses" in the past have been beaten while in police custody. Albanians have lost their jobs for refusing to sign loyalty oaths to the Serbian government or the new management which was installed by the Serbian authorities. Others have been dismissed from their jobs because they organized and participated in peaceful demonstrations. Some Albanians who have lost their jobs have also lost their apartments, in which their employers often hold a share. Approximately 300 Albanian families have been evicted from their homes without a court hearing, to which they are entitled. Dismissals of Albanians from their jobs and evictions from their homes have led to further economic and social marginalization of Albanians in Kosovo, where reportedly 86 percent of the population lives below the poverty line.[44]

The medical profession in Kosovo has also been purged of Albanians. Reportedly 2,000 Albanian medical personnel have been dismissed from their jobs. The quality of health care has deteriorated so drastically that cases of tetanus, diphtheria and child paralysis are appearing among the population. The delivery and receipt of humanitarian aid by local relief groups is impeded. In some cases, stocks of humanitarian aid have been confiscated by the Serbian authorities.

After the Serbian authorities revised the school curriculum so as better to reflect Serbian culture and history in Kosovo's education, ethnic Albanian students boycotted classes. The Albanians claimed that Albanian history and culture were reduced to a bare minimum so as to accommodate the Serbian curriculum. Moreover, ethnic Albanians object

---

[44] *Borba*, December 6, 1991.

306

to the institution of Serbian as the main language of instruction in Kosovo's schools. Although provisions are made for Albanian-language use in primary and secondary schools, Albanians claim that they are deprived of the right to use their language. Helsinki Watch urges the Serbian government to respect the rights of ethnic minorities in accordance with principles set forth in various documents of the Conference on Security and Cooperation in Europe (CSCE), particularly the two documents that summarize the results of the July 1991 experts' meetings on ethnic minority rights in Geneva.

* * *

Dear President Milošević and General Adžić:

This lengthy letter contains only a portion of the information on human rights abuses compiled by Helsinki Watch. We urgently call on you to end these violations.

We call upon the Yugoslav Army and Serbian forces in Croatia to:

• Investigate reports of summary executions and torture of civilians and disarmed combatants by Serbian military or paramilitary groups and to prosecute and punish all those guilty of such crimes.

  • Refrain from the indiscriminate and disproportionate use of force, which has caused thousands of civilian deaths and injuries, and cease all discriminate attacks against civilians -- including journalists -- and civilian objects.

  • Immediately and unconditionally release all civilians held hostage. We urge that all captured combatants be treated humanely and that torture and other mistreatment cease.

  • Make known the whereabouts of all missing persons abducted by Serbian forces.

  • Cease the robbing, pillaging, and forcible confiscation of homes and property.

  • Refrain from forcibly displacing persons for non-war related reasons and allow all persons forcibly displaced to return to their homes without reprisals or mistreatment against such persons.

  • Refrain from mobilizing members of the anti-war movement and political opposition in Serbia as a means of silencing government critics.

308

- Refrain from interfering with freedom of the Serbian press by demanding that it print the names of purported army deserters.

We call upon the Serbian government to:

- Investigate reports of harassment of, and attacks upon, anti-war activists, opposition groups, and the independent-minded media.

- Drop all criminal charges brought against Vuk Drašković for his role in organizing the March 1991 demonstrations in Belgrade.

- Cease all harrassment, arrest, demotion and dismissal of independent journalists and respect freedom of the press.

- Cease all arrests, prosecution and imprisonment of ethnic Albanians who have peacefully exercised their right to free speech and expression in Kosovo.

- Cease the mistreatment of Albanians held in detention.

- Immediately and unconditionally lift the ban against *Rilindja*.

- Cease all forms of discrimination against ethnic Albanians in Kosovo, including the arbitrary dismissal of Albanian workers from their jobs and their subsequent eviction from their homes.

Appendix E: Helsinki Watch Letter to Franjo Tudjman, President of the Republic of Croatia

February 13, 1992

His Excellency Franjo Tudjman
President of the Republic of Croatia
Radičev Trg 2
41000 Zagreb
Croatia

Dear President Tudjman:

The U.S. Helsinki Watch Committee is deeply concerned by reports of serious human rights abuses by forces responsible to the Croatian government and by individual extremists in Croatia. Our own investigations of these reports, conducted during a series of fact-finding missions to Croatia in the past year, indicate that many of these reports are well-founded. We call upon you to investigate the abuses enumerated in this letter and to punish those responsible for them. We call upon you to take immediate measures to ensure that such violations of human rights do not occur again.

The abuses described in this letter include violations of the laws of war in the current conflict between Croatian and Serbian forces and the Yugoslav army, including the summary execution of civilians and disarmed combatants; the torture and mistreatment of detainees; arbitrary arrests and disappearances; destruction of civilian property and the killing of journalists covering the war. In addition to violations connected with the war, Helsinki Watch has also documented restrictions on freedom of expression and the press and interference with the independence of the judiciary. Finally, we are gravely concerned about the harassment, discrimination and rising violence against Serbs not engaged in the armed conflict in Croatia.

310

Rules of War Violations in Croatia by Croatian Forces

Violations of the rules of war are often committed by local police officers and members of the Croatian army[1] in areas which are under heavy siege by Serbian forces and the Yugoslav army. Under international law, it is absolutely impermissible to summarily execute, mutilate or torture civilians or persons hors de combat.[2] Helsinki Watch holds the Croatian government
-- in particular the Croatian Ministries of Interior and Defense -- responsible for the acts of its armed forces.

Helsinki Watch is concerned that paramilitary forces of the Croatian Party of Rights are not sufficiently under the control of the Croatian government. Although steps have been taken by the Ministry of Defense to place such groups under Croatian government command, Helsinki Watch urges the Croatian authorities to ensure that such paramilitary groups do not operate independently without responsible military command.

---

[1] Recently, the Croatian National Guard (Zbora Narodne Garde - ZNG) has officially been renamed the Croatian Army and will be referred to as such herein.

[2] See article 3 common to the Geneva Conventions of 1949 and Article 4 of the 1977 Second Protocol Additional to the Geneva Conventions. At the invitation of the International Committee of the Red Cross, plenipotentiary representatives of the various parties to the conflict in Croatia -- including the Croatian government -- met in Geneva twice (on November 26-27 and December 19-20) and agreed to comply with the provisions of international humanitarian law. Helsinki Watch holds the Croatian and Serbian governments and the Yugoslav armed forces responsible for violations of the rules of war.

311

Summary Executions of Civilians and Persons Hors de Combat

September 21 - Karlovac

According to well-publicized news reports[3] ackowledged by the Croatian government, three soldiers who were serving their army terms, a Yugoslav army captain (Mile Peruača) and 17 Yugoslav army reservists -- most of whom were Serbs from Krnjak (municipality of Karlovac) and Vojnić -- left the town of Slunj in two army trucks and headed for a Yugoslav army garrison in Karlovac. En route, they were stopped by Croatian forces on a bridge over the Korana river and told to surrender. Several men were taken to police headquarters in Karlovac and later to Zagreb, where they were detained. The rest remained on the bridge waiting for a Karlovac police vehicle to come and pick them up. While they waited, the Croatian police officers beat their captives, particularly Captain Peruača and several reservists. One of the reservists, Svetozar Šarac, was hit in the face with a rifle butt and later lost an eye. A Croatian police officer, Mihajlo Hrasto, then ordered the captives to form a line, whereupon 13 of the soldiers were shot. Two of the soldiers managed to escape and one was later found wounded under the bridge.

Two of the Yugoslav army reservists, Svetozar Šarac and Dušan Mrkić, were treated in Karlovac hospital. Those killed were:

Jovan Sitić (25)
Božo Kozlina (37)
Nebojša Popović (24)
Mile Savić (37)
Milenko Lukač (32)
Slobodan Milovanović (25)
Svetoslav Gojković (32)
Miloš Srdić (43)
Zoran Komadina (27)
Mile Babić (42)
Vaso Bižić (36)

---

[3] The case was reported in the Serbian, Croatian, and foreign press. See also "Civilian and Non-Combatants Killed in Yugoslavia," United Nations Center for Human Rights, Geneva, p. 12.

Captain Mile Peruača (27)
Ensign Nikola Babić (43)

According to Željko Olujić, Croatia's Public Prosecutor, a member of the Croatian Army has been charged with the crime and is being held pending psychiatric examination.[4] He has been charged with murder.[5]

Mid-October - Gospić

According to Gospić residents interviewed by Helsinki Watch,[6] tensions between Serbs and Croats grew after the current Croatian government came to power in May 1990. Violence erupted on the evening of August 28-29, 1991, after a shoot-out between Serbs from the Krajina region[7] and Croats from Gospić. Since then, fighting has not subsided in Gospić and many people have been forced to flee the area or take shelter in their basements.

In late August, Milica Smiljanić -- a 42-year-old half-Serb, half-Croat from Gospić -- took refuge from the fighting in the basement of her mother-in-law's home on Vlade Kneževića 4 in Gospić. Eleven other people (ten Serbs and one Croat) also hid in the same basement. The twelve people hid in two separate rooms in the basement; Ms. Smiljanić, her husband Stanko, her mentally-ill brother-in-law Milan, her mother-in-law Bosiljka and an elderly woman, Milka Lemajić, hid in the same room. Željko Mrkić, Danica Barač, Radovan Barač, Radmilla Stanić, Luka

---

[4] Stephen Engelberg, "Yugoslavia's 'Pure Hatred'," *International Herald Tribune*, December 20, 1991, and "Villagers in Croatia Recount Massacre by Serbian Forces," *The New York Times*, December 19, 1991.

[5] The accused was charged under Article 35, clause 2(1), of the Croatian Criminal Code.

[6] Serbian residents who had fled from the Gospić municipality were interviewed in Belgrade on January 28-29, 1992. The population of the municipality of Gospić is 28,732, 64.3 percent of whom are Croatian, 31.1 percent Serbian, and 1.8 percent Yugoslav.

[7] The neighboring municipalities of Titova Korenica and Gračac are under the control of Serbian forces, which declared the area part of Krajina.

Šulentić, Marica Barač and her six-month old daughter, Jelena, hid in a second room.

On October 16, five members of the Croatian police entered the basement and first came into the room where the Smiljanić family was hiding. Four of the men wore olive ski masks over their faces while the fifth man had blond hair and wore glasses. All five men were dressed in uniforms worn by the Croatian police under the prior regime. All five carried AK-47 rifles. Ms. Smiljanić later told Helsinki Watch[8]:

> One of the men shot once at the ceiling, then pointed his gun at us and told us "Četniks"[9] to get out of the basement. We walked out of the room and into the hallway of the basement. One of the men put a gun to my back and told me to find Radovan Barač. His wife was Croatian and he worked in the local post office. I went to the other room and said, "Rajko, come out." No one opened the door but his mother, Danica, eventually came out and told the police officers to leave her son alone. One of the policemen pushed me aside and dragged Radovan Barač, his mother Danica, Radmilla Stanić, Željko Mrkić and Luka Šulentić from the room and told them to go upstairs. They also took my husband and brother-in-law, even though I pleaded with them to leave them alone.
>
> My mother-in-law, Milka Lemajić, Marica Barač and her child and I were left alone in the basement and the

---

[8] Interviewed in Belgrade on January 28, 1992.

[9] During World War II, the Četniks were Serbian forces engaged in the civil war against both the Croatian Ustaša and the communist partisans. The Croats commonly refer to the current Serbian insurgents as Četniks because they equate their current actions with the atrocities committed against Croats and Muslims during World War II. Some of the Serbian insurgents Helsinki Watch interviewed vehemently reject the label of "Četnik," claiming they are merely defenders of their land and not extremists. Others speak with praise of Vojislav Šešelj, leader of the ultra-right-wing Serbian Radical Party (Srpska Radikalna Stranka) and the Serbian Četnik Movement (Srpski Četnički Pokret).

policemen told us not to say anything to anyone. About two hours later, Luka Šulentić, the Croat, came back. Luka is deaf and because we have known each other for a very long time, I have learned to communicate with him through sign language. He told me that the police officers wanted to see everyone's identification cards and that my husband was cold; he was not wearing a coat when they dragged him out of the basement.

According to Dr. Zoran Stanković, a Yugoslav army officer and pathologist at the Military Hospital in Belgrade,[10] twenty-four bodies -- 15 men and nine women -- were found burned near the villages of Široka Kula and Perušić (municipalities of Gospić) in late December. Five more bodies were found nearby. The dead included the aforementioned Serbs who had been taken from the Smiljanić basement in Gospić.

According to Dr. Stanković, the victims were killed three kilometers from the village of Perušić and subsequently moved to Široka Kula by approximately 50 Serbian irregulars and five members of the Yugoslav army on December 27. All the victims were shot. Several who apparently did not die from the gunshot wounds were brutally executed. One person (Branko Stulić) appeared to have been stabbed in the back by a knife; a second individual was hit above the eye with either a bayonet or an axe; a third person (a woman) was shot in the head at close range; a fourth individual appeared to have had his skull broken by a heavy, blunt object. The bodies were then thrown into a pile, doused with gasoline and set on fire. According to Dr. Stanković, the bodies were approximately two months old when they were discovered.

The Croatian authorities are investigating the case and President Tudjman reportedly visited Gospić personally to inquire about the massacre. Helsinki Watch calls upon the Croatian government to hold accountable local commanders in Gospić -- particularly Tihomir Orešković, commander of the Croatian Army in Gospić, and Željko Bolf, the Gospić police chief -- for the actions of their troops.

---

[10] Interviewed on January 29, 1992, at the Military Hospital (Vojna Medicinska Akademija - VMA) in Belgrade. Helsinki Watch also spoke with family members who had come to identify the bodies of their family members and neighbors on the same day. Medical documents, videotapes and pictures also were examined.

November 15-25, Marino Selo (municipality of Pakrac)

At approximately 6:15 a.m. on November 15, members of the Croatian Army arrested 15 Serbs from the village of Kip (population 271, municipality of Daruvar), six from the village of Klisa (population 138, municipality of Pakrac) and one from the village of Batinjani (population 547, municipality of Pakrac). Most of those arrested were members of the Serbian insurgency, although they reportedly were unarmed at the time of their arrest. They were held in a hotel in the village of Marino Selo (population 364, municipality of Pakrac) and were guarded by 12 to 15 members of the Croatian Army. J.K.,[11] a 35-year-old man who was among those arrested in Kip, recounted his experience to Helsinki Watch:

> Four of the Croatian Guardsmen would get drunk frequently and beat all of us. I recognized them as being from the Pakrac-Daruvar area; one of them was named Rujić. They would take some of the captives out of the cell and tell them that they were going to be exchanged. They were taken outside and we heard gunfire. Those taken from their cells never came back. The Guardsmen who killed them made us bury the corpses. I buried seven men.

J.K. identified those he buried as:

Pero Popović, from Kip
Jovo Popović, from Kip
Pero Novković, from Kip
Milan Popović, from Kip
Savo Goljović, from Klisa
Nikola Krajnović, from Klisa
an unknown man from Klisa

Of the fifteen men from Kip who had been detained in the same cell, twelve were subsequently killed; they were either shot or beaten to death. In addition to those listed above, those killed included:

---

[11] J.K., who asked that his name not be used, was interviewed on January 29, 1992, at the Military Hospital (Vojna Medicinska Akademija - VMA) in Belgrade.

Branko Bunčić
Mijo Danojević
Nikola Gojković
Filip Gojković
Gojko Gojković
Mijo Gojković
Jovo Popović[12]

J.K., his 61-year-old father and another 35-year-old man were spared. They were taken to and detained in Daruvar on November 25-26, then to Bjelovar on December 10. On December 12, they were released in an exchange of prisoners that took place in Karlovac.

Helsinki Watch is also aware of two murders that have been investigated by the Croatian authorities. A restauranteur, Srbislav Petrova, was killed by members of the Croatian police force in the municipality of Pula. The police officers have been arrested and criminal charges have been filed against them. The murder of the Zec family in Zagreb in early January has also been investigated by Croatian authorities. The perpetrators have been arrested and an investigation by magistrates of the Zagreb district court is currently in progress.

Unexplained Deaths of Serbs

Helsinki Watch has received reports of Serbs who were killed shortly after being arrested by Croatian forces or whose bodies were found in Croatian-controlled territory. In some cases, the circumstances of the deaths remain unknown. In other instances, the available evidence implicates members of the Croatian police -- particularly in Sisak -- as having played a role in the deaths. Helsinki Watch calls upon the Croatian government to conduct thorough investigations of the deaths of the following individuals and to prosecute those found guilty of their murders:

● The corpse of Miljenko Djuričić, a 38-year-old Serb from Borovo Naselje, was found in the Danube River, near the village of Begeča, on July 17. According to the district prosecutor in Novi

---

[12] Two men with the same name were killed (see list of those buried by J.K.). The men were reportedly first cousins.

Sad, Djuričić was thrown into the Danube while still alive and his body -- which had been in the water for two to four days before it was discovered -- bore signs of torture. Djuričić had been arrested on July 13 by the Croatian police and interrogated. He was released on July 15 but was not seen alive thereafter.[13]

● Evica and Dušan Vila and their sons Marko and Željko were shot and their bodies discovered in Sisak.

● Vlado Bošić, a truck driver for "Slavijatrans" from Petrinja, was reportedly beaten to death. Reportedly, at a press conference, Djuro Brodarac, the Sisak police chief, claimed that the person who committed these crimes went beyond his orders but that he was not aware what type of -- if any -- disciplinary measures had been taken against the perpetrator.

● Milenko Djapa, a worker at the Sisak oil refinery, was murdered.

● Branko Oljača, a Serb who worked for the Croatian police force in Sisak, was murdered.

● Zoran Vranešević, a Serb who worked for the Croatian police force in Sisak, was murdered.

● Mico Čalić was a worker at the Sisak steel plant; his body was discovered in the Brezovići forest.

● Ilija Martić was reportedly killed at the entrance of a restaurant in Sisak.

● Nikola Arbutina, a worker at the "Graditelja" firm in Sisak, was murdered.

● Miloš Grubić, a retiree from the village of Blinjski Kut (population 500, municipality of Sisak), was reportedly held in

---

[13] Tanjug report dated July 20 reported by Agence France-Presse "Decouverte du cadavre d'un Serbe portant des traces de tortures," July 20, 1991.

318

the jail in Sisak; his body was subsequently found on the outskirts of the village of Komarevo.

- Damjan Zilić was a manager at the Sisak oil refinery; his body was discovered in the Jakuševac section of Zagreb.

Torture and Mistreatment in Detention

Croatian forces maintain more than nine detention centers throughout Croatia, including Bjelovar, Gospić, Zadar, Split, Rijeka, Slavonska Požega, Osijek and several in the municipalities of Karlovac and Zagreb[14]. Helsinki Watch has documented cases of torture and mistreatment of captives after they have been arrested and detained by the Croatian Army or police. In many cases, abuse of captives also takes place in local police stations. On the basis of numerous reports received by Helsinki Watch, Croatian forces in Sisak, Gospić and in areas of western Slavonia appear to be particularly brutal toward those held in custody.

J.K., who was among those arrested in Marino Selo,[15] was beaten during his detention. J.K.'s lower jaw and two ribs (the 7th and 8th ribs) were broken and all his teeth were knocked out. When Helsinki Watch spoke to J.K. and his doctor, surgery had been performed on his jaw and metal teeth had been implanted in his mouth.

---

[14] Helsinki Watch representatives visited detention centers in Osijek in August and in Zagreb in September. In both cases, Helsinki Watch representatives were permitted to speak with those held in custody privately and to examine their cells.

[15] See above case of summary executions in Marino Selo.

On November 26, Ivan K.[16] was arrested by three local police officers in the Zaprešić section of Zagreb. Ivan's ten year-old son also was taken to the police station, apparently because there was no one home at the time to look after him. Ivan reported that although he and his son were well-treated while at the Zagreb police station, he was never told of the reason for his arrest. Both Ivan and his son remained at the Zagreb police station from approximately 7:15 p.m. until 10:00 p.m., when they were taken by three men in camouflage uniforms to the Sisak police station.

> When we arrived at the police station in Sisak, I was hand-cuffed and taken to a room where five or six police officers started cursing at me, asking me how many Croats I had massacred, calling me a Četnik and threatening to put me in solitary confinement. My child was crying the entire time. I was then taken to a room on the first floor but they wouldn't let my son accompany me.[17]

> A woman in civilian clothing questioned me in the room about my brother Josip, who had been arrested in Sisak earlier in the day. A man in camouflage was also in the room. The lady asked me when was the last time I had gone to Banija. I told her that I was last there in late July when I went to visit my friends in Bosanski Novi and that my brother had accompanied me then. I went on to say that on July 26, shooting erupted and we fled to Croatian Kostajnica and that both my brother and I left

---

[16] Helsinki Watch interviewed Ivan K. and his sister in Zagreb on December 31, 1991. Both requested that their names and the name of their brother remain confidential because they fear reprisals from individual Croats. The names used are pseudonyms. Helsinki Watch will make the names of the tortured individuals known to the appropriate Croatian authorities in private.

[17] According to Ivan, the child was taken to a local orphanage where he was teased by other children and hit by one boy, apparently because he was Serbian. According to Ivan, he was fed and treated well by the nannies in the orphanage. The child reported that he had to sleep on a wooden bench without a blanket.

for Zagreb the following day. She asked me if my brother had participated in a massacre in Struga and Zamlača on July 26.[18] I told her that that was impossible because my brother had gone to Zagreb with me on that day. The man in camouflage kept provoking me by saying that we [Serbs] are all Četniks and that my brother killed those people [in Struga and Zamlača]. The lady also asked me if I was a member of any political party.

The questioning lasted for about 30 to 45 minutes and then I was taken to the jail where I was put in cell #4. It was about 1:00 a.m. There were several other men in the cell with me and every so often one of the guards would walk by and curse at us, telling us that we would end up in Belgrade.

That night, I heard someone being beaten in the hallway. Because the door to our cell only had a peephole, I couldn't see what was happening but I could hear everything. I recognized the voice of the man being beaten -- it was my brother, Josip. He kept saying "I'm not to blame," but they kept beating him and putting his head under water, I presume in a bucket. His torturers said, "This is only the first stage of your torture" and they kept calling out for someone to bring them a knife. I don't think they used a knife on him but threatened him only to scare him further. He was beaten from 11:30 p.m. to 5:30 a.m. and again between 9:00 a.m. and 12:30 p.m.

---

[18] Serbian insurgents launched an offensive from the town of Dvor against Croatian police in the village of Kozibrod on July 26, 1991. En route, the insurgents captured approximately 40 civilians and used them as human shields during their advance through the villages of Struga and Zamlača. A number of civilians were killed in the ensuing violence and three Croatian police officers who had surrendered to Serbian forces were summarily executed. See Helsinki Watch's "Yugoslavia: Human Rights in the Croatian Conflict," September 1, 1991, for an account of the incident.

At 1:00 p.m., the guards told me to get out of the cell and they handcuffed me. I was taken to the police station again, where the woman who had questioned me the night before told me that I was going home. I asked her about my brother and she answered that he was a war criminal. She told me that my son was at the orphanage and that I should go and get him. My son and I took the train back to Zagreb and I have been getting threatening telephone calls since then [i.e., since November 28]. Only yesterday my neighbor threatened me with physical harm and called me a Četnik.

The man's sister, Vesna, travelled to Sisak on November 29 to inquire as to the condition and whereabouts of her other brother, Josip, who remained in police custody and, she feared, was being tortured. She told Helsinki Watch:

A friend and I went to Sisak to find my brother, Josip. When we arrived at the Sisak police station, we were told that my brother was indeed at the police station being questioned. In fact, I caught a glimpse of him sitting next to the computer. We asked his interrogator if we could speak to him but were refused. Rather, we were told that he was being kept at the police station and that he was alive and well. We asked where he would be going and were told that he was being taken to investigatory court. We went to the court and waited for him to arrive. At 2:40 p.m. a police truck pulled up and my brother emerged. He was black and blue and his head was swollen. I started yelling and screaming. A secretary from the court, who was waiting for them at the stairs of the courthouse, was also crying. She said that many innocent people had been beaten this way. My brother said nothing to me; he was limping and walking slowly toward the courthouse.

On December 1, Josip spoke to his lawyer and on December 5, his family was allowed to visit him. As of February 11, Josip K. has not been charged. He is currently being held in investigatory detention at the Sisak district court.

Helsinki Watch also documented the abuse of Djordje Rkman who was physically abused by the Croatian Army. Rkman[19] was in charge of weapons inventory at the local territorial defense unit[20] for 15 years. He lived in the village of Šodolovci with his parents, wife and two children. While on vacation on July 7, at approximately 10:00 a.m., he was tending to chores in the fields when he heard fighting at the entrance to the village. He ran to the closest house -- 300 meters away -- for shelter. There were eight people inside the house, two grandmothers, one young woman, a boy, and four men. When they saw that the Croatian National Guard was shooting at the house, they ran upstairs for shelter. There had been some men hiding in the attic of this house with a machine gun who fled through the roof when the National Guard opened fire, he said, but he did not see them. The machine gun was abandoned in the room next to the civilians' hiding place.

Fifty to twenty members of the Croatian Army came into the attic, followed by a second group which beat the men. Rkman described his abuse to Helsinki Watch:

> All were in uniforms, all were [Croatian Army] soldiers. I was on the floor while they were beating me. I heard verbal harassment and threats. "Kill them now," one was saying. They put a gun to my forehead and were yelling "Četnik" at me. We were beaten for half an hour. We were then brought downstairs and they made us go out in the yard, where they made us lie down on our stomachs, hands on our heads. About 20 to 30 members of the Croatian Army randomly hit and kicked whoever they wanted. The women were not hit. I have not been to the doctor. It is hard for me to breathe. My lip and my head were cut and I cannot open my mouth very much.

---

[19] Rkman was interviewed in private in the Osijek jail on July 30, 1991. We requested to speak with him by name and the prison authorities complied.

[20] During Yugoslavia's communist era, territorial defense units consisted of a local reserve militia and armaments stored at the local level.

His upper right lip had a white scar on it.

We were then made to walk one to two kilometers with our hands behind our heads to their cars, where they beat us again.

They were handcuffed and taken to Djakovo, where the women were released. In Djakovo, they were individually interrogated.

When they saw I was beaten up, they took me to the hospital. While they were taking me down the hall in the police station, some of the police were yelling "Četnik" at me, kicking me in the sides as I went down the steps. I was also kicked in the courtyard of the hospital. But it was in the house where they broke my lip and my head. My left temple still hurts, as well as my ribs and back.

At the first aid station [in the hospital] they gave me two injections and stitched my face. I got two stitches on my mouth, two on my head, and two on my left cheek.

Arbitrary Arrests and Disappearances

In recent months, Serbian civilians have been arrested by Croatian authorities or abducted by individual Croatian extremists and their whereabouts remain unknown. Some have been missing for more than four months. Many arrests or abductions have been arbitrary: the criteria for arrest appear to be Serbian ethnicity; suspected or actual membership in the Serbian Democratic Party (Srpska Demokratska Stranka-SDS); current or prior membership in the Yugoslav People's Army[21] (Jugoslavenska Narodna Armija-JNA); or familial ties to a member of the JNA. Arbitrary arrests and the subsequent disappearances of Serbs usually take place in areas which are under heavy and prolonged

---

[21] Officers of the JNA who have switched sides in the conflict to assist or fight with Croatian forces have not been harassed. However, those members of the JNA who refuse to condemn the JNA's actions or support Croatian forces in the current war are frequently harassed.

attack by Serbian forces or the Yugoslav military. The abduction of Serbs appears to be particularly serious in the municipalities of Gospić and Sisak. Helsinki Watch has also received reports that Serbs are being abducted from Zagreb, Zadar and Daruvar. Helsinki Watch is deeply concerned both by the cases of disappeared persons and the growing frequency with which persons are vanishing in Croatia.

Helsinki Watch has documented the following reports of missing persons from Gospić and Sisak:

- On August 26, 1991, three uniformed men entered the apartment of the Rajšić family in Sisak and arrested Dragan Rajšić, a retiree. A warrant for his arrest was not presented. The three men -- the family believes they were members of the Croatian Army[22] -- returned to the family home later in the evening and asked Ms. Rajšić for her husband's weapons. Ms. Rajšić handed over a hunting rifle and two handguns, for which Mr. Rajšić reportedly had a license. They also asked for the gun's ammunition but Ms. Rajšić did not know where it was kept. The three men left and came back in ten minutes and found the ammunition and license, presumably after they were told by Mr. Rajšić where they were kept. Ms. Rajšić did not receive a receipt indicating that the weapons had been confiscated.

  The same evening, Mr. Rajšić's son, Dragoljub, inquired at the local police station, the Croatian Army headquarters, the Sisak district jail and the Sisak district court about his father's whereabouts and the reasons for his arrest -- this information was not disclosed to Rajšić. As of February 7, Dragan Rajšić remains missing.

- At approximately 8:00 a.m. on November 23, 1991, Vasilje Kovač, a 65-year-old colonel in the Yugoslav army, was taken by four men dressed in camouflage uniforms in Široka Kula (municipality of Gospić). His whereabouts remains unknown to

---

[22] Helsinki Watch spoke to the family's lawyer, Vladimir Ivković, in Zagreb on January 2, 1992.

his family or lawyer.[23]

In recent months, exchanges of prisoners held by Croatian or Serbian forces and the Yugoslav Army have taken place. According to international humanitarian and refugee organizations, it is estimated that Serbian forces currently hold eight times more prisoners -- including civilians -- than Croatian authorities. Helsinki Watch is concerned that Croatian authorities may abduct Serbian civilians and use them as prisoners for the purpose of exchange. Such action amounts to hostage-taking and is strictly forbidden under international humanitarian law.[24] Helsinki Watch urges the Croatian authorities to refrain from abducting Serbian civilians for the purpose of exchange.

Destruction of Civilian Property and Robbery

In Croatia, the destruction of civilian property has been used to frighten and intimidate people and to drive them from their places of residence. In the town of Vrpolje (municipality of Šibenik), Helsinki Watch representatives[25] examined the remains of three apartment buildings that were completely demolished by explosives. Graffiti and derogatory remarks demanding that all Serbs, Muslims, Albanians and Gypsies leave the area were scrawled on the walls.

Moreover, explosions have become commonplace in Croatia and, in most cases, property is destroyed for revenge. For example, if a Serb destroys a Croatian house one evening, a Croat will destroy a Serbian house the next evening and vice-versa. In May 1991, after Franko Lisica, a Croatian police officer from the village of Bibinje (municipality of Zadar), was killed, the Croatian villagers came to the nearby city of Zadar

---

[23] Ibid.

[24] Hostages are defined as "persons who find themselves, willingly or unwillingly, in the power of the enemy and who answer with their freedom or their life for compliance with the orders of the latter and for upholding the security of its armed forces." See International Committee of the Red Cross, *Commentary on the Additional Protocols of 1977*, (Geneva 1987) at 874.

[25] Helsinki Watch visited the Dalmatian and Knin regions in April, May, August and September 1991. Helsinki Watch visited Vrpolje in mid-August 1991.

and, in a riot, destroyed places of business owned by Serbs and Serbian and Yugoslav firms, such as the Yugoslav Airline (JAT) offices.[26]

In cases where individual extremists appear to be responsible for destruction of Serbian property, the Croatian authorities have sent inspectors to the scene of the damage, but few perpetrators have been apprehended. The Croatian insurance company has agreed to cover the losses suffered by the Serbian places of business destroyed in Zadar. Despite these steps, Helsinki Watch is concerned that not enough is being done to prevent individual destruction of civilian property.

Moreover, property -- usually but not exclusively belonging to Serbs -- has been destroyed after the proprietors have fled from regions of armed conflict and after Croatian troops assumed control. In December, Serbian paramilitary groups brutally massacred 43 civilians -- mostly elderly Croats -- in the villages of Vočin and Hum.[27] After Vočin was reclaimed by Croatian forces, individual Croats and members of the Croatian army destroyed and confiscated the property of Serbs who had fled from the area.[28] During a visit to Vočin on January 5, 1992, a Helsinki Watch representative saw two Croatian civilians loading a truck with belongings from a Serbian house. The village priest who accompanied the representative reprimanded the robber and told him to return the stolen articles but was rudely rebuffed. The priest reported the robbery to members of the Croatian army, who promised to look into the situation but did not send a patrol to investigate. Moreover, the priest and a number of people who had returned to the village told Helsinki Watch that individuals and members of the Croatian army had set several

---

[26] A Helsinki Watch representative visited Zadar on June 8, 1991.

[27] Helsinki Watch investigated and reported the killings in a letter to Slobodan Milošević, President of the Republic of Serbia, and General Blagoje Adžić, Acting Minister of Defense and Chief of Staff of the Yugoslav People's Army. The letter was delivered to representatives of the Yugoslav army and Serbian government on January 23 and 25, respectively, by Helsinki Watch representatives.

[28] Approximately 20,000 Serbs fled from parts of western Slavonia in late November, when Serbian forces were ordered to withdraw from the region by the Yugoslav army. Almost immediately thereafter, Croatian forces re-claimed the territory.

Serbian homes on fire in revenge for the December massacre in Vočin. Admittedly, most of the homes that were burned or otherwise demolished belonged to Croats and had been destroyed by Serbian paramilitaries during their occupation of the region. However, Helsinki Watch identified three Serbian houses that had been burned after the Croats reclaimed the village.

Helsinki Watch has received many reports in which individual Croats or members of the Croatian security forces have destroyed abandoned Serbian property after a village was re-taken by Croatian forces, particularly in western Slavonia. In some cases, discipline is not enforced by the troops' commanders, thereby encouraging pillaging, robbery and drunkenness among troops and individuals.[29] According to Serbs who have fled from western Slavonia,[30] Serbian homes and other property have been damaged in the following villages of western Slavonia: Čeralije, Macute, Bokane, Vočin, Komitnik, Hum, Sekulinci, Lisičine (municipalities of Podravska Slatina); Drenovac (municipality of Slavonska Požega); Pušina and Krašković (municipalities of Orahovica); Popovci (municipality of Pakrac); and Suhopolje (municipality of Virovitica). Although the extent of the damage is often exaggerated, Helsinki Watch found that Serbian property has intentionally been destroyed by individual Croats or members of the Croatian police or army.[31]

---

[29] In addition to western Slavonia, Helsinki Watch representatives also saw undisciplined and drunken Croatian soldiers in Dalmatia, particularly in Zadar and Split.

[30] Displaced Serbs from western Slavonia were interviewed in Belgrade on January 28-29, 1992.

[31] Helsinki Watch recognizes that damage to civilian property has been inflicted during battles between Serbian and Croatian forces in western Slavonia, particularly in the municipalities of Okučani, Novska, Pakrac and Nova Gradiška. In the cases enumerated in this section, Helsinki Watch refers to damage intentionally inflicted to civilian property after a lull in the fighting, not during a battle.

Killing, Assault and Harassment of Journalists

Helsinki Watch is concerned about the large number of journalists who have been killed, wounded, physically assaulted or otherwise attacked while reporting on the war in Croatia. According to the International Federation of Journalists (IFJ), Yugoslavia was "the most perilous site for journalists" in 1991.[32] The IFJ reported that some of the journalists killed in Yugoslavia were deliberately targeted because of their professional affiliation.[33]

Since July 26, 1991, at least 17 foreign and domestic journalists have been killed while covering the war in Croatia. Four journalists are missing and at least 28 have been wounded while covering the war in Croatia. At least 63 have been attacked and over 38 have been otherwise harassed (i.e., threatened, property confiscated).[34]

Deaths

Zoran Amidžić, Bora Petrović, Dejan Miličević and Sreten Ilić of Belgrade Television were killed while covering the war in Croatia under circumstances in which Croatian forces may have been responsible. The journalists were killed on October 9, 1991, on the road between Petrinja and Glina in circumstances that are still unclear. Various reports maintain that their car hit a land mine while other reports say that their car was ambushed by Croats using a shoulder-held grenade launcher.

---

[32]"Record Number of Journalists Reported Killed in 1991," Associated Press, January 6, 1992. According to the IFJ, of the 83 journalists killed worldwide in 1991, 21 were killed in Yugoslavia alone. More journalists have been killed since the IFJ released its report in late December.

[33] *Ibid.*

[34] The figures in this section were gathered in Helsinki Watch interviews with witnesses and from information provided by the International and American PEN Centers, the Committee to Protect Journalists, the Foreign Press Bureau in Zagreb and non-Yugoslav press and wire reports.

Disappearances

The whereabouts of four journalists remain unknown. While Siniša Glavašević and Branimir Polovina, a reporter and cameraman for Radio Vukovar, are presumed to have been captured by Serbian forces, the whereabouts of Viktor Nogin and Genadi Kurinoj, a reporter and a cameraman for Soviet Television, remain unknown. The Soviet journalists left Belgrade for Zagreb, via Osijek, on September 1, 1991, and have not been heard from since. They were driving a dark blue Opel Omega with diplomatic license plates. They are presumed to have been killed.

Helsinki Watch calls upon the Croatian authorities to investigate the deaths of the four aforementioned Serbian journalists and the disappearance of the two Soviet correspondents. Insofar as Croatian forces may have been responsible for their deaths, Helsinki Watch calls upon the Croatian government to prosecute vigorously those guilty of such crimes.

Harassment and Discrimination

A stridently nationalist election campaign in 1990 gratuitously inflamed Serbs in Croatia. The Croatian government did little to alleviate the Serbs' fear of persecution after it assumed power in late 1990. Through bombastic -- and in some cases racist -- rhetoric, the government-financed media and individual members of the Croatian government perpetuated nationalist hysteria in Croatia. Coupled with similar action by the Serbian government and media, violence between individual Serbs and Croats in Croatia is escalating not only on the battlefield, but also in areas which are not in imminent danger of attack. Indeed, the increase in individual harassment of, and discrimination against, Serbian civilians in Croatia is alarming.

Harassment

Critics of the Croatian government -- both Croats and Serbs -- have been harassed both by individual extremists and government officials. Members of the Serbian Democratic Forum (SDF)[35], the Serbian Democratic Party (SDS) and members of the Yugoslav army are especially targeted for such harassment. Helsinki Watch recognizes that many, though not all, SDS members are actively engaged in fighting against Croatian forces in Croatia. Insofar as such persons are active participants in the armed conflict, their arrests are permissible under international law.[36]

The Yugoslav army, navy and air force have suffered from mass desertions since the war began in Croatia. Many former JNA officials who are of Croatian origin have switched sides in the conflict and are actively engaged in the war effort against Serbian forces. Members of the Yugoslav armed forces who have deserted or switched sides are not harassed. Rather, those Yugoslav military officials who have not publicly sided with the Croats but continue to reside in Croatia (usually retired JNA officers), are frequently harassed and, in some cases, have disappeared.[37]

In some cases, a newspaper or magazine (most frequently *Slobodni Tjednik*) accuses various Serbs of being spies for the insurgents or members of the Yugoslav Army's counter-intelligence service (Kontra-obavještajna služba-KOS).[38] Individual Croat read the column and harass the named Serbs. Frequently, the named Serbs receive threatening telephone calls; some have been physically accosted by individual extremists.

In cases where victimized Serbs have reported physical harassment to the police, the authorities have responded in a variety of

---

[35] The Serbian Democratic Forum (SDF) was registered as an official organization--it is not a political party -- with the Croatian authorities in late December. SDF officials told Helsinki Watch that they experienced no difficulties in registering the organization.

[36] Under the rules of war, those actively participating in hostilities lose their civilian status and become combatants during the period of their combat participation, which includes defensive, as well as offensive action.

[37] See the case of Vasilije Kovač above.

[38] See *Slobodni Tjednik*, Number 66, Zagreb.

ways. In Zagreb and at the republican level, Croatian authorities have investigated such cases. However, few people are arrested or prosecuted for such offenses. On the local level, particularly in areas where Croatian forces are engaged in battle with Serbian forces and the Yugoslav army, harassment of local Serbs is rarely investigated by the local authorities. In some cases, local Croatian police and military agents are reportedly guilty of such harassment themselves.

Moreover, the Croatian police have summoned Serbs to local police stations for questioning, commonly referred to as "informative discussions" (*informativni razgovori*). Svetozar Livada, a retired sociology professor and member of the Serbian Democratic Forum (SDF), was interrogated by the police twice at Zagreb's police headquarters. Although Livada reported no mistreatment,[39] the grounds for his interrogation appear to be unfounded. According to Livada, he received a written request to come to police headquarters at Djordjičeva 19 at 9:00 a.m. on December 6, 1991. He was questioned about his research work regarding Archbishop Alojzije Stepinac and asked about his opinion of Croatia's newly promulgated law regarding ethnic minorities in Croatia.[40] The police also asked Livada about the origin of the Serbian Democratic Forum's financial support. On December 13 at 8:00 a.m., Livada received a telephone call asking him to come to the police station at 10:00 a.m. for another informative conversation, where he was questioned further about the same subjects.

Helsinki Watch believes that the questioning of Livada is without basis. Further, Helsinki Watch believes that such questioning is being used by Croatian authorities to intimidate members of the Serbian Democratic Forum, a legally registered organization which is not engaged in the armed conflict and seeks to represent the rights of law-abiding Serbian citizens in Croatia. Insofar as Croatian authorities are to question individuals, sufficient grounds must exist for such questioning. An

---

[39] Interviewed by Helsinki Watch in Zagreb on December 31, 1991.

[40] On December 4, 1991, the Croatian Parliament adopted a law which guarantees the human and cultural rights of ethnic and national groups or minorities in Croatia. (See "Ustavni Zakon o ljudskim pravima i slobodama i o pravima etničkih i nacionalnih zajednica ili manjina u Republici Hrvatskoj," *Narodne Novine Republike Hrvatske*, Broj. 65, 4. prosinca. 1991.)

individual's ethnic or political affiliations are not reasonable grounds for interrogation or arrest.

Helsinki Watch does not dispute the Croatian government's right to provide for its territorial defense and to take appropriate measures for such defense where necessary. However, Helsinki Watch is gravely concerned that the civil and political rights of various Serbs--and Croats who hold minority views--are being violated both by individual extremists and by government representatives in the name of national defense. Despite the fact that forces attacking Croatia are overwhelmingly Serbian, this in no way gives Croatian government officials or individuals the right to harass, attack or discriminate against Serbian civilians who are law-abiding citizens of Croatia. Helsinki Watch is concerned that such intimidation is forcing Serbs to flee from Croatia either to Serbian-occupied territory in Croatia and Bosnia or to Serbia proper. According to a Serbian lawyer in Zagreb[41], half of Zagreb's Serbs have fled because of harassment, or fear of harassment, by individual extremists. Helsinki Watch believes that the Croatian government has not done enough to ameliorate the tension between Serbs and Croats in Croatia in areas which are not occupied by Serbian forces. In some instances, local government officials have reportedly condoned, encouraged or perpetrated acts of violence or harassment against Serbian civilians.

Arbitrary Searches and Seizures

Croatian forces are responsible for the arbitrary search of homes and seizures of property, usually firearms for which the owner retains a license. Such searches often are conducted without warrants. In areas under siege, Croatian forces frequently search Serbian homes, purportedly for large caches of weapons. In some cases, the fact that a house is owned by a Serb appears to be sufficient cause to search the premises or an entire Serbian village. According to a 19-year-old woman from the predominantly Serbian village of Gornji (Upper) Gučani (population 92, municipality of Slavonska Požega):[42]

---

[41] Interviewed by Helsinki Watch in Zagreb on January 2, 1992.

[42] Interviewed by Helsinki Watch in Belgrade on January 21, 1992.

In early October, at about 4:00 p.m., armed villagers from the neighboring Croatian towns of Busnovi and Donji [Lower] Gučani blocked all the exits from Gornji Gučani, a predominantly Serbian village in which I lived. I was in my house at the time with my mother, grandmother and brother; my father was at work in Slavonska Požega at the time. About ten members of the Croatian Army walked from house to house searching every home in the village. Five soldiers came to my house and asked to search the premises. We asked them if they had a warrant and one of them replied, "We have too much work to do, we don't have time for those details." The five soldiers searched our house from top to bottom. They told us to hand over two guns which they thought we had in the house. My mother told them that we didn't have any weapons and after they searched the house again, they left peacefully. I knew the five soldiers, they were from the Slavonska Požega area.

Helsinki Watch does not dispute the Croatian government's right to take precautions against attack. While the authorities have the right to search a person's home, the reasons for such a search, and evidence to support the claim, must be presented to appropriate authorities, who must then issue a warrant, especially if the area to be searched is not under attack. The fact that a home belongs to a Serb does not constitute sufficient reason for a search of the premises. Moreover, searching an entire Serbian village is both arbitrary and discriminatory.

Discrimination in the Workplace

Because of the economic crisis, many workers of different nationalities have lost their jobs in recent months, while others have not been paid or have received their pay months late. Because of war damage or insolvency, closures and layoffs are becoming commonplace throughout Croatia. However, many claim that they have lost their jobs for ethnic, as opposed to economic, reasons.

Helsinki Watch has received reports of discrimination in the work place in Croatia. Much of the discrimination does not appear to be government-sponsored, but privately organized. For example, individual Croats, particularly in the coastal cities of Split and Šibenik, have

334

authored and organized the signing of "loyalty oaths" to the Croatian government. The loyalty oaths are typically written by Croatian workers and presented either to all employees or only to Serbian workers for signatures. Those who refuse to sign -- mostly Serbs -- are threatened with dismissal or are, in fact, fired from their jobs.

The "loyalty oath" campaign originated with Croats who claimed that Serbian colleagues who worked with them were the same individuals who fought on the side of the Serbian insurgents, particularly in Knin. They accused their Serbian colleagues of manning barricades and shooting at Croats in the evening and then coming to work the next day with the same Croats at whom they shot the night before.

The Croatian Ministry of Labor and Social Welfare has documented cases of loyalty oath signature campaigns in ten enterprises throughout Croatia, including the TEF (Tvornica elektroda i ferolegura) and TLM (Tvornica lakih metala) plants in Šibenik, the ship-building factory in Split and the Slavija enterprise in Zagreb. Helsinki Watch has also received reports of such campaigns in the Zadranka firm in Zadar and at the Jadrantours enterprise in Split.

The Croatian government and the Croatian Parliamentary Committee for the Protection of Human Rights have condemned the signing of loyalty oaths and have required the reinstatement of those who have lost their jobs because they refused to sign such oaths. The practice of loyalty oaths appears to have been particularly abused in the spring and summer of 1991, but has greatly diminished since then. Helsinki Watch has not received any recent reports of loyalty oath campaigns organized by Croats.

Helsinki Watch welcomes the condemnation of loyalty oaths by the Croatian government. We also urge the authorities to take disciplinary actions against those who have required the signing of loyalty oaths and to take steps -- at the republican and local levels -- to prevent similar campaigns in the future. Dismissing a worker because of his or her failure to sign a loyalty oath to a government violates the right to freedom of expression. Moreover, using loyalty oaths to weed out Serbs is discriminatory. If individuals are engaged in illegal activity, the authorities should conduct an investigation into the illegal offense, rather than dismiss an individual because he or she is of Serbian ethnicity or is suspected of supporting the Serbian insurgents.

Discrimination in the Police Force

Helsinki Watch is concerned that ethnic criteria are applied by the Croatian Ministry of the Interior to hire and dismiss Serbian police officers. During the communist era, the vast majority of the police officers in Croatia were Serbian. According to the Croatian Ministry of the Interior, Serbs accounted for approximately 75 percent of the Croatian police force despite the fact that they comprised only 11.5 percent of the republic's population. Since the new Croatian government has taken power, the police forces have been greatly enlarged and the ratio between police officers of Serbian and Croatian origin has been reversed; Serbs constitute approximately 23 percent.

The Croatian Ministry of the Interior contends that the numbers have not been reversed because Serbs were fired from their jobs but because more Croats were recruited. Slavko Degoricija and Milan Brezak, former and current Deputy Interior Ministers, told Helsinki Watch that no one has been fired from police jobs simply because of nationality. They contend that three factors have influenced the reversal in the composition of the police. First, after the new Croatian government decided to change the insignia on the police uniform from a communist red star to the traditional Croatian coat of arms, many Serbs quit, claiming that they would not wear the new insignia because they equated the coat of arms with the fascist Croatian regime during World War II. Second, some Serbs quit the Croatian police force to fight on the side of the Serbian insurgents in Croatia. Third, when the Croatian police force was being augmented, according to Brezak and Degoricija, an effort was made to rectify the disproportionate representation in the police forces by establishing "national parity and equal representation" in the police force.

Indeed, in the past nineteen months, both the active and reserve units of the Croatian police force have been greatly enlarged. The Croatian government justifies the increase in their security forces by pointing to the Serbian insurgency, the Serbian bias of the JNA and the JNA's dismantling of Croatia's territorial defense units.[43]

---

[43] Helsinki Watch is aware that, early in 1990, the Yugoslav People's Army (JNA) confiscated most of the weapons that were part of Croatia's territorial defense (teritorijalna obrana - TO), a local defense force separate from the federal army. When the new Croatian government came to power, and after the TO's

Although Helsinki Watch does not dispute the Croatian government's right to increase and strengthen its police force, it is concerned that Serbs are being excluded and dismissed because of their nationality. Helsinki Watch interviewed several insurgents who admitted that they had quit their jobs with the Croatian police to join the Serbian insurgency. However, it is difficult to believe the Ministry of the Interior's assertion that of the 11,000 Serbs who worked for the Croatian police during the communist regime, 6,000 left of their own accord.

Helsinki Watch has documented one such case in which disciplinary action was taken against twelve Serbian police officers in Zadar because they walked out of a meeting led by deputy police chief, Perica Jurić. According to official documents from the Zadar police station and disciplinary committee,[44] Jurić gave a speech at a meeting of police officers in Zadar on October 30, in which he stated that a number of police officers would have to be dismissed because of a surplus of labor. During the meeting, Jurić reportedly insulted a number of police officers and made comments that were considered arrogant, prejudiced and unprofessional by approximately fifty workers, all of whom walked out of the meeting. Of those who walked out -- reportedly both Croats and Serbs -- disciplinary action appears to have been taken only against the twelve Serbian police officers because they "created dissatisfaction and disquiet among other workers" after they walked out of an "official meeting which they were obliged to attend as employees of the police force."[45] Charges were subsequently dropped against one police officer

---

weapons had been confiscated, both active and reserve police units in Croatia were strengthened.

[44] See Republika Hrvatska, Ministarstvo Unutarnjih Poslova, Sekretarijat za Unutarnje Poslove Zadar, Broj 511-17-01-9649/1-1990, Zadar, 08.studenog.1990 and Broj DS-01-30/20-1990, Zadar, 20.11.1990. See also Republika Hrvatska, Ministarstvo Unutarnjih Poslova, Policijska Uprava Zadar, Broj. DS-01-30/19-1990, Zadar, 26.12.1990; Broj DS-01-30/20-1990, Zadar, 4.1.1991; and Broj DS-01-30/22-1990, Zadar, 17.1.1991. See also "Zapisnik," Broj DS-01-30/19-1990, 18.12.1990, završen u 17,10, i 24.12.1990, završen u 15,20 sati.

[45] The Secretariat for Interior Affairs of Zadar brought charges against the twelve police officers who were accused of violating Article 84(1), points 3, 10 and 13, of the Law of Interior Affairs (i.e., "Zakon o unutrašnjim poslovima," *Narodne Novine Socijalisticke Republike Hrvatske*, Broj 55, 26. prosinca 1989, as adopted,

and nine were fined. Two police officers were fired because they had spoken to the press[46] "about the official business of the police station without permission," i.e., the meeting in question. One of the two who was fired was accused of having used restricted firearms without the knowledge or permission of his superiors.[47]

While Helsinki Watch does not dispute the right of the police to maintain order within its ranks, we are concerned that actions against the twelve Serbian police officers was used to harass and intimidate the men. Helsinki Watch believes that the proceedings and subsequent penalties were not justified as a means of disciplining officers; instead, they interfered with their freedom of expression. Moreover, disciplinary action

---

amended and revised in "Zakon o izmjenama Zakona o unutrašnjim poslovima," *Narodne Novine Republike Hrvatske*, Broj 47, 14. studenoga 1990). The charges were considered and decisions were set forth by a disciplinary committee (i.e., disciplinski sud za radnike Radne zajednice Policijske uprave Zadar i Policijskih stanica Biograd na moru, Benkovac, Obrovac i Pag). The committee's decisions are set forth in three separate judgements (i.e., presude): Republika Hrvatska, Ministarstvo Unutarnjih Poslova, Policijska Uprava Zadar, Broj. DS-01-30/19-1990, Zadar, 26.12.1990; Broj DS-01-30/20-1990, Zadar, 4.1.1991; and Broj DS-01-30/22-1990, Zadar, 17.1.1991. Charges against Mirko Kalanj were dismissed for lack of sufficient evidence. The following police officers were fined: Jovo Vujasinović, Borivoj Mucalj, Nikica Subotić, Saša Bubalo, Željko Babić, Slaven Rašković, Milan Gajica, Slobodan Grbić and Nevenko Tintor. (All the aforementioned men, except Gajica and Vujasinović, had 15 percent of their pay withheld for a period of three months. Gajica and Vujasinović each had 15 percent of their pay withheld for four and six months, respectively.) Damir Basta and Miroslav Macura were dismissed from their jobs.

[46] The comment was made at a press conference in Knin on November 1, 1990, (as reported in "Neka se sazna prava istina," *Slobodna Dalmacija*, November 2, 1990) and on the daily news program of Croatian Television on November 18, 1990.

[47] As a member of the special forces of the Croatian police, Miroslav Macura was licensed to carry and operate a Hekler automatic weapon while on duty and only with the permission of his commander. When Macura went off-duty, he took the weapon home with him and fired three bullets in the village of Crno without the knowledge or permission of his superiors. (See Republika Hrvatska, Ministarstvo Unutarnjih Poslova, Policijska Uprava Zadar, Broj DS-01-30/22-1990, Zadar, 17.1.1991.)

appears to have been taken only against the Serbs and not against the Croats who walked out of the meeting, thus discriminating against workers on the basis of nationality.

Failure to Prosecute a Killing

On July 1, the Chief of Police of Osijek, Josip Reihl Kir (a Croat), and two elected officials (one Serb and one Croat) were killed. One other Serbian official was reportedly wounded by a Croatian reserve police officer.[48] This officer, Antun Gudelj, was known to be a Croatian extremist. He reportedly shot at the officials' car from behind a police barricade in Tenja. Although many reserve and regular police officers were at the scene, no one detained the killer, who is still at large. The victims, seen as moderates, were trying to negotiate a peaceful settlement to the violent Tenja disputes.[49]

Osijek mayor Zlatko Kramarić told Helsinki Watch[50]:

> The Serbs asked for a meeting with Kir, but Kir did not use his political acumen when he agreed to talk to the Serbs in Tenja [on July 1]. The Croats there, who are pretty radical, would view that as aiding the Serbs.
> The man who shot Kir, Antun Gudelj, had just had his

---

[48] Those killed with the Chief of Police were Goran Zopundzija (a Croat), vice-president of the executive branch of Osijek's government, and Milan Knežević (a Serb), president of Tenja's town council and member of Osijek's district council. Wounded at the same time was Mirko Tubić (a Serb), a member of Tenja's town council.

[49] The town of Tenja (population 7,664, a municipality of Osijek), is divided into the old and new sections. Old Tenja is predominantly Serbian while new Tenja is comprised of both Serbs and Croats. On July 7, 1991, seven people were killed in a gun battle between Serbs and Croats. (See Marcus Kable, "Five Die in Serb, Croat Battle; EC Seeks to Avert Yugoslav War," Reuters Information Service, July 7, 1991, and Stephen Engelberg, "Five Die as Croats and Serbs Trade Fire," *The New York Times*, July 8, 1991.) Sporadic violence had erupted in late June between Tenja's Serbs and Croats.

[50] Kramarić was interviewed in his office on July 29, 1991.

house burned and his father captured on that day[51] and he was not psychologically stable. One can understand but not exonerate his anger.

During Kir's visit, three barricades had been erected in Tenja: one was manned by the active Croatian police, another by the Croatian reserve police -- most of whom were members of the Croatian Democratic Union (Hrvatska Demokratska Zajednica - HDZ), and a third was controlled by the Serbian insurgents. Kir and his colleagues passed through these barricades without difficulty on their way to Tenja. While Kir was at the insurgents' headquarters, the Serbs told Kir that they had been warned of an impending attack by the Croatian police. Kir, claiming he had no knowledge of this, returned to talk to his men. They reportedly told him that no attack was planned.

On his way back to deliver the message to the Serbs, as he passed again through the HDZ-controlled barricade, Kir and two others were shot dead.

A Croatian reserve police officer[52] told Helsinki Watch:

I was there on July 1 when Kir was shot and I saw the bodies. I was about 100 meters away on patrol. I did not have a good view of the scene but I heard the shooting and ran over.

Kir was killed at the entrance to new Tenja. A reserve police officer killed them because the driver refused to stop the car. Many others were there and saw what happened, including the Croatian police.

The investigating magistrates of the district court in Osijek told Helsinki Watch that a warrant is out for Gudelj's arrest but that he has not yet been apprehended.

---

[51] See Helsinki Watch's "Yugoslavia: Human Rights Abuses in the Croatian Conflict," September 1991, for an account of the Antun Gudelj's father's treatment and torture while held by Serbian insurgents.

[52] Interviewed on July 30, 1991, in Osijek.

The Croatian authorities are obligated to investigate, apprehend and charge those responsible for crimes such as the killing of Kir and the other two officials. Because they called up and armed reserve police officers, the Croatian government has a heightened duty to prosecute acts allegedly committed by these officers.[53]

Interference with the Independence of the Judiciary and Politically-Motivated Court Proceedings

The Case of Dobroslav Paraga and Milan Vuković

Dobroslav Paraga, leader of the ultra right-wing Croatian Party of Rights (Hrvatska Stranka Prava-HSP), has frequently criticized the Croatian government for its alleged ill-preparedness for, and laxity toward, the Serbian insurgency in Croatia. Under Paraga's leadership, the Croatian Party of Rights formed an armed wing called the Croatian Armed Forces[54] (Hrvatske Oružane Snage-HOS), which engages in military operations against Serbian forces. Although the Croatian government has forbidden the formation of such paramilitary units and claims that HOS forces are now under the command of the Croatian Ministry of Defense, the degree to which the Croatian government exercises control over HOS forces remains ambiguous. Likewise, the

---

[53] Despite public suspicion, Helsinki Watch found no evidence to suggest that the murder of Ante Paradžik, Vice-President of the Croatian Party of Rights, had been politically motivated. Paradžik was shot at a police checkpoint by a Croatian police officer who had seriously wounded an unarmed Yugoslav army officer at a checkpoint ten days before. It appears that the officer irresponsibly used his weapon in both cases and that no political motive existed in either instance. Croatian officials failed to take disciplinary measures against the police officer after his shooting of the Yugoslav army officer; however, murder charges have been brought against the police officer for the killing of Paradžik. Helsinki Watch urges the Croatian authorities to take appropriate measures to ensure that the shooting of the Yugoslav army officer not go unpunished.

[54] Although this group operates under the name of the "Croatian Armed Forces," it does not represent the legitimate military forces of the Croatian government. Hereinafter, Paraga's troops will be referred to by their Croatian acronym, HOS.

estimated number of HOS troops varies widely from between 300 to 2,000.

In early October, HOS troops took over a building in central Zagreb by force and placed a cannon in front of the building. Despite public outcry, no charges were filed against Paraga or his troops at the time and the Croatian Party of Rights was allowed to establish its headquarters in the seized building.

Later that month, Paraga began calling vociferously for the ouster of President Tudjman. On November 25, criminal charges were filed against Paraga and his deputy, Milan Vuković. Both men were charged with inciting an armed rebellion[55] and illegally obtaining weapons.[56] Due to lack of evidence, charges of organizing an armed rebellion were dropped against Paraga and Vuković by a district court on December 4, a decision which was subsequently confirmed by the Croatian Supreme Court on December 13. The lesser charges of illegally purchasing weapons remained in force.[57] Vuković was charged and released on November 25, 1991. Paraga was detained and released on December 4. after the district court rejected the public prosecutor's [i.e., the government's] contention that Paraga remain in investigatory detention. The case remains in the investigatory phase.

Helsinki Watch does not dispute the charges brought against Paraga and Vuković nor the right of the Croatian government to try both men. However, Helsinki Watch questions the delay in bringing charges, which implies that the motivation to bring charges against Paraga was political rather than legal. Action was taken against Paraga only after he

---

[55] See Article 236f(1) and (2) of Croatia's Criminal Code.

[56] See Article 209(2), of Croatia's Criminal Code.

[57] Court documents state that Paraga and Vuković illegally sought to purchase 185,000 DEM (approximately $US114,000) worth of weapons, including five sniper guns, 100 AK-47's, 10 pistols 27,000 bullets and 36 mines on September 10, 1991, from Stjepan Palijan, president of the district council of Križevci. The weapons were to be used to arm and equip Paraga's HOS forces. (See "Rješenje," Poslovni broj, I.KIO-I-311/91, Okružni Sud Zagreb, Istražni Odjel, 2. prosinca 1991; "Rješenje," Poslovni broj, XXI-II-Kv.-691/91/KIO.I-311/91, Okružni Sud Zagreb, Istražni Odjel, 4. prosinca 1991; and "Rješenje" Broj IV-Kz-124/1991-4, Vrhovni Sud Republike Hrvatske, 13. prosinca 1991.)

called for the ouster of President Tudjman's government. Criminal proceedings appear to have been brought against Paraga because he exercised his right to free speech and not because he was responsible for the organization, training and arming of illegal paramilitary groups and forcible breaking and entering. No action was taken against Paraga in October, when HOS troops used force to assume control of a building in downtown Zagreb. Helsinki Watch believes that action should have been taken against Paraga and HOS forces in October, immediately after HOS forces took forcible control of the building and placed a cannon in central Zagreb. Likewise, the Croatian government's attempt to bring HOS paramilitaries under the control of the Croatian Defense Ministry should have come much earlier.

The Case of Mile Dedaković

On November 18, 1991, the city of Vukovar fell to Serbian forces. For much of the three-month siege of Vukovar, Mile Dedaković (a.k.a. Jastreb) was commander-in-chief of Croatian defense forces in Vukovar. Approximately one week before Vukovar's fall, Dedaković was reassigned to the nearby city of Vinkovci, where he served as commander-in-chief of Croatian forces for the Vukovar and Vinkovci-Županja region. After Vukovar fell, two commissions -- one in Parliament and another in the government -- were formed to investigate the reasons for the defeat of Croatian forces.

In late November, Dedaković was arrested by the Croatian military police,[58] who beat him in custody. Dedaković was charged with attacking the constitutional order of the Republic of Croatia[59] by the military authorities and was subsequently taken to civil court for trial. When Dedaković was taken to Zagreb district court on December 3, the

---

[58] The Office of Intelligence and Security (Sigurnosno Informativna Služba-SIS) of the Croatian Ministry of Defense is responsible for the military police and gathering of military intelligence. As a member of the Croatian armed forces, Dedaković was subject to military, rather than civil, rules of conduct and procedure and therefore was detained and questioned by the military police for a longer period of time than stipulated under Croatian criminal and civil law.

[59] Dedaković was initially charged under Article 236a of the Croatian Criminal Code.

presiding judge saw that Dedaković had been severely beaten in detention.[60] The civil authorities demanded to know who was responsible for Dedaković's maltreatment and the Croatian authorities have begun an investigation into the matter.

The district court dropped charges against Dedaković for attacking Croatia's "constitutional order" due to lack of sufficient evidence. However, the court charged Dedaković and two accomplices[61] for abusing their official positions[62] to embezzle money (approximately $US 1 million) which was to have been used to buy weapons for Vukovar's defense.

Dedaković was taken into custody by civil authorities and placed in civil detention at the Zagreb district court. On December 24, Zagreb district court Judge Emir Midžić (47) ruled that sufficient evidence did not exist for Dedaković to remain in investigatory detention and he was released on his own recognizance pending completion of the magistrate's investigation. On the evening of December 24, Judge Midžić was served with a draft notice to report immediately for combat duty. He was sent to the battlefield near Letovanović. He was released from military service approximately three weeks later and is currently attending to his judicial duties.

Helsinki Watch calls upon the Croatian government to ensure that those responsible for Dedaković's mistreatment are punished. Moreover, Helsinki Watch is gravely concerned that Croatian government authorities ordered the mobilization of Judge Letovanović because said authorities disapproved of Dedaković's release. Colleagues of Judge Midžić claim that he had received threatening telephone calls from Croatian government officials who were upset that charges against

---

[60] The court's medical examiner confirmed that Dedaković was maltreated.

[61] Dedaković, Ljiljana Toth and Nikola Toth, the latter the commander of the Fourth Battalion of the Croatian National Guard and member of the Vukovar Defense Command from August 29 to November 13, were charged and arrested for the same offense.

[62] Dedaković was charged under Article 222 of the Croatian Criminal Code.

344

Dedaković had been reduced.[63] Helsinki Watch believes that the mobilization of Judge Midžić may have been politically motivated. Such an action grossly interferes with the independence of the judicial system and shows an utter disrespect for the rule of law.

Restrictions on Freedom of the Press

The war has had a devastating effect on freedom of the press and, to a lesser extent, freedom of expression in Croatia. Harassment of and economic pressure against independent-minded journalists and publications is also a problem.

On October 30, 1991, President Tudjman signed a presidential decree "on the distribution of information in the event of a state of war, or an immediate danger to the independence and unity of the Republic of Croatia."[64] The Croatian Parliament adopted the decree on November 2, 1991. The decree establishes rules of conduct for the foreign and domestic press covering the war in Croatia. The decree does not call for the censorship of all news, only information related to defense matters during times of war. Nevertheless, Helsinki Watch believes that such a decree seriously violates freedom of the press.

The decree calls for the formation of a committee (the Information Headquarters of the Republic of Croatia) which would coordinate and supervise press activities. The committee consists of the Minister of Information, media experts appointed by the Minister of Information and other government-appointed officials.[65] The decree places Croatian Television and Radio under the direct control of the Croatian Government[66] and designates certain newspapers to be "war

---

[63] Helsinki Watch spoke to colleagues of Judge Midžić in early January 1992, who asked that their names be kept confidential because they feared dismissal from their jobs for disclosing such information.

[64] "Uredba o Informativnoj Djelatnosti za Vrijeme Ratnoga Stanja ili u Slučaju Neposredne Ugroženosti Neovisnosti i Jedinstvenosti Republike Hrvatske," Register No. 57, Number 1134/91, Zagreb, October 30, 1991.

[65] *Ibid.*, Article 3.

[66] *Ibid.*, Articles 4 to 6.

dailies" which would also be subordinated to government control.[67] The decree demands that all media comply with instructions issued by the republic's Information Headquarters, local administrative bodies and respective regional defense centers.[68] Thus, in effect, the decree establishes censorship panels at both the republican and local level.

The decree places severe restrictions on journalists reporting on the war. Permits must be issued by respective regional defense centers before a journalist can report news from the battlefield[69] and any information regarding Croatian security forces or defense-related news must be approved by a body of the Croatian Armed Forces.[70] Reporting military secrets, calls for the forcible overthrow of the government, and information considered harmful to the defense of Croatia is prohibited. If a publication violates the above regulations, government authorities are empowered to seize all copies of the publication; such action cannot be appealed.[71] Moreover, foreign journalists may be held liable for violating the censorship rules and foreign radio and television programs can only be broadcast with the permission of the Croatian Ministry of Information.[72]

Journalists may be sentenced to a maximum of five years of imprisonment for reporting military information without the permission of the Croatian Armed Forces. Continued publication after banning by

---

[67] *Ibid.*, Article 7.

[68] *Ibid.*, Article 8.

[69] *Ibid.*, Article 10.

[70] *Ibid.*, Article 11. The Fund for Free Expression, a sister organization of Helsinki Watch, has criticized press and speech restrictions imposed by the United States military during the U.S. campaign in the Persian Gulf in early 1991. The restrictions imposed by the U.S. government during Operation Desert Storm were also criticized by the U.S. press community and a host of other civil rights organizations. (See The Fund for Free Expression, "Freedom of Expression and The War: Press and Speech Restrictions in the Gulf and F.B.I. Activity in the U.S. Raise First Amendment Issues," January 28, 1991.)

[71] *Ibid.*, Article 13.

[72] *Ibid.*, Articles 15 and 16.

346

the Ministry of Information is punishable by a prison term of up to five years; distribution of a banned publication is punishable by a prison term of up to three years in prison. The refusal by an editor-in-chief to broadcast or publish a government communique is punishable by a prison term of up to one year, as is the unapproved broadcast of foreign media.[73]

An issue of *Slobodni Tjednik*[74] was recently banned by the Croatian government, because it transcribed a telephone conversation between President Tudjman and Mile Dedaković, former commander of Croatian forces in the besieged city of Vukovar.[75] According to *Slobodni Tjednik*'s transcription of the conversation, delivery of weapons for the defense of the besieged city was promised. The article implies that, although military aid was promised, such aid never arrived.

Despite the adoption of the presidential decree by the parliament, the Croatian government has made no case for the imposition of press restrictions. The Croatian government has failed to prove that the press has in anyway obstructed military operations or endangered national security. The promulgation of the decree is a step backward, rather than a step toward the development of democracy in Croatia. Helsinki Watch is concerned that such restrictions may have been imposed to minimize coverage of civilian and combatant injuries and deaths and material damage inflicted not only by Croatian security forces, but also by the Serbian insurgents and the Yugoslav army, whose victories might reflect poorly on the Croatian government's ability to provide for its peoples' defense, thus weakening the current government. Helsinki Watch does not dispute the right of the Croatian government to provide for its territorial defense. However, Helsinki Watch believes that the rights to freedom of speech, expression and the press should not be subordinated for military purposes.

---

[73] *Ibid.*, Articles 17-21.

[74] *Slobodni Tjednik*, Number 94, Zagreb January 8, 1992. Helsinki Watch retains a copy of this issue.

[75] For a description of Dedaković's case, see above section on interference with the independence of the judiciary and politically motivated court proceedings.

Helsinki Watch is also concerned about actions taken by the Croatian authorities against *Glas Slavonije* (Voice of Slavonia), an Osijek-based newspaper. In the past, *Glas Slavonije* was independent and not directly controlled by the government. On July 25, 1991, the paper was placed under the control of the government, precipitating the resignation of the editor-in-chief, Drago Hedl, and the managing director, Vladimir Kokeza. The next day, the commander of Croatian forces in Slavonia, Branimir Glavaš, entered the paper's offices with ten heavily armed members of the Croatian Army. Glavaš ordered all those present to leave.[76] Shortly thereafter, Glavaš -- a military official -- and other government-appointed members of the paper's executive board installed new management at *Glas Slavonije*.[77] Helsinki Watch deplores the methods used by government forces to assert control over *Glas Slavonije*, particularly the armed intervention at the newspaper's offices. The current war in Croatia in no way gives local military or political authorities the right to use force to interfere with freedom of the press.

Helsinki Watch is concerned that the Croatian government -- both at the republican and local levels -- is trying to silence critical or independent publications through intimidation and economic pressure. A journalist for the Split-based daily newspaper, *Slobodna Dalmacija*,[78] expressed his concern to Helsinki Watch that the newspaper was being pressured to enter the government's fold or go out of business.

> In the summer of 1990, *Slobodna Dalmacija* restructured itself as a share-holding company and all government assistance and involvement ceased after it became a private enterprise. Our circulation is high and we're a profitable firm. Whereas many other Croatian dailies provide access to government or right-leaning opposition groups, *Slobodna Dalmacija* prints columns and articles by, and interviews with, left-of-center opposition figures.

---

[76] See Committee to Aid Democratic Dissidents in Yugoslavia, *CADDY Bulletin*, No. 66, August 1991, p. 9, and "Krici i Šaputanja iz Glasa Slavonije," *Slobodna Dalmacija*, August 1, 1991, p. 11.

[77] *Ibid.*

[78] Interviewed on June 8, 1991, in Split.

348

The government and right-wing opposition groups do not appreciate our editorial policy. We consider ourselves objective and they view us as "Bolshevik." The government still considers *Slobodna Dalmacija* a public enterprise, despite the fact that we became a private company months ago. They are trying to co-opt the private and independent press and put it under the government's wing.

Local and republican government officials, some of whom belong to the conservative wing of the Croatian Democratic Union (Hrvatska Demokratska Zajednica — HDZ) have tried to discredit the paper with the public.[79] In May 1991, Marko Bitanga, a local HDZ leader, expressed his desire to become director of *Slobodna Dalmacija*. However, his bid was "roundly defeated by a unanimous vote of the paper's journalists."[80] Thereafter, Bitanga attacked the daily in HDZ's party publication.[81] *Slobodna Dalmacija* responded with a series of articles in late May.[82] On June 8, the director of the Committee for Information of Croatia's Parliament attacked *Slobodna Dalmacija* during an interview with Radio Split, criticizing the paper for opposing the "interests of Croatia's people and the state."[83]

---

[79]For example, see the following articles in *Slobodna Dalmacija* for the position of Marin Mihanović, vice president of the district council of Split: "Kako prilagoditi glavne urednike," October 1, 1990 (which reprints an interview with Mihanović in *Nedjeljna Dalmacija*); and "Neprijateljske Novine," October 12, 1990. For a rebuttal of Mihanović's statements, see the following articles by Viktor Ivančić in *Slobodna Dalmacija*: "Gospodo Novinasi Novinari Okanite se Iluzija!" October 1990; "Ventilatori nisu vječni," September 25, 1991, and "Politički barbarizam," October 4, 1990.

[80] Committee to Aid Democratic Dissidents in Yugoslavia, *CADDY Bulletin*, No. 65, June 1991, p. 13.

[81] "Jeli slobodna *Slobodna Dalmacija*," *Glasnik*, May 17, 1991, pp. 6-7.

[82] Committee to Aid Democratic Dissidents in Yugoslavia, *CADDY Bulletin*, No. 65, June 1991, p. 13.

[83] *Ibid.*

Helsinki Watch does not dispute the right of individuals and groups to voice their opinions of *Slobodna Dalmacija* or other publications. However, Helsinki Watch is concerned that statements made by public officials against the paper are part of a campaign to intimidate its journalists, discredit the paper, and place it under government control. Helsinki Watch believes that such methods by government officials are a serious detriment to freedom of the press in Croatia.

In recent months, Croatia has undertaken a number of steps to privatize former state enterprises, including the media. Although there is wide support for privatization throughout Croatia, media privatization may actually result in increased, rather than decreased, government involvement in the press. Indeed, Helsinki Watch is concerned that the Croatian government is using economic means to close publications that are critical of the government.

In its effort to privatize the economy, the Croatian government's Agency for Restructuring and Development is overseeing the re-organization of twelve Vjesnik publications.[84] The government agency created a committee which will take over the financial and property-related management for each of Vjesnik's publications. The committee is comprised of four government appointees. Each publication has the right to appoint one person to the committee but that individual will only be consulted about issues directly affecting the representative's respective publication. The committee will have the right to replace managing directors but, according to Zdravko Mršić, the former director of the Agency for Restructuring and Development, "the content and editorial decisions of the papers will remain in the hands of the current editors."[85] Milovan Šibl, Director of the Croatian News Agency HINA, and a member of the aforementioned committee, has said that the

---

[84] The publishing house Vjesnik publishes a combined total of 18 newspapers and magazines, of which only two are profitable (i.e., the evening daily *Večernji List* and the magazine *Arena*.) See "Crne vijesti iz *Vjesnika*," *Nedjeljna Dalmacija*, June 2, 1991, p. 14.

[85]"Upad u Vjesnik," *Danas*, June 4, 1991, p. 28-29 and "Crne vijesti iz *Vjesnika*," *Nedjeljna Dalmacija*, June 2, 1991, p. 14.

committee "will not interfere with the editorial decisions of the respective publications."[86]

Despite such assurances, many journalists are afraid that the government will force the closure of certain publications, not simply for economic reasons, but also because they publish articles critical of the Croatian government. In particular, Helsinki Watch is concerned that the Croatian government is trying to drive *Danas* out of business for political reasons. During both the communist and current regimes, *Danas* published articles from dissident and opposition groups which were criticized by the government. In recent months, *Danas* has had economic problems and is no longer a profitable publication of the Vjesnik publishing house. For this reason, the committee of the Agency for Restructuring and Development sought to close *Danas*, claiming that it was bankrupt. On August 21, a court rejected the committee's proposal.[87] Although *Danas* was not closed, it was denied access to Vjesnik's printing presses in mid-September, allegedly because *Danas* had not paid its bills.[88] Currently, *Danas* uses the printing facilities of the *Delo* publishing house in Ljubljana, Slovenia.

Helsinki Watch is concerned that economic insolvency is being used as an excuse to close publications for political reasons. Although *Danas* has indeed had financial difficulties for some time, so too have fifteen of Vjesnik's other publications, almost all of which are feature magazines.[89] Helsinki Watch is concerned that *Danas* has been among

---

[86]"Upad u Vjesnik," *Danas*, June 4, 1991, p. 28-29. Šibl was interviewed by Helsinki Watch in Zagreb on May 28, 1991.

[87]Committee to Aid Democratic Dissidents in Yugoslavia, *CADDY Bulletin*, No. 66, August 1991.

[88]"Obavijest Čitateljima," *Danas*, October 1, 1991, p. 6.

[89] In addition to *Danas* and the only two profitable publications (*Večernji List* and *Arena*), Vjesnik's other publications include *Vjesnik, TOP, Draga, Erotika, Studio, Start, Svijet, Mila, Astro, Vikend, Auto-klub, Sportske novosti, Sport magazin, Izborov magazin,* and *Video-Studio*. All fifteen publications are experiencing economic difficulties. See "Crne vijesti iz *Vjesnika*," *Nedjeljna Dalmacija*, June 2, 1991, p 14.

351

the first of Vjesnik's publications to be targeted for closure by the government because of its independent and critical editorial policy.

Journalists who have criticized the Croatian government or nationalist policies have been harassed and physically abused by Croatian extremists who regard criticism of Croatian nationalism tantamount to treason. Journalists for the Zagreb-based weekly *Danas* and the Split-based daily *Slobodna Dalmacija* are the most frequently targeted for such harassment. On May 26, 1991, Josko Celar, a reporter for *Slobodna Dalmacija*, was "physically assaulted on the island of Murter and vilified as being anti-Croatian."[90] Also, in late June, Jadran Marinković, a reporter for Radio Split was demoted. During the Croatian elections in 1990, Marinković was a candidate of the Party of Democratic Change (Stranka Demokratskih Promjena-SDP), the former communist party. Marinković's superiors apparently disapproved of comments he made about Radio Split. He was told that "all radio employees are strictly forbidden to discuss the internal affairs of the station at any time, anywhere." Only the "responsible editor, with the consent of those who are in charge in Zagreb," could comment on the internal activities of the station.[91] Helsinki Watch is convinced that these claims have been used by the Croatian authorities as a pretext to demote Marinković because of his political beliefs and affiliation with the SDP.

Croatian government officials -- both at the republican and local levels -- have also harassed journalists who are critical of the Croatian government's policies. A journalist[92] for the now-defunct Zadar-based youth magazine *Fokus* wrote an article in which the journalist asserted "that forces were working behind Tudjman's back," namely that people in Tudjman's government were clandestinely working against him. After the article appeared in *Fokus* in October 1990, the author was harassed for four months. According to the journalist:

---

[90] See Committee to Aid Democratic Dissidents in Yugoslavia, *CADDY Bulletin*, No. 65, June 1991, p. 14.

[91] *Ibid.*

[92] For fear of further harassment, the journalist asked that his/her name be withheld. The journalist, a Croat, was interviewed by Helsinki Watch in April 2, 1991, in Zadar.

Shortly after my article was published in early October, the Mayor of Zadar called my editor and me to his office. He asked how I knew that forces were working behind Tudjman's back and he asked me to reveal my source of information but I refused. In late October 1990, I started to get anonymous telephone calls. The voice was always the same and he called every day. The caller would recite where, when and with whom I had been the day before, so I had reason to believe that I was being followed. The calls were persistent and they unnerved my family, particularly my father. The day my grandmother died, the entire family was in mourning and this man called. My mother asked him to please leave us alone today; my grandmother had just died and we didn't need to be upset further. Surprisingly, the caller apologized, explaining that he was being told to call by government officials.

On November 29, 1990, I received a telephone call from Vladimir Šeks [Vice-President of the Croatian Parliament] personally. He demanded that I come to Zagreb the next day but I told him I had plans for tomorrow. He replied that I would "suffer the consequences for my actions." Šeks called once again but I refused to be intimidated and told him that I was not going to Zagreb to be questioned. A few days later, the anonymous telephone calls started again. After my lawyer asked the authorities to trace the telephone calls, the caller stopped calling for about twenty days but he started harassing me again.

The Croatian government has also taken steps to curb freedom of expression. In May 1991, a criminal investigation was initiated in Zagreb against Mirjana Jakelić, President of the Croatian chapter of the League of Communists -- Movement for Yugoslavia (Savez Komunista-Pokret za Jugoslaviju). Zagreb's district public prosecutor charged Jakelić under Article 197(1) and Article 225(1)(2) of the Croatian Criminal Code with "willfully spreading false rumors" because she publicly blamed

President Tudjman for the murder of a soldier in Split[93] and distributed leaflets opposing the May 19 referendum on Croatia's independence.[94] Although court proceedings have not been initiated, charges against Jakelić have not been dropped.

Helsinki Watch believes that freedom of speech should never be hindered, unless said speech is a direct and immediate incitement to acts of violence.[95] Although Jakelić's actions and speech may be offensive to some, she was peacefully exercising her right to free speech.

The Croatian Ministry of Information has tried to close the Zagreb offices of *Borba*, a Belgrade-based daily. Serbian newspapers are no longer available in Croatia due to transportation problems posed by the war and political rivalries between the two republics. The Croatian authorities have not allowed Yutel, a pan-Yugoslav television program to broadcast because government officials declared that it was anti-Croatian.

---

[93] On May 6, 1991, Sasko Gesovski, a 19-year-old Macedonian soldier of the Yugoslav army, was killed by gunfire during an anti-army demonstration by 30,000 people in Split. (See "Soldier Shot Dead in New Yugoslav Violence," Reuters Information Services, May 6, 1991.)

[94] Charges brought against Jakelić are enumerated in "Rješenje," Broj XXV KIO-1207/91.8, Republika Hrvatska, Okružni Sud Zagreb, Istražni Odjel, June 3, 1991. See also "Autogol Hrvatske Pravde," *Danas*, June 4, 1991, and Committee to Aid Democratic Dissidents in Yugoslavia, *CADDY Bulletin*, No. 65, June 1991, p. 12.

[95] Any restriction on the content of expression must be based on direct and immediate incitement to acts of violence, discrimination or hostility against an individual or clearly defined group of persons in circumstances in which such violence, discrimination or hostility is imminent and alternative measures to prevent such conduct are not reasonably available. For this purpose, "violence" refers to physical attack; "discrimination" refers to the actual deprivation of a benefit to which similarly situated people are entitled or the imposition of a penalty or sanction not imposed on other similarly situated people; and "hostility" refers to criminal harassment and criminal intimidation. Helsinki Watch considers any law or prosecution that is not based on a strict interpretation of incitement to be presumptively a violation of the right to free expression. [Human Rights Watch, Hate Speech Policy.]

Other Concerns

Helsinki Watch also is concerned about the establishment of a secret police force, attacks on the Jewish community and restrictions on freedom of movement in Croatia. Moreover, Helsinki Watch is concerned that the Croatian authorities are gerrymandering areas of Croatia so as to decrease the level of Serbian representation in a given municipality. Helsinki Watch condemns any such action by the Croatian government and urges that all those displaced by the war -- including Serbian families -- be allowed to return to their homes in Croatia without fear of persecution and reprisals.

Helsinki Watch is concerned about the formation of the Office for the Protection of Constitutional Order (Ured za Zaštitu Ustavnog Poredka), which is headed by Josip Manolić. The newly formed office is responsible for gathering intelligence and counter-intelligence activities in Croatia. Helsinki Watch urges that such a government body not be used to violate the civil, political and other basic human rights of Croatia's citizens.

In August, the Jewish community center in Zagreb was badly damaged by a bomb. The Jewish cemeteries in Zagreb and Split also were vandalized during the summer of 1991. The Croatian government responded immediately and investigated the matter, offering an award for any information leading to the arrest of the perpetrator(s). Unfortunately, no one has yet been arrested.

Freedom of movement has been restricted by the Croatian government due to the war. All draft-age males must obtain permission before leaving their place of residence. Such restrictions of freedom of movement were meant to ensure that males do not avoid the draft, should the area be mobilized. However, persons living in besieged areas also must obtain approval before leaving such areas. Milica Smiljanić[96] -- a half-Serb, half-Croat -- had to obtain permission from the local command in Gospić before leaving the area. According to Ms. Smiljanić:

> Because of the fighting, I could not go to work for several weeks. We stayed in the basement the entire time. When I finally went to work on November 6, my

---

[96] See above case regarding the summary execution of 24 persons from Gospić.

director, a Croat, saw that I looked ill and had lost about 20 pounds. He asked me what he could do to help. I asked him to get me a permission slip so I could go to Zagreb. My director called Dr. Dražen Jurković, the commander of Croatian forces in Gospić. Dr. Jurković was in Zagreb, but when he returned three days later, my director took me to see him. I told Jurković that I was going to Zagreb for medical attention and he then gave me a permission slip to leave.[97]

* * *

Dear President Tudjman:

Helsinki Watch welcomes the Croatian government's efforts to investigate reports of human rights abuses committed by its troops on territory which it controls. It also welcomes the condemnation of loyalty oath campaigns by the Croatian government and the Parliamentary Committee for the Protection of Human Rights and the investigation of such activities by the Croatian Ministry of Labor and Social Welfare. Helsinki Watch commends the speed with which Croatian authorities apprehended the perpetrators of the crime, who appear to be agents of the Croatian government. Helsinki Watch calls upon the Croatian government to vigorously prosecute those guilty of both crimes. Željko Olujić, Croatia's Public Prosecutor, has stated that magistrates were investigating "wide-spread reports that gangs of Croats were abducting Serbs in towns under siege by the Yugoslav Army."[98] Helsinki Watch welcomes calls by you and other Croatian government officials for non-governmental and international monitoring of Croatia's human rights record.

---

[97] Helsinki Watch retains a copy of the permission slip, which was signed by Dražen Jurković and issued on November 9, 1991, at Gospić's command headquarters (i.e., Krizni Štab).

[98] Stephen Engelberg, "Villagers in Croatia Recount Massacre by Serbian Forces," *The New York Times*, December 19, 1991.

Despite such welcome steps by the Croatian government, we remain convinced that stronger and immediate action must be taken to stop human rights abuses from escalating in Croatia. In particular, we urge the Croatian government to purge its armed forces of extremists who act without orders and commit egregious violations of human rights, including the summary execution of civilians and the brutal beating of prisoners. The Croatian government is responsible for actions committed by its agents, including the Croatian army and police, and is therefore responsible for such human rights abuses. It is bound to bring paramilitary groups under government supervision or disband them so as to prevent such groups from committing human rights abuses. Individual extremists who are guilty of similar offenses must also be punished, in accordance with the law. Helsinki Watch urges the Croatian government to take concrete steps to lend effect to the recently promulgated Constitutional Law on Human Rights and Freedoms and the Rights of National and Ethnic Communities or Minorities in the Republic of Croatia.[99] We also urge the Croatian government to take steps to ameliorate the tensions between Serbs and Croats in Croatia.

In summary, we call upon the Croatian government to:

- Investigate reports of summary executions and torture of civilians and disarmed combatants by Croatian forces and individual extremists, prosecute and punish all those guilty of such crimes, and take disciplinary measures against the perpetrators' immediate superiors, insofar as it can be established that human rights abuses are being condoned -- or possibly encouraged -- by local military or police commanders.

- Make known the whereabouts of all missing persons abducted by Croatian forces.

- Investigate the deaths and disappearances of journalists in Croatia, especially in cases where Croatian forces may have been responsible for such acts.

---

[99] "Ustavni Zakon o ljudskim pravima i slobadama i o pravima etnickih i nacionalinih zajednica ili manjina u Republici Hrvatskoj," *Narodne Novine Republike Hrvatske*, Broj 65, 4. prosinca 1991.

357

- Take measures to bring to an end the robbing of homes and property.

- Allow all civilians displaced by the war, including Serbs, to return to their homes without fear of reprisals.

- Cease all arbitrary searches and seizures of property by members of the Croatian armed forces and police. Insofar as such searches are necessary, a warrant must be issued beforehand.

- Instruct the newly-formed military police to enforce discipline among the military cadres and to ensure that all members of the Croatian military and police behave in a responsible manner.

- Release immediately persons being held without charges or on charges that are considered unfounded by an independent court of law.

- Cease all questioning, intimidation and other harassment of Serbs who are engaged in peaceful political and civil activities in Croatia.

- Arrest and prosecute the killer(s) of Josip Reihl Kir, Goran Zopundzija and Milan Knežević.

- Investigate reports of harassment of, and attacks upon, Serbian civilians and others.

- Ensure that ethnic or national criteria are not used to hire or dismiss workers, in both the governmental and non-governmental sectors.

- Cease all interference with the independence of the judiciary.

- Repeal the censorship decree, respect freedom of the press throughout Croatia, and refrain from using force, the threat of criminal prosecution, harassment and intimidation or political criteria to impede freedom of the press or expression.

- Cease any efforts at gerrymandering territory so as to decrease Serbian representation in a given region.

- Arrest and prosecute those responsible for attacks against the Jewish community center in Zagreb and the Jewish cemeteries in Zagreb and Split.

- Respect the right to freedom of movement, especially for those unfit or ineligible for combat duty.

- Refrain from using the Office for the Protection of Constitutional Order as a tool through which to violate the civil and political rights of Croatia's citizens.

Helsinki Watch would like to have an opportunity to discuss our human rights concerns with you in person. Please consider this a formal request for such a meeting. If you will indicate a convenient time for such a meeting, we will arrange to send a delegation to Zagreb for this purpose.

Sincerely,

Jonathan Fanton
Chair

Jeri Laber
Executive Director